Identification and Assessment in Early Intervention

Infants & Young Children Series

Edited by

James A. Blackman, MD, MPH

Professor of Pediatrics
Director of Research
Kluge Children's Rehabilitation Center and Research Institute
Department of Pediatrics
University of Virginia
Charlottesville, Virginia

AN ASPEN PUBLICATION®
Aspen Publishers, Inc.
Gaithersburg, Maryland
1995

Library of Congress Cataloging-in-Publication Data

Identification and assessment in early intervention /
edited by James A. Blackman.
p.   cm.
Articles reprinted from infants and young children.
Includes bibliographical references and index.
ISBN 0-8342-0644-7
1. Child development deviations—Diagnosis.   2. Developmentally
disabled children—Rehabilitation.   I. Blackman, James A.
II. Infants and young children.
[DNLM: 1. Child Development Disorders—diagnosis—collected works.
2. Child, Exceptional—collected works.   WS 350.6 I19 1995]
RJ135.I34   1995
618.92'0075—dc20
DNLM/DLC
for Library of Congress
94-24184
CIP

Editorial Services: Ruth Bloom

Library of Congress Catalog Card Number: 94-24184
ISBN: 0-8342-0644-7
Series ISBN: 0-8342-0652-8

Printed in the United States of America

1   2   3   4   5

Table of Contents

Preface

Early intervention cannot exist without an effective identification process. The components of this process include both specific identification methods and, more importantly, an identification system that guarantees equal access and efficient transition to assessment and services when indicated.

There has been much debate about identification methods. Some have criticized developmental screening instruments as too insensitive. Others worry that they overidentify children, fearing overload on service-providing agencies, premature labeling with "failure," and possibly unnecessary worry for parents.

Some screening tests, say critics, take too long to administer; others are too cursory or do not detect subtle developmental dysfunction. Furthermore, they say, many are culturally insensitive and those administering them have insufficient training. The validity of parent report via developmental screening questionnaires is questioned.

These are the legitimate objections we grapple with despite knowing that some sort of practical screening methodology is mandatory. Those pioneers who persisted with the grueling task of developing and refining screening instruments have given us a basis to work with, perhaps not perfect, but something tangible. To them we should be grateful. In time their efforts will yield improvements in our ability to detect developmental problems early while overcoming many of the objections cited above.

A second challenge is orchestrating the many individuals, agencies, locations, and funding streams that are involved in community screening activities. With limited resources we cannot afford to duplicate efforts any more than fail to identify a child in need. The system of screening, therefore, is as important as the particular techniques employed.

While sorting out the best approaches, diversity is welcome and should be encouraged: informal vs. formal screening; mass vs. selected screening; direct testing vs. parent questionnaires; brief vs. more extended screening procedures. Through experimentation we will achieve a menu of possibilities that can be adapted to varying circumstances.

The next step in early intervention assessment elicits the same concerns and questions, only on a more intense level. The benefits or risks of appropriately or poorly conducted assessments are potentially greater than in screening. Since assessment often determines eligibility for services as well as the content and frequency of these services, no wonder this topic has been at the center of the early intervention debate since Public Law 99-457 was enacted.

The articles in this volume represent a wealth of experience in developing, implementing, and evaluating many aspects of screening and assessment.

Through these experiences with children and families with a variety of developmental concerns in heterogeneous circumstances, our early intervention efforts will advance and mature.

James A. Blackman, MD, MPH
Editor

Identification and treatment of very young children with hearing loss

Jane R. Madell, PhD
Director of Audiology
Department of Audiology
New York League for the Hard of
 Hearing
New York, New York

HEARING LOSS in infants is one of the most common disabilities in the United States. Mild to severe sensorineural hearing loss is reported[1-3] to occur in 1 in 380 to 750 births. In graduates of neonatal intensive care units, hearing loss is present in 1 in 25 to 50.[4,5]

IDENTIFICATION OF HEARING LOSS

There is no disagreement about the necessity to identify hearing loss at an early age because hearing is the primary channel for learning spoken language.[6,7] Reduced ability to hear is known to adversely affect the development of speech and language skills. Children with mild hearing loss and no other handicapping conditions frequently display communicative and academic problems.[8,9] As the degree of hearing loss increases, so usually do these problems. Early identification permits early habilitation, which should reduce the devastating effect of hearing loss.

Several authors,[10-12] including JM Greenstein et al (written communication, September 1977), have reported significant benefits when hearing loss is identified early and habilitation is begun in a timely fashion. Unfortunately, there is often an extensive delay in identifying hearing-impaired children.[13-16] For children with no other complicating problems, delay in identifying hearing loss may be due to the reluctance of physicians to refer them for audiologic evaluation. One recent study indicated that physicians delayed in referring children for audiologic evaluation an average of 7.8 months after parents first expressed concern about their children's hearing. The problem is compounded for children with developmental disabilities. Although data indicate that between 32% and 78% of these children also have some degree of hearing loss,[17,18] referral for early audiologic evaluation is not routine. Both parents and professionals may be confused by the developmental disability and may not recognize sings of hearing loss or may attribute their concerns about response to sound to the developmental disability and not to impaired hearing.

The New York League for the Hard of Hearing evaluates many children enrolled in programs for the developmentally disabled who have not had hearing tests. Of these children, 70% were identified as having some degree of hearing impairment. The League suspects one reason for the delay in obtaining evaluations is that some professionals may not look beyond their own area of specialization in evaluating a child and, therefore, may overlook evidence of hearing loss. Each professional must be sensitive to any factor that may affect a child's devel-

Inf Young Children 1988; 1(2): 20–30

1

opment. While delay in diagnosis of hearing loss is tragic in all cases, it is particularly so for children with multiple handicaps because it further decreases the child's chances of reaching his or her fullest potential. Hearing testing must be a routine part of the diagnostic workup when a child is being evaluated for developmental disabilities.

TESTING A CHILD'S HEARING

Routine hearing screening is conducted by a number of different professionals, including audiologists, speech-language pathologists, physicians, and nurses; but any child for whom hearing is a concern needs a diagnostic evaluation by a pediatric audiologist and otologist. The otologist will determine if there is a medical condition interfering with hearing that requires treatment. Routine otologic evaluation is essential for developmentally disabled children whether or not hearing loss is present. Children with Down Syndrome and other developmental disabilities have a high incidence of otitis media (middle-ear disease), even when they are asymptomatic.[18,19] Routine otologic care is essential to prevent other problems from developing.

Behavioral observation audiometry

A number of different testing techniques are valuable in assessing hearing in children. Space does not permit a full description of the techniques used in pediatric audiologic evaluations, but a brief summary might be beneficial. For children with a developmental age of less than 6 to 8 months, behavioral observation audiometry (BOA) is the initial method of evaluation.[8] With this technique, testing is done in a sound-proof room. The child is placed in an infant seat lying on a table or in another position in which the child is comfortably at rest and easily visible to the audiologist. A variety of well-calibrated and acoustically defined stimuli are presented. Stimuli may include acoustically defined sound toys (squeak toys, bells, rattles, drums, whistles) and such calibrated stimuli as audiometric warbled tones of different frequency and intensity, voice, and music. Responses include changes in sucking, respiration, limb movement, general alertness, and possibly searching for the sound. In the hands of an experienced audiologist, it is possible to rule out a significant hearing loss or to determine the extent of hearing loss with a good degree of accuracy.

Visual reinforcement audiometry

Once a child has reach a developmental level of 6 to 7 months, testing can be easily accomplished using visual reinforcement audiometry (VRA).[20] The child should be seated comfortably with his or her attention directed to the front, using a toy or other interesting object, while sound stimuli are presented. Seat the child in a highchair whenever possible, since that appears to facilitate observing the child. It is also possible to use an infant seat or to sit the child on a parent's lap. (Caution must be taken when the child sits on a parent's lap, because any movement on the part of the parent may signal to the child that a sound is present, which could confuse test interpretation.)

Test stimuli may be presented through loudspeakers or earphones. In VRA, a moving toy or a light is paired with the initial sound presentations so that the child begins to associate the toy or light with the sound and look for the toy when the sound is presented. Once the child has made the association, testing can begin. The child will look up at the toy when a sound is heard and continue playing when no sound is heard. At each frequency to be tested, the audiologist presents stimuli of different intensities and observes whether the child responds until the threshold is determined. Test results are reliable and valid.

Obtaining accurate behavioral testing on developmentally disabled children who are functioning at a developmental age below 7 to 8 months is sometimes difficult. The combination of hearing loss and other disabilities may make it difficult to specifically determine accurate hearing levels. Once the child has reached the developmental age of 7 to 8 months and it becomes possible to use VRA as the test method, thresholds can be determined with better accuracy. Some children who have cognitive developmental levels of 7 or 8 months do not have sufficient neck control to enable them to turn their heads toward a toy or light, required for VRA testing. Standard VRA testing will not be appropriate for these children, but the technique can be modified so valid and reliable results can be obtained.

BOA and VRA testing sometimes reveal thresholds that indicate slightly poorer hearing than may, in fact, exist. As children grow older and become more responsive to auditory stimuli, it is not uncommon to find that thresholds improve by about 10 dB.

The audiologist must know the child's developmental age in order to select the appropriate test method; chronologic age is less important. This is especially critical when developmental delays are a consideration. A child with a chronological age of 9 months and a developmental age of 5 months should be tested with BOA. Testing such a child with VRA would probably result in an error in diagnosing the degree of hearing loss. If the child's developmental level is not clear, it might be useful to obtain a developmental evaluation for the child prior to completing testing. The developmental evaluation will need to take the possibility of hearing loss into account.

Auditory brainstem response testing

Auditory brainstem response testing (ABR) is often recommended as the test of choice for infants since it is considered to be an objective test procedure.

(EDITOR'S NOTE: An article on infant audiologic screening using ABR is included in *Infants and Young Children,* vol. 1, no. 1, July 1988.) As commonly used, ABR assessment often only tests high-frequency stimuli. Once a child has passed infancy, testing requires sedation because the child must lie quietly during the procedure, and results are difficult to evaluate for children with neurologic disorders.[21] While ABR is a useful procedure, it should be used only as part of a complete best battery that includes behavioral techniques.

WHEN A CHILD IS IDENTIFIED AS HEARING IMPAIRED

While hearing loss may be suspected by many people, the loss should be confirmed by an audiologist. Results from the audiologic and otologic evaluations usually determine the degree and type of hearing loss. This information, in conjunction with other diagnostic tests, is used to plan a habilitation program.[22] Program planning is best done as a team effort. The team should include an audiologist, otologist, speech-language pathologist, psychologist, physical therapist, occupational therapist, and special education teacher. Others, such as a neurologist, psychiatrist, or augmentative communications specialist, may be added as appropriate. While all may not be needed for each child, input from all appropriate professionals ensures that no area is being overlooked in developing an appropriate plan.

The involvement of the parents is crucial at all steps in the planning and at all future stages of treatment. The identification of hearing loss in a child is likely to be extremely stressful for them. This is especially true when the child has already been identified as having other disabilities. It is one more thing that must be dealt with. It probably means additional therapy; it certainly means that the child will have to wear hearing aids, which some parents feel is further indication to the world at large that something is wrong with their child. Other parents may be relieved when a hearing loss is identified. The hearing loss may be viewed as the explanation for some of the developmental delays and may be accompanied by a belief that remediating the hearing loss will cure other developmental problems. Counseling is essential in helping parents sort out their feelings at this critical time.[23]

AMPLIFICATION

When a hearing loss has been identified, a program of habilitation must be initiated as quickly as possible to minimize delays in developing speech, language, and auditory skills. Selection and fitting of appropriate amplification are the first steps. The essential function of any amplification system is to make speech as audible as possible for the hearing-impaired child. If the child is to employ the normal auditory mode for the development of speech and language, then he or she will have to hear as much of the speech signal as possible for as long as possible.

Who needs a hearing aid?

There is general agreement that anyone with a moderate hearing loss or worse will have difficulty communicating in most situations without assistance. If the loss is conductive (caused by damage to the outer and middle ear) and can be corrected surgically or medically, amplification is not indicated. If the loss is sensorineural (caused by damage to the inner ear), the child should be fit for amplification as quickly as possible.

When the hearing loss is mild, there may be some question about fitting the child with amplification. Recent research[9,24–28] has demonstrated that mild or unilateral hearing loss can cause more problems than originally thought. A child with a mild hearing loss will respond to many sounds, may turn when called, and will begin to develop speech and language. However, he or she will have difficulty hearing when the speaker is at a distance and when there is background noise. Listening will generally be more difficult, and speech and language may be affected. Sometimes poorer-than-expected school performance may be the most apparent consequence of a mild hearing loss.[9,28]

Clinical experience has indicated that even children with mild losses benefit from amplification. Parents and school staff report that, after receiving amplification, children are more alert and that speech and language development improves. Amplification should be considered for all children with mild hearing losses, especially for those who demonstrate a language delay respective to their developmental level or poorer-than-expected academic performance. Since time is so critical in providing assistance to developmentally disabled children, these children would seem to be best served by moving quickly to fit them with amplification. If, on reevaluation, it is determined that hearing is better than previously thought, amplification can be removed. On the other hand, if the fitting of amplification is delayed, valuable time may have been lost.[10–12] If amplification is being fit when the audiologist is not absolutely certain of the degree of hearing loss, caution must be exercised in the fitting to be certain that the amount of amplification is not enough to cause any additional hearing loss. After a trial period of amplification, a determination can be made as to its value by assessing how the use of amplification has affected the child's vocalizations, attention to auditory stimuli, and development of language.

Children with fluctuating conductive hearing loss due to middle-ear disease present a unique challenge. Auditorily, these children have more difficulties than a child with a mild sensorineural hearing loss because their hearing is always changing. On days when hearing is not compromised, they will function well. On other days, not as well. This is confusing and frustrating for the child, parents, and everyone involved. Some audiologists and otologists recommend hearing aids for use on a temporary basis only when hearing is compromised. This can work well since it enables the child to have fairly consistent hearing regardless of the status of the middle ear. It requires, however, that the parents accept responsibility for being alert to the child's hearing status to be able to determine when amplification is needed.

Types of hearing aids

If a hearing aid is determined to be appropriate, then amplification should be fit as quickly as possible. Once otologic treatment, if appropriate, is completed, earmold impressions can be taken of the child's ear and the impressions sent to an earmold laboratory for fabrication. When the earmold returns from the laboratory, the process of hearing-aid selection can begin. Optimally, a child should be wearing amplification within two weeks of the time the hearing loss is identified.

Several types of hearing aids are available. Cosmetics is often a factor in selection of hearing aids for adults, but it should not be a factor where children are concerned. Hearing aids fall into three basic categories: aids that fit in the ear (ITE), in the canal (ITC), behind the ear (BTE), and on the body (body-worn). ITEs and ITCs are not generally recommended for children. They are expensive to use, since they need to be remade frequently as the child's ear grows; they are very small, and there is a danger that they might be swallowed; and they do not offer the number of adjustments available in the larger types of aids.

BTE hearing aids

BTE hearing aids are the type most commonly fit on children. They are available in a variety of power settings, so they can be used for different degrees of hearing loss from mild to severe. Most have controls that permit the audiologist to adjust various electroacoustic parameters as the child grows older and more information about the hearing loss becomes available. BTEs are appropriately fit on children with losses from mild to severe. While many audiologists also fit them on children with profound hearing losses, they may not always provide the most benefit. BTE aids are cosmetically more acceptable than body-worn hearing aids, and some have as much power; but all the available power cannot be used because of problems caused by feedback.

Feedback is the high-pitched whistle that occurs when some of the sound being delivered through the earmold is fed back into the hearing-aid microphone, is reamplified, and escapes once again from the earmold. Feedback is a particular problem for children because of the rate at which their ears grow and because of the soft cartilage in the outer ear. The earmold may be feedback-free when it is first fabricated; but often within weeks, the ear will have grown sufficiently to loosen the earmold and produce feedback. Even if the mold is sufficiently tight, sound may radiate through the soft cartilage of the outer ear causing feedback. This problem can be solved most easily by increasing the distance between the hearing-aid microphone and the receiver. With BTE aids, the microphone and the receiver are located within centimeters of each other. With body aids, the microphone is located on the chest and the receiver is at the ear, usually 12 to 15 in apart.

Body-worn hearing aids

Only a small number of body-worn hearing aids are fit on children, but they may be the best possible hearing aid for many children with severe to profound hearing losses. Body-worn hearing aids will minimize feedback because of the increased distance between the ear and the hearing-aid microphone. In addition, the cord attached to the aid allows the aid to be used as a close-talking microphone. The parent, speech-language pathologist, or other person working with the child can place the unit close to the mouth when speaking to the child, reducing the negative effects of distance and improving the quality of the sound the child receives.

Another factor favoring the use of body-worn hearing aids is their ease of operation and manipulation. Because a body-worn aid is larger than a BTE aid and is worn on the chest, it is easier for the child to see, adjust, and learn to care for. For children with dexterity problems, body-worn aids may offer the only opportunity for them to be responsible for their amplification.

Once a child reaches second or third grade, the social pressure to hide the hearing aid often becomes very strong, and it becomes necessary to change from body-worn to BTE hearing aids. By this time, it may be easier to overcome some of the earmold problems that were present at a younger age.

Assistive listening devices

A variety of assistive devices can be used alone or in conjunction with hearing aids to enhance a child's ability to receive speech information. The most common one for children is a frequency-modulated (FM) system. This is a two-part system in which the parent, teacher, or other caregiver wears a microphone-transmitter and the child wears an FM receiver. The sound is broadcast from the microphone-transmitter to the receiver via FM radio waves, exactly as in an FM radio. The sound received will be clear and undistorted by the effects of distance and background noise since the FM microphone is located close to the talker's mouth. Every hearing-impaired child in a class or group situation will benefit from the use of an FM system. Some audiologists are recommending FM systems as the primary amplification for hearing-impaired children with severe or profound losses. For these children, the FM system appears to be making a significant difference in the amount of auditory learning that takes place. Research in this area is in progress.

Some children with very profound hearing losses are not able to make good use of any auditory information. For these children, it is sometimes beneficial to use a vibrotactile device. A number of tactile devices are available, and they continue to be developed. Tactile devices can offer valuable assistance to a limited population of children and adults with profound hearing loss.

Cochlear implants

An exciting technologic development is the cochlear implant. It is a device intended to bypass the cochlea (the part of the ear that is severely damaged in many patients with profound sensorineural hearing loss) and stimulate the auditory nerve more directly. This is accomplished by implanting one or more electrodes in the cochlea. A microphone is placed behind the ear and a speech processor (the size of a large, body-worn hearing aid) is worn on the chest or in an outside pocket. Cochlear implants are attached to the implanted portion of the unit by a magnet just under the skin above the ear.

Children have been receiving implants on an experimental basis since 1980. Currently two cochlear implant systems are available for children. The House Ear Institute in Los Angeles, California developed a single-channel implant that has been used for children since 1980. In 1986, a multichannel device, developed by Nucleus Corporation in Lane Cove, Australia, became available for implantation in children. Cochlear implants are devices to be used in children with bilateral, very profound, or total sensorineural hearing loss who receive no benefit from amplification. The children must be at least 2 years of age, have an IQ within normal limits; have no significant handicaps that would adversely affect functioning with the implant; have good family support; and, most important, have demonstrated that they could not make satisfactory progress in auditory development even with training.

The benefit a child receives from an implant varies, depending on the length of time the child has had the hearing loss and the type of communication mode the child uses, among other things. The most successful candidates seem to be children who have recently lost their hearing and who communicate orally. With an implant, children are expected to have increased awareness and alertness to sound and improved speech-reading skills. Most children develop the ability to detect the number of syllables present in a word and to detect differences in duration using only the implant. Some children have developed the ability to understand some speech without clues and to use the telephone. Work with adults seems to indicate that the multichannel implant is able to provide more assistance than the single-channel implant, but more information is needed before this can be said definitively. Much is being learned about cochlear implants and more information can be expected in the next few years. Presently, cochlear implants are not for everyone—only for a very small group of children.

What can be expected from hearing aids?

Basically, hearing aids make sounds louder. Many hearing aids have adjustments that permit the audiologist to modify the frequency response and output to provide more amplification at certain frequencies than at others. By using knowledge of the child's hearing loss, it is theoretically possible to adjust the hearing aid to compensate for the loss. Unfortunately, this cannot always be done satisfactorily. Although it is possible to substantially improve the signal the child hears, no hearing aid will fully compensate for the hearing loss because the child is listening through a damaged auditory system. Fortunately, the English language is sufficiently redundant so a hearing-impaired child with good language can still understand the message, even if only part of the signal is heard, by using the existing language base to fill in the gaps. Speech–language therapy can assist the child in learning to interpret minimal auditory clues to maximize the information received.

Even under ideal circumstances, hearing aids work well only when the speaker is within 2 to 3 ft of the listener and when there is no background noise. As the distance between the speaker and the listener increases, the intensity (loudness) of the speaker's voice decreases. The softer the signal, the more difficult it will be for the signal to be heard. In addition to the problem of distance, the problem posed by background noise must be considered. All persons have difficulty with background noise, but the problem is greater for those with hearing loss.[29] It is essential that conditions be arranged to maximize the amount of auditory information a hearing-impaired child receives. Infants will often be very close to the caregiver most of the time that communication is taking place so the effects of distance and noise are minimal. As children get older and more independent, the listening situation changes frequently, and they are often at a greater distance than 2 to 3 ft. Once this happens, the child does not receive a good auditory signal. Exactly how much the signal is compromised depends on the degree of the hearing loss and the amount of background noise present. Essentially, this situation is the reason that FM systems are recommended.

Mild hearing loss

Children with mild hearing losses traditionally have not been fit with hearing aids because it was assumed that they could receive a sufficient amount of sound without amplification.[30] Boney and Bess[31] and others have demonstrated that, in the presence of background noise, children with minimal hearing losses had twice as much difficulty with speech recognition as their normal-hearing peers. When this is added to the difficulties affecting a child with developmental disabilities, a very good case can be made for fitting these children with hearing aids for general use and FM systems for use in any group-listening situation.

Moderate hearing loss

A child with a moderate hearing loss will hear speech if the speaker is fairly close or if speech is loud. It will probably be somewhat distorted and will be significantly affected by the problems of distance and background noise. The child's speech is a good indicator of the sounds the child is able to hear, and speech production may be a good diagnostic indicator of speech perception. For the child with a developmental disability, other factors may also affect speech production. It is essential that children with moderate hearing losses be provided with hearing aids for general use and an FM system for use in group situations.

Severe hearing loss

A child with a severe hearing loss will hear very little without amplification. He or she will hear speech close to the ear and may hear loud speech at close distances. This child will not hear speech at normal conversational levels when the speaker is 2 ft away without hearing aids. With appropriate amplification and training, a child with a severe hearing loss can develop excellent auditory skills and be able to understand speech without visual clues (lipreading). Many children with severe hearing losses are able to use the telephone and are able to understand unclued material with their hearing aids in quiet situations. In noisy classrooms, it is essential that they use FM systems to maximize listening. Obviously, a developmental disability can significantly affect the progress made by a child with a severe hearing loss.

Profound hearing loss

Children with profound hearing losses vary greatly in their ability to function. Some have hearing throughout the frequency range and function very much like children with severe hearing losses. Others have hearing in only a small portion of the frequency spectrum, usually the low frequencies, and are able to receive only limited auditory clues. They may be able to identify certain vowels and recognize rhythm, inflection, and the number of syllables present in a word. However, even this limited information can be beneficial and can improve their ability to speechread and to modulate their own voices. Some children with hearing only in the low frequencies develop speech recognition ability for clued material (such as picture identification) and some develop speech recognition for unclued material.[22] Distance and noise severely degrade these children's ability to use auditory information, so the importance of good hearing aids and FM systems cannot be sufficiently stressed. As with other categories of hearing loss, the presence of a developmental disability affects the child's progress.

ROLE OF SPEECH–LANGUAGE THERAPY

The speech–language pathologist plays a critical role in the treatment of any child with a developmental delay. The role with a child who has a hearing loss is even more critical. The speech–language pathologist will develop a plan for speech and language stimulation that will be implemented in cooperation with the special educator and parents or caregivers. The speech–language pathologist must carefully monitor the child's developing use of audition. In most facilities, this individual will be the one to monitor the hearing-impaired child's hearing aids and FM system since he or she will see the child more frequently than the audiologist. Along with the audiologist, the pathologist will assist parents or caregivers, teachers, and therapists in understanding what the child can and cannot hear with and without amplification and will assist other personnel in understanding how to maximize the child's auditory functioning. The speech–language pathologist and audiologist will monitor the child's auditory development and assist the parents and other personnel in developing it to its fullest potential.

•   •   •

For all children, hearing loss must be identified as soon after birth as possible to minimize the speech and language delays associated with it. There is even greater urgency to identify hearing loss early in children with developmental disabilities, since they are already at risk for these delays. Once the loss is identified, hearing aids and FM systems should be fit as quickly as possible, preferably within a few weeks of the time the loss is identified. As soon as amplification is fit, remediation can begin.

REFERENCES

1. Simmon FB: Identification of hearing loss in infants and young children. *Otolaryng Clin North Am* 1978;11:19–26.
2. Downs MP: The rationale for neonatal hearing screening, in Swigart ET (ed): *Neonatal Hearing Screening.* San Diego, College-Hill Press, 1986, pp 21–30.
3. Martin JAM, Moore WJ (eds): *Childhood Deafness in the European Community.* Luxembourg, Office for Official Publications of the European Communities, 1979.
4. Cox LC, Hack M, Metz DM: Auditory brain stem response audiometry in the very low birthweight infant: Incidence and risk factors. *Ear Hear* 1984;5:47–51.
5. Stein L, Ozdamar O, Kraus N, et al: Follow-up of infants screened by auditory brainstem response in the neonatal intensive care unit. *J Pediatr* 1983;103:447–453.
6. Fry D: The role and primary of the auditory channel in speech and language development, in Ross M, Giolas T (eds): *Auditory Management of Hearing Impaired Children.* Baltimore, Md, University Park Press, 1978.
7. Ross M, Brackett D, Maxon A: *Hard of Hearing Children in Regular Schools.* Englewood Cliffs, NJ, Prentice-Hall, 1982.
8. Northern J, Downs MP: *Hearing in Children,* ed 3. Baltimore, Md, Williams & Wilkins, 1984.
9. Bess FH, Tharpe AM, Klee TM, et al: Unilateral sensorineural hearing loss in children. *Ear Hear* 1986;7:3–54.
10. Ling D: Recent developments affecting the education of hearing impaired children. *Public Health Rev* 1975;4:117–152.
11. Ling D, Milne M: The development of speech in hearing-impaired children, in Bess FH, Freeman BA, Sinclair JS (eds): *Amplification in Education.* Washington, DC, Freeman, 1981.

12. Markides A: Age at fitting of hearing aids and speech intelligibility. *Br J Audiol* 1986;20:165–167.

13. Coplan J: Deafness: Ever heard of it? Delayed recognition of permanent hearing loss. *Pediatrics* 1987;79:206–213.

14. Elssmann S, Matkin N, Sabo M: Identification of congenital sensorineural hearing impairment. *Hear J* 1987;40(9):13–17.

15. Luterman D, Chasin J: The pediatrician and the parent of the deaf child. *Pediatrics* 1970;45(1):115–116.

16. Parving A: Early detection and identification of congenital/early acquired hearing disability. Who takes the initiative? *Int J Pediatr Otorhinolaryngol* 1984;2:107–117.

17. Stein, et al: Hearing loss in an institutionalized mentally retarded population. *Arch Otolaryngol* 1987;113:32–35.

18. Balkany T, Downs M, Krajicek M: Hearing loss in Down's syndrome, in Gerber S, Mencher G (eds): *Early Diagnosis of Hearing Loss.* New York, Grune & Stratton, 1978.

19. Brooks DN, Wooley H, Kanjilal GC: Hearing loss and middle ear disorders in patients with Down's syndrome (mongolism). *J Ment Defic Res* 1972;16:21–29.

20. Matkin ND: Behavioral methods in pediatric audiometry: Past, present, future. *Annals Otol Rhinol Laryngol* 1980;89 (suppl 74):50–52.

21. Resnick SB, Friedrich B: Considerations in applying ABR measurements to the multiply handicapped/neurologically impaired pediatric population. *Bioacoustics Instruments.* Columbia, Md, Bioacoustics Instruments, Inc., 1986.

22. Boothroyd A: *Hearing Impairment in Young Children.* Englewood Cliffs, NJ, Prentice-Hall, 1982.

23. Luterman D: *Counseling Parents of Hearing Impaired Children.* Boston, Little, Brown, 1979.

24. Logan SA, Bess FH: Amplification for school-age hearing-impaired children. *Semin Hear* 1985;6(3):309–321.

25. Quigley S, Thomure F: *Some Effects of Hearing Impairment on School Performance.* Springfield, Ill, Illinois Office of Education, 1968.

26. Reynolds L: The school adjustment of children with minimal hearing loss. *J Speech Hear Disord* 1955;20:380–384.

27. Sarff L: An innovative use of free field amplification in regular classrooms, in Roser R, Downs M (eds): *Auditory Disorders in School Children.* New York, Thieme-Stratton, 1981.

28. Bess FH: The minimally hearing impaired child. *Ear Hear* 1985;6:43–47.

29. Finetzo-Heiber T, Tillman T: Room acoustic effects on monosyllabic word discrimination ability for normal and hearing impaired children. *J Speech Hear Res* 1978;21:440–458.

30. Ross M, Giolas T: Effects of three classroom listening conditions on speech intelligibility. *Am Ann Deaf* 1971;116:580–584.

31. Boney SJ, Bess FH: Noise and reverberation effects in minimal bilateral sensorineural hearing loss. Presented at the American Speech-Language-Hearing Association Convention, San Francisco, November 16–19, 1984.

The assessment of cognition/intelligence in infancy

Terri L. Shelton, PhD
Assistant Professor of Psychiatry and
  Pediatrics
Department of Psychiatry
University of Massachusetts Medical
  Center
Worcester, Massachusetts

THE COGNITIVE assessment of infants, like intelligence testing in general, has its roots in the intelligence testing movement of the late 19th and early 20th centuries. Since that time interest in the development and use of infant cognitive assessment instruments has mushroomed. The passage of Public Law 99-457 in October of 1986, the Education of the Handicapped Act Amendments, established early intervention services for infants from birth through 3 years of age in all states. This legislation also has contributed to an even greater interest in identifying techniques that can be used to document developmental delay, to identify infants at risk, to plan intervention services, and to evaluate their effectiveness.

In light of this growing interest, this article will review the development of infant cognitive assessment and will briefly describe some of the tests in current use. Basic considerations in choosing and administering infant intelligence/cognitive assessment instruments will be discussed along with a review of factors that affect the interpretation of the results of these evaluations. Finally, the usefulness of cognitive assessment will be discussed, including the use of information in an interdisciplinary team, the predictive validity of tests, and new approaches to assessment.

HISTORIC OVERVIEW

Psychometric instruments

Arnold Gesell[1] was the pioneer of infant assessment. Although most infant cognitive assessment instruments that were later developed included many of the items developed by Gesell, his primary purpose in developing the scales was to identify those infants in need of assistance in the area of welfare and hygiene. The initial scales, published in 1925,[1] consisted of 144 items in four general areas: motor, language, adaptive, and personal/social behavior. The purpose of the scales was broad and clinical. An updated version of the scales was published in 1974 by Knobloch and Pasamanick[2]; it provided more adequate norms for infants from 1 month to 5 years of age. Although Gesell viewed the environment as important, he thought that development was primarily influenced by genetics and the maturational process. While the scales do not yield a specific level of cognitive abilities, but rather developmental quotients in the different areas, the Gesell scales provided the basis for many other assessment instruments, such as the Brunet-Lezine

Inf Young Children 1989; 1(3): 10–25
© 1989 Aspen Publishers, Inc.

Scale,[3] published in 1951 and largely used in Europe, and the Griffiths Scale of Mental Development, published in 1954.[4]

In contrast to Gesell's broad conceptualization of development, Cattell[5] specifically set out to develop a standardized assessment of infant cognitive abilities that could be a downward extension of the Stanford-Binet. While Cattell used many of the items from the Gesell, she eliminated those thought to be unduly influenced by home training or large muscle control. She made the scoring more objective and standardized the test for infants from birth through 30 months. Like Gesell, the theoretical underpinnings of the test seemed to emphasize the inherent abilities of the infant and to diminish the role of the environment.

Bayley[6,7] also used the Gesell schedules as a starting point in her first California First Year Mental Scale, published in 1933. In its present form the scales include both mental and motor scales and a behavior record for evaluating infants aged 1 month to 30 months. The Bayley scales are perhaps the most widely used of the formal infant intelligence scales, and there is a large body of research documenting the reliability and validity of the scales. Although initially the development of the scales seemed to reflect a more unitary view of intelligence, over time Bayley's concept of intelligence began to change. Intelligence, as measured by these scales, seemed to be viewed as emergent throughout infancy and functionally unique at different ages. In fact, Kohen-Raz's[8] scalogram analysis of the Bayley scales yields five scales that are very similar to the scales typically found on Piagetian-based sensorimotor instruments.

Sensorimotor scales

With the translation of the work of Piaget into English came a new theoretical approach to the study of infant development and to the assessment of cognition/intelligence in infants as well. The previous approaches by Bayley, Cattell, and Gesell assumed that intelligence was more or less a unitary trait and that development was nonhierarchical. In contrast, Piagetian theory viewed development as a series of hierarchical, qualitatively different stages, dependent on the infant's interaction with his or her environment.

Three major assessment scales based on Piagetian theory have been developed: the Casati-Lezine Scale,[9] the Albert Einstein Scales of Sensorimotor Development by Corman and Escalona,[10] and the Infant Psychological Development Scales (IPDS) by Uzgiris and Hunt.[11] The Casati-Lezine test measures object search, the use of intermediaries, object exploration, and the combination of objects. The Einstein scales are designed for infants between 1 month and 2 years of age and assess skills in prehension, object permanence, and functioning in three-dimensional space. The IPDS is appropriate with infants aged 1 month to 2 years and is comprised of six scales: (1) visual pursuit and permanence of objects, (2) means of obtaining desired environmental events, (3a) vocal imitation, (3b) gestural imitation, (4) operational causality, (5) construction of object relations in space, and (6) schemes for relating to objects. In contrast to non–Piagetian-based scales, no developmental quotients or deviation IQ scores are obtained. Rather, infants are characterized with respect to their most advanced performance on each subscale. The IPDS appears to be as reliable and valid as the other psychometric approaches. Although the IPDS has not really been standardized, Uzgiris and Hunt[11] note that the various levels of cognitive organization are of psychologic significance in their own right and "need not be based on the individual's comparative status in a statistical distribution."[11px]

Concurrent with the development of Piagetian-based instruments in the 1960s and 1970s was the development of assessment instruments in several other areas: (1) neonatal assessment, (2) screening instruments, (3) assessment of skills for special populations, and (4) assessment-based programming instruments. Clearly the impetus for many of these instruments has been and will continue to be the growing interest in early intervention techniques, the need to identify infants at risk, and the survival of infants born prematurely or with disabilities. A brief description of selected and frequently used instruments in each of these categories appears in Appendix A. Appendix B is a checklist for assessing infant cognition. Further accounts of the historic development of infant assessment as well as current trends can be found elsewhere.[12–14]

BASIC CONSIDERATIONS IN INFANT ASSESSMENT

Purpose

The assessment of infant cognition or intelligence can be useful in a variety of ways: to document delay or risk status, to design an intervention program, to provide valuable pretreatment and posttreatment information for research or treatment regarding the effectiveness of a therapeutic intervention, or to predict future abilities. Therefore it is extremely important that an examiner first identify the function or purpose of the assessment. The purpose will determine not only the type of test (eg, screening, in-depth assessment) but also the necessary test characteristics (eg, time needed, reliability). Once the examiner's purpose is clear, it also is important to examine the purpose for which the assessment instrument was designed and to try to match these as much as possible. As measurement often deals with intangible variables that are not always directly observable, constructs such as cognition, intelligence, and personality must be measured indirectly. Each test author makes theoretical assumptions about this variable or construct. Information on the theoretical underpinnings of the particular test as well as other test characteristics, such as item selection and reliability and validity estimates, should be available in the test manual's description of the construction of the test.

Skills of the examiner

In choosing an assessment instrument, the examiner should evaluate whether he or she has the necessary training and experience to administer the instrument. Because of the special demands inherent in evaluating infants, examiners should have experience testing very young children and infants in general. For example, it is important to know techniques for eliciting the best performance from the infant, to make the family feel comfortable, and to know when to interrupt or to discontinue testing. In addition to general experience, experience with specific populations is equally important to recognize the limitations of infant assessment, to interpret the test results, and to use the information to assist caregivers or for intervention. For example, specific experience in evaluating infants with cerebral palsy or with sensory impairments and in interpreting test results is critical, particularly in light of the fact that few existing infant assessment techniques have been developed specifically for infants with these disabilities.

Familiarity with the specific assessment instrument is required as well. Because the attention span and interest level of infants are brief, a good working knowledge of the assessment instrument can speed the administration of the items, maximizing the chance that the infant's optimal performance is obtained. Many of the assessment instruments specify the level of expertise needed. For example, the Bayley Scales of Infant Development[7] should not be administered by anyone who is not trained in developmental or intellectual testing. In contrast, the Hawaii Early Learning Profile (HELP)[15] can be administered by an early interventionist who needs no particular training in test construction or developmental testing per se. At a basic level, however, all examiners should know the limitations of the testing instrument, how representative the infant's performance was, and how well they administered the test so that these factors can be considered in the interpretation of results.

The professional discipline of the examiner can vary. There are psychologists, nurses, early interventionists, special educators, among others, who can be competently trained examiners of infant cognitive abilities. However, the ability to interpret the results and to communicate these findings to the infant's parents and to other professionals is as important as the ability to choose and to administer the test. Because of these reasons it is often advisable to choose a developmental or clinical psychologist or other professional with specific knowledge of test construction and limitations of intellectual testing and with the clinical skills necessary to interpret and relate in a clear but compassionate way what may be distressing news to the family. Because the results of a cognitive assessment are important for other developmental areas, the examiner should also have a working knowledge of other developmental areas so that the results can be communicated to other professionals, such as a physical therapist or physician, in a meaningful way.

Standardization sample

In addition to matching the purpose of the assessment to the theoretical under-pinnings of the test itself, it is important to determine whether the characteristics of the child being evaluated are similar to those of the group for whom the test was developed or standardized. Standardization is a mechanism for attaching meaning to raw scores and for making comparisons between and among individuals. Some-times it is not possible to find an assessment instrument whose standardization sample is comparable to the characteristics of the infant being evaluated, espe-cially when evaluation of infants with chronic illness or multiple disabilities is becoming more common. Nevertheless, when these infants are being evaluated, this factor should enter into the interpretation of the results.

Performance

Another consideration is the type of performance one is interested in obtaining. Cronbach[16] distinguished between measures of maximum or best performance and measures of typical performance. For example, the Brazelton Neonatal Behavioral Assessment Scale[17] is designed to examine the infant's best performance, and spe-cific conditions are outlined that must be met before the infant's performance is considered optimal. Measures of typical performance, such as tests of personality, habits, or interests, are designed to examine an individual's usual, representative, or typical behavior.

Psychometric issues

Psychometric issues, such as reliability and validity, should enter into the choice of an assessment instrument. Reliability refers to the consistency and accu-racy of measurement, that is, what proportion of an infant's score can be attributed to chance or error and what proportion is a "true score." There are a number of ways to estimate reliability (eg, test-retest, alternate forms, split half, and coeffi-cient alpha). For example, if an infant is to be reevaluated in the near future, the test-retest reliability of a particular instrument would be an important consider-ation. A test with good test-retest reliability would give the examiner greater con-fidence that the results obtained on the second evaluation were a valid representa-tion of the infant's abilities and not reflective of error or chance fluctuations in the test itself. All estimations of reliability are reported in the form of a correlation coefficient (eg, Pearson r) and range from 0 to 1.00. The closer a reliability coeffi-cient is to 1.00 the better. However, because some degree of chance or error enters into every assessment, a reliability of 1.00 is rarely obtained. Reliabilities between .70s and .90s indicate that the test is generally stable and accurate.

While good reliability is an essential characteristic of an assessment instrument, the information it provides is useless if the test lacks validity. Validity is the relationship between the variable or trait being measured and the procedures used to measure it. In other words, does the test measure what it says it does? There are three major types of validity: content, criterion-related, and construct. Content validity is whether the test covers the material it is supposed to cover. Criterion-related validity, such as concurrent or predictive validity, relates to the comparison of test scores with some external variable or "criterion" known or believed to measure the same variable or attribute.

Similar to reliability, the correlation coefficient is the usual index of criterion validity. Unlike the reliability coefficient, the value of the validity coefficient must be squared to determine the percentage of the infant's score that is due to chance fluctuations and the percentage thought to be a true reflection of the infant's abilities. For example, suppose the relationship or correlation between an infant's score on a test of cognitive abilities at 12 months of age and an intellectual assessment at 6 years of age is .70. Squaring .70 results in .49. This number indicates the proportion of variance shared in common by the two tests. Thus 49% of the infant's score is believed to be based on the infant's cognitive abilities; 51% is attributable to error, chance, plus the effects of some other undetermined variables.

How high a validity coefficient should be will vary. Obviously the higher the validity coefficient the more confidence the examiner can place on the results of the test being an accurate reflection of the infant's abilities. Given the choice between two measures where everything else is equal, it would be better to choose the one with the higher criterion validity.

Construct validity examines the *meaning* of the test. It is determined by examining the relationship of the test to the variables the test is intended to assess as well as the relationship to those that should have no relationship to the domain underlying the instrument. Construct validity cannot be determined on the basis of any one study but is best demonstrated by an accumulation of supportive evidence from different sources over time. For example, the construct validity of an infant assessment instrument would be determined by demonstrating high positive correlations or a strong relationship with other measures of intelligence and a low correlation or minimal relationship with a measure of a presumably unrelated trait or variable, such as temperament.

INTERPRETATION OF TEST RESULTS

Criterion versus norm referencing

Assessment instruments differ on whether test scores are left as raw scores or are translated into criterion-referenced or norm-referenced scores. Raw scores alone provide no stable point of comparison between individuals since scores might indicate what is a normal or expected performance on a particular test. To aid in interpreting the infant's score, the raw score can be translated. In criterion-referenced instruments, the raw score is translated into a statement about how that child's performance compares with a specified behavioral criterion established for that specific test. The principal use of criterion referencing has been in the development of mastery learning tests. The tests are designed to measure whether an individual has or has not attained mastery of a specific content area. The content of these criterion-referenced measures is usually designed to test acquisition of a relatively small domain of content and skills. Age-equivalent scores, mental age, ratio intelligence quotients, and some developmental quotients are examples of criterion-referenced scores. The advantage of these conversions is that they are readily understandable and are suitable when one is interested in whether an infant has acquired a specific skill. However, criterion-referenced tests should not be used if one is interested in comparing an infant's performance to the average performance of a group of infants in general. When this type of information is desired, norm-referenced instruments are more appropriate.

Most norm-referenced measures are based on an overview of some broad content domain (eg, intelligence), in contrast to the criterion-referenced tests that examine a specific skill (eg, fine motor). For example, the Early Learning Accomplishment Profile (Early LAP, see Appendix A), a criterion-referenced measure, is designed to provide a record of the child's existing skills in the major developmental areas. The Bayley Scales of Infant Development,[7] a norm-referenced instrument, provides a comparison of an infant's mental and motor abilities with those of other infants. Norm-referenced scores are most commonly reported as percentile ranks, z-scores, t-scores, stanines, and deviation intelligence quotients.

Correction for prematurity

Since an increasing number of the infants whose cognitive abilities are being evaluated have bene born prematurely, another consideration in the interpretation of results is the issue of correction for prematurity. There continues to be debate over whether one uses an infant's gestational or chronologic age in the calculation of the scores and how long one uses this conversion. It has typically been the practice to correct for prematurity during the first two years of life.[18–20] However, there is growing evidence that this may not be the most appropriate practice. Caputo et al,[21] Siegel,[22] and others have indicated that correction for the degree of prematurity appears to be appropriate in the first few months or during the first year. However, a slightly more accurate prediction is achieved by using the uncorrected scores. As the Siegel[22] study points out, biologic immaturity alone is not the only consideration. Environmental influences, low birth weight, neurologic insult, among others, influence test scores. Furthermore, the degree of prematurity is a consideration. It might be more appropriate to correct for prematurity longer if the child was born at 28-weeks gestation than if the child was born at 34 weeks. In addition, as the medical conditions under which premature infants are born improve over time, correction for prematurity must be constantly reevaluated.

Whatever the correction method used, it is important to discuss with the child's family the child's current rate of development and what rate would be necessary for the infant to "catch up" in the future. Many parents have reported disappointment when an early prediction of catching up was not accurate. The box is an example of how the infant's rate of development can be explained.

At the January evaluation this infant was only one month beyond his or her gestational age and three months behind his or her chronologic age. If the infant gains one month of skills for each month of life until the next evaluation, he or she will still be three months behind his or her chronologic age, but the relative percentage of delay (75% v 83%) would be less. To catch up with his or her chronologic age by the next evaluation, the infant would need to gain nine months of skills in only six months time—an accelerated rate of development. Sharing this type of discussion with the family can be helpful in setting realistic expectations for the infant's development. Continuing to use a child's gestational age for some time (eg, until 3 years of age) without some type of discussion about the infant's rate of development can place the family at risk for bitter disappointment when the child does not make up all the delay. It can, in some cases, lead the family to be disappointed with what may in fact be a good rate of development (eg, month-for-month gain).

Testing situation

When choosing an assessment instrument and when interpreting the results the examiner should consider where the child is being evaluated. Evaluation results obtained during an assessment in familiar surroundings such as the child's home may be very different from those obtained on the same child in unfamiliar or po-

---

Premature Infant's Rate of Development

Date of evaluation	January		June
Chronologic age (CA)	12 months	+6 months	18 months
Gestational age (GA)	10 months	+6 months	16 months
Cognitive development	9 months	+6 months	15 months
Percentage of delay (CA)	75%		83%
Percentage of delay (GA)	90%		94%

tentially disruptive settings (eg, developmental evaluation clinic). These factors are critical in the interpretation of the results for a child of any age but particularly for an infant.

The timing of the evaluation also is an important factor. If one has any flexibility in scheduling a cognitive evaluation, it would be important to contact the family to determine when the infant normally naps or feeds. Trying to elicit the infant's interest in a structured task during a regular naptime is less likely to yield the best performance.

Since many infants receiving cognitive evaluations may have other health difficulties, possibly as the result of prematurity, the infant's health status should be considered. Was the infant fatigued following several developmental or medical evaluations? Does the infant have an ear infection or some other acute condition that may be affecting his or her performance? While it is not always possible to schedule the evaluation when these factors are not concerns, some mention of them in the interpretation of the results is important. Conferring with other professionals who have ongoing contact with the infant or who may have evaluated the infant earlier in the day or asking the parents if the infant's performance was representative or typical of what they see at home are ways in which the representatives of the infant's performance can be estimated. Some statement about how valid the test results are thought to be should be included in every developmental evaluation report.

Parent's report

Asking parents about the representativeness of their infant's performance will automatically lead to the question of whether to include, and how to include, the parent's report in the interpretation of results. Historically, professionals' estimation of the validity of a parent report has been that parents overestimate their child's abilities. As a result a parent's report typically has not been included in the analysis of results or in the report.

Furthermore, the differences in perspective are not usually discussed or reconciled, often leading professionals to label the parents as denying the child's true developmental limitations and the parents to discount the examiner's results because they did not account for skills not displayed in the artificial testing situation.

There are many benefits for including a parent's report. First, it is a source of important and accurate information about the child's abilities. While referring to a parent report about parent–child interaction, Maccoby and Martin's[23] comment is applicable to the assessment of an infant's cognitive abilities as well.

Using parents as informants has great potential advantages. For assessment of behavior that varies considerably across situations or behavior that is usually not displayed in public, reliable observational data are difficult to obtain and parent interviews are often the only viable alternative. Parents have an opportunity to observe their children and the patterns of interaction in their families over extended periods of time in a broad range of situations. Thus by virtue of their daily participation in the family system, parents have access to a truly unique body of information about the family, and it is reasonable to tap into this information by questioning them.[23(p16)]

There is growing evidence that there is not much difference between the parent and the professional perspective, and where different the parents' perspective may be more accurate. For example, in one study by Honzik et al,[24] use of mothers' reports contributed to more accurate findings. Infants who were suspected, based on birth records, of having neurologic impairment vocalized with greater frequency during their cognitive evaluations at 8 months of age than was true of the normal control group. Honzik et al[24] concluded that the infants in the control group were more inhibited by the strangeness of the test situation and vocalized less in the test situation, thus failing the vocalization items on the Bayley. On the Griffiths and the Gesell scales, the mothers' reports of vocalizing would have been credited, thus leading to a more accurate representation of the infant's skills.

In many cases parents give the child more credit for emerging skills than do professionals and because of their ongoing contact with the infant may be in a better position to note whether the strangeness of the testing situation has hampered the child's test performance. Often the difference between a parent's report and a professional observation may not be in the behavior noted but in the interpretation of the behavior. Parents' definition of "talking" may be quite different from that of a professional. Nevertheless, a skilled interviewer can help the parent to identify what behavior they have interpreted as talking and to discuss the interpretation that the professional would make of this behavior. Another source of disagreement is whether the skill is well-established or whether the skill is emerging, with the infant relying more on the cues of the situation. Again, this is often seen in the interpretation of the infant's understanding of verbal requests. The parent may see the infant make anticipatory moves when the infant is told that he or she will be going outside. The parent reports that the infant understands this statement. However, when administered in the testing situation, without the behavioral environmental cues of the parent standing at the door, holding a coat, and reaching out his or her arms for the infant, the infant does not appear to understand. While the infant may not demonstrate enough understanding to be credited on a developmental evaluation, he or she is demonstrating emerging knowledge, and the correlation between the verbal command and the environmental cues is one way this knowledge of verbal commands can develop. Thus both the parent and professional are accurate, and both pieces of information are important in evaluating the child's development and in planning development evaluations.

A parent's report can be included in the developmental report in a number of ways. Some developmental assessments, such as the Brunet-Lezine,[3] do provide for the inclusion of a parent's report. Professionals may also want to score a developmental evaluation in two ways: (1) using only those behaviors that were observable in the testing, and (2) giving credit for a parent's report. In many cases the resulting developmental age or developmental quotient is not that different.

By including a parent's report, the professional has access to valuable information not readily accessible in the testing situation that can serve as a guide in planning interventions and in deciding whether the intervention should take place in the home or in a center-based program. Perhaps more importantly, the inclusion of a parent's report and discussion of different perspectives lays the groundwork for a collaborative relationship between the professional and parent rather than the adversarial one that can often develop when the parent feels the results are widely discrepant from his or her view. While there are some circumstances in which the parent's estimation is extremely overinflated, simply discounting the parent's perspective will not likely end this problem. A sensitive discussion of the behaviors in question will be more likely to lead to a mutual understanding. This agreement is essential if parents are to collaborate on the intervention as well.

USEFULNESS OF INFANT COGNITIVE ASSESSMENT

As mentioned above, the cognitive assessment of infants can serve many purposes. First, it provides an estimate of the way a child currently thinks about the world and processes information. This information, in turn, can be used in planning developmental interventions. Care must be taken that the developmental activity or intervention (eg, block building) is not the same as the task used to assess the attainment of that skill (eg, builds tower of eight cubes). "Teaching the test," as it is sometimes called, not only leads to inflated tests scores and splinter skills but really does not address or remediate the underlying delay or difficulty.

The results of a cognitive assessment can be helpful in other ways as well. Along with results of developmental evaluations in other areas (eg, gross motor, speech–language), it is a critical factor in basing expectations for the development of self-help or adaptive skills. For example, it would be inappropriate to consider beginning toilet training with a 3-year-old whose cognitive, gross motor, and speech–language skills are delayed at a 1-year level. The scores also are helpful in basing expectations for the child's behavior in areas such as attention span or interest in toys.

Professionals from other disciplines may find this information useful as well. In the absence of evaluations in other developmental areas, a skilled examiner can use the results of an infant's performance in a cognitive evaluation as a screen to identify those infants in need of additional testing of motor or speech–language skills. In addition, the results can be used in the planning of developmental interventions in other developmental areas.

The assessment of an infant is itself an intervention. Parental observations of the assessment can help parents and other family members gain an understanding of and insight into the child's needs and strengths. The information can, for example, enable parents to set expectations, to better understand the child's communicative cues, and to incorporate this information into the child's daily routines. The assessment process also provides an opportunity for parents and family members to ask questions and to clarify concerns about the infant's development. The Brazelton Neonatal Assessment Scale is a good example of how an assessment has been used in this manner.

Predictive validity

The results of a cognitive assessment can, in some cases, provide an estimate of the child's overall future intellectual abilities. How well evaluations of cognitive abilities during infancy predict performance on later intellectual tests has been a critical issue in the field since the inception of infant assessment. The method used to assess the predictive validity is interage correlations. As with most assessments, not just infant tests, the longer the time period between evaluations, the lower the correlation or relationship between the test scores. The result of these cumulative findings has been that in some circles infant cognitive assessments have not been regarded as predictive of later intelligence or that the tests were not really measuring cognition or intelligence.

Despite these views there are many theories and much research to support the predictive validity and overall usefulness of infant assessment. Ironically many of the early developers of infant assessment instruments, such as Gesell, indicated that they never intended tests to measure intelligence and therefore they should not be expected to predict later IQ. In addition, many theorists have stated that high correlations between infant assessment and the measurement of later intelligence should not be expected because infant intelligence may not be a unitary concept. Piaget and others have theorized that mental functioning undergoes qualitative changes over time, making the issue of prediction a moot point. Thus the skills being evaluated with infant tests (eg, sensorimotor), while important for later functioning, are not the same skills measured on tests of intellectual functioning at a later age (eg, visual-motor skills, verbal reasoning).

Perhaps the most convincing argument for the predictive validity of infant assessments is the research that documents that for infants with moderate to severe developmental delays the predictive validity is much greater.[13,25–29] These findings are consistent, regardless of whether the "low score is due to chromosomal aberrations (eg, trisomy 21), infection (rubella during pregnancy), injury, perinatal anoxia, or generalized abnormality of unknown etiology."[19(p97)] Honzik[13] also notes that while infant mental tests can be helpful in the diagnosis of neurologic lags or the effects of an impoverished or enriched environment, infant tests have more limited predictive validity when the infant scores are high. According to Honzik, "precocity in infancy may reflect early maturing or the effects of a great deal of stimulation rather than higher potential for later above-average cognitive functioning."[13(p97)]

There are many ways to further improve the diagnostic value of infant assessments. Periodic evaluations as well as the interpretation of the results in light of other developmental tests or related factors (eg, parent's socioeconomic status, degree of prematurity, health) can provide a more complete picture of the infant's current status and of those factors that may have long-term effects on the development of the infant's cognitive abilities.

FUTURE DIRECTIONS

Where is the field of infant cognitive assessment going? One direction seems to be a more thorough evaluation of other factors that interact with and relate to the development of cognitive abilities. The previous research on attachment and temperament continues along with more in-depth studies into parent–child relationships and factors that fall under the general heading of infant mental health.[30,31]

A second focus is on improving the ability of infant assessment techniques to predict development later on. McCall[25] and others have suggested several ways in which prediction can be improved, including using existing infant assessment techniques but augmenting them with additional information, such as the health status of the infant or developmental data on other related skills such as speech and language development; the use of frequent periodic assessments to identify abnormal patterns of development that can serve as markers for future developmental delay; or the inclusion of test items in the assessment battery that have been shown to be associated with specific abnormalities or risk conditions (eg, poor social responses, seizures, odd postures or movements).

A third area seems to relate to the age-old question of the continuity/discontinuity of development. There continues to be investigation into techniques that assess abilities in infancy that are assumed to be present in later childhood. The development of measures to assess sensory processing, such as attention, discrimination, and memory, seem to be the most promising at this time. One example of this approach is based on the early research by Fantz and Nevis[32] and others that demonstrated differences in visual processing among infants without developmental delay, those at risk, and those with identifiable delays. Fagan and his colleagues[33] have developed a screening device that assesses an infant's ability to discriminate among pictures being shown, to remember a picture previously seen, and to visually fixate to the novel stimulus. Because it is thought that perceptual and memory processes are necessary for successful performance on intellectual evaluations at a later age, documentation of an infant's competence in theses areas were hypothesized to be predictive of later functioning. In fact, the available research on this screening instrument has yielded prediction rates clearly better for this approach than for other standardized assessment devices such as the Bayley scales. While the Fagan test does not obviate the need for more thorough developmental evaluations, it does show promise as a reliable and valid screening instrument and perhaps sets the stage for more assessment measures based on this theoretical perspective.

Another possible direction for the field of infant cognitive assessment is evident in the work of Als[34] and Duffy et al,[35] which uses a combination of behavioral assessment and traditional neurophysiologic measures. Als' APIB,[34] the Assessment of Preterm Infant's Behavior, has been combined with Duffy and colleagues'[35] brain electrical activity mapping (BEAM) technique to examine the diagnostic value of this combined approach. The BEAM uses computerized topographic mapping to develop a visual picture of EEG and evoked potential (EP) data (for additional information see the article by Karniski in the "Technology" section of this issue). In one study by Duffy and Als[36] both measures were used to distinguish between two groups of infants—five neurologist-referred infants and one pediatrician-referred infant judged on the APIB to be the least behaviorally competent (eg, autonomic instability, difficulty in modulating tone, posture, and movement) from five pediatrician-referred infants who were judged to be the most behaviorally competent. These infants were then studied in a neurophysiology laboratory, and the results were used to generate topographic maps. The two groups were successfully distinguished by use of the BEAM. The authors conclude that the data suggest that direct observations of behavioral clustering do appear to have correlates in measures of brain electrical activity and that topographic display can be helpful in identifying differences between these behavioral clusters. Clearly more thorough investigation and development are needed, but the combination of techniques could prove to be a valuable technique in the early identification of those infants at risk for later neurologic and behavioral difficulties, such as learning disabilities.

•   •   •

The field of infant cognitive assessment has come a long way from Gesell's first scale in 1925. While all the existing instruments can be criticized to some degree, there are a number of well-standardized, reliable, and relatively valid instruments available that are appropriate for use in documenting delay or risk status, for research, for planning intervention, or for predicting future development. Certainly continued refinement and restandardization with existing instruments are needed as well as the development of techniques for use with infants with special needs (eg, cerebral palsy, visual impairment). The recent work of Fantz and Nevis,[32] Fagan et al,[33] Als,[34] Duffy et al,[35] Duffy and Als,[36] and others reflect advancement in this area. As the need for more refined and additional infant assessment techniques grows, particularly with the establishment of more early intervention programs through Public Law 99-457 and the increased survival of infants with special needs becomes apparent, care must be taken so that the basics of good test construction, the need for solid testing skills and responsible test interpretation, and an appreciation of the complexity of infant cognitive development are not disregarded.

REFERENCES

1. Gesell A: *The Mental Growth of the Preschool Child.* New York, Macmillan, 1925.

2. Knobloch H, Pasamanick B: *Gesell and Amatruda's Developmental Diagnosis: The Evaluation and Management of Normal and Abnormal Neuropsychologic Development in Infancy and Early Childhood,* ed 3. New York, Harper & Row, 1974.

3. Brunet O, Lezine PUF: *Le Developpement Psychologique del al Premiere Enfance.* Issy-les-Moulineaux, France, Editions Scientifiques et Psychotechniques, 1951.

4. Griffiths R: *The Abilities of Babies.* New York, McGraw-Hill, 1954.

5. Cattell P: *The Measurement of Intelligence of Infants and Young Children.* New York, Psychological Corporation, 1940.

6. Bayley N: Mental growth during the first three years. *Genetic Psychology Monographs* 1933;14:1–92.

7. Bayley, N: *Bayley Scales of Infant Development.* New York, Psychological Corporation, 1969.

8. Kohen-Raz, R: Scalogram analysis of some developmental sequences of infant behavior as measured by the Bayley Infant Scale of Mental Development. *Gen Psychol Monographs* 1967;76:3–21.

9. Casati I, Lezine I: *Les Etapes de L'Intelligence Sensori-Motrice.* Paris, Editions du Centre de Psychologie Appliquée, 1968.

10. Corman HH, Escalona SK: Stages of sensorimotor development: A replication study. *Merrill-Palmer Q* 1969;15:351–361.

11. Uzgiris IC, Hunt JMcV: *Toward Ordinal Scales of Psychological Development in Infancy.* Champaign, Ill, University of Illinois, 1975.

12. Lewis M, Sullivan MW: Infant intelligence and its assessment, in Wolman BB (ed): *Handbook of Intelligence: Theories, Measurements, and Application.* New York, Wiley, 1985.

13. Honzik MP: Measuring mental abilities in infancy: The values and limitations, in Lewis M (ed): *Origins of Intelligence.* New York, Plenum, 1983, pp 67–106.

14. Brooks-Gunn J, Weinraub M: Origins of infant intelligence testing, in Lewis M (ed): *Origins of Intelligence.* New York, Plenum, 1983, pp 25–66.

15. *Hawaii Early Learning Profile Activity Guide (HELP). Enrichment Project for Handicapped Infants.* Palo Alto, Calif, VORT Corporation, 1979.

16. Cronbach LJ: *Essentials of Psychological Testing,* ed 3. New York, Harper & Row, 1970.

17. Brazelton TB: *Neonatal Behavioral Assessment Scale.* Clinics in Developmental Medicine, Philadelphia, Lippincott, 1973, No. 50.

18. Hunt JV: Predicting intellectual disorders in childhood for preterm infants with birthweights below 1501 grams, in Friedman SL, Sigman M (eds): *Preterm Birth and Psychological Development.* New York, Academic Press, 1981, pp 84–102.

19. Hunt JV, Rhodes L: Mental development of infants during the first year. *Child Dev* 1977;49:204–210.

20. Parmelee A, Schulte F: Developmental testing of preterm and small-for-date infants. *Pediatrics* 1970;17:125–146.

21. Caputo DV, Goldstein KM, Taub HB: Neonatal compromise and later psychological development: A 10-year longitudinal study, in Friedman SL, Sigman M (eds): *Preterm Birth and Psychological Development.* New York, Academic Press, 1981, pp 36–73.

22. Siegel LS: Correction for prematurity and its consequences for the assessment of the very low birth weight infant. Child Dev 1983;54:1176–1188.

23. Maccoby EE, Martin JA: Socialization in the context of the family: Parent-child interaction, in Hetherington EM (ed): *Handbook of Child Psychology.* New York, Wiley, 1983, vol 4.

24. Honzik MP, Hutchings JJ, Burnip SR: Birth record assessment and test performance at eight months. 1965;109:416–426.

25. McCall RB: Toward an epigenetic conception of mental development in the first three years of life, in Lewis M (ed): *Origins of Intelligence.* New York, Plenum Press, 1976, pp 97–122.

26. Goodman J, Cameron J: The meaning of IQ constancy in young retarded children. *J Genet Psychol* 1978;132:109–111.

27. Vanderveer B, Scheweid E: Infant assessment: Stability of mental functioning in young retarded children. *Am J Ment Defic* 1974;79:1–4.

28. Drillien C: A longitudinal study of the growth and development of prematurely born children. Part VII: Mental development 2–5 years. *Arch Dis Child* 1961;36:233–240.

29. Ireton H, Thwing E, Gravem H: Infant mental development and neurological status, family socioeconomic status, and intelligence at age four. *Child Dev* 1971;41:937–945.

30. Field T: Affective and interactive disturbances in infants, in Osofsky JD (ed): *Handbook of Infant Development,* ed 2. New York, Wiley, 1987, p 972.

31. Emde RN: Infant mental health: Clinical dilemmas, the expansion of meaning, and opportunities, in Osofsky JD (ed): *Handbook of Infant Development,* ed 2. New York, Wiley, 1987, pp 1297–1320.

32. Fantz RL, Nevis S: Pattern preferences and perceptual-cognitive development in early infancy. *Merrill-Palmer Q* 1967;13:77–108.

33. Fagan JF, Singer LT, Montie JE, et al: Selective screening device for the early detection of normal or delayed cognitive development in infants at risk for later mental retardation. *Pediatrics* 1986;78:1021–1026.

34. Als H: Toward a synactive theory of development: Promise for the assessment and support of infant individuality. *Infant Ment Health J* 1982;3:229–243.

35. Duffy FH, Burchfiel JL, Lombroso CT: Brain electrical activity mapping (BEAM): A method for extending the clinical utility of EEG and evoked potential data. *Ann Neurol* 1979;7:412–420.

36. Duffy FH, Als H: Neurophysiological assessment of the neonate. An approach combining brain electrical mapping (BEAM) with behavior assessment (APIB), in Brazelton TB, Lester BM (eds): *New Approaches to Developmental Screening of Infants.* New York, Elsevier Science, 1983, pp 175–196.

37. Frankenburg W, Dodds J: The *Denver Developmental Screening Test*. Denver, University of Colorado Medical School, 1975.

38. Ireton HR, Thwing EJ: *Minnesota Child Development Inventory (MCDI)*. Minneapolis, Behavior Science Systems, Inc, 1974.

39. Stillman R (ed): *The Callier-Azusa Scale*. Dallas, Tex, South Central Regional Center for Services to Deaf-Blind Children, 1977.

40. Bluma SM, Shearer MS, Frosham AH, et al: *Portage Guide to Early Education (No. 12)*. Portage, Wis, Cooperative Educational Agency, 1976.

41. Glover ME, Preminger J, Sanford A: *Early Learning Accomplishment Profile* (Early LAP). Winston-Salem, Kaplan Press, 1978.

Appendix A

Selected infant assessment instruments

PSYCHOMETRIC INSTRUMENTS

Bayley Scales of Infant Development

The mental scale (162 items) measures sensory-perceptual acuities and discriminations; early acquisition of object constancy and memory, learning and problem-solving ability; vocalizations and the beginning of verbal communications and classifications. The motor scale (81 items) measures the degree of control of the body, coordination of the large muscles and finer manipulatory skills of the hands and fingers. The tester must be a trained examiner. Test is standardized with established reliability and construct validity. It is appropriate for infants aged 1 month to 30 months.

SENSORIMOTOR INSTRUMENTS

Infant Scales of Psychological Development

Inspired by Piaget's writings on infant intelligence, this instrument assesses an infant's achievement as a sequence of ordered levels of intellectual functioning. A series of six scales include visual pursuit and the permanence of objects, the development of means for obtaining desired environmental events, development of operational causality, the construction of object relations in space, the development of gestural and vocal imitation. The tester should have early intervention experience. Information concerning standardization, reliability, and validity is available in the manual. Appropriate for infants from birth to 2 years of age.

SCREENING INSTRUMENTS

Denver Developmental Screening Test[37]

Largely based on the Gesell schedules, the test (105 items) is an individually administered screening inventory designed to identify children with developmental delays. It measures four aspects of functioning: adaptive, fine and gross motor, language, and personal-social development. It yields an overall summary label. The tester can be a trained professional or paraprofessional. The test is standardized with established reliability and construct validity. Appropriate for infants and young children from birth through 6 years of age.

Minnesota Child Development Inventory[38]

This 320-item inventory provides a developmental profile based on summary scores for each of the following content areas: gross/fine motor, receptive/expressive language, person-social, and situation comprehension. The tester is the parent. The inventory has been standardized, and there is reliability and validity information.

ASSESSMENT INSTRUMENTS WITH SPECIAL POPULATIONS[39]

Callier-Azusa Scale

The scale (551 items) is composed of subscales in the following areas: motor development, perceptual and cognitive development, daily living skills, language development, and socialization. Each subscale is composed of sequential steps describing developmental milestones. Space is provided for comments by the teacher. The tester is the teacher/interventionist. The test is an observationally based tool, yielding a developmental profile. The test has been standardized from other tests and reliability is available from the author. There is no information on validity. The scale is appropriate for use with children from birth to 4 years of age who are deaf, blind, or severely and profoundly disabled.

ASSESSMENT-BASED PROGRAMMING INSTRUMENTS

Hawaii Early Learning Profile Activity Guide (HELP)

The HELP (585 items) assesses infants in six areas of development: gross/fine motor, expressive language, cognitive, social-emotional, and self-help. The HELP chart allows for a visual representation of the child's functional level in each domain. The accompanying activities guide provides suggested intervention activities accompanying specific developmental ages. Standardization is based on the items drawn from other tests, and there is limited information on reliability and validity. The test is appropriate for children from birth to 3 years of age.

Portage Guide to Early Education[40]

The Portage Guide is comprised of three parts: a checklist, a manual, and cards to be used in teaching behaviors included in the checklist. The checklist (580 items) is to be used as an assessment tool to pinpoint existing developmental strengths as well as areas of need. The tester is the interventionist, and there is limited information on standardization, reliability, and validity. Appropriate for children from birth to 6 years of age.

Early Learning Accomplishment Profile[41]

The Early LAP (412 items) is designed to provide the parent or teacher with a simple criterion-referenced record of the child's existing skills in all the major developmental domains. It identifies the next appropriate step in development and gives detailed instructions for reaching this objective. The tester is unspecified. Standardization is based on items from other tests, and there is limited information on reliability and validity.

Appendix B

Checklist for assessing infant cognition

Purpose or goals of test

- Screening
- Assessment of cognitive abilities
- Assessment of all developmental areas
- Assessment-based programming instrument

Ages of children for which test is intended

Test administration

- Time to administer
- Who administers (eg, professional, paraprofessional, parent)
- Acceptability
- Cost
- Necessary testing conditions

Test construction

- Type of test or procedure (eg, interview, checklist, inventory, observation)
- Acceptability of standardization sample to infant
- Reliability (eg, test-retest, alternate forms)
- Validity (eg, construct, content)

Test scoring and interpretation

- Optimal *v* typical performance
- Criterion-referenced *v* norm-referenced

A hierarchy of motor outcome assessment: Self-initiated movements through adaptive motor function

Stephen M. Haley, PhD
Acting Director
Medical Rehabilitation Research and
 Training Center in Rehabilitation
 and Childhood Trauma
Assistant Professor
Tufts University School of Medicine
Boston, Massachusetts

Mary Jo Baryza, MS
Research Assistant
Medical Rehabilitation Research and
 Training Center in Rehabilitation
 and Childhood Trauma
Instructor
Tufts University School of Medicine
Boston, Massachusetts

MOVEMENT EDUCATION and treatment are integral parts of most intervention and educational programs for young children with developmental deficits. A comprehensive and multidimensional motor assessment strategy for young children that emphasizes consistent monitoring of progress is essential for program refinement and successful motor gains. Although some evidence supports the effectiveness of motor programming,[1,2] many studies have not been able to demonstrate the benefits expected from motor intervention.[3] Much of the criticism of evaluation studies has been directed toward the limited spectrum of measurement variables used to monitor an individual child's progress or conduct program evaluation research.[4] Many questions remain regarding the specific effects of motor deficit remediation, yet little attention has been given to the issues related to the selection of appropriate outcome measures. The purpose of this article is to describe a broad framework for the conceptualization of motor outcome variables that can be used for the assessment of motor programming. The fundamental importance of matching outcome measures to treatment and intervention goals for individual children will also be stressed.

The remediation of motor deficits in young children can take a variety of forms. Motor programs may involve general stimulation activities; curriculum-based programming to improve developmental skills; specific treatment procedures by occupational or physical therapists to improve posture and motor control; or individualized training, such as the use of a prosthetic device for the development of upper-extremity functional skills. In most cases, motor programs are multifaceted, involve a wide spectrum of short-term and long-term outcome goals, and are derived from both narrow and broad-based curricula.[5]

This work of the Medical Rehabilitation Research and Training Center in Rehabilitation and Childhood Trauma was supported in part by Grants H133B80009 and H133G80043 from the National Institute on Disability and Rehabilitation Research, US Department of Education.

Inf Young Children 1990; 3(2): 1–14
© 1990 Aspen Publishers, Inc.

For a specific child, outcome variables are often identified at a number of programmatic levels. An example is a child who has significant problems in walking a distance of 50 ft as a result of balance deficits. Changes in the quality of walking (improved control of stepping, more normal base of support) can be measured and related to the intervention program. Standing balance tests may also be used to determine improvements in stability and resistance to stumbling and falling. At a more functional level, recording the actual decrease in the frequency of falls or the amount of time needed to walk 50 ft provides an indication of adaptive change. Collectively, multiple outcome measures not only provide information on child improvement, but also suggest patterns of interdependence among different levels of outcome variables. Consistent efforts to capture progress at many levels through a comprehensive series of outcome measures provides the intervener with data that are essential for evaluation and refinement of the motor program.

MOTOR OUTCOME ASSESSMENT HIERARCHY

Motor outcome variables can be classified into several categories. Fig 1 depicts five levels of motor outcome variables:
1. self-initiated movements,
2. prefunctional motor determinants,
3. motor performance and motor control variables,
4. motor skills, and
5. adaptive motor function.

This classification scheme derives its bases from a number of different viewpoints. First, the hierarchy arranges motor variables from a subcomponent level of analysis to motor activities involving a series of complex tasks. The teaching of new motor skills is often predicated on the building of various components into integrated activities, and thus the hierarchy represents progression from a microanalysis of movement components to a macroanalysis of motor function. Moreover, the hierarchy is consistent with a traditional clinical viewpoint of the importance of underlying motor components. Campbell and Stewart[6] discussed a motor skill acquisition model that included underlying components of movement, activation of desired muscle contractions, and translation of movements into functional and cognitively directed movements. In their model, detailed motor assessment data were needed to identify precise entry points of intervention and to provide an exact picture of motor status. In addition, global measures were recorded to help interviewers understand the relationship between component behaviors and functional outcomes.

Second, the motor outcome assessment hierarchy is consistent with a classification scheme defined by the World Health Organization.[7] This scheme, which defines outcome parameters at the levels of impairment, disability, and handicap, has been applied conceptually to pediatric assessments.[8,9] Impairments are isolated deficits that interfere with the execution of movement, such as muscle contractures, loss of an extremity, or a specific balance or coordination deficit. The term disability refers to the inability to complete daily activities, such as dressing, eating, or moving freely in the environment. Handicap is a term that refers to the limitation in the performance of a social role, depending on the age of the child and social demands placed on him or her. A young child may be considered to have a handicap if he or she is unable to play with peers or is unable (because of physical impairments) to attend a preschool or nursery program.

Third, the hierarchy includes outcome levels with increasingly greater relevance to ecologic needs and the requirements of the child's actual environment.[10] Specific motor competencies and skills tested in an early intervention or classroom environment are viewed as measuring only the capability of the child, rather

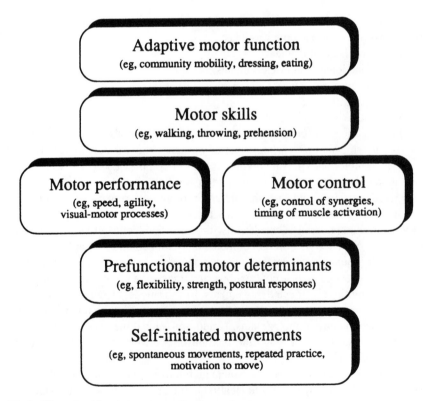

Fig 1. Hierarchy of motor assessment outcomes.

than the true motor performance during daily routines. From an ecologic perspective, interest is focused on what actually occurs in the home and on how new motor skills taught in the classroom or intervention program are generalized into the child's relevant environment.

The motor outcome assessment hierarchy represents a comprehensive framework for the identification of motor outcome assessments for multiple disciplines and purposes. A multilevel content assessment in the motor area permits various levels of specificity for different documentation, treatment planning, and child and program monitoring needs. Selected measures will be described that provide examples of standardized (if available) and nonstandardized measurement systems at each level of the hierarchy.

Self-initiated movements

Movement is a fundamental component of early development. Professionals working with children who have motor delays often forget that whereas movement is spontaneous for the nonhandicapped child, many children with motor and cognitive delays do not display a repertoire of self-initiated movements. Limiting factors may be cognitive, behavioral, or neuromotor in origin. Nevertheless, the paucity of movement may pose a serious problem for motor learning and overall developmental progress. The ability and willingness of a child to initiate movement are essential ingredients for the learning and acquisition of new motor skills. Normal children learn to move by constantly experimenting with new movement challenges. This type of outcome measure has generally been overlooked in clinical research or service provision for children with motor deficits. Touwen[11] considered the evaluation of spontaneous movements to be an important component of a developmental motor evaluation. He viewed the trial-and-error process in movement exploration and the variability of movement as strong indicators of normal motor development. Such systems of treatment as neurodevelopmental therapy are frequently directed toward giving the child the opportunity to experience and practice new movements that he or she could not otherwise experience.[12] Yet only fragmented attempts to develop measurement systems to document self-initiated and spontaneous movement changes have been reported.[13–18]

More recently, Haley[19] developed a standard protocol to document by videography self-initiated movement activity in infants. This protocol, the Analysis of Movement Activity in Infants, is designed to measure gross motor movements, especially antigravity and mobility patterns. Spontaneous movements of infants under nonstimulating and stimulating conditions (toys, encouragement of parents) are recorded for short intervals. Videotapes are scored for the amounts of time an infant spends in the static, intermediate (weight shift from support surface), transitional (movement from one developmental position to another), and mobility (progression to a new location) phases. Continuous real-time measurement is used to determine the relative frequency and duration probability of antigravity, transitional, and complex movements. Using this system, Baryza[20] identified specific movement characteristics that differentiate children with motor deficits from nonhandicapped comparison children. Efforts are currently under way by Baryza to evaluate the capability of the system to detect movement changes in a group of handicapped infants after intensive intervention programs. Continued development of measure or measurement systems is needed in this outcome domain to improve the documentation of self-initiated movement changes as a result of motor programming.

During the motor learning of any task, whatever the age of the child, practice and the correction of errors are vital to new skill acquisition.[21] Active movements and continual practice are particularly important to enable new motor patterns to emerge. For some children, self-motivation to move may not be strong, and therefore environmental reinforcements must be added as part of the motor program.[22,23] Attention to improving the frequency of practice to enable a new neuromotor pattern to become established may be an essential part of the motor program. Rates of functional practice can be important outcome variables to document if the motor program is initially directed toward increasing the rate of active functional motor responses.

Prefunctional motor determinants

A number of physical and motor variables have been suggested as important prefunctional measurements of the development of voluntary motor abilities:
- flexibility,
- force generation,
- postural reflexes and reactions,
- biomechanical aspects of posture, and
- growth variables.

Unfortunately, there is no straightforward formula for the degree of these components that is necessary for the achievement of certain motor skills and functions. In fact, the relationship of prerequisite variables to motor skill and function is complex and may be specific to different patterns of motor dysfunction. For example, most children with a strong asymmetrical tonic neck reflex are unable to walk. However, some children with athetoid cerebral palsy walk independently by making use of the reflex. The pattern may be abnormal, but it is very functional. Prefunctional motor determinants are outcome measures describing the component behaviors that may be required for the development of the functional motor capabilities of the child.

Flexibility and range of motion of the spine and extremities are obvious necessities for the execution of normal movements. For some children, a very important outcome measure of the motor program is the maintenance or restoration and improvement of flexibility or the prevention of contractures. Although range-of-motion measurements by therapists are common clinical procedures, extreme care must be taken to standardize measurements and to periodically assess procedural reliability, particularly in regard to children with strong spasticity.[24]

Postural stability and movement require adequate levels of force production in muscles. Force generation and extremity strength are difficult measurements to obtain accurately in the younger child. Strength in the infant and young child is often estimated by the ability to maintain antigravity postures such as prone extension and quadruped. Functionally related strength measures have been developed for the older child with muscular disease who is able to follow commands,[25] as part of motor proficiency tests[26] (see the section on motor performance/motor control) and by use of hand-held force transducers.[27]

Postural reflexes and reactions are considered important elements of normal motor development. Although they may be more directly related to the maturation of the nervous system than that of motor capabilities,[28] some evidence supports the notion that the development of postural reactions is closely correlated with motor skill development.[29,30] Normalization of postural tonus has frequently been the focus of much developmental intervention,[31] but its accurate measurement in infants is quite subjective. Detailed descriptions of clinical evaluation techniques and outcome measures of postural reflexes and reactions and of postural tonus are available.[28,32–35]

The biomechanical aspects of posture can be principal outcome measures in children with severe disabilities. A child's alignment over the base of support while sitting or standing influences the use of upper extremities and overall motor control. Altering posture, avoiding misaligned positions, and providing a better support system through either improved postural control or supportive equipment are prominent outcome measures to document, particularly if postural alignment is related to functional goals.

Growth measurements have recently been used to differentiate children with cerebral palsy from a normal group.[36] A long-term outcome of a motor stimulation program may be the improvement of overall growth, muscle mass, and body proportions. Although patterns of growth are influenced by multiple factors, such as general health, nutritional status, and environmental conditions, improvement in anthropometric measures may provide an important index of change that could be directly related to a motor intervention program.

Motor performance/motor control

Outcome variables of motor performance and control emphasize discrete, qualitative motor requirements, the processes of movement generation, and control of movement in the infant and young child. Motor performance variables refer to factors that influence the execution of movement. Five general motor performance requirements have been identified through research on normal children ranging in age from 4 through 15 years:

1. speed,
2. precision,
3. strength,
4. balance, and
5. coordination.[37]

The Bruininks-Oseretsky Test of Motor Proficiency[26] was an outgrowth of these motor performance factors, and it provides a standardized approach to measuring these components in school-age children. Campbell[38] identified additional performance outcome variables for children with motor deficits, including abnormal resistance to movements (often due to abnormal timing of muscle pairs), overactive responses to sensory input, and inability to perform selective and precise movements. Recently, the Tufts Assessment of Motor Performance[39] was developed to assess performance requirements underlying functionally related skills in children and adults with severe physical disabilities. Factor analysis of adult and pediatric scores has identified functionally related performance factors of grasp and release, manipulation, use of a typewriter, use of fasteners, dynamic balance, mat mobility, locomotion, and wheelchair skills. Unfortunately, motor or functional performance components have not been identified specifically through empirical studies in infants and preschool children.

New advances in technology, along with a greater appreciation of motor control processes, have led to an emerging clinical interest in evaluating the mechanisms that control movements. Increased use of instrumentation is regarded as an important refinement in our ability to evaluate and treat children.[38] Most of the present instrumentation is restricted to research applications, and yet many of the new approaches to understanding motor control can be applied to the clinical evaluation of infants and young children. For example, although Heriza[40,41] required expensive technology to monitor and record infant kicking, her work has provided clinicians with a much better understanding of the qualitative variables that are important to examine. Similarly, investigation of the control of upright balance has provided the clinician with a better framework from which to determine the nature of the balance control deficit (ie, somatosensory, vestibular, or visual).[42,43] Continued development of these measures and further work on their applications to clinical assessment will likely improve our ability to understand, assess, and teach children better control of their movements.

Motor skills

Motor skills are discrete tasks that are the result of motor learning or practice.[44] In contrast to adaptive motor function, motor skills are defined as tasks performed outside the context of environmental demands. For example, most standardized developmental tests are assessments of motor skills.[45–47] These tests sample skills such as crawling, sitting upright, hopping, kicking a ball, grasping a raisin, and putting rings on a ring stack. Most early intervention and early childhood educational programs rely heavily on the use of developmental skill assessments for description of changes in a child. Motor milestone tests are very appropriate for detecting delays in individual children or for monitoring the progress of children who deviate only slightly from a normal developmental course.[48] Assessment instruments are now being extended into the adaptive and functional areas for use with children who have moderate and severe handicaps.[9,49]

Adaptive motor function

Assessments of adaptive motor function measure the ability of the child to perform necessary daily activities. The focus of the assessment is to determine the independence and maximization of function performed within the limitations imposed by the child's level of disability. For example, walking is a motor skill that is sampled on most developmental milestone tests. However, the concept sampled by a functional test is mobility in the environment, regardless of whether the child walks normally, uses an ambulatory aid, or moves in the environment via wheelchair. Functional outcome variables are focused on complex environmental demands such as eating, dressing, and bowel and bladder management. For many young children with severe physical handicaps, functional variables are more relevant and sensitive to change than motor skill variables. A number of standardized instruments for adaptive assessments of young children are available,[9] and, recently, new instruments that sample adaptive motor function in the infant and young child have become available.[8,50] For example, the Pediatric Evaluation of Disability Inventory (PEDI)[50] is a new functional assessment instrument for infants and young children aged 6 months through 7 years. Item content includes self-care skills, bowel and bladder control, transfers, mobility (indoor and community), communication, and social function. The PEDI is designed to identify the child's functional ability along three scales:
1. functional skill level,
2. modifications or adaptive equipment (ie, braces and wheelchair) used, and
3. caregiver assistance.

OUTCOME EVALUATION

To illustrate how one would choose outcome measures on the basis of this hierarchical model, the case is presented of a 1-year-old boy, Mark, referred to an early intervention program. Intake information indicated that he did not roll, did not reach or bring his hands to his mouth, and had no vocalizations other than crying. Mark was functioning at or below a 6-month age level in the motor domain. After initial evaluations by a multidisciplinary team, it was decided that a general motor stimulation program coupled with specific intervention by a physical and occupational therapist was needed to help improve motor functioning.

Long-range goals were established to stimulate overall motor activity and function, improve self-care and mobility skills, and decrease Mark's dependence on his parents for mobility and self-care. Baseline adaptive motor function was recorded via the PEDI.[50] Short-term goals were established for the factors that were felt to be limiting the improvement of Mark's overall motor function. Thus, a series of simultaneous baseline measures were taken at lower levels of the hierarchy to monitor progress in the motor domains to which specific intervention was initially directed.

Mark had very few spontaneous movements and showed little inclination to explore the environment. It was decided that the facilitation of movement experiences was needed, and his parents were taught to stimulate and reinforce self-initiated movement. A baseline analysis of his movement activity[19] was made and recorded on videotape. It was further hypothesized that Mark had serious limitations in the hierarchical level of prefunctional determinants. Clinical evaluation indicated that his postural tone was low, and he lacked righting and equilibrium reactions to help himself maintain stable postures. The physical therapy program was devoted to improving postural tone and developing these postural reactions. Clinical assessments of postural tone and of righting and equilibrium reactions were recorded to help determine if physical therapy intervention was making an impact in these areas. Because Mark appeared to have serious motor deficits in the gross motor area, but also appeared to have more immediate potential to develop fine motor skills, occupational therapy was directed toward improving eye-hand coordination and grasp. A motor skill test (Peabody Development Motor Scales)[47] was performed to establish a baseline for gross and fine motor skills.

Mark was evaluated again at 2 years of age. His spontaneous movements had improved, and he had developed a strong interest in manipulating objects with his hands. Marginal improvements were noted in postural tone and reactions. His fine motor skills were markedly improved, as new supported-sitting equipment had provided him with the postural stability to practice these skills. Mark's improvements in fine motor skills were carried over into his daily routines, and he required less assistance in self-care skills. Mobility skills, particularly transfers, were improving. All of these positive changes were easily documented by comparison with the comprehensive baseline data taken at initial admission to the program and at subsequent intervals. During Mark's second year in the program, new emphasis in the occupational therapy program was placed on the motor performance variables of speed and accuracy in reaching. As no standardized test was available to assess reaching components in a child of this age, careful descriptions of baseline performance were defined so that progress could be monitored.

At the age of 3 years, Mark was ready to leave the early intervention program, and a final evaluation was performed. Adaptive motor function as measured by the PEDI had significantly improved (Figs 2 and 3.) Analysis of Mark's scores on the PEDI indicated a progression from a level of almost no functional skills and complete dependence to a level of improving functional skills and good use of adaptive equipment. Although Mark's long-term goals were focused on functional and adaptive gains, a number of short-term goals (improvement of self-initiated movements, postural tone and reflexes, fine motor performance and skills) had been established at different levels of the hierarchy. Outcome measures were established for these individual goals, as they were the specific targets of intervention. Improvement in adaptive motor function was the ultimate goal for Mark, and assessment of all levels of the hierarchy helped to define, monitor, and refine the motor program.

Although Mark's motor program may seem logical and straightforward, it is often difficult to establish outcome assessment priorities. A serious dilemma in the selection of motor outcomes exists as a result of the unclear relationship between lower levels of the motor hierarchy and gains in adaptive motor function. The factors that underlie various motor disorders are often very difficult to uncover, and the extent to which a specific deficit can be related to a functional behavior is often dependent on the severity of the deficit and the relevance of that deficit to a particular functional activity.[51]

Different training philosophies may be expected to emphasize different levels of the hierarchy.[51] In the example of Mark, the motor program was directed at multiple levels but primarily at the most basic levels. This represents a systems approach, in which basic levels of motor function are addressed but are integrated as closely as possible with functional goals. One extreme point of view is that intervention at the most basic levels (self-initiated movements, prefunctional determinants) has the most generalized and profound impact. This viewpoint assumes that underlying skills must be developed before overall motor function can be improved. An opposite extreme would be to train only at the functional level, and not to attempt to improve postural control or any other performance or skill level. The latter approach assumes that underlying components of movement are not important or relevant for the improvement of functional gains. Much more research and systematic clinical documentation are needed to determine the most effective and efficient approaches for infants and young children with different patterns of motor dysfunction at different ages.

The selection of outcome variables differs with respect to the level of detail needed, the scope of the outcome variables, and the intended audience for the outcome measures.[10] The degree of detail of outcome measures should be greatest

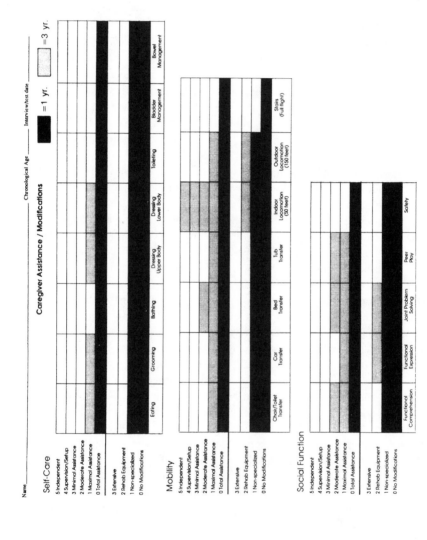

Fig 2. Change in functional skills and behaviors as measured by the Pediatric Evaluation of Disability Inventory.

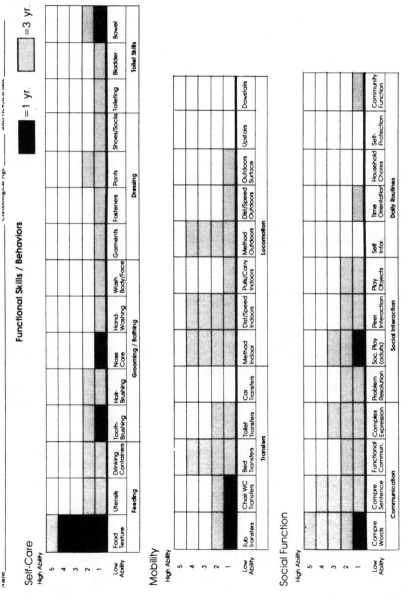

Fig 3. Change in caregiver assistance and use of modifications as measured by the Pediatric Evaluation of Disability Inventory.

if the primary purpose of the outcome analysis is to determine changes in specific qualitative movement components or discrete skills. Less detailed outcome measures are needed if the focus of treatment is to improve independence or daily endurance. For some children who require a major emphasis on motor programming, the scope of outcome measures encompasses not only detailed assessments, but also the development of more functionally related goals. In other children whose program has little emphasis on motor skills, a less comprehensive series of outcome measures should be developed. Physical and occupational therapists may develop more detailed outcome measures for intricate program monitoring and change, whereas more global measures of motor progress may be acceptable to teachers or program administrators. The appropriate assessment of the motor domain with regards to degree of detail, scope, and intended audience establishes a more thorough base for planning treatment and developing a successful overall motor program.

ADDITIONAL CONSIDERATIONS

Additional considerations in carrying out an assessment plan include the technical characteristics of outcome measures, the importance of linkage of outcome measures with intervention goals, and the need for multidimensional assessment of infants and young children.

Characteristics of outcome assessments

Neisworth and Bagnato[52] promoted a multipurpose model of assessment, in which measurements can serve distinct functions, including description, prediction, educational and treatment planning, and evaluation and monitoring of progress. For example, these same authors[53-55] presented a comprehensive assessment model for children with acquired brain injury that incorporated multiple domains of motor behavior used for multiple purposes. Although the linking of various assessments for multiple purposes promotes a synchronous and parsimonious approach to the overall evaluation process, care must be taken to use outcome assessments correctly. For example, Rosenbaum and colleagues[56] cautioned against the use of assessments for multiple purposes unless the instruments are specifically designed for those purposes or unless validity has been established for each application. A major concern is the use of developmental scales for the assessment of change when those scales have been developed primarily to describe a child's status or to categorize children via norm-based standard scores.[56]

Outcome assessments for the monitoring of motor progress should be chosen on the basis of the ability to detect meaningful clinical change.[57] Not all assessment instruments are designed to measure change: some are best suited to describe motor deficits or to differentiate individuals from normative status, and others are more adept at predicting outcome or classifying future group status.[58] The determination of the responsiveness of an instrument to change is often a difficult clinical judgment as few motor instruments have supporting validity data. The responsiveness of an instrument should be evaluated on the basis of

- intended purpose of the instrument or validity data (if any),
- the inclusion of items most likely to change or develop over time,
- a sufficient number of scale values to detect fine gradations of change (eg, partial completion of items) if ordinal level measurements are used, and
- the use of quantitative variables that incorporate interval-level measurements.[56,59]

Outcome measures should adhere closely to acceptable standards of reliability, validity, clinical acceptance, and feasibility.[58]

Linkage of outcome measures and intervention

Outcome measures should be closely linked to the focus of the intervention.[48,49] Although this appears to be an obvious necessity, practitioners often collect information in the motor domain that is easily obtainable, rather than that which is most pertinent to the individual child's goals. There is little agreement as to the most salient components of a motor outcome evaluation for young children, but the hierarchy introduces a framework to help organize outcome assessments. Development of a broad motor assessment battery that includes qualitative, quantitative, and adaptive child measures has been strongly advocated.[33,34,38] In addition, specific outcome measures should be used if an individual child's physical or motor goals are not adequately evaluated in a motor assessment battery. Comprehensive outcome assessments incorporate both the immediate and the long-range focuses of the child's motor program.[33] The amount, specificity, and frequency of outcome data collection are influenced by the severity of the child's motor deficits, the program philosophy, and the resources of the program.[60] A comfortable balance point between the provision of service and the collection of assessment data to monitor progress and adjust intervention programs must be defined appropriately within each program to ensure the most effective use of limited program time.

Although educators and early intervention specialists have advocated a strong link between assessment measures and developmental curricula,[48,49] Campbell and colleagues cautioned against an overreliance on the use of developmentally based curricula for program planning and outcome assessment.[6,23] Part of this concern is related to the need to teach children with neuromotor disabilities alternative methods of achieving adaptive skills, which are not considered in developmental curricula. Moreover, the milestone sequence of normally developing motor skills does not necessarily represent the appropriate mix of skills that a child with motor delays must attain in order to learn functional movement skills.[31] Most developmental curricula do not include prerequisite movement components necessary to achieve motor milestones.[6] Unfortunately, very little progress has been made in the determination of empirically established prerequisite components for important functional motor skills for young children.[61,62]

The establishment of appropriate outcome measures for children undergoing motor programming can be complicated. Change in motor function is a product of a series of complex and interlocking forces, including central nervous system development and maturation; evolution of new motor patterns; changes in the environmental expectations, task demands, or motivating factors; alterations in parental behavior and support; and overall social and cognitive development. In some cases, change may not be a reasonable goal, and a successful outcome might be the maintenance of existing motor function, a decrease in the rate of deterioration, or the prevention of a likely complication secondary to a movement disorder.[63]

Outcomes other than the specifically motor may need to be considered for full assessment of the impact of motor change. For example, an indirect effect of the enhancement of motor skills may be an improvement in self-esteem and social function.[38,64] A further broadening of outcome measures may include the effect of the program on parents or caregivers.[65] Parents are often enlisted to help effect and sustain changes in the motor status of children, either by teaching them specific skills or by promoting a more stimulating environment for the development of improved mobility. Outcome measures designed to evaluate the effectiveness of these moderator variables will help to determine the factors that have positively influenced a child's motor abilities. Even when a child's movement behavior has not improved markedly, caregiver practices and ease of care by the parents are important outcome variables to document. The hierarchy of motor variables discussed in this article was necessarily limited to child-centered variables, but a similar hierarchy of pediatric psychosocial and parent outcome variables could also be developed as valid sets of moderator variables to determine the effects of motor programming.

Multidimensional assessment

Many children with motor impairments also have complex cognitive, behavioral, and other deficits. The entire complex of developmental delays in a child must be assessed by a knowledgeable and multidisciplinary team that measures multiple domains of behavior from multiple sources.[22,52] Multidisciplinary teams must establish programming priorities and develop a consensus as to the most important goals for the child and family.[66] Motor goals become secondary priorities if improvement in other domains of development is critical for the immediate safety, school placement, or primary interest of the child or parent. Similarly, motor goals may emerge as a high priority if immediate preventive or safety issues surface or if the child and parent appear to want to resolve motor issues before other programming can begin.

• • •

This article has presented a hierarchical framework of motor outcome measures for use in programs for infants and young children. The hierarchy promotes the systematic measurement of outcomes for individual children and for programs, the organization of outcome data on the basis of an individual child's goals, and the relation of intermediate levels of the hierarchy to improvement in adaptive motor function. Until more research is available to guide interveners in motor programming efforts, the process of outcome assessment will have to be systematic and thorough. Through the application of a hierarchical framework and the development of a sufficient outcome assessment data base, programs will be able to improve their efficiency, effectiveness, and understanding of the impact of motor programming directed at various levels of the motor skills hierarchy.

REFERENCES

1. Ottenbacher K, Petersen P. The efficacy of early intervention programs for children with organic impairment: A quantitative review. *Eval Program Plan.* 1985;8:135–146.

2. Ottenbacher KJ, Biocca Z, DeCremer G, et al. Quantitative analysis of the effectiveness of pediatric therapy: Emphasis on the neurodevelopmental treatment approach. *Phys Ther.* 1986;66:1095–1101.

3. Harris SR. Early intervention for children with motor handicaps. In: Guralnick MJ, Bennett FC, eds. The effectiveness of early intervention for at-risk and handicapped children. Orlando, Fla: Academic Press, 1987.

4. Harris S. Early intervention: Does developmental therapy make a difference? *TECSE.* 1988;7(4):20–32.

5. Sparling JJ. Narrow and broad-spectrum curricula: Two necessary parts of the special child's program. *Inf Young Children.* 1989;1:1–8.

6. Campbell P, Stewart B. Measuring changes in movement skills with infants and young children with handicaps. *J Assoc Sev Hand.* 1986;11(3):153–161.

7. World Health Organization. *International Classification of Impairments, Disabilities and Handicaps.* Geneva: World Health Organization, 1980.

8. Granger CV, Hamilton BB, Kayton R. *Guide for the Use of the Functional Independence Measure for Children (Wee-FIM) of the Uniform Data Set for Medical Rehabilitation.* Buffalo, NY: Research Foundation, State University of New York, 1988.

9. Haley SM, Hallenborg S, Gans BM. Functional assessment in young children with neurological impairments. *TECSE.* 1989;9:106–126.

10. Brown M, Gordon W, Diller L. Rehabilitation indicators. In: Halpern AS, Furher MJ, eds. *Functional Assessment in Rehabilitation.* Baltimore: Paul H. Brooks, 1984.

11. Touwen B. Variability and stereotyping in normal and deviant development. In: Apley J, ed. *Care of the Handicapped Child, Clinics in Developmental Medicine.* London: Spastics International Medical Publications, 1978:67.

12. Stern FM, Gorga D. Neurodevelopmental treatment (NDT): Therapeutic intervention and its efficacy. *Inf Young Children.* 1988;1:22–32.

13. Pickler E. Learning motor skills on the basis of self-induced movements. In: Hillmith JH, ed. *Exceptional Infant: Studies in Abnormalities,* vol 2. New York: Bruner/Mazel, 1971.

14. Horton M, McGuinnes J. Movement notations and the recording of normal and abnormal movements. In: Holt K, ed. *Movements and Child Development, Clinics in Developmental Medicine.* London: Spastics International Medical Publications, 1975:65.

15. Downs FS, Fitzpatrick JJ. Preliminary investigation of the reliability and validity of a tool for the assessment of body position and motor activity. *Nurs Res.* 1976;25:404–408.

16. Brand HL, Rosenbaum P. Recording children's movements: The development of an observational method. In: Holt KS, ed. *Movement and Child Development. Clinics in Developmental Medicine.* London: Spastics International Medical Publications, 1975:65.

17. Hopkins B, Prechtl HFR. A quantitative approach to the development of movements during early infancy. In Prechtl HFR, ed. *Continuity of Neural Functions from Prenatal to Postnatal Life. Clinics in Developmental Medicine.* London: Spastics International Medical Publications, 1984: 94.

18. Phillips S, King S, DuBois L. Spontaneous activities of female versus male newborns. *Child Dev.* 1978;49:590–597.

19. Haley SM. Assessment of motor performance. In: Wilhelm IJ, ed. *Advances in Neonatal Special Care.* Chapel Hill, NC: Division of Physical Therapy, University of North Carolina at Chapel Hill, 1986.

20. Baryza MJ. Quantity of spontaneous movement in handicapped infants. Boston, Mass: Boston University; 1989. Thesis.

21. Wolff, P. Theoretical issues in the development of motor skills. In: Lewis M, Taft LT, eds. *Developmental Disabilities Theory, Assessment and Intervention.* New York: Spectrum Publications Medical & Scientific Books, 1982.

22. Bricker W, Campbell P. Interdisciplinary assessment and programming for multihandicapped students. In: Sailor W, Wilcox B, Brown L, eds. *Methods of Instruction for Severely Handicapped Students.* Baltimore: Paul Brookes, 1980.

23. Campbell P, McInerney W, Cooper M. Therapeutic programming for students with severe handicaps. *Am J Occupat Ther.* 1984;38(9):594–602.

24. Harris S, Hurthun S, Krukowski L. Goniometric reliability for a child with spastic quadriplegia. *J Pediatr Orthop.* 1985;5:348–351.

25. Vignos PJ. Rehabilitation in progressive muscular dystrophy. In: Lichts S, ed. *Rehabilitation and Medicine.* New Haven, Conn: Licht Publisher, 1968.

26. Bruininks RH. *Bruininks-Oseretsky Test of Motor Proficiency.* Circle Pines, Minn: American Guidance Service, 1984.

27. Stuberg WA, Metcalf WK. Reliability of quantitative muscle testing in healthy children and in children with Duchenne muscular dystrophy using a hand-held dynamometer. *Phys Ther.* 1988;68:977–982.

28. Stengel TJ, Attermeier SM, Bly L, Heriza CB. Evaluation of sensorimotor dysfunction. In: Campbell SK, ed. *Pediatric Neurological Physical Therapy.* New York: Churchill Livingstone, 1984.

29. Molnar G. Analysis of motor disorders in retarded infants and young children. *Am J Ment Defic.* 1974;55:393–398.

30. Haley SM. Postural reactions in infants with Down syndrome: Relationship to motor milestone development and age. *Phys Ther.* 1986;66:17–22.

31. Campbell P, Clegg K, McFarland L. Measuring motor behavior. In: Stevens-Dominquez M, Stremel-Campbell K, eds. *Ongoing Data Collection for Measuring Child Progress.* Monmouth, Ore: Western States Technical Assistance Resources, 1982.

32. Chandler L, Andrews M, Swanson M. *Movement Assessment of Infants.* Rolling Bay, WA: Movement Assessment of Infants, 1980.

33. Scherzer A, Tscharnuter I. *Early Diagnosis and Therapy in Cerebral Palsy: A Primer on Infant Developmental Problems.* New York: Marcel Dekker, 1982.

34. Wilson JM. Cerebral palsy. In: Campbell SK, ed. *Pediatric Neurologic Physical Therapy.* New York: Churchill Livingstone, 1984.

35. Connolly BH, Montgomery PC. *Therapeutic Exercises in Developmental Disabilities.* Chattanooga, Tenn: Chattanooga Corporation, 1987.

36. Campbell SK, Wilhelm IJ, Slaton DS. Anthropometric characteristics of young children with cerebral palsy. *Pediatr Phys Ther.* 1989;1:105–108.

37. Krus PH, Bruininks RH, Robertson G. Structure of motor abilities in children. *Percept Mot Skills.* 1981;52:119–120.

38. Campbell S. Assessment of the child with CNS dysfunction. In: Rothstein JM, ed. *Measurement in Physical Therapy.* New York: Churchill Livingstone, 1985.

39. Gans BM, Haley SM, Hallenborg SC, et al. Description and interobserver reliability of the Tufts Assessment of Motor Performance. *Am J Phys Med Rehabil.* 1988;67:202–210.

40. Heriza C. Organization of leg movements in preterm infants. *Phys Ther.* 1988;68:1340–1346.

41. Heriza CB. Comparison of leg movements in preterm infants at term with healthy full-term infants. *Phys Ther.* 1988;68:1687–1693.

42. Shumway-Cook A. Dynamics of postural control in the child with Down syndrome. *Phys Ther.* 1985;65:1315–1322.

43. Shumway-Cook A, Woollacott MH. The growth of stability: Postural control from a developmental perspective. *J Mot Behav.* 1985;17:131–147.

44. Schmidt RA. *Motor Control and Learning: A Behavior Emphasis.* Champaign, Ill: Human Kinetics, 1982.

45. Bayley N. *The Bayley Scales of Infant Development.* New York: Psychological Corporation, 1969.

46. Schafer DS, Moersch MS, eds. *Developmental Programming for Infants and Young Children.* Ann Arbor: University of Michigan Press, 1981.

47. Folio R, Fewell RR. *Peabody Developmental Motor Scales.* Allen, Tx: DLM Resources, 1983.

48. Bagnato S. Developmental scales and developmental curricula: Forging a linkage for early intervention. *TECSE* 1981;1(2):1–8.

49. Bagnato SJ, Neisworth JT, Munson SM. *Linking Developmental Assessment and Early Intervention: Curriculum-based Prescriptions.* 2nd ed. Rockville, Md: Aspen Publishers, 1989.

50. Haley SM, Faas RM, Coster WJ, Webster H, Gans BM. *Pediatric Evaluation of Disability Inventory: Examiner's Manual.* Boston: New England Medical Center, 1989.

51. Whyte J. Outcome evaluation in the remediation of attention and memory deficits. *J Head Trauma Rehabil.* 1986;1:64–71.

52. Neisworth J, Bagnato S. Assessment in early childhood special education: A typology of dependent measures. In: Odom SL, Karnes BM, eds. *Early Intervention for Infants and Children with Handicaps: An Empirical Base.* Baltimore: Paul H. Brooks, 1988.

53. Bagnato S, Neisworth J. Tracing developmental recovery from early brain injury. *Remed Spec Edu.* 1986;7(5)31–36.

54. Bagnato S, Neisworth J. Efficacy of interdisciplinary assessment and treatment for infants and preschoolers with congenital and acquired brain injury. *Anal Intervent Dev Disabil.* 1986;5:107–128.

55. Bagnato S, Neisworth J. Neurodevelopmental outcomes of early brain injury: A follow-up of fourteen case studies. *TECSE.* 1989;9(1):72–89.

56. Rosenbaum PL, Russel DJ, Cadman DT, Gowland C, Jarvis S, Hardy S. Issues in measuring changes in motor function in children with cerebral palsy. *Phys Ther.* 1990;70:125–131.

57. Guyatt GH, Walter SD, Norman G. Measuring change over time: Assessing the usefulness of evaluative instruments. *J Chronic Dis.* 1987;40:171–180.

58. Law M. Measurement in occupational therapy: Scientific criteria for evaluation. *Can J Occup Ther.* 1987;54(3):133–138.

59. Cole K, Swisher V, Thompson M, Fewell R. Enhancing sensitivity of assessment instruments for children: Graded multidimensional scoring. *J Assoc Sev Hand.* 1985;4:209–213.

60. Bricker D, Littman D. Intervention and evaluation: The inseparable mix. *TECSE.* 1982;1(4):23–33.

61. Fishkind M, Haley SM. Independent sitting development and the emergence of associated motor components. *Phys Ther.* 1986;66:1509–1514.

62. Montgomery PC, Connolly BH. Norm-referenced and criteria-referenced tests in pediatrics and application to task analysis of motor skills. *Phys Ther.* 1986;66:1873–1876.

63. Gans BM. Rehabilitation of the pediatric patient. In: DeLisa JA, ed. *Rehabilitation Medicine: Principles and Practice.* Philadelphia: Lippincott, 1988.

64. Kopp C. Perspectives on infant motor system development. In: Bornstein M, Kessen W, eds. *Psychological Development from Infancy: Image to Intention.* Hillsdale, NJ: Lawrence Erlbaum Associates, 1979.

65. Allen D. Measuring rehabilitation outcomes for infants and young children: A family approach. In: Fuhrer MJ, ed. *Rehabilitation Outcomes Analysis and Measurement.* Baltimore: Paul H. Brookes, 1987.

66. Orlando C. Multidisciplinary team approaches in the assessment of handicapped preschool children. *TECSE.* 1981;1(2):23–30.

Assessment of sensory, emotional, and attentional problems in regulatory disordered infants

Georgia A. DeGangi, PhD
Director of the Cecil and Ida Green
  Research and Training Institute
Reginald S. Lourie Center for Infants
  and Young Children
Rockville, Maryland
Clinical Instructor
Department of Pediatrics
Georgetown University
Washington, DC

IN RECENT YEARS, growing attention has been directed to the clinical importance of fussy or difficult behaviors in infants. Two lines of investigation currently are contributing to the understanding of these behaviors. One view integrates clinical and theoretical perspectives. Greenspan[1-3] described infants with homeostatic and regulatory disorders and postulated that they are at risk for specific types of psychopathology and learning difficulties. The other view has focused on temperament as an important variable that affects a child's behavioral style.[4] Infants with difficult temperament have been described as reacting negatively to social interactions,[5] to demonstrate aggressive and conflictual behaviors at 2 year of age,[6] and to display a heightened reactivity to negative environmental overstimulation such as noise confusion.[5] The etiology of difficult temperament has often been debated; however, studies of parental personality and home environments have found that these variables do not seem to influence difficult temperament,[7] thus supporting the notion that there are distinct infant characteristics that account for difficult behaviors.

Research investigating the clinical significance of negative temperamental characteristics has been limited, primarily due to the heavy reliance on parent report measures and lack of reliable and valid observational techniques.[8,9] Although some constitutionally based traits are transient in nature and resolve once the child develops internal self-organizational mechanisms,[10] other traits are not transient. The developmental histories of preschool and school-aged children with learning and perceptual difficulties often include an early history of difficult temperament including symptoms such as irritability, poor self-calming, and sensitivity to touch.[11] Similarly, it has been reported that infants with early sensorimotor deficits, particularly hypersensitivity to stimulation, developed emotional difficulties in the school-age years.[12,13] Additionally, negative temperamental traits (eg, distractibility, difficult temperament) in infancy have also been linked with reactive depression in late adolescence.[14]

Recent theorists view constitutionally based individual differences as reflecting individual reactivity and self-regulatory processes.[15,16] Many young infants' problems in attaining homeostatic functions resolve with maturity. For example, infants frequently display sleep disturbances or colic that resolves spontaneously by 5 or 6 months of age. At the same time, there is increasing interest in infants older

Inf Young Children 1991; 3(3): 1–8

than 6 months who exhibit fussiness, irritability, poor self-calming, intolerance for change, and a hyperalert state of arousal. Using Greenspan's[1-3] clinical constructs, these infants recently have been recognized as regulatory disordered.[17] Often these infants are hypersensitive or hyposensitive to sensory stimuli including auditory, tactile, visual, and vestibular stimulation.[18] Regulatory disordered infants are commonly observed in clinical practice and exhibit deficits in psychological processes (eg, sustained attention) and physiological organization (eg, lack of appropriate physiological suppression to cognitive or sensory challenges).[17] It has been suggested that disorders of regulation involve maladaptive responses to early organization of sensory and affective-thematic experiences.[19]

Research has substantiated that difficult or fussy infants have different behavioral and psychophysiological profiles[18]; however, there is virtually no research investigating the clinical significance of these negative characteristics. Therefore, a series of clinical studies of regulatory disorders was initiated. An initial study of the psychophysiological characteristics of regulatory disordered infants revealed that as a group, the sample did not differ significantly from their normal counterparts at 8 to 11 months of age; however, the regulatory disordered infants tended to have higher baseline vagal tone with a lack of suppression of vagal tone during sensory and cognitive stimulation.[18] This finding suggests that some regulatory disordered infants have difficulty regulating autonomic nervous system functions and have physiological hyperreactivity to environmental stimulation.

A longitudinal study was recently conducted to investigate the long-term significance of fussy babies diagnosed as regulatory disordered at 8 to 11 months of age (DeGangi GA, Porges SW, Sickel R, Greenspan SI. June 1990. Unpublished data). These infants exhibited sleep disturbances, hypersensitivities to sensory stimulation, irritability and poor self-calming, and mood and state deregulation. Examination of group differences revealed that children initially identified as regulatory disordered differed significantly from their normal peers in perceptual, language, and general cognitive skills at 4 years of age. Although the regulatory disordered sample did not differ from their normal counterparts in developmental parameters during infancy, at 4 years of age, five of the nine regulatory disordered infants displayed either motor or overall developmental delays. A high incidence of vestibular-based sensory integrative deficits (eg, poor bilateral coordination and postural control), tactile defensiveness, motor planning problems, hyperactivity, and emotional and behavioral difficulties were present in the regulatory disordered population. The findings imply that regulatory disordered infants are at high risk for later perceptual, language, sensory integrative, and behavioral difficulties in the preschool years.

DEVELOPMENT OF REGULATORY PROCESSES

The early regulation of arousal and physiological state is critical for successful adaptation to the environment. The development of homeostasis is important in the modulation of sensory reactivity, emotional responsivity, and attentional capacities.[20-24] The foundations of self-regulation lie in the infant's capacity to develop homeostasis in the first few months of life when the infant learns to take interest in the world while simultaneously regulating arousal and responses to sensory stimulation.[19] Self-regulatory mechanisms continually develop and refine over the first two years of life. Some of the important milestones include the formation of affective relationships and attachments, purposeful communication, an understanding of causal relationships, and development of self-initiated organized behaviors.

It is generally recognized that self-regulatory mechanisms are complex and develop as a result of physiological maturation, caregiver responsivity, and the infant's adaptation to environmental demands.[25] In the early stages of development, the caregiver soothes the young infant when distressed and facilitates state organization.[26] As the child develops, the caregiver attaches affective meanings to situations and provides social expectations and values related to specific emotional responses.[27] The development of action schemes (eg, vocalizations, self-distractions, or other motor responses), cognitive organization (eg, representational thinking, self-monitoring) and motivation, and external support from caregivers have been proposed as key elements in attainment of emotion regulation, a key element in the development of self-regulation.[28]

SYMPTOMS OF REGULATORY DISORDER

A regulatory disorder is defined by persistent symptoms that interfere with adaptive functioning. Typically, the regulatory disordered infant displays problems in sleep, self-consoling, feeding, arousal, mood regulation, or transitions. Some infants may exhibit minor transitory difficulties in any of these areas due to maturational difficulties or parental mismanagement.

An initial investigation of the epidemiological factors related to regulatory disorders examined the perinatal and medical histories of 27 regulatory disordered infants and 59 normal infants. The presence of frequent headaches during the pregnancy ($\chi^2 = 4.66$, $p < .05$) and the wrapping of the umbilical cord around the infant's neck during delivery ($\chi^2 = 10.25$, $p < .01$) occurred in a high proportion of the sample of regulatory disordered infants. The presence of headaches during pregnancy may reflect stress or anxiety in the mother. Medical diagnoses of eating problems ($\chi^2 = 4.05$, $p < .05$), elimination problems ($\chi^2 = 5.34$, $p < .05$), colic ($\chi^2 = 10.24$, $p < .01$), and frequent colds ($\chi^2 = 6.74$, $p < .01$) were present as well in the regulatory disordered sample (DeGangi GA. June 1990. Unpublished data).

Sleep disturbances

A large number of children with regulatory disorders have difficulty regulating sleep–wake cycles. Persistent sleep disorders have been found to result in biochemical changes in stress hormones and biological rhythms and in states of arousal.[29] Fussy and irritable behaviors may occur during the day because the infant is overtired and unable to fall and stay asleep. Some sleep disorders are physiologically based, while others result from parental mismanagement. Children with sleep deficits exhibit a high state of arousal and are unable to inhibit their alert state to allow for sleep. Sometimes the child is not able to fall into a deep rapid eye movement sleep and wakes frequently throughout the night.

Difficulty self-consoling

Most infants can self-calm by bringing their hand to their mouth to suck, touching their hands together, rocking, or looking or listening to preferred visual or auditory stimuli. These behaviors are often unavailable to regulatory disordered infants. Once upset, the infant requires extreme efforts to calm down. The caregiver may spend from two to four hours a day attempting to calm the infant. With older infants, severe temper tantrums are often present.

Feeding difficulties

The feeding problems exhibited by the regulatory disordered infant usually include difficulty establishing a regular feeding schedule, distress related to feeding including regurgitation, refusal to eat, and other feeding problems not related to specific allergies or food intolerance. Resistance to eating a variety of food textures often emerges after nine months. Some infants spit out lumpy food or refuse to eat anything but a few preferred foods, usually with firm and crunchy or pureed textures. Occasionally growth retardation or failure to thrive may be diagnosed secondary to the feeding disturbance.

Hyperarousal

Along the continuum of sleep disturbances is the problem of hyperarousal. Many regulatory disordered infants become very disorganized during the transition from one activity to the next. Strong reliance on routines and constant need for structure are common problems. A common characteristic of hyperarousal is a high need for novelty and distractibility to sights, noise, or movement. Some regulatory disordered infants notice details in the environment that are not normally noticed. The infant may appear overwhelmed by sensory input and may cry or avert his or her gaze to avoid contact. Parents often describe their infant as intense, wide-eyed, or "hyper." Frequently the child will go from one toy to another, often not playing with any toy long enough to develop a toy preference.

Mood lability

The most pervasive traits of the regulatory disordered infant are fussiness, irritability, an unhappy mood state, and a tendency to quickly escalate from contentment to distress. Often the parents are unable to determine what causes the fussiness. Maternal perception of difficultness may be confirmed through the use of temperament scales (eg, Bates' *Infant Characteristics Questionnaire*, fussy-difficult subscale[30]). When the parents do not view their child as difficult despite clinical evidence of mood deregulation, further investigation is needed to determine if such problems as parental inexperience, denial, or maternal depression exist. In many cases, the fussiness and irritability are very disruptive to the family and result in a high degree of family stress.

ASSESSMENT STRATEGIES

An expanded model of assessment should include three stages: (1) evaluation of infant performance in sensorimotor and regulatory processes affecting functional learning and behaviors, (2) incorporation of parental observations regarding the influence of an infant's behaviors on his or her functioning within the family and home environment, and (3) examination of parental characteristics (eg, personality dimensions, interaction styles) and parental availability to be involved in the assessment and treatment process.

The intake interview

The diagnostic process begins with a comprehensive intake interview conducted by a child psychiatrist and a pediatric nurse to evaluate parental concerns and parental perception of the child. The interview is useful in determining the presence of primary or secondary parental emotional problems, marital conflicts, or other contributing factors that may affect the parent–child dyad. The parent's presenting concerns are assessed through the use of a comprehensive symptom checklist that contains questions related to sleep, self-calming, feeding, sensory responses (ie, touch, movement), communication and language, and emotional responses. The checklist is structured in such a way that it is possible to determine the extent of the problem and changes in behavioral patterns over development. In addition, the *Parenting Stress Index*[31] is administered to provide a measure of child characteristics (eg, adaptability, demandingness) and dimensions of parent stress (eg, depression and sense of competence).

The home visit

A home visit is conducted by a pediatric nurse to observe characteristics of the home environment, resources available to the family, and any particular life styles or cultural values that may affect the family's management of their difficult child. The child's behaviors, as well as mother–child interactions, are observed in the familiar setting of the home. In addition, further parental concerns can be ascertained. Parents often feel free to discuss personal issues that may affect their relationship to the child in the security of their home.

Clinical assessment of the fussy infant

A comprehensive diagnostic assessment is conducted to evaluate constitutional factors that may contribute to the child's regulatory difficulties. Instruments are used to provide five different types of information related to the development of infants, toddlers, and young children with regulatory difficulties:

1. sensory processing and reactivity, including measures of responses to touch, movement, tactile discrimination, and adaptive motor functions, evaluated with the *Test of Sensory Functions in Infants*[32];
2. sustained attention, including the ability to initiate and hold interest in novel tasks;
3. mother–infant interactions during symbolic and sensory play activities, evaluated with the *Greenspan-Lieberman Observation Scale (GLOS)*[33];
4. developmental cognitive and communication skills, evaluated with the *Bayley Scales of Infant Development* mental scale[34]; and
5. physiological responses using cardiac vagal tone[35] (eg, the interaction of the rhythmic component of the heart rate pattern, transitory respiratory changes), a potential index of the quality of arousal and attentional responses.

DIFFERENTIATION OF TYPES OF REGULATORY DISORDERS

Using the information derived from the intake interview, symptom checklist, home visit, and various diagnostic tests, the child's adaptive developmental mechanisms, organizational behaviors, and regulatory difficulties can be described. A "neurobehavioral" model, originally developed by Porges,[35] is useful in explaining the different types of regulatory disorders. Four levels of regulatory disorders have been delineated based on the level of organizational mechanisms available to the child. In addition, a distinct category has been defined to explain the "late regulator," or the infant with transitory regulatory difficulties.

Level 1 represents basic organization of physiological and sensory systems. It refers to the infant's capacity to regulate a rhythmic heart rate and respiration pattern and his or her ability to register sensory inputs (eg, basic perception of touch, movement, sound, and sights). A disorder at this level would involve a severe developmental disorder with dysfunction of major neurological and sensory functions (eg, blindness, profound retardation).

Level 2 reflects the dynamic coordination of physiological and sensory systems and provides the basis for homeostatic functioning. Functions at this level involve arousal or alertness to stimuli and coordination of respiration and heart rate needed for state control or basic information processing. Intersensory integration, such as the capacity to organize inputs from two or more sensory channels (eg, visual and tactile), occurs at this level.

Severe and persistent regulatory disorders are observed when developmental processes are compromised at this level. Such disorders include significant sleep and state control problems (eg, hyperalertness to sights, noises, touch) and severe behavioral distress (eg, high degree of irritability). The child is unable to self-soothe or to internalize soothing experiences from the caregiver. Symptoms include extreme hypersensitivity to sensory stimulation and inability to synthesize sensory inputs from two or more modalities (eg, visual–tactile integration). As a result, difficulty tolerating touch and movement from the caregiver and inability to explore objects through the senses are common. Physiological deregulation may occur, causing the child to be hyperactive to incoming stimuli. Hyperactivity and attentional deficits may result as well.

Level 3 represents the infant's ability to organize overt behaviors in response to environmental stimulation and involves his or her capacity to organize psychological processes in noncontingent situations (eg, manipulation of objects in play). An infant with a level 3 regulatory disorder is unable to develop self-regulatory mechanisms and relies strongly on other-regulation (eg, structure from the caregiver, routines). The infant may be able to be soothed by others, but he or she can only remain regulated as long as the mother or caregiver provides this input. Hypersensitivities are often present but are less pervasive than those observed at level 2. For instance, the child may learn to use one particular sensory channel to develop self-soothing (eg, rocking), but the child may overuse the behavior, weakening its capacity to soothe the child. The infant displays a very limited range of adaptable behaviors and intense frustration. Play behaviors tend to be stereotypic and show little diversity (eg, banging or mouthing objects rather than engaging in symbolic play). When presented with a challenging situation, the child may lack the problem-solving ability needed to develop strategies to act effectively on the object.

Level 4, the highest level of organization, reflects the infant's ability to integrate and respond to contingent events and situations. This level is highly dependent on the infant's capacity to regulate affective expression and to respond to social interactions adaptively. The level 4 regulatory disorder is manifested in high reactivity to affective or social situations. The child may respond aversely to affective expressions from others. For instance, the parent may find that raising his or her voice to discipline the child even slightly provokes a temper tantrum. As a result, parents often find it very difficult to set limits. The child has a high need for

Table 1. Types of regulatory disorders

Neurobehavioral level of development	Type of regulatory disorder
1. Basic organization of physiological and sensory systems	Severe sensory or developmental disorder
2. Dynamic coordination of physiological and sensory systems; basic homeostatic functions	Persistent and severe regulatory disorder with sensory hypersensitivities, mood and state deregulation; difficulties utilizing regulation from others
3. Organization of overt behaviors in noncontingent situations	Mild to moderate regulatory disorders; ability to utilize regulation from others; may be able to use one sensory regulatory mechanism
4. Organization of contingent responses in social situations	Affective and mood deregulation with or without sensory component

predictability and structure in the environment and resists changes in routine or new challenges. Often the child exhibits extremes in moods with a limited range of affective modulation.

Children who do not necessarily fit the classic picture of regulatory disorders are termed "late regulators." The child's affect changes from an unhappy, unsettled state to a happy and content state once the child masters a developmental challenge such as crawling, walking, or talking. The late regulator's need to be in charge or to be his or her own self-regulator seems extremely important. A discrepancy or unevenness in development seems to cause the child to be frustrated or unhappy, but once development levels, the child self-regulates. Generally, the late regulator is highly intense and overreactive to the environment but not hypersensitive to sensory stimulation. Table 1 presents the author's working model of the types of regulatory disorders.

•   •   •

Disorders of regulation appear to be based in problems associated with sensory processing, communicative intent, state control and arousal, physiological regulation, and emotion regulation. Identifying infants with regulatory difficulties is crucial in light of recent research suggesting that this group of infants is at high risk for later perceptual, language, sensory integrative, and emotional and behavioral difficulties in the preschool and school-age years.

During infancy, the regulatory disordered infant is often normal in developmental skills; however, difficulties are apparent in behavioral organization and adaptive functioning. A comprehensive assessment of the regulatory disordered infant should include measures of sensory processing, mother–infant interactions during play, sustained attention, communication, and physiological responses. Parent characteristics (eg, personality dimensions, interactional styles) and the parent's availability to be involved in the assessment and treatment process need to be addressed.

REFERENCES

1. Greenspan SI. *Psychopathology and Adaptation in Infancy and Early Childhood: Principles of Clinical Diagnosis and Preventive Intervention.* New York, NY: International Universities Press; 1981.

2. Greenspan SI. A model for comprehensive preventive intervention services for infants, young children, and their families. In: Wieder S, Lieberman AF, Nover RA, Lourie RS, Robinson M, eds. *Infants in Multirisk Families: Case Studies of Preventive Intervention.* New York, International Universities Press; 1987.

3. Greenspan SI. *The Development of the Ego.* Madison, Conn: International Universities Press; 1989.

4. Thomas A, Chess S. The role of temperament in the contributions of individuals to development. In: Lerner RM, Busch-Rossnagel NA, eds. *Individuals as products of Their Development: A Life-span Perspective.* New York, NY: Academic Press; 1981.

5. Wachs TD, Gandour MJ. Temperament, environment, and six-month cognitive-intellectual development: A test of the organismic specificity hypothesis. *Int J Behav Dev.* 1983;6:135–152.

6. Lee CL, Bates JE. Mother-child interaction at age two years and perceived temperament. *Child Dev.* 1975;56:1314–1325.

7. Daniels D, Plomin R, Greenhalgh J. Correlates of difficult temperament in infancy. *Child Dev.* 1984; 55:1184–1194.

8. Bates JE. The concept of difficult temperament. *Merrill-Palmer Q.* 1980;26(4):299–319.

9. Carey WB. Practical applications in pediatrics. In: Kohnstamm GA, Bates JE, Rothbart MK, *Temperament in Childhood.* New York, NY: Wiley; 1989.

10. Thelen E. Self-organization in developmental processes: Can systems approaches work? In: Gunnar M, ed. *Systems in Development: The Minnesota Symposium in Child Psychology.* Hillsdale, NJ: Erlbaum; 1989:22.

11. Ayres AJ. *Sensory Integration and the Child.* Los Angeles, Calif: Western Psychological Services; 1979.

12. Fish B, Dixon WJ. Vestibular hyporeactivity in infants at risk for schizophrenia. *Arch Gen Psychiatr.* 1978;35:963–971.

13. Walker E, Emory E. Infants at risk for psychopathology: Offspring of schizophrenic parents. *Child Dev.* 1983;54:1269–1285.

14. Chess S, Thomas A, Hassibi M. Depression in childhood and adolescence: A prospective study of six cases. *J Nerv Ment Dis.* 1983;171:411–420.

15. Rothbart MK. Temperament and development. In: Kohnstamm GA, Bates JE, Rothbart MK, eds. *Temperament in Childhood.* New York, NY: Wiley; 1989.

16. Strelau J. *Temperament, Personality, Activity.* London, England: Academic Press; 1983.

17. DeGangi GA, DiPietro JA, Greenspan SI, Porges SW. Psychophysiological characteristics of the regulatory disordered infant. *Infant Behav Dev*. To be published, 1991.

18. DeGangi GA, Greenspan SI. The development of sensory functioning in infants. *Phys Occup Ther Pediatr*. 1988;8(3):21–33.

19. Greenspan SI, Porges SW. Psychopathology in infancy and early childhood: Clinical perspectives on the organization of sensory and affective-thematic experience. *Child Dev*. 1983;55:49–70.

20. Als H, Lester BM, Tronick EZ, Brazelton TB. Towards a research instrument for the Assessment of Preterm Infants' Behavior (APIB). In: Fitzgerald H, Lester BM, Yogman MW, eds. *Theory and Research in Behavioral Pediatrics*. New York, NY: Plenum; 1982.

21. Brazelton T, Koslowski B, Main M. The origins of reciprocity: The early mother-infant interaction. In: Lewis M, Rosenblum L, eds. *The Effect of the Infant on Its Caregiver*. New York, NY: Wiley; 1974.

22. Field T. Gaze behavior of normal and high-risk infants and during early interactions. *J Am Acad Child Psychiatry*. 1981:308–317.

23. Sroufe LA. Socioemotional development. In: Osofsky J, ed *Handbook of Infant Development*. New York, NY: Wiley; 1979.

24. Tronick EZ. Emotions and emotional communication in infants. *Am Psychol*. 1989;44(2):112–119.

25. Rothbart MK, Derryberry D. Development of individual differences in temperament. In: Lamb ME, Brown AL, eds. *Advances in Developmental Psychology*. Hillsdale, NJ: Erlbaum; 1981.

26. Als H. Patterns of infant behavior: Analogs of later organizational difficulties? In: Duffy FH, Geschwind N, eds. *Dyslexia: A Neuroscientific Approach to Clinical Evaluation*. Boston, MA: Little, Brown; 1982.

27. Kopp CB. The growth of self-regulation: Parents and children. In: Eisenberg N, ed. *Perspectives in Developmental Psychology*. New York, NY: Wiley; 1987.

28. Kopp CB. Regulation of distress and negative emotions: A developmental view. *Dev Psychol*. 1989;25:343–354.

29. Weissbluth M. Sleep-loss stress and temperamental difficultness: Psychobiological processes and practical considerations. In: Kohnstamm GA, Bates JE, Rothbart MK, eds. *Temperament in Childhood*. New York, NY: Wiley; 1989.

30. Bates JE. *Infant Characteristics Questionnaire. Revised*. Bloomington, Ind: Indiana University; 1984.

31. Abidin RR. *Parenting Stress Index*. Charlottesville, Va: Pediatric Psychology Press; 1986.

32. DeGangi GA, Greenspan SI. *Test of Sensory Functions in Infants*. Los Angeles, Calif: Western Psychological Services; 1989.

33. Greenspan SI, Lieberman A. Infants, mothers and their interactions: A quantitative clinical approach to developmental assessment. In: *The Course of Life: Psychoanalytic Contributions towards Understanding Personality Development: Vol 1. Infancy and Early Childhood*. Washington, DC: Government Printing Office; 1980. Pub No ADM 80–786.

34. Bayley N. *Bayley Scales of Infant Development*. New York, NY: Psychological Corp; 1969.

35. Porges SW. Heart rate patterns in neonates: A potential diagnostic window to the brain. In: Field TM, Sostek AM, eds. *Infants Born at Risk: Physiological and Perceptual Processes*. New York, NY: Grune & Stratton; 1983.

Use of parent-completed developmental questionnaires for child-find and screening

Jane K. Squires, PhD
Assistant Professor
Center on Human Development
University of Oregon
Eugene, Oregon

Robert Nickel, MD
Clinical Director
Regional Services Center
Child Development and Rehabilitation
    Center
Oregon Health Sciences University
Eugene, Oregon

Diane Bricker, PhD
Professor
Director
Early Intervention Program
Center on Human Development
University of Oregon
Eugene, Oregon

COMPLETION OF developmental questionnaires by parents of infants and young children is a promising strategy to improve current child-find and screening systems. Public Law 99-457 requires that comprehensive child-find systems be developed and that systematic screening of infants for early identification be undertaken. One potentially effective and economical way to meet these specifications is through parent involvement in the developmental assessment of their children. The Revised Parent Developmental Questionnaire (RPDQ),[1] the Infant/Child Monitoring Questionnaires (ICMQ),[2,3] and the Revised Denver Prescreening Developmental Questionnaire (RDPDQ)[4] are all examples of parent-completed questionnaires currently used in child-location programs and for developmental screening in medical offices.

This article reviews the advantages of involving parents in the developmental assessment of their infants and children and outlines guidelines for eliciting valid and reliable information from parents. Current tools are reviewed, and examples of their implementation in child-find and screening programs are described.

WHY USE PARENTS?

Parental input in screening and assessment systems for infants and toddlers is advantageous for several reasons. First, parents possess information often unavailable to professionals, such as developmental histories, personality characteristics, social-emotional adjustment, and functioning in the home environment. Parents witness a larger sample of their children's behavior than is observed in a classroom, clinic, or assessment situation. Information form parents assists in providing a comprehensive picture of the children and enhances the validity and reliability of a developmental assessment, especially for very young children. Multisource assessments, with information contributed by parents and family

Inf Young Children 1990; 3(2): 46–57

63

members as well as teachers, physicians, and therapists, are necessary for a complete and accurate picture of a child's functioning and are mandatory for young children with handicaps.[5]

Second, Public Law 99-457 intends that parents be partners in the development and delivery of services to their children. Procedures that formally require parental input in the initial screening and assessment of their children help ensure this involvement from the beginning.

Third, parental input may also be cost-effective for a child-find or screening system.[6] The completion of questionnaires by parents preserves professional assessment time for those infants about whom questionnaires are not appropriate (eg, infants whose parents are unable to read or provide accurate information about their children). In addition, the use of parents in first-level screening allows larger numbers of infants to be followed with limited resources, while practitioners concentrate on the smaller population of infants with suspected problems.

Fourth, parents may increase their knowledge about child development[7] and their involvement in developmental activities.[8] Answering questions about their children's current status may alert parents to important developmental phenomena to be encouraged and may give them ideas about games or strategies to elicit these important skills. The involvement of parents in screening and initial assessments may also result in their increased participation in their children's intervention program.[9]

Finally, the use of parents to screen their children's development also benefits early intervention personnel, particularly medical practitioners. Physicians are in a unique position to identify preschool-aged children with disabilities through regular preventive health checkups. Physicians overwhelmingly support early identification to increase the success of early intervention services with young children.[10] A committee of the American Academy of Pediatrics recommends developmental assessment at every encounter with children from infancy to 5 years.[11] Unfortunately, most physicians tend to rely on clinical rather than formal testing, which may not be sufficient for early identification of children with disabilities.[10,12] Developmental questionnaires completed by parents provide a formal review of their children's skills, encourage the parent to discuss any developmental concerns with the physician, and help the physician recognize and attend to parental concerns. Developmental testing is then scheduled for infants who receive a suspect rating on the parent-completed questionnaire.

ARE PARENTS ACCURATE?

Although some practitioners have been wary about the validity and reliability of parent-supplied information,[13] current research supports the accuracy of parental reports on young children. Gradel et al,[14] Coplan,[15] Donnelly et al,[16] Sexton et al,[17] and Sonnander[18] have examined the degree of agreement between parent and professional assessment of children who are normal and disabled. These investigators have arrived at two important conclusions. First, they found that parents are generally accurate when estimating their children's current developmental level. Second, discrepancies between parent and professional evaluations of children occur most often with emerging items, items close to the ceiling of an assessment, or items related to behaviors affected by the testing situation (eg, unfamiliar language or social requests).

Lichtenstein and Ireton[9] discussed four factors affecting the reliability and validity of parental reports about their child's development. The first factor is the nature of information that is requested: as noted above, parents are most reliable if asked to assess a current, observable behavior that does not involve an inference. Wenar[19] and Dale et al[20] found that mothers are not reliable in recalling historical events, such as those associated with pregnancy and early childhood illnesses. To maximize accuracy, parents should be asked questions that focus on newly acquired skills that are used frequently.[20]

The second factor is the method of obtaining information: structured interviews, questionnaires, and inventories generally yield more reliable information that unstructured, open-ended interviews. If directions to parents are clear and specific, and if descriptions of behavior are requested, the information is likely to be of better quality. Lengthy questionnaires yield more reliable and valid information; however, if a questionnaire is too long, cooperation or concentration may be adversely affected. An instrument must be long enough to ensure accuracy, yet short enough to retain parents' attention.

The third factor is the child's characteristics. Lichtenstein[21] found that reports about first-born children were more predictive of school performance than were reports about later-born siblings. However, research in this area is limited. The influence on parent reports of other characteristics, such as gender, age, and type of disability, has yet to be established.

The fourth factor is the characteristics of the parents themselves. Research findings on the accuracy of parents' reports are contradictory in terms of the relationship between accuracy and the variables of socioeconomic status (SES) and education level. Using the Minnesota Child Development Inventory (MCDI),[22] Sturner et al[23] found that reports from low-SES parents on child development level were less valid than reports from higher-SES parents. The reports from low-SES parents were compromised, because these parents omitted more items than higher-SES parents. In contrast, Lichtenstein[21] found that preschool screening reports from low-SES parents had validity equal to or greater than that of reports from higher-SES parents in predicting teacher rating of kindergarten performance. Eisert et al[24] also found that MCDI information provided by low-SES parents was highly correlated with the results of a battery of cognitive tests administered by professionals. Using the RPDQ, Knobloch et al[1] concluded that both well-educated and poorly educated parents can accurately answer questions about their children's developmental status and can provide professionals with useful assessment information. Frankenburg et al[25] reported that the Denver Prescreening Developmental Questionnaire (DPDQ) was more accurate when completed by parents with a high school education than by parents without a high school education.

It is also important than parents have the capacity to respond to requests for information. A questionnaire will not yield useful information from parents with poor reading skills, and an interview may be inappropriate for parents who have poor oral communication skills. Questionnaires that are not culturally sensitive may yield a poor quality of information and may not produce an accurate picture of child functioning.

Parent-completed developmental questionnaires may be inappropriate for some parents for other reasons. Information about child functioning reported by parents whose mental function is impaired as a result of substance abuse, developmental disabilities, or psychologic disturbances may not be valid or reliable. If a practitioner has concerns about the home environment, a home visit or a visit by the parents to a center for an evaluation may help the practitioner to know how the family is functioning. For the homeless and those who frequently change residences, strategies other than mailing or completing questionnaires in the home will be necessary. Alternative strategies include completion of questionnaires in a welfare or Women's, Infants' and Children's (WIC) office or reliance on physician information such as that collected by the Washington State High-Priority Infant Tracking Program.[26,27]

PARENT-COMPLETED QUESTIONNAIRES

Information on selected parent-completed developmental questionnaires and inventories is shown in Table 1.[6,28,29] Examples from each of the instruments appear in the Appendix.

Frankenburg et al[4,28] developed parent questionnaires that serve as first-level screening tools. The DPDQ and, more recently, the RDPDQ contain items adapted from the Revised Denver Developmental Screening Test (RDDST).[29] The RDDST is widely used by professionals and paraprofessionals to screen children from birth to 6 years of age.[30] The RDPDQ is designed as the first step of a two-step approach, in which the screening completed by parents is followed by administration of the RDDST if the parent questionnaire reflects possible developmental delays. The RDPDQ is designed to be completed in a medical office or clinic prior to a well-child visit, and it currently enjoys wide use.

The RDPDQ contains questions on the developmental range from birth to 6 years of age. Parents are instructed to answer questions until a ceiling of three consecutive "no responses" is reached. Initial data reported by Frankenburg et al[4]

Table 1. Information on selected parent-completed questionnaires

Instrument	Age range	Purpose/ description	Reliability	Validity
Communication Development Inventory (CDI) Short Form[1]	12–24 months	CDI Short Form includes five nonoverlapping word lists of 123 words	High, correlations among five word lists	Correlations r > 0.94 with CDI WORDS
Infant/Child Monitoring Questionnaires (ICMQ)[2]	4–36 months	The I/CMQs contain 35 items in areas of fine motor, gross motor, communications, adaptive, personal-social skills; questionnaires available at 4, 8, 12, 16, 20, 24, 30, 36 months; 10–15 minutes to complete	Interrater >0.85; test-retest >0.90	Concurrent validity with Gesell, Bayley, Stanford-Binet = 0.86–0.91; sensitivity = 0.43–0.94; specificity = 0.83–0.94
Language Development Survey (LDS)[3]	24 months	LDS is a vocabulary checklist containing 300 words and general questions about word combinations	Test-retest >0.86; Cronbach's alp = 0.99	Concurrent validity with Bayley and Reynell Scales = 0.87; specificity = 0.87; sensitivity = 0.86
Minnesota Child Development Inventory (MCDI)[4]	6 months–6 years	The MCDI contains 320 items in areas of general development, gross motor, expressive language, language competency situation comprehension, self-help, and personal-social skills; lengthy for a screening instrument	Internal consistency = 0.90	Concurrent validity with standard-ized measures = 0.50–0.76; sensitivity = 0.76; specificity = 0.76

(continues)

Table 1. Continued

Instrument	Age range	Purpose/ description	Reliability	Validity
Revised Denver Prescreening Developmental Questionnaire[5]	0–6 years	Items taken from Revised Denver Developmental Screening Test (RDDST); parents answer questions until celing of 3 consecutive no-responses reached	Test-retest >0.80; interobserver >0.80	Concurrent validity with RDDST; identified 84% of non-normal on original DDST.
Revised Parent Developmental Questionnaires[6]	6–36 months	Items from Gesell in areas of gross motor, adaptive language, and personal-social skills	Not reported	Concurrent validity with Gesell; underscreening = 2.6%–10%; overscreening = 6%

[1]Reznick JS, Goldsmith L. A multiple form word production checklist to assess early language. *J Child Lang.* 1989;16:91–100.

[2]Bricker D, Squires J, Mounts L. *Infant/Child Monitoring Questionnaires.* Eugene, Ore: University of Oregon, Center on Human Development, 1990.

[3]Rescorla L. The language development survey: A screening tool for delayed language in toddlers. *J Speech Hear Disord.* 1989;54:587–599.

[4]Ireton H, Thwing E. *Minnesota Child Development Inventory.* Minneapolis: Behavior Science Systems, 1974.

[5]Frankenburg W, Fandel A, Thornton S. Revision of the Denver Prescreening Developmental Questionnaire. *J Pediatr.* 1987;57:744–753.

[6]Knobloch H, et al. The validity of parental reporting of infant development. *Pediatrics.* 1979;63:873–878.

comparing the RDPDQ with the RDDST indicated that the RDPDQ identified 84% of children that were identified as non-normal by the RDDST. Test-retest and interobserver reliability were reported to be >0.80.

Meisels[30] and Borowitz and Glascoe[31] recommended caution in using the RDDST with some populations because of the test's reported low sensitivity for identification of preschool-age children with disabilities. The RDDST was also reported[32] to have low specificity for biologically vulnerable infants. The relationship between the RDDST and the RDPDQ requires that similar caution be taken in using the RDPDQ with some groups of infants and young children.

Another parent-completed questionnaire is the RPDQ.[1] Items on this questionnaire are derived from the Gesell Developmental and Neurologic Examination in gross motor, fine motor, language, adaptive, and social-emotional skill areas. To study validity, Knobloch et al[1] mailed questionnaires to parents of 526 high-risk infants who were 28 weeks old; the questionnaires were completed in the home, returned, and scored by professional examiners. The infants received complete developmental and neurologic evaluations at 40 weeks of age. Knobloch et al[1] reported low underscreening and overscreening rates when the RPDQ results were compared with results using the Gesell examination. They also found that parents from a wide range of education and social backgrounds answered the RPDQ reasonably well.

Public health nurses in 18 counties in New York State are using the RPDQ as part of the statewide Infant Health Assessment Program (IHAP). These nurses help parents complete the questionnaire in the home when the infants are 6 months of age and again when the children are 30 to 36 months old. About 2,500 at-risk infants are currently being monitored via this parent-completed questionnaire. Nurses in the IHAP program feel that, in addition to providing screening information, the questionnaire affords them a natural opportunity to teach parents about development and to model appropriate behaviors.

A third parent-completed questionnaire is the ICMQ,[2,3] which comprises a set of eight questionnaires completed by parents at 4-month intervals until the child is 24 months old, and then again when the child is 30 and 36 months old. (Alternative ICMQ forms for completion when the child is 6 and 18 months old are also available.) Each questionnaire contains 35 questions that address gross motor, fine motor, communication, personal-social, and adaptive skill areas. Questions are simply worded and accompanied by illustrations when appropriate. The ICMQs are designed to be completed by parents at home and can be distributed in a postage-paid, mail-back format.

Validity and reliability studies of more than 400 infants have been reported by Bricker et al.[2,3,6] Validity, as measured by the agreement between the infant's classification based on the parent-completed questionnaire and a criterion measure (eg, Bayley Scales of Infant Development,[33] Stanford-Binet Intelligence Test,[34] or Revised Gesell Developmental Schedules[35]), was high, ranging from 86% to 91%. Underscreening and overscreening rates were low, ranging from 0% to 6% and from 3% to 11%, respectively. Sensitivity—that is, the proportion of infants correctly identified by the screening tool as abnormal—ranged from 0.43 at 4 months to 0.94 at 12 and 16 months; overall sensitivity was 0.63. Specificity, the proportion of infants correctly excluded by the screening tool as normal ranged from 0.83 at 24 months to 0.94 at 12 and 16 months, and the overall specificity was 0.91. Test-retest and interobserver reliability were reported to be >0.85. The cost of maintaining the questionnaire system (mailing and scoring questionnaires and completing follow-up phone calls) was about $2.50 per questionnaire (Squires J. May 1987. Unpublished data).

The ICMQs are currently being pilot tested in several states as part of the child-find and screening efforts associated with the implementation of Public Law 99-

457. For example, the North Dakota Early Childhood Tracking System is in the initial phase of implementing the ICMQs statewide and is currently observing about 550 children from birth to 3 years of age with follow-up of 5,000 children proposed for full implementation. Questionnaires are mailed to the parents' homes, and the initial return rate is about 75%. Additional questionnaires are collected during home visits and in WIC offices. Children who are screened as abnormal by the ICMQs are referred to the local early intervention team for further evaluation. Data from the initial phase have not yet been analyzed.

The Southwest Minnesota High-Priority Infant Follow-Along Project, operating in an 18-county area, is observing about 100 infants in its initial pilot phase. Community health service agencies in each county use a computer program to mail and keep track of outgoing and incoming ICMQs. In addition, letters to parents and developmental information for parents covering the next questionnaire period are generated by the computer. Those children screened as abnormal on the ICMQs are given a further assessment by the community health service agency and are referred to the county interagency early intervention committee for design of an intervention program with parents when warranted. Although no data have been analyzed to date, the public health nurses involved in the program have responded favorably to the use of parent-completed questionnaires and consider them valuable as a teaching tool.

From 1984 to 1988, the Oregon Developmental Monitoring Project used the ICMQs as part of a regional follow-up project for high-risk infants in 10 counties in central and southern Oregon. This project was coordinated in each county by community health nurses. The children who were rated on the ICMQ as abnormal were tested with the Revised Developmental Screening Inventory (RDSI).[35] In a comparison study with the RDSI, the specificity of the ICMQs (4-, 8-, 18-, and 36-month questionnaires) was 0.90 or greater, and the sensitivity ranged from 0.82 to 0.91 for all questionnaires except the 4-month ICMQ.[36] As an extension of this project, the ICMQs continue to be used in 15 Oregon counties in the Care Coordination Program of the Child Development and Rehabilitation Center.

The MCDI[22] is a parent-completed tool in which parents are asked to answer 320 questions with "yes" or "no," depending on whether the child has acquired the behavior or not. Skill areas include general development, gross motor, fine motor, expressive language, language comprehension, situation comprehension, self-help, and personal-social skills. The MCDI is usually completed in a clinic setting with the assistance of a professional. It was standardized on a sample of nearly 800 children aged 6 months to 6 years. Studies on concurrent validity[37–39] and predictive validity[40] have found that the parent-completed MCDI yields accurate outcomes.

Parent-completed inventories specific to language functioning currently are being used successfully in physicians' offices and clinics. The Language Development Survey (LDS)[41] is a vocabulary checklist designed for use as a screening tool in the identification of language delays in 2-year-old children. It contains a vocabulary checklist of about 300 words grouped in categories (eg, food, toys, animals, body parts) and general questions about word combinations (eg, "Does your child combine two or more words in phrases?"). The LDS inventory takes parents about 10 minutes and can be completed in a pediatric waiting room or clinic setting, in the home, or in other appropriate settings. Psychometric studies conducted by Rescorla[41] in pediatric and hospital clinic settings with a wide variety of SES groups (N = 549) reported high test-retest reliability and Cronbach's alpha coefficients. Concurrent validity, using the Bayley Scales of Infant Development and the Reynell Expressive and Receptive Language Scales, was also high. Rescorla found the LDS to be a good clinical tool when used as part of the 24-month pediatric examination. Because of the flexibility and short administration time of the instrument, it is generally well suited to child-find and screening endeavors. Vocabulary checklists can be read to nonreading (or orally translated to non-English-speaking) parents by a paraprofessional or professional.

Several groups supported by the MacArthur Foundation[20,42,43] (and Dale PS. January 1990. Unpublished data) developed the Communication Development Inventories (CDI), a series of parent-completed inventories for assessment of infant and toddler language. One instrument in this inventory, CDI WORDS, contains checklists for parental assessment of expressive language. Dale et al[20] reported high validity for a version of CDI WORDS, when they used the Bayley Scales of Infant Development as the criterion measure. Reznick and Goldsmith[43] developed a checklist of 123 words, CDI WORDS Short Form, which is suitable for parental completion at home or prior to a clinic or physician's office visit. Reznick and Goldsmith found high correlations between this shortened checklist and the longer CDI WORDS. Revised norms for the CDI for infants and toddlers are under development, as are shortened versions of each instrument, which will be suitable for screening.

In addition to developmental questionnaires, questionnaires assessing temperament,[44-47] behavior,[48] personality,[49] and the home environment[50] have been developed for parents. Although it is not within the scope of this paper, research on these questionnaires generally supports the usefulness of information from parents.

•   •   •

Parent-completed questionnaires represent a low-cost strategy for including parents in the assessment process. They can be used in a variety of ways for child-find and developmental screening, depending on the needs and resources of a program or state. Physicians' offices and screening clinics are among the sites at which parent-completed developmental questionnaires can be used. Moreover, many questionnaires can be mailed to the parent's or caregiver's home or completed in conjunction with a home visit by a nurse or caseworker. If parents have no permanent address or a disorganized home environment, questionnaires can be completed in a waiting room or with the help of a paraprofessional prior to a clinic or office visit.

The need for low-cost child-find and screening systems is underscored by the increasing numbers of infants who are at risk for developmental delays and as a result of reduced federal and local budgets.[51] Parent-completed questionnaires are being used in several states as part of statewide child-find and screening efforts. These questionnaires represent flexible, cost-effective means of obtaining developmental information about infants and young children who are at risk. Although no single test or method will satisfy the multiple needs of large child-find and screening programs, parent-completed questionnaires should be included as a fundamental strategy.

REFERENCES

1. Knobloch H, Stevens F, Malone A, Ellison P, Risemberg H. The validity of parental reporting of infant development. *Pediatrics.* 1979;63:873–878.

2. Bricker D, Squires J, Kaminski R, Mounts L. The validity, reliability, and cost of a parent-completed questionnaire system to evaluate at-risk infants. *J Pediatr Psychol.* 1988;13(1):55–68.

3. Bricker D, Squires J. A low-cost system using parents to monitor the development of at-risk infants. *J Early Intervent.* 1989;13(1):50–60.

4. Frankenburg W, Fandal A, Thorton S. Revision of the Denver Prescreening Developmental Questionnaire. *J Pediatr.* 1987;57:744–753.

5. Bagnato S, Neisworth J, Munson M. *Linking Developmental Assessment and Early Intervention: Curriculum Based Prescription.* 2nd ed. Rockville, Md: Aspen Publishers, 1989.

6. Bricker D, Squires J. The effectiveness of screening at-risk infants: Infant monitoring questionnaires. *Top Early Childhood Spec Educ.* 1989;9(3):67–85.

7. Squires J. *Validity, Reliability and Impact of Developmental Questionnaires Completed by At-risk Mothers.* Eugene, Ore: University of Oregon; 1988. Dissertation.

8. Hunt J, Paraskevopoulos J. Children's psychological development as a function of the accuracy of their mother's knowledge of their abilities. *J Genet Psychol.* 1980;136:285–298.

9. Lichtenstein R, Ireton H. *Preschool Screening: Identifying Young Children with Developmental and Educational Problems.* Orlando, Fla: Grune & Stratton, 1984.

10. Shonfoff JP, Dworkin PH, Leviton A, Levin MD. Primary care approaches to developmental disabilities. *Pediatrics.* 1979;64(4):506–514.

11. Green M, ed. Committee on psychosocial aspects of child and family health, 1980–1985. *Guidelines for Health Supervision.* Elk Grove Village, Ill: American Academy of Pediatrics, 1985.

12. Korsh B, Cobb K, Ashe B. Pediatricians' appraisals of patients' intelligence. *Pediatrics.* 1961;6:990–1003.

13. DuBose RF, Langley MD, Stagg V. Assessing severely handicapped children. *Focus on Except Child* 1977;9:1–13.

14. Gradel K, Thompson M, Sheehan R. Parental and professional agreement in early childhood assessment. *Top Early Childhood Spec Educ.* 1981;1:31–40.

15. Coplan J. Parents' estimates of child's developmental level in high-risk population. *Am J Dis Child.* 1982;136:101–104.

16. Donnelly B, Doherty J, Sheehan R, Whittemore C. A comparison of maternal, paternal, and diagnostic evaluations of typical and atypical infants. Presented at Handicapped Children's Early Education Program/Division for Early Childhood Conference, December 1982. Washington, DC.

17. Sexton D, Miller J, Murdock J. Correlates of parental-professional congruency scores in the assessment of young handicapped children. *J Div Early Child.* 1984;8(2):99–106.

18. Sonnander K. Parental developmental assessment of 18-month-old children: Reliability and predictive value. *Dev Med Child Neurol.* 1987;29:351–362.

19. Wenar C. The reliability of developmental histories. *Psychosomat Med.* 1963;25:505–509.

20. Dale PS, Bates E, Reznick JS, Morisset C. The validity of a parent report instrument of child language at twenty months. *J Child Lang.* 1989;16:239–249.

21. Lichtenstein R. Predicting school performance of preschool children from parent reports. *J Abnorm Child Psychol.* 1984;12(1):79–94.

22. Ireton H, Thwing E. *Minnesota Child Development Inventory.* Minneapolis: Behavior Science Systems, 1974.

23. Sturner R, Funk S, Thomas P, Green J. An adaptation of the Minnesota child development inventory for preschool developmental screening. *J Pediatr Psychol.* 1982;7:295–306.

24. Eisert D, Spector S, Shankaran S, Faigenbaum D, Szego E. Mothers' reports of their low birth weight infants' subsequent development on the Minnesota child development inventory. *J Pediatr Psychol.* 1980;5(4):353–364.

25. Frankenburg W, Coons C, Ker C. Screening infants and preschoolers to identify school learning problems. In: Edgar E, Haring N, Jenkins J, Pious C, eds. *Mentally Handicapped Children.* Baltimore: University Park Press, 1982.

26. Sells CJ. *High-priority infant tracking project.* Seattle, Wash: Child Development and Mental Retardation Center, University of Washington, 1986.

27. Berman C, Birq P, Fenichel E, eds. *Keeping Track: Tracking Systems for High Risk Infants and Young Children.* 2nd ed. Washington, DC: National Center for Clinical Infant Programs, 1989.

28. Frankenburg W, Van Doorninck W, Liddell T, Dick N. The Denver prescreening developmental questionnaire (PDQ). *Pediatrics.* 1976;57:744–753.

29. Frankenburg W, Goldstein A, Camp B. The revised Denver developmental screening test: Its accuracy as screening instrument. *J Pediatr.* 1971;79(6):988–995.

30. Meisels S. Can developmental screening tests identify children who are developmentally at risk? *Pediatrics.* 1989;83(4):578–585.

31. Borowitz KC, Glascoe FP. Sensitivity of the Denver developmental screening test in speech and language screening. *Pediatrics.* 1986;78:1075–1078.

32. Sciarillo W, Brown M, Robinson N, Bennett F, Sells C. Effectiveness of the Denver screening test with biologically vulnerable infants. *Dev Behav Pediatr.* 1986;7(2):77–83.

33. Bayley N. *Bayley Scales of Infant Development.* New York: Psychological Corp, 1969.

34. Thorndike RL, Hagen EP, Sattler JM. *Stanford-Binet Intelligence Scale.* 4th ed. Chicago: Riverside, 1985.

35. Knobloch H, Stevens F, Malone A. *Manual of Developmental Diagnosis: The Administration and Interpretation of the Revised Gesell and Armatruda Developmental and Neurological Examination.* New York: Harper & Row, 1980.

36. Nickel RE. *The Oregon Developmental Monitoring Project for High Risk Infants—Final Report.* Eugene, Ore: Child Development and Rehabilitation Center, Oregon Health Sciences University, 1989.

37. Ireton H, Thwing E, Currier S. Minnesota child development inventory: Identification of children with developmental disorders. *J Pediatr Psychol.* 1977;2:18–22.

38. Gottfried A, Guerin D, Spencer J, Meyer C. Concurrent validity of the Minnesota child development inventory in a nonclinical sample. *J Consult Clin Psychol.* 1983;51:643–644.

39. Saylor CF, Brandt BJ. The Minnesota child development inventory: A valid maternal-report form for assessing development in infancy. *Dev Behav Pediatr.* 1986;7(5):308–311.

40. Colligan R. Prediction of reading difficulty from parental preschool report: A 3-year followup. *Learning Disability Q.* 1976;4:31–37.

41. Rescorla L. The language development survey: A screening tool for delayed language in toddlers. *J Speech Hear Disord.* 1989;54:587–599.

42. Synder L, Bates E, Bretherton I. Content and context in early lexical development. *J Child Lang.* 1981;8:565–582.

43. Reznick JS, Goldsmith L. A multiple form word production checklist to assess early language. *J Child Lang.* 1989;16:91–100.

44. Carey W, McDevitt S. Revision of the infant temperament questionnaire. *Pediatrics.* 1978;61:735–739.

45. Rothbart MK. Measurement of temperament in infancy. *Child Dev.* 1981;52:569–578.

46. Worobey J. Convergence among assessments of temperament in the first month. *Child Dev.* 1986;57:47–55.

47. Hagekull B, Bohlin G, Lindhagen K. Validity of parental reports. *Inf Behav Dev.* 1984;7:77–92.

48. Achenback TM, Edelbrock CS. *Child Behavior Checklist.* Bethesda, Md: National Institute of Mental Health, 1982.

49. Wirt RD, Lachar D, Klinedinst JK, Seat PD. *Personality Inventory for Children.* Los Angeles: Western Psychological Services, 1977.

50. Coons C, Gay E, Fandal A, Ker C, Frankenburg W. *The Home Screening Questionnaire Reference Manual.* Denver: Ladoca Publishing Foundation, 1981.

51. Szanton E. *Infants Can't Wait: The Numbers.* Washington, DC: National Center for Clinical Infant Programs, 1986.

Appendix

Examples from selected parent-completed developmental questionnaires

MINNESOTA CHILD DEVELOPMENT INVENTORY*

If the question describes your child's present or past behavior, answer yes.
1. Walks without help.
2. Unbuttons one or more buttons.
3. Says two or more words clearly.
4. Rides tricycle using pedals.

Reprinted with permission from Ireton H, Thwing E. Minnesota Child Development Inventory. Minneapolis: Behavior Science Systems, 1974.

REVISED DENVER PRESCREENING DEVELOPMENTAL QUESTIONNAIRE†

44. Plays Pat-A-Cake
    Can your baby play "pat-a-cake" or wave "bye-bye"
    without help? Answer **No** if you need to help him/her
    by holding his/her hands.
    | | **Yes** | **No** | (13) | PS |

45. Dada or Mama, Specific
    Does your child say "da-da" when (s)he wants or see his/her
    father? Does your child say "ma-ma" when (s)he wants or
    sees his/her mother? Answer **Yes** if your child says *either*.
    | | **Yes** | **No** | (13-1) | L |

46. Stands Alone Well
    Can your baby stand alone without having to hold on to
    something for *30 seconds* or more?
    | | **Yes** | **No** | (13-3) | GM |

(Left margin: 9–24 Months (R-PDG))

---

†Reprinted with permission from Frankenburg W, Fandal A, Thornton S. Revision of the Denver Prescreening Developmental Questionnaire. J Pediatr. 1987;57:744–753.*

REVISED PARENT DEVELOPMENTAL QUESTIONNAIRE[‡]

Does your child?   Yes   No

N.   No longer go about on her hands and knees but walk
        alone all the time, without pulling up first?

(56w) Climb into a couch or an adult chair?

O.   Fall very little when walking?

(15m) Climb on a chair or a stool in order to reach things?

P.   Walk down stairs if you hold 1 hand?

(18m) Walk into or step on a large ball, after you have
        shown her how to kick it?

[‡]*Reprinted with permission from Knobloch H, Stevens F, Malone A, Ellison P, Risemberg H. The validity of parental reporting of infant development. Pediatrics. 1979;63:873–878.*

COMMUNICATION DEVELOPMENT INVENTORY (CDI) SHORT FORM

Check the words you have heard your child use.

List 1	List 2	List 3
New	Sticky	High
Green	Sick	Red
Fast	Sad	Noisy
Quiet	Gentle	Hard
Awake	Better	Black
White	Loud	Old
First	Poor	Slow

LANGUAGE DEVELOPMENT SURVEY

Please check off each word your child says.

Vocabulary checklist

ANIMALS		ACTIONS		HOUSEHOLD	
bear	cow	bath	cough	bathtub	crib
bee	dog	breakfast	cut	bed	cup
bird	duck	bring	dance	blanket	door
bug	elephant	catch	dinner	bottle	floor
bunny	fish	clap	doodoo	bowl	fork
cat	frog	close	eat	chair	glass
chicken	horse	come	feed	clock	knife

PERSONAL		CLOTHES		MODIFIERS	
brush	pencil	belt	jacket	all gone	clean
comb	penny	boots	mittens	all right	cold
glasses	pocketbook	coat	pajamas	bad	dark
key	tissue	diaper	pants	big	dirty
money	toothbrush	dress	shirt	black	down
paper	umbrella	gloves	shoes	blue	good
pen	watch	hat	slippers	broken	happy

INFANT MONITORING QUESTIONNAIRE*—8

Diane Bricker, Jane Squires, and Linda Mounts with assistance from Ruth Kaminski, Robert Nickel, and LaWanda Potter

III. Fine motor

(Be sure to try each activity with your child.)

	Yes	Some-times	Not Yet	
1. Does your baby reach for a crumb or Cheerio and touch it with her finger or hand? (If she already picks up a small object, check "yes" for this item.)	❑	❑	❑	_____
2. Does your baby pick up a small toy, holding it in the center of her hand with her fingers around it?	❑	❑	❑	_____
3. Does your baby *try* to pick up a crumb or Cheerio by using her thumb and all her fingers in a raking motion, even if she isn't able to pick it up? (If she already picks up a crumb or Cheerio, check "yes" for this item.)	❑	❑	❑	_____

Developmental screening: Rationale, methods, and application

Frances P. Glascoe, PhD
Child Development Center
Department of Pediatrics
Vanderbilt University
Nashville, Tennessee

PUBLIC LAW 99-457, which extends public special education services to infants and preschoolers, is predicated on the early identification of young children who have preexisting conditions that make them high risk for developmental delays or who are already experiencing delays in one or more developmental domains. Detecting the latter type of child is the focus of this article. The purpose is to assist professionals in finding the best available answers to essential questions about early detection: What are the features of developmental delay? How does it change over time? Which measures are most accurate? Which are most applicable to various settings—schools, departments of public health, pediatric offices, and so forth? The article emphasizes practical issues in detecting young children with developmental problems while listing directions for training and further research.

ASSUMPTIONS

Despite the fact that there are differences across states in how delays are defined and measured, the concepts of developmental delay and early detection have a number of commonalities that are consistent from state to state. These are listed below along with several working assumptions drawn from current research:

1. In young children, development may be malleable because it is easily influenced by positive forces such as early intervention as well as by adverse environmental conditions including limited family resources, lack of education, or parental anxiety.[1-4]

2. Young children without any early signs of developmental delays may exhibit deficits as they grow older.[4,5] Certain developmental domains become prominent as children mature, particularly language in late infancy, and preacademics in older preschoolers. It is only when there is an untimely absence or attenuation of skills in these domains that a delay or disorder can be recognized. This means that the older the child, the greater the chance of delay or disorder.[6]

3. In order to monitor age-related changes in children's development, repeated screening is necessary (as is already the policy of the American Nurses' Association and the American Academy of Pediatrics). Repeated screening should be provided to all children including those who receive early intervention services. This will help ensure the earliest possible detection of developmental delays as well as distribute parsimoniously precious intervention resources.

4. Not all developmental domains are equally important indicators of current or future functioning. Approximately 90% of school-age children receiving special

Inf Young Children 1991; 4(1): 1–10
© 1991 Aspen Publishers, Inc.

education services have either speech-language impairments, mental retardation, or learning disabilities.[7] The fact that these disabilities all involve deficits in various types of language skills adds credence to the fact that language is a critical indicator of development as well as a strong predictor of subsequent success in school.[8] Motor skills, in contrast, are not as highly correlated with general functioning, although motor milestones should not be confused with motor tone, abnormalities in which are sometimes associated with school difficulties.[9–11] While it is important to screen all aspects of development, the probability of detecting children with the most common types of emerging disabilities is greater when expressive and receptive language delays are carefully screened.

5. Standardized screening tests of development are preferable to informal assessment (eg, checklists, reviews of milestones, or clinical judgment). Studies of professionals who rely on nonstandard screening techniques exclusively show that they miss the majority of children with developmental problems.[12,13] This may be due to inconsistent use of these informal measures, poor selection of items, lack of data on how to interpret results, etc. When informal techniques are used, they should be coupled with standardized measurement.[14–16]

6. Because development, whether delayed or typical, is often inconsistently expressed, it is advisable to use measures that rely on multiple sources of information (parent report, direct elicitation, and observation) wherever possible. Children usually demonstrate more sophisticated skills when in familiar settings. This largely explains why parents' descriptions may appear inflated relative to measured performance. Accounting for such variability encourages professionals to view development not as a fixed point but, more appropriately, as a range of functioning. This lends confidence to the interpretation of screening test results, helps reconcile differing perspectives between parents and professionals, and facilitates parental involvement. Similarly, the use of multiple screening measures rather than a single test is advisable (and encouraged within PL 99-457 for the determination of eligibility) because it reduces error and helps ensure that all domains of development are assessed.

7. In many states, screening tests rather than diagnostic tests are used to establish children's eligibility for programs, diagnostic testing being provided only after enrollment. This means that professionals without extensive experience in developmental assessment act as gatekeepers to early intervention services. Training in developmental screening is necessary to ensure that those who administer measures acquire a careful, respectful appreciation for the integrity of tests as well as recognizing the need for precision in their administration, scoring, and interpretation.[17]

METHODS

Having established a framework for issues in developmental detection, it is important to consider desirable characteristics of screening tests. In the marketplace of screening, there is no correlate to the Food and Drug Administration for ensuring that only well-constructed and accurate measures are available to consumers. Professionals charged with selecting from among the competing array of tests must learn to recognize and demand quality measures. They must do so in a market that is in great flux. Publishers and test authors, anticipating the growing national demand for screening tests, have revised many older tests and devised new ones. While several of these tests are promising and clearly capitalize on the pitfalls of previous instruments, independent validity studies on the accuracy of these new and improved measures inevitably lag behind instrument development. Such studies are extremely helpful in establishing how well each test detects children with and without problems—critical information not always provided in test manuals.

Quality screening tests can also be recognized by various guidelines derived from *Standards for Educational and Psychological Tests*[18] established by the American Psychological Association and elaborated by researchers specializing in developmental screening.[19–23] These standards include:

Sensitivity. Sensitivity is an indicator of how well a test identifies children with delays. Ideally, a minimum of 80% of children found to have developmental problems when given a comprehensive diagnostic test battery should also have failing scores on a screening test.

Specificity. Specificity is an indicator of how well a test identifies children without delays. At least 90% of the children found to have typical development on diagnostic testing should pass a screening test.

Positive predictive value. It is acceptable and even necessary for screening tests to fail more children than actually have problems since this helps ensure that fewer children with delays are missed. Positive predictive value is the percentage of children who, after failing a screening test, are actually found to have developmental problems when administered diagnostic tests. The reciprocal of positive predictive value is the over-referral rate. When the over-referral rate is more than 1½ to 2 times the number of truly delayed children, the screening test should be thought of as a prescreen, usually a very brief measure that identifies a subset of children who are likely to fail screening. Prescreens are popular in medical settings because they can be given quickly to all patients any may reduce by as much as two-thirds the numbers targeted for lengthier screening tests.

Reliability. High levels of reliability show that a test can be administered identically by different examiners, all of whom can interpret and score children's responses in the same way. Without such interexaminer reliability, test results cannot be compared across children or to test norms. Reliability across examiners is established by having different examiners test the same child. Scores are then compared and 80% or greater agreement is expected.

It is also important to know whether the same behavior can be elicited from the same child with any consistency. Testing children twice, 1 to 4 weeks apart, and comparing their performances on each item establishes test-retest reliability. Correlations of approximately 0.9 or at least 80% agreement in performance are preferred.

Stratification/sampling. In order to decide the significance of an individual child's performance on a test, examiners compare each child's scores to numerical or decision-making tables provided in the test manual. These tables were generated by administering the test to a large group of children, called the normative sample, whose performance becomes the test's norms. The norms indicate the typical distribution of results (eg, what percentage of children pass or fail). Ideally, the normative population for a test should be representative of the country in which the test will be given. In the United States, representativeness is determined by the US census, which lists racial, geographic, and socioeconomic distributions. In addition to emulating these distributions, at least 100 children per age interval (usually 6 to 12 months) should be included. The term test standardization is often used to refer to the process of normative sampling and reliability assessment.

Validity. There are many types of validity. Concurrent validity should be established by comparing each subtest from a screening test to diagnostic measures of that domain. Correlations of 0.6 or greater are preferable. In contrast, content validity is not demonstrated by statistical analyses but rather by practical considerations about the test. For example, it is important to have a subtest for each domain listed in PL 99-457 (cognitive, physical, language, self-help, psychosocial). Each subtest should produce a range of scores that comply with state requirements for defining developmental delay (eg, cutoffs, standard deviation units, percentage of delay, etc.). Subtest items should sample a range of realistic behaviors clearly related to the domain measured and selected on the advice of relevant professionals, or drawn from developmental research or from a broad range of well-established tests (eg, diagnostic tests of speech-language development, motor skills, adaptive behavior, academics, etc.). While it is not necessary for screening tests to show statistical evidence of their predictive or criterion-related validity, it is helpful if tests measure carefully, and weight heavily, those domains that are closely linked to future school performance (ie, preacademic skills and language).

Miscellaneous. There are a number of other features desirable in screening tests: Test materials should be interesting and colorful to children and not so numerous as to make locating them overly challenging to the examiner. The manual should be designed so that it is easy to locate each subtest. Directions should be highlighted to enhance their visibility during test administration. Test protocols, norms, and scoring procedures should be simple and clear in order to reduce computational error. Examiner training requirements and practice exercises should be thoroughly described. Test manuals should describe how to explain results to families with distinct recommendations for avoiding use of diagnostic labels. Examiners should be directed, on the basis of score patterns, to make specific types of referrals (eg, delays only in language suggest referral to a speech and hearing center, whereas multiple delays suggest a need for comprehensive evaluations, and motor delays indicate a need for a medical examination or physical therapy evaluation, etc.). Finally, it is helpful if tests have a prescreening component—a set of items or a subtest that busy professionals can use to quickly check the development of all patients, clients, or students in order to determine if further screening is needed.

APPLICATIONS

Below is a review of selected screening instruments. The standards described above are considered for each. The list of tests selected is not exhaustive but includes recent additions to the screening market or measures with high levels of specificity and sensitivity. Additional reviews may be found in a number of other sources.[19–23]

Battelle Developmental Inventory Screening Test

The Battelle Developmental Inventory Screening Test (BDIST)[24] is a subset of items drawn from the comprehensive Battelle Developmental Inventory. The BDIST is designed for children 6 months to 8 years of age. It has several scoring options that should fit the differing state criteria (the test has been adopted for use under PL 99-457 by Utah, California, New Hampshire, Maine, and Montana) and individual scores are produced for each of the seven subtests (personal-social, adaptive, gross and fine motor, receptive and expressive language, and cognitive). Many items have alternative methods of administration: interview, observation, or direct elicitation. This is helpful, particularly in medical settings where children are often fearful, sick, sleepy, or recalcitrant. Modifications are described for screening children with visual or physical handicaps. The use of basals and ceilings keeps testing and scoring time to around 30 to 35 minutes. The presence of subtest scores helps specify the types of referrals needed and there are careful guidelines for explaining test results to parents.

Perhaps because the test is relatively new it lacks many features that would make it easier to use, such as thumb tabs for ease in changing subtests. That interview items are interspersed with direct items makes it difficult to maintain children's attention and behavior. Directions are clear and easy to locate although examiners must create their own wording on parent report items. This means that well-developed interviewing skills are essential. Training exercises are provided in the manual but are quite time-consuming. The test can be purchased with or without stimuli. The former is quite expensive and the latter challenging to locate and difficult to organize.

The norms include children with geographic, racial, and socioeconomic diversity and were recently revised in response to independent research critical of score calibrations. Because of this, there is little current evaluation of the test's sensitivity and specificity. That which exists is promising. A study using a small sample (N = 22) of 6- to 78-month-old children from pediatric practices showed that the expressive language subtest was 88% sensitive to language problems and 100% specific in detecting normal language.[15] Another study of 80 30- to 72-month-old children drawn from day-care centers and developmental evaluation clinics showed that total BDIST scores were 90% sensitive and 80% specific to any handicapped condition (using criteria from PL 94-142). This research also showed that the Communication and Cognition subtests can be used alone since they were each 80% sensitive and 86% specific to diagnoses. However, the Battelle age equivalents were found to be significantly lower than those derived from diagnostic measures. This suggests that states relying on percentage of delay scores should compute these only when children have already failed based on cutoff scores. Otherwise, overidentification may result.[25]

Infant Monitoring System

The Infant Monitoring System (IMS)[26] is a unique measure designed to be mailed to families at regular intervals, at 4, 8, 12, 16, 20, 24, 30, and 36 months of age. There are separate norms for boys and girls. Items are clearly written and many are illustrated so that parents can elicit very specific behaviors from their children. The potential for inflated results is minimized by having parents indicate "yes," "sometimes," or "not yet" for each item. The test is then returned to the sender for scoring and interpretation. The manual contains thoughtfully written sample letters for informing parents of their child's progress and suggesting specific types of referrals. The IMS has five subtests assessing communication, gross and fine motor, adaptive, and personal-social skills. Cutoff scores are produced for each and performance below the second standard deviation results in referral. The IMS is ideal for medical settings since the measurement intervals coincide with well-child exam schedules and could be mailed along with reminder letters encouraging families to make or keep health visits. The IMS can also be used to follow children on high-risk registries.

Due to the recency of publication, the only validity studies are those conducted by the authors. However, standardization is reasonably thorough and there are high rates of sensitivity and specificity to scores on the Gesell.

Developmental Profile II

The Developmental Profile II (DP-II)[27] is designed for children between 0 and 9½ years of age. It has five subtests that measure gross and fine motor skills, self-help, social-emotional, cognitive-academic, and expressive-receptive language skills. Each subtest produces age-equivalent, pass-fail, and months-differential scores (which coincide with standard deviation units). Items can be administered by interviewing parents or by directly eliciting behavior from children. The latter method is lengthy and users must create complicated and less than portable test kits. While the interview version is easier, it presents a different set of challenges. Items use sophisticated vocabulary and syntax and rewording is necessary. Parental responses must often be probed since the yes-no response format may produce inflated scores unless "sometimes" or "if I help him" answers are scored as "no." These problems are easily overcome with well-developed interviewing skills but the DP-II should probably not be used by paraprofessionals unless they have been thoroughly trained.

Nevertheless, the DP-II is useful in settings where direct measurement of children's behavior is impossible. Another attractive feature is that the Academic Subtest can be easily used for prescreening because it samples several areas of development (cognitive, preacademic, language, and fine motor skills) and takes only 5 minutes to administer and score. For the Academic Subtest and the DP-II as a whole there are insufficient items sampling prereading and articulation and limited guidelines for test interpretation and referral. However, the computer-scored version includes a printout that can be modified for interpreting to parents.

The DP-II has adequate standardization using over 3,000 children stratified by race and socioeconomic status, although most resided in urban areas of the Midwest. The numerous validity studies reported in the manual include those by researchers other than the author. These and other studies[21] show that the DP-II correlates highly with a host of diagnostic measures of intelligence, achievement, language, and fine motor skills. While this suggests that sensitivity and specificity should be high, further study is needed on this potentially valuable instrument.

Denver-II

When the original Denver Developmental Screening Test was written in the late 1960s, there did not yet exist the body of research showing that young children with language delays needed detection and intervention if they were to succeed in school. As a consequence, the original Denver was designed to identify only that 3% of the population with multiple domain delays suggestive of mental retardation. Thus, it is not surprising that subsequent research showed the test failed to detect half the children with developmental problems, particularly those with language delays.[28–30]

The Denver-II,[31] published in 1990, is a response to independent validity research and represents an extensive revision of the original Denver. The new test is standardized on 2,096 children stratified by age, race, socioeconomic status, and urban versus rural areas of residence, although all lived in Colorado. The language sector is substantially changed with the inclusion of items tapping expressive language skills including articulation. A brief behavior scale has also been added in which examiners rate compliance, interest, fearfulness, and attention. These may be helpful in assessing psychosocial development. Old test kits can be updated inexpensively by purchasing the two new stimuli, as well as the new manual protocols.

The Denver-II retains the structure of the original test with four domains or subtests (language, fine-motor/adaptive, personal-social, and gross motor) designed to be given to children between 0 and 6 years of age. Multiple measurement methods continue to be used including parent report, observation, and direct elicitation. Scoring is complicated. Each item receives a pass/fail/refusal score and a secondary set of classifications in relation to the child's age (normal, advanced, caution, delay, no opportunity). These classifications are used to determine overall test performance (normal, abnormal, questionable, untestable).

Despite the changes and improvements in the Denver-II there continue to be a number of serious limitations. Preacademic and academic skills are not assessed, which, as the authors themselves suggest, means that the test may not detect children with emerging or existing learning disabilities. The fact that the domains do not coincide with the usual categories of development means that the Denver-II may not be convenient for indicating developmental delay under PL 99-457. Last but foremost, the test is published without any information on its validity, sensitivity, or specificity. The authors contend these standards are established by the test's standardization (its reliability and the percentage of normal/abnormal/questionable results for the normative sample). Although such information is important (and promising, in that older children and those with lower socioeconomic status fail more often) it constitutes only a fraction of the standards for psychometric tests. Absent are studies comparing the Denver-II to diagnostic instruments in order to show its sensitivity, specificity, or concurrent validity. For this reason it seems prudent to wait for the results of independent research on the Denver-II before using the measure.

Birth to Three: Assessment and Intervention System

Like the Denver-II, Birth to Three[32] is published without research on its reliability, validity, sensitivity, specificity, etc. It is standardized on 360 children from the southeastern and western United States, stratified only by gender and area of residence. The test has five subtests, which tap a range of motor, cognitive, social, self-help, and language skills. Each subtest produces percentile, standard, and stanine scores. Item scoring uses an interesting system (pass, emerging, fail) but the item sample is both unusual and limited such that a 3-year-old might pass the language subtest using only two word utterances. Directions are vague and hard to locate in the manual. A thorough revision and restandardization would need to be undertaken to rectify the problems of this measure, and its use cannot be recommended.

Minnesota Child Development Inventories

The Minnesota Child Development Inventories (MCDI)[33] is actually a series of screening tests including the Infant Development Inventory (0 to 15 months), the Early Child Development Inventory (1 to 3 years), and the Preschool Development Inventory (3 to 6 years). In its entirety, the MCDI is sufficiently long (320 items) to be considered more an assessment device than a screening test. However, the smaller Inventories function as screens and have significantly fewer items (60 to 80).

All the Inventories use a parent report format. Each has a General Development Section—a series of yes-no questions covering language, comprehension, fine and gross motor skills, and personal-social development. A single cutoff score, corresponding to a 30% delay, stratified by age and gender, indicates whether referral is needed. Each Inventory also has a Possible Problems Section which uses a similar format to identify behavioral, health articulation, sensory, and emotional difficulties. Several open-ended questions require parents to describe their child, list any concerns, and indicate whether there are any preexisting problems or handicaps. A procedure called the Developmental Review provides a thoughtful mechanism for completing the Inventories face-to-face. A Developmental Map is provided on which development is charted and parents' observations noted, and with which developmental strengths and weaknesses can be discussed and interpreted.

The MCDI was standardized on 796 white children from suburban Minneapolis. Most parents had at least a high school education. Although this is not a representative sample, a large number of validity studies show that the Inventories do what they were intended to do—detect children at risk for school failure. Specifically, these studies show the Inventories have acceptable levels of sensitivity (77% to 88%) and moderate levels of specificity (65% to 77%).[34–36]

A revision of the MCDI is planned (Harold Ireton, PhD, personal communication, January 1991). This will improve standardization and specificity, provide better organization of items, and may offer subtest scores for ease in making referrals and determining eligibility for services. However, in its current form, the Inventories are ideal for use in mass mailings and medical waiting rooms. A tape-recorded version and a simplified answer sheet could be devised for use where illiteracy is common.

Early Screening Profile

The Early Screening Profile (ESP)[37] was published in September 1990 and designed for children ages 2 through 6 years. It approaches ideals in test construction and is one of the few tests that include in their manuals independent studies of their sensitivity and specificity. Unfortunately, these data show the ESP to be greatly lacking in sensitivity. One study found that it detected only 27% to 61% of children known to have handicapping conditions. This is an especially unfortunate finding for a test with as many thoughtful features as the ESP. For example, it has subtests measuring language, articulation, cognition, motor, self-help, social, and behavior skills, as well as home environment and health. The language and cognitive subtests appear to account for much of ESP's insensitivity and it seems likely that the items themselves are to blame since they seem removed from typical life behaviors. Nevertheless, parts of the test may continue to be useful in screening psychosocial development or family needs.

Developmental Indicators for Assessment of Learning-Revised

The Developmental Indicators for Assessment of Learning-Revised (DIAL-R)[38] is a well-established screen for children between 2 and 6 years of age. Its subtests tap three of the five domains listed in PL 99-457: motor, language, and cognitive skills. Items thoroughly sample the dimensions of each domain (ie, expressive and receptive language as well as articulation; gross and fine motor skills; cognitive and academic skills). All items directly elicit behavior from children, a task made easier because of the interesting and colorful test materials. Directions are clear and easy to locate. Percentiles are produced for each subtest and for the test as a whole. There are well-defined guidelines for interpreting test behavior and for explaining test results to parents. Suggestions for follow-up and intervention activities are included. The test can be used for individual or mass screening. Each approach is described in the manual and a separate program can be purchased from the publisher to aid in the training of paraprofessionals. The DIAL-R is well standardized, capitalizes on the strengths of the original DIAL, and is supported by a number of validity studies.[21]

CONCLUSIONS

From the preceding reviews, there is clearly a wide range of measures on the market, some of which approach standards for test construction. The more promising tests show that development can be measured with reasonable accuracy. Nevertheless, more research is needed, particularly on the accuracy of tests according to children's ages and the prevalence of developmental delays. Such information will help authors improve the sensitivity and specificity of instruments. Longitudinal research is also needed to assess the unique patterns of early screening test performance in relation to subsequent diagnosis. Such studies will answer such essential questions as what are the early developmental features of children later found to have mild mental retardation? Studies of these and other patterns should include measures of environmental variables (eg, parents' level of education, presence of parental mental retardation or mental illness, etc.) thought to affect or covary with developmental status. Knowing the combined effects of interdevelopmental and extradevelopmental variables should help states refine eligibility criteria and ensure the inclusion of all children likely to develop handicapping conditions.

The measurement of development occurs in a variety of settings: in departments of public health, in homes, in classrooms, at health fairs, and in pediatric offices. Accordingly, test authors should consider how to tailor measures so that they fit a range of applications. Some existing and possible modifications were described above and included tape recordings of tests relying on parent report; the availability of items standardized for both parental report/observation or direct elicitation so that development can be checked even when behavior is problematic; and items that can be modified for children with physical and sensory handicaps so that all domains of their development can be screened. The increased availability of brief prescreening subtests for each larger measure will help ensure that tests are useful to professionals for whom issues in development are secondary to other roles (eg, health counseling).

Almost every measure needs improvement in usability. Numerous challenges are placed on those attempting to screen young children: behavior must be managed, toys and other materials retrieved, directions located, protocols marked, parents interviewed, redirected, interpreted to, etc. Test authors can ease the burden by printing directions in boldface type, clearly marking the beginning and end of subtests so that users can more easily find their place, delineating exact wordings for interview items, minimizing the numbers of toys and other test stimuli even while enhancing their interest to young children, separating interview from direct items so that children's interest can be maintained, simplifying protocols and scoring procedures, etc. Such modifications will improve the ability of examiners to administer tests in a standardized, reliable, and valid manner.

Test authors must also recognize that, more than ever, individuals without backgrounds in psychometry, developmental or educational measurement, are using screening instruments. Therefore, training procedures for each measure should be carefully defined. Such instruction should cover not only basics in the administration of items, but also the importance and meaning of standardized procedures, interviewing techniques, methods of child behavior management, examples of interpreting test results to families, and documentation of scores in test reports. Videotapes and publisher-sponsored training workshops should be made increasingly available. Retraining is also important. One study showed the importance of "periodic retraining and repeated proficiency checks"; otherwise the exactness of test administration decreases over time.[17] Publication of parts of tests (eg, protocols without manuals) should be discouraged since it contributes to casual and often inappropriate use of standardized measures.

• • •

Development may be best conceived as a moving target. A skilled marksperson using superior weapons is more likely than one who is untrained and poorly armed to hit the bull's-eye—in this case, detect accurately the presence or absence of developmental delay. Given that PL 99-457 proffers something of a right to early intervention, it is foreseeable that litigation may result not only from failure to screen, but failure to screen well. Worse still is loss of human potential or needless parental concern. Thus, it is imperative for professionals responsible for identifying young children with delays to select a quality screening test and to become skilled in its use.

REFERENCES

1. Gallagher JJ, Ramey CT. *The Malleability of Children.* Baltimore, Md: Brookes Publishing; 1987.

2. Aylward GP. Environmental influences on the developmental outcome of children at risk. *Inf Young Children.* 1990;2:1–9.

3. Infant Health and Development Program. Enhancing the outcomes of low-birth weight, premature infants. *J Am Med Assoc.* 1990;263:3035–3042.

4. Meisels SJ, Wasik BA. Who should be served? Identifying children in need of early intervention. In: Meisels SJ, Shonkoff JP. eds. *Handbook of Early Childhood Intervention.* Cambridge, Mass: Cambridge University Press; 1990.

5. Aylward GP, Gustafson N, Verhulst SJ, Colliver JA. Consistency in diagnosis of cognitive, motor and neurologic function over the first three years. *J Pediatr Psychol.* 1987;12:77–98.

6. Bell RQ. Age-specific manifestations in changing psychosocial risk. In: Farran DC, McKinney JC. eds. *Risk in Intellectual and Psychosocial Development.* Orlando, Fla: Academic Press; 1986.

7. Algozzine B, Korinek L. Where is special education for students with high prevalence handicaps going? *Excep Child.* 1985;51:388–394.

8. Horn WF, Packard T. Early identification of learning problems: A meta analysis. *J Educ Psychol.* 1985;77:597–607.

9. Kaminer R, Jedrysek E. Early identification of developmental disabilities. *Pediatr Ann.* 1982;11:427–437.

10. Bottos M, Barba BD, Stefani D, Pettena G, Tonin C, D'Este A. Locomotor strategies preceding independent walking: prospective study of neurological and language development in 424 cases. *Dev Med Child Neurol.* 1989;31:25–34.

11. PeBenito R, Sanatello MD, Faxas TA, Ferretti C, Fisch CB. Residual developmental disabilities in children with transient hypertonicity in infancy. *Pediatr Neurol.* 1990;5:154–159.

12. Korsch B, Cobb K, Ashe B. Pediatricians' appraisals of patients' intelligence. *Pediatrics.* 1961;29:990–995.

13. Dearlove J, Kearney D. How good is general practice developmental screening. *Br Med J.* 1990;300:1177–1180.

14. Glascoe FP, Altemeier WK, MacLean WE. The importance of parents' concerns about their child's development. *Am J Dis Child.* 1989;143:855–958.

15. Glascoe FP. Can clinical judgement detect children with speech-language problems? *Pediatrics.* 1991;17:317–322.

16. Glascoe FP, MacLean WE, Stone WL. The importance of parents' concerns about their child's behavior. *Clin Pediatr.* In press.

17. Frankenburg WK, Goldstein AD, Camp BW. The Revised Denver Developmental Screening Test: Its accuracy as a screening instrument. *J Pediatr.* 1971;79:988–995.

18. American Psychological Association. *Standards for Educational and Psychological Tests.* Washington, DC: APA; 1985.

19. Lichtenstein R, Ireton H. *Preschool Screening: Identifying Young Children With Developmental and Educational Problems.* Orlando, Fla: Grune & Stratton; 1984.

20. Meisels SJ, Provence S. *Screening and Assessment: Guidelines for Identifying Young Disabled and Developmentally Vulnerable Children and Their Families.* Washington, DC: National Center for Clinical Infant Programs; 1989.

21. Wolery M. Child find and screening issues. In: Bailey DB, Wolery M. eds. *Assessing Infants and Preschoolers with Handicaps.* Columbus, Ohio: Charles E. Merrill; 1989.

22. Barnes KE. *Preschool Screening: The Measurement and Prediction of Children at Risk.* Springfield, Ill: Charles C Thomas; 1982.

23. Glascoe FP, Martin ED, Humphrey S. A comparative review of developmental screening tests. *Pediatrics.* 1990;86:547–554.

24. Newborg J, Stock JR, Wnek L, Guidubaldi J, Svinicki J. *Battelle Developmental Inventory Screening Test.* Allen, Tex: DLM-Teaching Resources; 1984.

25. Wossum D. The validity of the Battelle Developmental Inventory Screening Test for early detection of developmental disorders. *Dissertation Abstracts International.* Lubbock, Tex: Texas Tech University. In press.

26. Bricker D, Squires J, Mounts L. *Infant Monitoring System.* Eugene, Ore: Center for Human Development, College of Oregon; 1989.

27. Alpern G, Boll T, Shearer M. *Developmental Profile II.* Los Angeles, Calif: Western Psychological Services; 1980.

28. Meisels SJ. Can developmental screening tests identify children who are developmentally at risk? *Pediatrics.* 1989;83:578–585.

29. Borowitz KC, Glascoe FP. Sensitivity of the Denver Developmental Screening Test in speech-language screening. *Pediatrics.* 1986;78:1075–1078.

30. Meisels SJ, Shonkoff JP. eds. *Handbook of Early Childhood Intervention.* Cambridge, Mass: Cambridge University Press; 1990.

31. Frankenburg W, Dodds J, Archer P, et al. *The Denver II.* Denver, Colo: Denver Developmental Materials; 1990.

32. Bangs TE, Dodson S. *Birth to Three: Assessment and Intervention System.* Allen, Tex: DLM-Teaching Resources; 1986.

33. Ireton H, Thwing E. *Minnesota Child Development Inventories.* Minneapolis, Minn: Behavior Science Systems; 1979.

34. Guerin D, Gottfried AW. Minnesota Child Development Inventories: Predictors of intelligence, achievement and adaptability. *J Pediatr Psychol.* 1987;12:595–609.

35. Chaffee CA, Cunningham CE, Secord-Gilber M, Elbard H, Richards J. Screening effectiveness of the Minnesota Child Development Inventory expressive and receptive language scales: Sensitivity, specificity, and predictive value. *Psychol Assess: AJ Consult Clin Psychol.* 1990;2:80–85.

36. Creighton DE, Suave RS. The Minnesota Infant Development Inventory in the developmental screening of high-risk infants at eight months. *Can J Behav Sci.* 1988;20:424–433.

37. Harrison PL, ed. *Early Screening Profile.* Circle Pines, Minn: American Guidance Service; 1990.

38. Mardell-Czudnowski C, Goldenberg D: *Developmental Indicators for Assessment of Learning-Revised (DIAL).* Edison, NJ: Childcraft Educational Corporation; 1983.

Using biologic and ecologic factors to identify vulnerable infants and toddlers

Thomas T. Kochanek, PhD
Department of Special Education
Rhode Island College
Providence, Rhode Island

Stephen L. Buka, ScD
Harvard School of Public Health
Boston, Massachusetts

DESPITE THE superior technologic standing of the United States worldwide, and in spite of significant advances in public health standards and medical intervention capacity, our ability to prevent disabling conditions in children remains surprisingly primitive.[1] To a significant extent, the failure of prevention efforts is attributable to an absence of effective screening and early identification models. While clear linkages have been discovered between specific bacterial agents and biologic disorders (eg, pneumonia), this is not true for the origin of developmental disabilities in young children.[2]

FORMULATION OF MODELS

While early conceptual models of screening[3] presumed that elevated risk for disability arose from a range of adverse circumstances surrounding the birth process and, moreover, were confined to the child independent of context, numerous studies[4-7] have demonstrated that single-factor (eg, anoxia, low birth weight, intraventricular hemorrhage) predictive models are plagued with error. Recent longitudinal investigations[8-10] have confirmed that competency in early childhood is not linearly related to status in later life and, furthermore, that a wide array of rearing conditions and factors are more powerful determinants of outcome than biologic insults.[11] In short, early identification models must include information on not only biologic circumstances, but also the social and familial environment within which a child interacts.[12]

Although universal consensus exists around this conclusion, available epidemiologic data reveal exceedingly low identification rates of developmentally disabled children from birth to 3 years of age.[13] In fact, the number of disabled infants and toddlers reported (ie, 1% of the total birth cohort) represents a very small proportion of children later identified as handicapped at 10 years of age (ie, 17% of enrolled public school youngsters[14]). Furthermore, this prevalence rate of 1% is remarkably incongruent with the observed rates of occurrence of disability in children from birth to 3.[15] Simply stated, a small percentage of children eventually determined to be disabled after entry into school are identified during the infant/toddler period.

The research on which this article is based was principally supported by a Handicapped Children's Early Education Project Grant Award (#G008730278) from the US Department of Education.

These data have prompted considerable discussion in the pediatric community,[16,17] and have given birth to the clinical concept of "developmental surveillance."[18,19] This evolutionary process, intended to be integrated into child health supervision visits, is not restricted to an examination of a child's developmental competence, but also includes information concerning family traits, social support, and factors in the home that may adversely affect growth and development. While the merits of such a conceptual model are widely endorsed,[20,21] specific applications of this approach are rare and necessitate thoughtful development and decision making. For example, such surveillance models require careful selection of child and family measures and establishment of operational procedures for risk determination. Additionally, large-scale population based studies are essential in evaluating the reliability and validity of alternative risk classification methods.[18]

The concept of developmental surveillance has received additional notoriety through the reauthorization of the Education of the Handicapped Act (Public Law 99-457, Part H), in which states are prompted to implement comprehensive screening initiatives in order to accurately and promptly identify children who experience significant developmental delay, or who have established conditions (eg, chromosomal, neurologic disorders) resulting in such delays. In addition, states may elect to identify and serve children at risk of having developmental delays if appropriate early intervention services are not provided. While valid early identification models for infants and toddlers are scarce, recent publications[22] provide important guidance to those developing screening systems. More specifically, recommendations for experimental models have advanced the following essential concepts.

Screening as services

The sole purpose of screening is to *not* exclude children and families from service systems. Alternatively, screening should be viewed as the initial step in service provision and, as such, is designed to gather information concerning child and family needs and ensure linkage with appropriate community based resources and programs.

Multifaceted screening components

Numerous research studies have repeatedly verified that learning, behavioral, and social competence in adolescence cannot be predicted independent of the child's caretaking experiences.[11] As such, screening models must not only include information on biologic circumstances and developmental competence, but must also be amplified to assess family needs, strengths, resources, support systems, and the quality and quantity of the child/parent relationship.

Multiple information sources

Predictive validity studies[8,22] have indicated that early identification models that rely on single factors are replete with decision-making error. Consequently, reliable screening systems must include not only multiple sources (eg, combination of biologic, developmental, and environmental factors) but also multiple reporters (eg, professionals, parents, family members) of information.

Periodicity

Because of significant variation in child developmental pathways as well as ongoing changes in family status, all children and families should participate in screening on multiple occasions between birth and 3 years of age. Judgment regarding the need for further evaluation should be based upon evidence of jeopardy at individual time points as well as from determination of cumulative risk.

Dual-level screening

Several investigations have concluded that single-stage screening models focusing upon adverse, macroscopic factors (eg, low birth weight, respiratory distress) are highly likely to overidentify children in need of early intervention services. As a corrective, the merits of two-tiered models have been advanced,[23] in which essential, valid information can be collected at two levels of specificity in order to determine the need for in-depth, multidisciplinary team evaluation.

A project embodying the principles advanced above has been recently underwritten by the US Department of Education and entitled Preschool Early Detection and Infant Classification Technique (PREDICTS).[14] Major questions this project was designed to address are as follows:

- What factors within a population based screening system for newborns determine the need for in-home follow-up?
- For children and families receiving follow-up screening visits, what measures (ie, child and family) determine the need for referral to an early intervention program?
- What is the prevalence of children and families identified with vulnerabilities at each level of the screening process?
- Are the factors that determine vulnerability constant, or are they dependent upon the age at which the data are collected?

The primary purposes of this paper therefore are: (1) to briefly present the conceptual design of the serial, multivariate, dual-level screening process used within PREDICTS, (2) to report the prevalence of vulnerable children identified by the risk determination process used within this population based model, and (3) to isolate specific child and family factors that accounted for the identification of the high-risk group within the infant and toddler period.

METHOD

Procedure

Consistent with the concepts advanced in developmental surveillance, the PREDICTS model is designed as a two-tiered, multidimensional, ongoing process that involves systematic data collection of child and family status. Level 1 screening, the first stage of the process, is intended to be population based and involves the collection of information at four time points (ie, neonatal period and at 6, 12, and 24 months of age). The newborn component is completed within the hospital by nursing staff, and subsequent Level 1 screens are integrated into well-child care visits, at which time data are collected by physicians. It is important to note that data presented herein focus upon the newborn component of the screening model only.

The objective of Level 1 screening is simply to identify children in need of more in-depth follow-up and, as such, is brief and intended to include highly significant, nonredundant, macroscopic components. Four domains of information, representing 12 specific risk factors, are included within the newborn component. One risk factor, family history, is treated as a single dimension within the decision-making algorithm; however, it is based upon five pieces of information (ie, parents with histories of mental health treatment, child protective services, developmental disabilities, chronic illness, or substance abuse).

Level 2 screening, conducted within the home, is a comprehensive process that includes information on the child's developmental competence; family strengths, needs, and support systems; and the generic quality of the caregiving environment. The primary goal of Level 2 screening is to identify children in need of a multidisciplinary team evaluation in an early intervention program. Data presented in this paper include results of Level 2 screening from a variety of different referral sources, including Level 1 screening.

Although details regarding the rationale for instrument selection are presented elsewhere,[24] specific measures used within Level 2 screening are as follows.

Mullen Scales of Early Learning

The Mullen Scales of Early Learning (MSEL)[25] is a developmental test that assesses a young child's learning abilities and patterns. The test is designed to measure a broad set of developmental processes that analyze both visual and language skills at receptive and expressive levels. Intended for children from infancy through 68 months, the test provides quantitative information on receptive and expressive performance in visual and language modalities, and qualitative information on organizational skills.

Developmental Profile II

The Developmental Profile II (DP-II)[26] is an inventory designed to assess a child's development in five areas of functioning: physical, self-help, social, academic, and communication. The test is intended for use with children from birth through 9 years, and may be administered by both parent interview and direct testing of the child.

Family Resource Scale

The Family Resource Scale (FRS)[27] is a self-report inventory designed to measure the adequacy of resources in households with young children. The scale has 30 items ordered form most to least basic, and for each, a five-point Likert scale expresses the severity of each need. Therefore, beyond the qualitative, clinical outcome data, two quantifiable expressions are derived: (1) total number of needs, and (2) perceived severity of identified needs.

Family Support Scale

The Family Support Scale (FSS)[27] measures the extent to which different sources of support exist and are helpful to families rearing young children. The scale includes 18 items that identify the availability of various sources of informal and formal support and, if available, their perceived helpfulness. In addition to the clinically relevant data derived from the instrument, two quantifiable outcomes are evident: total number of available supports and parental perceptions of helpfulness.

Home Observation for Measurement of the Environment (HOME)

The HOME[28] inventory is a 45-item scale with items clustered into six subscales: emotional and verbal responsiveness, acceptance of child, organization of physical and temporal environment, provision of appropriate play materials, maternal involvement with the child, and opportunities for variety in daily stimulation. Information needed to score the scale is obtained through a combination of observation and interview of the child's primary caregiver, completed in the home with the child present and awake. Data elements of each stage of the screening process are summarized in the box.

Operationally, the Level 1 protocol for newborns involved the recording of status information abstracted form the birth certificate and medical chart. All data

Levels 1 and 2 Screening Components

	Level 1 screening			
	Neonatal period	6 months	12 months	24 months
Established conditions				
Chromosomal anomaly				
Genetic disorder				
Inborn errors of metabolism				
Neurological disorders				
Sensory impairments				
Infectious diseases				
Congenital malformations				
Toxic exposure				
Developmental delay				
Child characteristics				
Birth weight	X	—	—	—
Gestational age	X	—	—	—
Apgars	X	—	—	—
NICU treatment	X	—	—	—
No. and length of hospital admissions	—	X	X	X
Growth parameters	—	X	X	X
No. of confirmed instances of otitis media	—	X	X	X
Hearing assessment	—	X	X	X
Vision assessment	—	X	X	X
DDST-R	—	X	X	X
Lead screening	—	—	X	X
Parental demographics				
Maternal education	X	—	—	—
Maternal age	X	—	—	—
Maternal marital status	X	—	—	—
No. of persons living in home	X	—	—	—
Parental characteristics				
No/inadequate prenatal care	X	—	—	—
Developmental disabilities	X	—	—	—
Mental health tx.	X	X	X	X
Child protective services	X	X	X	X
Substance abuse	X	X	X	X
Chronic illness	X	X	X	X

Level 2 screening

Child characteristics
    Mullen Scales of Early Learning* (MSEL) or Developmental Profile II (DP-II)
Parental characteristics
    Family Resource Scale† and Family Support Scale
Mother/Child Interaction
    Home observation for measurement of the environment (HOME)‡

*MSEL used for children from birth to 16 months. DP-II used for children from 17 to 36 months.
†Dunst CJ, Trivette CM, Deal A. *Enabling and Empowering Families: Principles and Guidelines for Practice.* Cambridge, Mass: Brookline Books; 1988.
‡Caldwell B, Bradley R. Home observation for measurements of the environment. Little Rick, Ark: University of Arkansas; 1984.

were recorded by trained public health nurses within 72 hours after delivery, and no specific examination or interview of the infant or parent was required. Locating the source information and completing the protocol required approximately 15 to 20 minutes per child. Twelve individual risk factors were recorded, and defined criteria (ie, cut points) were developed for all factors that are specified in other documents.[29] These factors were incorporated into a risk determination algorithm which assigned equal weight to all factors, both biologic and environmental. It is important to note, however, that due to their rare occurrence and suspected significance, three factors were given special weight: known established condition, very low birth weight, and extended intensive care unit hospitalization. Therefore, occurrence of any of these three factors resulted in referral for Level 2 screening.

Level 1 screening risk classifications

Three distinct risk classifications were derived from the Level 1 screening process. Positive findings for individual risk factors were defined according to predetermined criteria (eg, birth weight < 1,500 g).

- Risk Positive: Two or more positive findings; children eligible for Level 2 screening.
- Risk Suspect: One positive finding; children eligible for periodic phone monitoring and subsequent Level 1 (Toddler) screenings.
- Risk Negative: No positive findings; children eligible for subsequent Level 1 (Toddler) screenings.

All Level 1 (Neonatal), Risk-Positive children and families were eligible for Level 2 screening. These home visits were also conducted by trained public health nurses, required, on average, 1 to 1½ hours, and typically included anticipatory guidance as well as linkage between identified needs and community based resources. it is important to note that Level 2 screenings were fully integrated into the existing statewide maternal and child health system and as such, did not constitute a new costly enterprise. Details regarding the organization, management, and funding of this program are presented elsewhere.[30]

Level 2 screening risk classifications

Final decisions pertaining to early intervention program referral from Level 2 screenings were made in accordance with the following criteria:

- Risk Positive: Significant developmental delay, or mild developmental delay *and* evidence of substantial unmet needs, extreme social isolation, and/or significant deprivation in the caregiving environment. Refer to early intervention program for team assessment.

- Risk Suspect: Mild developmental delay, or marginal evidence of unmet needs, social isolation, and/or deprivation in the caregiving environment. Refer to other health, educational, and social service programs.
- Risk Negative: Child level of functioning is age appropriate and no evidence of unmet family needs. Children eligible for subsequent Level 1 (Toddler) screenings.

Sample

All children born between March 1988 and April 1990 and residing within any of the nine target communities in Rhode Island were eligible for participation in this screening initiative. All deliveries occurred in two hospitals. Of the families who were approached regarding participation in this project, the levels of compliance approximated 80% and 70%, for each hospital respectively. Examination of a small sample of nonparticipating families revealed no significant selection biases. Nonparticipating families were comparable in terms of race, social class, and risk group assignment. Thus, it was presumed that findings for Level 1 (Neonatal) screening were generalizable to the regions within which the data were collected.

Within the 25-month enrollment period of this project, 3,363 infants received Level 1 screenings. Of these 1,636 (49%) were female, 3,182 (95%) were white, and 151 (5%) were low birth weight. With regard to parental traits, mothers reported an average educational attainment of 13 years, were approximately 27 years of age at delivery (260 or 8% were below age 20), and 514 (15%) were single. With regard to the representativeness of the study sample within the nine target communities, vital statistics data reveal remarkable similarities between the sample and entire resident population. For all births occurring within these communities in 1987, 96% were white, 5% were low birth weight, 8% of the mothers were below age 20, and 14% were single.

RESULTS

Level 1 (neonatal) screening

Results of risk classification related to Level 1 screening as well as the distribution of individual factors within groups are presented in Table 1. Data first of all indicated that 975 (29%) children were designated as Risk Positive. Of these, 45 children were identified by the presence of an established condition (eg, chromosomal anomaly, neurologic disorder), and this constituted approximately 5% of the Risk-Positive group and 1% total sample.

Within the child characteristics domain, approximately 5% of the total population screened evidenced positive findings for one risk factor, and an additional 1%

had two or more positive findings. The most frequently occurring condition was intensive care unit stay of greater than 48 hours, which accounted for 13% of the Risk-Positive group.

With regard to parent demographics, 632 children (19% of the total sample) were identified with two or more risk factors. The most prevalent positive findings occurred for mothers with first-born children, unmarried mothers, and parents with low levels of educational attainment. Finally, within the parent characteristics domain, 189 infants were judged as Risk Positive, primarily due to no/inadequate prenatal care as well as evidence of risk within the family history (eg, child protective services, developmentally disabled parents, inpatient psychiatric hospitalization).

While Table 1 is useful in that it presents differences among risk groups on individual factors, it does not clearly portray the composition of the Risk-Positive group, that is, those with verifiable vulnerabilities who warrant follow-up services. Fig 1 graphically presents findings for Risk-Positive children only, and reveals the proportion accounted for by various components of risk. It is again important to note that due to the infrequent occurrence of positive findings within the child characteristics domain, the algorithm was modified to include all children who were low birth weight *or* remained in the neonatal intensive care unit (NICU) for more than 2 days. These were the only two factors that singularly determined assignment to this group. Of significance in Fig 1 is that of 975 infants, 20% were identified through child related factors, while the remainder were classified according to parental data (young, single, poorly educated). In short, within the newborn phase of the surveillance process, if parental information were eliminated from the protocol, 80% of the Risk-Positive group would be excluded from follow-up services.

Level 2 screening

Findings for all children who have received Level 2 screenings are presented in Table 2. Of the 932 children included, 393 (42%) were identified as Risk Positive in Level 1 (Neonatal) screening, 254 (27%) were direct referrals from the child protective service agency (ie, Department of Children and Their Families [DCF]), and 285 (31%) were referred by health care providers and child care agencies owing to concern regarding the child's developmental progress. Mean chronological ages at the time of in-home screening were 6.8 (Level 1), 19.0 (DCF), and 12.7 (Other) months, respectively.

Several important results are evident in this table. Of all children receiving Level 2 screenings, 234 (25%) were determined to be Risk Positive and in need of a multidisciplinary team evaluation in an early intervention program. Of interest, however, is that significant differences are evident across referral sources in that three times as many children were determined to be Risk Positive in the DCF and Other groups as compared to the Level 1 group. It would appear that this is attrib-

Table 1. Level 1 screening results by risk group

	Risk Positive (%)	Risk Suspect (%)	Risk Negative (%)	Total (%)
Total	975 (29)	297 (9)	2091 (62)	3363 (100)
Established conditions	45 (5)*	0	0	45 (1)
Child characteristics				
One risk factor	151 (16)	9 (3)	0	160 (5)
More than one risk factor	29 (3)	0	0	29 (1)
Birth weight <1500 g	17 (2)	0	0	17 (0.5)
Small for gestational age BWT 1500–2500 g and gestational age >37 wks	42 (4)	7 (2)	0	49 (2)
APGAR scores 1 min and 5 min both <7	24 (3)	2 (1)	0	26 (1)
NICU STAY >48 hrs	129 (13)	0	0	129 (4)
Parent demographics				
One risk factor	267 (27)	218 (73)	414 (20)	899 (27)
More than one risk factor	632 (65)	0	0	632 (19)
Mother's age				
<18	185 (19)	1 (0.3)	0	186 (6)
>38	48 (5)	61 (21)	0	109 (3)
Parents' education				
<11 yrs	292 (20)	95 (32)	0	387 (12)
Marital status				
Not married	555 (57)	61 (21)	0	616 (18)
Prior live births				
None	736 (76)	0	414 (20)	1185 (35)
>5	2 (0.2)	0	0	2 (0.1)
Parent characteristics				
One risk factor	236 (24)	70 (23)	0	306 (9)
More than one risk factor	189 (19)	0	0	189 (6)
Family history	152 (16)	41 (14)	0	193 (6)
Early prenatal care No visits before 5 months	231 (24)	6 (2)	0	237 (7)
Total prenatal care <6 visits	260 (27)	23 (8)	0	283 (8)

*Number of children (percentage of risk group).

utable to not only the nature of the referral source, but also the age at which screening was completed. This is clearly evident in Fig 2, which portrays the composition of the Level 2 Risk-Positive group by referral source as well as reason for risk determination.

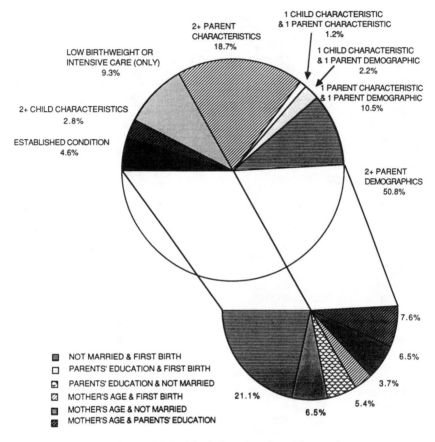

Fig 1. Composition of 975 Risk-Positive infants from Level 1 screening.

Evident in Fig 2 is the finding that of the Risk-Positive group overall, 63% were identified by significant developmental delay (ie, MSEL and DP-II), while the remainder were so classified owing to mild delays in addition to evidence of significant unmet family needs (FRS), social isolation (FSS), or concern about the quality of the caregiving environment (HOME). Clearly, 37% of the Risk-Positive group would have been missed had it not been for the inclusion of family centered information in the screening model and decision-making equation.

Also of importance in Fig 2 is that the underlying reasons for Risk-Positive determination vary by referral source. More precisely, while 43% of the Level 1 referred group evidenced significant developmental delay, 68% of both the DCF

Table 2. Outcomes of Level 2 screening by referral source

	Source of referral							
	Level 1		DCF*		Other		Total	
Final disposition	N	(%)	N	(%)	N	(%)	N	(%)
Risk Positive	46	(12)	88	(35)	100	(35)	234	(25)
Risk Suspect	47	(12)	59	(23)	42	(15)	148	(16)
Risk Negative	300	(77)	107	(42)	143	(50)	550	(59)
Total	393		254		285		932	

*Department of Children and Their Families.

and "Other" referrals were found to have such delays. Again, while this is not surprising given the nature of these referral sources as well as the age at which the screening data were collected, preliminary findings appear to justify the critical importance of both child *and* family components in the screening process and, furthermore, underscore the importance of multiple referral pathways in statewide surveillance systems.

Data in Table 3 present the Level 1 (Neonatal) status of the 46 children who received Level 2 screenings and were judged Risk Positive. Of significance is the fact that while 26% of the group were identified by child related traits (eg, established condition, low birth weight [LBW], NICU stay) and in all probability would have been identified absent the Level 1 screening process, the remainder of the group revealed the need for follow-up through family centered information. That is, without the inclusion of family centered information in the screening process, 74% of the children ultimately identified as demonstrating verifiable risk would *not* have been identified.

Overall, therefore, preliminary data collected over a 2-year period revealed that implementation of a population based, child and family focused screening process has identified approximately one of three newborns in need of follow-up examination. Furthermore, of those screened within a home based model that assessed child competence in addition to family resources, strengths, and supports, approximately 25% were determined to be in need of in-depth team assessment. While follow-up studies are currently underway of children who have received team evaluations in early intervention, these preliminary data are useful in estimating both the prevalence and cost of such a multivariate decision-making model.

It is also critical to note, however, that the prevalence of identified children can easily be modified by adjusting the algorithm. As an illustration, Fig 3 represents the effects of removing both individual factors and complete domains from the Level 1 (Neonatal) screening process. For example, if all child characteristics were removed

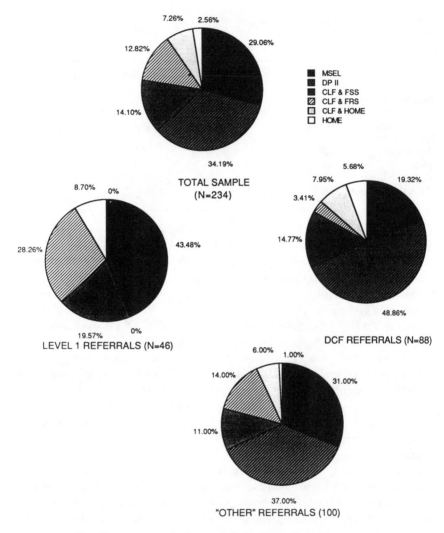

Fig 2. Composition of Level 2 Risk-Positive children.

from the equation, approximately 26% of the population would be judged as Risk Positive. Conversely, if all parent demographics were eliminated, only 11% would be determined Risk Positive. Furthermore, modification of cut points for individual factors also yields not only a different prevalence rate, but also a group with remarkably different presenting characteristics and needs. In short, while data presented herein relate to one expression of a decision-making process, adoptions of such a model can

Table 3. Level 1 status of Level 2 Risk-Positive children

	N	(%)
Child related	12	(26)
Established condition	3	(7)
≥2 child characteristics	1	(2)
LBW or NICU	8	(17)
Family related	34	(74)
≥2 parent characteristics	15	(33)
1 child and 1 parent characteristic	1	(2)
1 child and 1 parent demographic	1	(2)
1 parent characteristic and 1 parent demographic	2	(4)
≥2 parent demographics	15	(33)
Total	46	

involve far more restrictive or inclusive criteria dependent upon the resources and service systems available in specific states.

DISCUSSION

The inherent challenge within any screening initiative is to seek measures that will accurately identify all cases that later become symptomatic. In searching for children who are developmentally disabled or at substantial risk for manifesting later learning or behavioral problems, effective paradigms must taken into account the interaction of the individual and experiential context. The purpose of this project was to translate this principle into a functional process that could be efficiently integrated into an existing well-child-care surveillance system. Preliminary outcomes from approximately 3,400 newborns provide several noteworthy findings for both policymakers and researchers.

For policymakers, outcomes of this study are particularly important in that widespread fear may be unfounded regarding the high cost and prevalence rates presumed to be associated with biologic and ecologic population based screening models. Specifically, following newborns through a comprehensive child- and family-focused screening process identified only 4% (ie, 29% at Level 1 and 12% at Level 2) of the total population who were subsequently referred to early intervention programs. Furthermore, since all referred children are not deemed eligible for service, the prevalence of need for early intervention may not be as intimidating to states as originally assumed. It is also important to note that these findings emerge from a system that is designed to identify all three groups of children referenced in PL 99-457 (Part H) (ie, developmentally delayed, established condition, and substantially at risk).

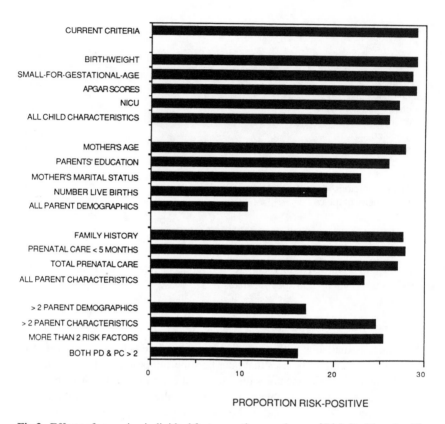

Fig 3. Effects of removing individual factors on the prevalence of Risk-Positive classification at Level 1 screening.

While this finding may be encouraging to states with broad early childhood visions of which Part H is a component, it is critical to note that the above findings are for children primarily less than 1 year of age. Level 2 screening data indicate that approximately one of three toddlers (ie, 18 to 24 months) screened are determined to be Risk Positive and in need of a multidisciplinary team evaluation. Overall, data suggest that prevalence is heavily dependent upon both child age and the assessment measures used, and that as states attempt to estimate prevalence rates, prospective population based models similar to PREDICTS would seem to be essential to accurate forecasting.

A second major implication for policymakers is that such comprehensive screening models applied to entire populations further underscore the importance of the interagency underpinnings of Part H. Clearly, vulnerable children and families emerge from such models who are not eligible for early intervention services, yet they warrant some form of intervention (eg, therapeutic day care, parent education and support programs). Comprehensive, multidimensional screening initiatives also demand broad-based, accessible early childhood service options, and the two are inseparable and must be considered concomitantly by system developers.

For the research and clinical community, data appear to validate that the origins of vulnerability reside within both the biologic and ecologic domains. More precisely, for infants with verifiable developmental delay at Level 2 screening, 74% of this group were identified as newborns through the parental component of the screening process. While it must be acknowledged that accurate identification of children requiring early intervention and, longitudinally, those needing special services after school entry, are the key dependent measures in any screening effort, and that such outcome data are essential to generating more robust statistical measures (ie, sensitivity and specificity), preliminary data presented herein are viewed as encouraging. Additional follow-up studies are urgent in order to verify the validity of such comprehensive models, and to more carefully examine the predictive accuracy of particular elements within the screening paradigm.

Data also suggest that the prevalence of developmentally disabled and high risk children varies considerably by age, and that specific measures contribute differently to decision making dependent upon the age at which they were collected. Newborns who emerge from such surveillance models differ from those identified at 18 months of age, and while this finding provides further credence to the need for serial, multivariate screening, it also suggests the need for further experimentation with alternative measures and heterogeneous, cross-cultural populations.

Finally, Werner,[31] after years of impressive longitudinal research on risk factors, has concluded that assessment processes must focus upon resiliency as well as risk, that is, at identifying protective factors in the individual and environment that reduce vulnerability. Such factors include intrafamilial and extrafamilial support systems and opportunities to establish a close bond with caretakers who provide noncontingent positive attention. A major asset of biologically and ecologically based surveillance models is that they prompt attention to such protective factors and constitute an important step toward implementing comprehensive preventative programs. The essence of risk research requires an investment not only in those who become disabled but also in others who manifest unexpected strengths, and in attempting to understand the genesis of these strengths. PL 99-457 (Part H) provides an enormously rich and unique opportunity to conduct such investigations, and this must become a vital research enterprise in the decade ahead.

REFERENCES

1. Rutter M. Prevention of children's psychosocial disorders: Myths and substance. *Pediatrics.* 1982;70:883–894.

2. Sameroff A, Fiese BH. Transactional regulation and early intervention. In: Miesels SJ, Shonkoff JP. eds. *Handbook of Early Childhood Intervention.* New York, NY: Cambridge University Press; 1990.

3. Pasamanick B, Knobloch H. Epidemiological studies on the complications of pregnancy and the birth process. In: Caplan G. ed. *Prevention of Mental Disorders in Children.* New York, NY: Basic Books; 1961.

4. Gottfried AW. Intellectual consequences of prenatal anoxia. *Psychol Bull.* 1973;80:231–242.

5. Papile L, Munsick-Bruno G, Schaefer A. Relationship of cerebral intraventricular hemorrhage and early childhood neurological handicaps. *Pediatrics.* 1983;103:273–277.

6. Stewart AL, Reynolds E, Lipscomb A. Outcome for infants of very low birthweight: Survey of world literature. *Lancet.* 1981;1:1038–1041.

7. Bierman-van Eenderburg M, Jurgens-van der Zee A, Olinga A. Predictive value of neonatal neurological examination: A follow up study at 18 months. *Dev Med Child Neurol.* 1981;23:296–305.

8. Broman S, Bien E, Shaughnessy P. *Low achieving children: The first seven years.* Hillsdale, NJ: Erlbaum; 1985.

9. Nichols DL, Chen T. *Minimal brain dysfunction: A prospective study.* Hillsdale, NJ: Erlbaum; 1981.

10. Kochanek TT, Kabacoff RI, Lipsitt LP. Early identification of developmentally disabled and at-risk preschool children. *Except Child.* 1990;56:528–538.

11. Werner E, Smith R. *Vulnerable but Invincible.* New York, NY: McGraw-Hill; 1982.

12. Sameroff A, Chandler M. Reproductive risk and the continuum of caretaking casualty. In: Horowitz F, Hetherington M, Scam-Salapatek S, Siegel G. eds. *Review of Child Development Research.* Vol 4. Chicago, Ill: University of Chicago Press; 1975.

13. Meisels SJ, Wasik B. Who should be served? Identifying children in need of early intervention. In: Meisels SJ, Shonkoff JP. eds. *Handbook of Early Childhood Intervention.* New York, NY: Cambridge University Press; 1990.

14. Kochanek TT. Preschool early detection and infant classification technique (PREDICTS). Providence, RI: Rhode Island College; 1987.

15. Gortmaker S, Sappenfield W. Chronic childhood disorders: Prevalence and impact. *Pediatr Clin North Am.* 1984;31:3–18.

16. Meisels SJ. Can developmental tests identify children who are developmentally at risk? *Pediatrics.* 1989;83:578–585.

17. Dworkin PH. Developmental screening—expecting the impossible? *Pediatrics.* 1989;83:619–622.

18. Dworkin PH. British and American recommendations for developmental monitoring: The role of surveillance. *Pediatrics.* 1989;84:1000–1010.

19. Developmental surveillance. *Lancet.* 1986;1:950–951. Editorial.

20. Hall DM. ed. *Health for all children: A programme for child health surveillance.* Oxford, England: Oxford University Press; 1989.

21. American Academy of Pediatrics, Committee on Practice and Ambulatory Medicine. Recommendations for preventative pediatric health care. *Pediatrics.* 1988;8:466.

22. Meisels SJ, Provence S. *Screening and Assessment: Guidelines for Identifying Young Disabled and Developmentally Vulnerable Children and Their Families.* Washington, DC: National Center for Clinical Infant Programs; 1989.

23. Frankenburg W. The Denver approach to early casefinding. In: Frankenburg W, Emde R, Sullivan JW. *Early Identification of Children at Risk.* New York, NY: Plenum; 1985.

24. Kochanek TT, Friedman DH. *Incorporating Family Assessment and Individualized Family Service Plans into Early Intervention Programs; A Developmental, Decision Making Process.* Providence, RI: Rhode Island College; 1988.

25. *Mullen Scales of Early Learning.* Cranston, RI: TOTAL Child, Inc, 1984.

26. *Developmental Profile II.* Los Angeles, Calif: Western Psychological Services, 1984.

27. Dunst CJ, Trivette CM, Deal AG. *Enabling and Empowering families.* Cambridge, Mass: Brookline, 1988.

28. Caldwell BM, Bradley RH. Home Observation for measurement of the environment. *Administration manual.* Little Rock, Ark: Univ Arkansas, 1984.

29. Kochanek TT. *Operations Manual and Coding Forms for Level I and Level II Screening Procedures in Project PREDICTS.* Providence, RI: Rhode Island College; 1988.

30. Kochanek TT. *The Family Outreach Program.* Providence, RI: Rhode Island College; 1990.

31. Werner EE. Children of the garden island. *Sci Am.* 1989;260(April):106–111.

Conceptualization and measurement of disablement in infants and young children

Wendy J. Coster, PhD, OTR/L
Assistant Professor
Department of Occupational Therapy
Sargent College of Allied Health
  Professions
Boston University
Boston, Massachusetts

Stephen M. Haley, PhD, PT
Assistant Professor
Tufts University School of Medicine
Director of Research
Medical Rehabilitation Research and
  Training Center in Rehabilitation
  and Childhood Trauma
New England Medical Center
Boston, Massachusetts

INVESTIGATORS from various disciplines recently have argued that interventions for infants and young children must be functionally focused; that is, they must concern themselves with assisting the young child and his or her family to achieve more satisfactory performance of meaningful daily activities.[1-5] Within early intervention programs, a notable shift in functionally based and adaptive curricula has begun to take place.[6] Although this emphasis on functional training has gained considerable support, implementation requires that a clear framework for the conceptualization of function in children be available for reference. To date, however, such a framework has not been presented.

This article examines the suitability of available conceptual models of function and its counterpart, disablement, for application to young children. We argue that the unique characteristics of the developing child require modification of frameworks developed for adults. We also argue that such a modified framework can begin to resolve some of the confusion surrounding the term *function* and may provide a useful structure by which clinicians and researchers can think more clearly about the problems faced by children with disabilities. Finally, we contend that a sound conceptual framework is an essential foundation for the development of functional assessment instruments for infants and young children.

CONCEPTUALIZATION AND THE MEASUREMENT PROCESS

Efforts to describe the functional performance of infants and young children require a clear conceptual framework for what it is that one is attempting to represent. Although most professionals in the field probably share a common understanding of the term *function,* such a broad term is not sufficient as a conceptual guide. A framework must be developed that specifies the relevant phenomena en-

Supported in part by a Mary E. Switzer Rehabilitation Research Fellowship (WJC) and grants H133B00009 and H13G80043 from the National Institute on Disability and Rehabilitation Research, Department of Education.

Inf Young Children 1992; 4(4): 11–22
© 1992 Aspen Publishers, Inc.

compassed by the concept and the relations among them and that also helps identify the meaningful dimensions or categories for measurement.

The development of a conceptual framework is viewed as the initial and most
important step in the process of measurement. For the sake of clarity in our discussion
of this process, we adopt the terminology of Wood.[7] Wood uses the term *disablement*
to describe the overall spectrum of experiences related to limitations in function. The
term *disability,* by contrast, designates specific functional limitations as defined by a
particular conceptual framework.[8] A working model of the conceptualization of disablement in infants and young children leads directly to the development of appropriate measurement constructs and the creation of clinical assessments. These clinical
assessments may be focused on one or more distinct purposes: diagnostic, discriminative, or evaluative.[9] The accuracy and validity of the conceptual model can then be
tested and refined by a series of empiric studies. The findings from these studies
should help either confirm or suggest changes in the initial conceptual framework and
lead to further advances in the measurement constructs and subsequent versions of
the clinical assessment. This circular and interdependent process of conceptual and
measurement refinement is the hallmark of behavioral descriptions of complex phenomena such as function in children (Fig 1).

CONCEPTUAL FRAMEWORKS FOR FUNCTION AND DISABLEMENT

Within the adult rehabilitation literature, the most widely accepted system for
defining function is the one provided by the World Health Organization (WHO).[5]
The description of function in this model is given through a hierarchy that includes
three components. Impairment is defined as a limitation or abnormality in anatomic, physiologic, or psychologic processes (eg, impairment of visual acuity or
paralysis of a limb). Disability is a deficit in the performance of integrated daily
activities (eg, walking or dressing). Handicap is defined as a deficit in social roles

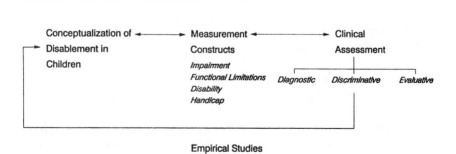

Fig 1. Importance of conceptualization in the measurement process.

that leads to a decrease in the quality of life (eg, inability to attend nursery school or day care or to participate in customary social activities of the family). Functional outcome measures, in these terms, assess "any restriction or lack of ability to perform an everyday activity in a manner or within the range considered normal for the person of the same age, culture, and education."[5(p143)]

The three components of the WHO system are hierarchic in the sense of representing increasingly complex, integrated activities. However, the classification system is not a simple linear sequence in the sense that the presence of difficulties at one level automatically defines difficulties at the other levels. For example, one can have an impairment but not be disabled, as in the case of a child with a traumatic below-elbow amputation who nevertheless, with the aid of a prosthesis, performs all daily activities satisfactorily. The model thus recognizes that there are multiple influences other than the presence of an impairment that determine the functional performance of the individual. In particular, the presence of handicap is viewed as a function of the circumstances in which the child finds himself or herself, not just the result of the child's personal capacities. For example, whether the child is restricted in activities at day care is a function both of his or her functional capabilities and the accessibility of the physical environment. One important consequence that follows from adoption of the WHO framework is that a conceptual shift is made from focusing on normality to focusing on function.

Subsequent discussions of the WHO taxonomy have identified inadequacies in the distinctions among the different components of the model.[10] Recently, it has been suggested that the framework proposed by Nagi[11,12] is conceptually clearer.[13] In particular, Nagi proposes an intermediate component that bridges impairment and disability, which he terms functional limitations, and defines as limitations on the person's "ability to perform the tasks and obligations of his usual roles and normal daily activities."[11(p102)] Disability is defined as a pattern of overall behavior that is less than adequate to meet normal role performance expectations. This definition requires that a limitation have social consequences before it is identified as a disability.

The Nagi model also more readily accommodates the range of information required for representing the different levels of disablement in children. In particular, the inclusion of the functional limitation level allows separate measurement of the components of complex functional tasks, which may ultimately contribute to a better understanding of the sources of disability. Even so, the Nagi model does not adequately distinguish between the performance of complex tasks, such as eating or dressing, and the performance of social roles, such as attending school or otherwise participating in one's community. We would separate these levels of functional performance and label the former disability and the latter social role performance. Although the definition of the latter is quite similar to the WHO handicap level, the term *handicap* is viewed as having denigrating connotations in the United States, and a more positive category label is preferable.[10] Fig 2 presents our working conceptual model for disablement in young children.

FURTHER ADAPTATIONS OF THE MODEL FOR CHILDREN

The specification of these major categories of disablement is an important advance in defining the domain of functional performance. As it stands, however, the model only provides a broad description of the categories of functional performance. An adequate working model for educational and therapeutic intervention must also encompass the additional personal characteristics, such as age, gen-

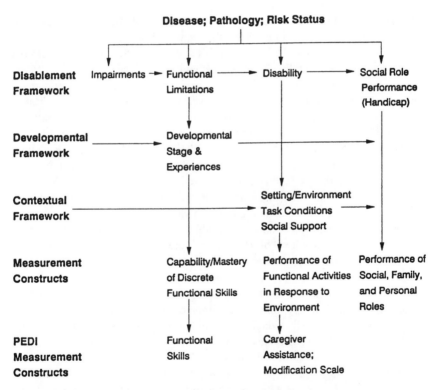

Fig 2. Working conceptual model of disablement in childhood. Adapted with permission from Haley SM. Motor assessment tools for infants and young children: A focus on disability assessment. In: Forrsberg H, ed. *Treatment of Children with Movement Disorders: Theory and Practice.* Medicine and Sport Science Series, Vol. 36, Hebbelink M, Shephard RJ, eds. Basel, Switzerland: Kargel Publishers (in press).

der, and temperament, that influence performance; risk factors affecting the child; and the environmental and social characteristics that determine both the expectations and supports available for functional performance. Although proponents of both the WHO and the Nagi models clearly acknowledge the role of such influences in the disabling process, this part of the model remains the least clearly explicated. For the Nagi model to be truly useful as a conceptual guide for describing children's function, these influences must be incorporated more clearly. In addition, the development of a model for children must address two other critical issues: the incorporation of a developmental framework, and consideration of contextual influences.[14]

Incorporating developmental information into the model

Measurement of each component of the model of disablement depends on identifying deviations from the norm. When the focus is children, the definition of the norm must encompass not only the cultural or social definition of expectations but also what is developmentally appropriate behavior given the child's age. This requirement is especially crucial at the point when a model is translated into a measurement tool, whether it be focused on measuring functional limitations, disability, or handicap. The measurement of performance must be done against a background of what is known about the order and timing of appearance of functional skills as well as relevant quantitative and qualitative changes that occur with maturation and/or learning. Indeed, it is not even relevant to consider certain tasks until the age when that skill is typically acquired. For example, it would be meaningless to ask about a 2-year-old's ability to cross streets alone or to dial a telephone. The relevant tasks that define function vary across age groups.

Both the proponents of the models of disablement and relevant research support the need to measure each level of function separately because the links among the components are not straightforward[2,12,15] and may vary across different age groups. To date, however, most developmental research has focused on describing the emergence and elaboration of component processes such as visual memory or manual grasp (most closely linked to the impairment level). The development of function has not been well studied. Thus, we know much less about the developmental changes in daily activities of play or self-care in relation to changes or impairments in memory or in manual skills.

Although measures that purport to measure function or adaptive skills exist, the items chosen for the instruments are designed more to identify the existence of a developmental lag than to describe the functional abilities of the child. This difference in conceptualization is most clear in the limited choice of items along which a functional dimension is measured: The items may carry developmental significance (something more difficult can now be done), but they may or may not carry significant implications in terms of functional limitation or disability. An example to illustrate the difference in conceptualization is as follows: Behavioral change with age in mobility can be measured by means of items such as learning to walk, run, jump, and skip. A change from walking to skipping indicates that the child has indeed acquired new competencies, but the implications of this change for the child's overall function are not clear. On the other hand, a change from walking while holding on to walking while carrying an object may significantly alter the child's ability to participate in family and peer activities. Thus, at the point when the concept of function becomes operationalized into measurement tools, we must ensure that the items chosen represent the most meaningful units of development change in function as described by the model.

Incorporating contextual information into the model

A second aspect that must be more fully elaborated in a model of child disablement is the interrelation between function and the social and physical environment. With adults, it may be reasonable to set the (culturally expected) level of independence as a standard for determining health. Dependence then becomes a measure of disablement. This approach has limitations even with adults, however, because it does not recognize that interdependence is an essential feature of all societies.[5] Overreliance on dependence as a criterion for assessing health, therefore, can lead to an inappropriate focus on the child as the source of the functional disability rather than on the disability as a result of an unsatisfactory match between what the child can do and what the environment supports. The view that one adopts has profound implications for how intervention goals are formulated. In the first case, efforts are directed primarily toward helping the child conform more closely to the norm, often through specialized treatment. In the latter case, efforts may be directed toward influencing both the environment (eg, by changing accessibility and social attitudes) and the child's performance to achieve a more functional outcome.

It is even more crucial to consider the role of the social context in developing a model for childhood disablement. Almost all children's functional activities take place under the supervision or instruction of others and in environments set up and controlled by adults. Thus, children's functional performance is intricately involved with what this social and physical environment affords. As investigators have shifted their focus to studying children in these natural contexts, it has become clear that joint management of functional tasks by adult and child is the normative pattern.[16] The functional performance of the child must therefore be characterized as a transactional process, not just as a set of fixed skills that the child either does or does not have.

Recognition of the child's embeddedness in his or her social context is reflected in recent policy articulated in Public Law 99-457, which mandates that early intervention services be family focused. Gallimore and colleagues[17] and Tharp and Gallimore[18] have also presented a framework for reconceptualizing how we assess the function of children with disabilities and their families. If this shift is to be incorporated more widely into the educational and rehabilitative framework, however, we also will need to conceptualize our measurement of function in a way that incorporates description of the participation of other people and of the physical environment in facilitating (or hindering) function.

Fig 2 summarizes our working conceptual model of childhood disablement. The major components draw from Nagi,[11,12] WHO,[5] and Pope and Tarlov[10] and reflect levels of impairment, functional limitation, disability, and social role performance as well as risk factors and individual characteristics. In addition, we have indicated that at each level of performance both developmental status and physical and social context must enter into the assessment of whether function is satisfactory or not.

MEASUREMENT CONSTRUCTS FOR CHILDHOOD DISABLEMENT

Although the general outline of a conceptual framework has now been laid out, further specification will be required to enable measurement of the different aspects of function that it represents. Indeed, unless a framework can be translated into meaningful measurement constructs, its usefulness as a conceptual guide for clinical reasoning and research will remain quite limited. Operationalization of the constructs requires determination of the relevant context domains that should be sampled and, within these domains, what dimensions (or observable units of behavior) should be the focus. This issue was touched on earlier and is now discussed in more detail, with our own work developing the Pediatric Evaluation of Disability Inventory (PEDI)[19] being used for illustration. We concentrate on defining the functional limitation and disability components of the model and end with a discussion of some issues that will need to be addressed in defining the concept of social role performance in children.

Defining functional limitations

The first task in defining functional limitations is to specify the relevant domains to be sampled. The WHO's broad domains of function include behavior, communication, personal care, locomotion and body disposition, dexterity, and situational tolerance (tolerance of environment). The Functional Independence Measure (FIM),[20] which is widely used in adult rehabilitation, incorporates the domains of self-care, sphincter control, mobility, locomotion, communication, and social cognition. One relevant measurement issue at this level is whether these groupings represent coherent, unitary constructs, in which case an overall summary measure of function such as the FIM provides would be conceptually meaningful. Recent literature in the area of functional assessment has emphasized the importance of unidimensionality in scale construction and the development of an interpretable summary score.[21,22]

Once the basic domains are defined, each must be defined in terms of more discrete tasks before measurement of functional limitations can proceed. This task requires specification of the particular skills that have functional importance in daily life: For example, self-care may be broken down into self-feeding, toileting, and so forth. For children, the skills selected to be part of a measure may have to be tailored to a particular context. For example, although bathing is a functional self-care skill that is relevant at home, it has little functional meaning at day care or nursery school. Conversely, the ability to put on outdoor clothing may be an important functional skill at day care but may be less critical than putting on shirt and pants at home. Table 1 provides an illustration form the PEDI of content areas chosen to have reasonably broad applicability across home and school contexts for infants and young children.

Skills need to be further specified in terms of graded intervals if the measurement intends to show relative movement along the dimension of increasing function. For example, lesser to greater function in using eating utensils may be broken down into items ranging from finger feeding up to use of a knife. A good measure of function will have to integrate two requirements into the final scaling: first, the identification of meaningful units of functional capability, and second, developmental information about the order of accomplishment and age-relevant expectations of the units included. The Box gives an example of the functional skills sampled in the dressing area of the self-care domain on the PEDI. Rasch Scale techniques[23] were used to establish the order of item difficulty and the degree to which a summary score adequately represents a child's performance along a coherent functional continuum. Tables based on data from a sample of normal children allow comparison of a child's functional performance with what is expected at his or her level of development.

Defining disability

As discussed earlier, it is necessary to incorporate a distinction between disability and social role performance into a pediatric framework. In our proposed framework, disability would refer to limitations in performing complex, integrated activities required for one's social role, whereas the overall performance of social roles would be measured separately. Thus, a preschool child with poor ability to recognize and avoid safety hazards in his or her environment would be described

Table 1. Functional skills content of the PEDI

Self-care domain	Mobility domain	Social function domain
Types of food textures	Floor locomotion	Comprehension of word
Use of utensils	Chair/wheelchair transfers	meanings
Use of drinking containers	Opening and closing doors	Comprehension of sentence
Toothbrushing	In and out of car	complexity
Hairbrushing	Bed mobility	Functional use of expressive
Nose care	Stand/sit in tub or shower	communication
Handwashing	Method of indoor locomotion	Complexity of expressive
Washing body and face	Distance/speed indoors	communication
Pullover/front-opening	Pull/carry objects	Problem resolution
garments	Method of outdoor	Social interactive play
Fasteners	locomotion	Peer interactions
Pants	Distance/speed outdoors	Self-information
Shoes/socks	Locomotion on outdoor	Time orientation
Toileting tasks	surfaces	Household chores
Control of bladder function	Scooting up and down stairs	Self-protection
Control of bowel function	Walking up and down stairs	Community function

Reprinted with permission from Haley SM, Coster WJ, Ludlow LH, et al. *Pediatric Evaluation of Disability Inventory (PEDI).* Boston: New England Medical Center; 1992.

---

as having a disability. If the child were restricted from attending community recreational activities with his or her peers because of this poor safety judgment, he or she would be assessed as having a role limitation.

The development of measures at the level of disability also requires decisions about the appropriate behaviors to be sampled and the scale or content to be used as the measure of disability. As indicated earlier, one common approach has been to measure the level of assistance required during the ordinary performance of a complex activity along the dimension from total assistance to complete independence. To the extent that level of assistance may provide a measure of the caregiving or of the burden of care, it can serve as an indicator that carries social significance. As discussed earlier, however, there are also problems inherent in the use of assistance as a measure of disability. Although level of assistance is treated as a measure of the child's limitations, it is, in fact, also a measure of the capability of the child's caregivers to judge and then provide the appropriate and necessary support. This limitation is especially problematic when level of assistance is determined through caregiver report. If the caregiver misjudges the degree of assistance the child needs (ie, is either overprotective or underprotective), the child's assessment will misrepresent his or her capability for function. These problems are especially significant when one is attempting to use caregiver assistance as a measure of disability in children. It is an accepted reality that children

---

Example of Functional Skill Items from the PEDI Self-Care Domain: Dressing*

Assists, such as putting arms through shirt
Removes socks and unfastens shoes
Assists, such as pushing legs through pants
Tries to assist with fasteners
Removes pants with elastic waist
Removes T-shirt, dress, or sweater
Puts on unfastened shoes
Assists with clothing management
Puts on pants with elastic waist
Puts on socks
Puts on T-shirt, dress, or sweater
Puts on and removes front-opening shirt, not including fasteners
Snaps and unsnaps
Removes pants, including unfastening
Buttons and unbuttons
Puts shoes on correct feet; manages Velcro fasteners
Puts on and removes front-opening shirt, including fasteners
Puts on pants, including fastening
Zips and unzips, separates and hooks zipper
Ties shoelaces

*Items are listed in order of increasing difficulty based on normative data.

---

normally require assistance of some kind to accomplish their daily activities and that the degree required differs considerably as a function of normal variations among children, for example in such things as temperament, and as a function of the different circumstances of family lives (eg, the degree of time pressure in the daily schedule). The difficulty, in terms of measurement, is to specify what constitutes assistance beyond the expectable level.

In developing the PEDI, we used caregiver assistance during performance of complex activities as our measure of disability (Table 2). To obtain reliable and interpretable responses from caregivers, we found that we needed to develop different operational definitions of assistance appropriate to each separate content area. For example, the nature and type of assistance typically given during dressing is quite different from the assistance that may be given to keep the child safe while out on a walk. Dressing often involves hands-on assistance and selection of easy-to-manage clothing. In contrast, caregivers assist the child to remain safe by staying vigilant, making rapid interventions when a hazard such as a crossing is encountered, and restricting the child to particular environments such as a fenced backyard.

Data collected with the PEDI on normal children confirm the importance of distinguishing functional capability/limitation and disability (as measured by assistance).[19] Although the functional skills sampled represent the essential components of the complex activities measured under caregiver assistance, attainment of

Table 2. Complex functional activities assessed with the Caregiver Assistance Scale on the PEDI

Self-care domain	Mobility domain	Social function domain
Eating	Chair/toilet transfers	Functional comprehension
Grooming	Car transfers	Functional expression
Bathing	Bed mobility/transfers	Joint problem solving
Dressing upper body	Tub transfers	Peer play
Dressing lower body	Indoor locomotion	Safety
Toileting	Outdoor locomotion	
Bladder management	Stairs	
Bowel management		

Reprinted with permission from Haley SM, Coster WJ, Ludlow LH, et al. *Pediatric Evaluation of Disability Inventory (PEDI)*. Boston: New England Medical Center; 1992.

the highest levels of functional skill almost always preceded attainment of independence in the overall activity. For example, by 3 years of age most children were reported to show the capability to plan and carry out joint activities with a peer. At the same age, however, only a small percentage were reported as independently (ie, without adult involvement) able to play cooperatively on a regular basis with one or more same-age peers. We interpret these data as validation of the distinction made in the model between the ability to do a particular task (functional capability/limitation) and the ability to carry out the integrated activity of which that task is a component (disability). Additional studies are underway that will examine to what extent different reporters (eg, parents and clinicians) agree on the child's level of capability and need for assistance.

Other potential measurement dimensions of performance need to be considered and tested for their conceptual validity as measures of disability. We need to determine the qualities of a performance that best represent what is meant by function. Some possibilities include the ability to initiate activities at the correct time, in the correct situation, and with sufficient frequency; the ability to complete them in the required time; and the degree to which undesirable or inappropriate behaviors interfere with the completion of daily activities. It is also important to recognize that different measurement dimensions may be appropriate for different aspects of function. For example, we found that it was quite difficult for caregivers of a toddler with limited language skills to characterize the level of assistance they provided when trying to understand the child's communications. Although it is obvious to observers that the caregiver is putting in extra effort when trying to clarify a toddler's messages, there may be a better way to capture these limitations. It will be important not to let the desire for a uniform measurement scale, such as assistance, obscure the important differences that exist among the various functional activities to be measured.

Defining social role performance (handicap)

The WHO framework defines the dimension of handicap in terms of what the authors call "survival roles."[5(p193)] The model identifies six such roles: orientation, physical independence, mobility, occupation, social integration, and economic self-sufficiency. It is recommended that an individual's current degree of disadvantage be assessed for each role to allow the construction of a profile. All these roles, except economic self-sufficiency, potentially can be applied to children, and in fact the examples given in the WHO framework include several that are specific to children. For example, in the occupation category, a child who could attend regular school but who had disabilities that prevented participation in certain activities would be described as having curtailed occupation.

There have been few attempts to examine the suitability of this existing framework for describing handicap in children or to develop a method for measurement of this dimension in terms relevant to intervention. A notable exception is the Nordic Neuropaediatric Association's adaptation of the WHO handicap dimension for children 6 to 7 years.[24] Interestingly, they have converted the social integration category into a dimension labeled social interaction. New definitions and criteria more appropriate for children have been established for classifying the level of handicap. This new coding format has been used successfully in a sample of 6- to 7-year-old children[25] but has yet to be examined for younger children.

Because the level of role performance is the most deeply intertwined with existing social and cultural conditions, the task of developing a method for characterizing both the child's current situation and the factors contributing to the existing disadvantage will be exceedingly complex. Although education and therapy teams are engaged in this task on a daily basis as they prepare individualized education and intervention plans for children with disabilities, a comprehensive system for recording this information that could be applied across diverse settings has yet to be developed.

CONCEPTUALIZATION AND THE PURPOSES OF CLINICAL ASSESSMENT

The focus of a conceptual framework for disablement in children may shift depending on the specific purposes for functional assessment. These include diagnosis and intervention planning, discrimination of normal from abnormal or delayed development of functional performance, and evaluation of change in response to educational or therapeutic intervention.

One important function of a classification system is to facilitate the categorization of the manifestations of disease or impairment in uniform terms. This categorization enables clear communication among individuals concerned with functional performance or disablement, which can then facilitate a number of other goals. Most important, a clear classification system forms the foundation for a model of the functional problems faced by a child or group of children and helps clarify the questions that will need to be addressed to build a better understanding of those problems.

Decisions about who is a candidate for services, what type of services are most appropriate, the role of particular disciplines in providing services, and the measures to be used to evaluate the outcome of those services are also tied to the framework used in defining or classifying the problem initially. Conceptual confusion and/or differences in definitions among the individuals concerned with this type of classification may result in difficulty in achieving a coherent intervention plan because it will not be possible to agree upon the essential problems, proper goals, or measures of progress for the child.[2,15] For example, in the case of a young child with a movement limitation, one approach is to define the problem at the impairment level, in terms of altered tone or tendency to become fixed in primitive reflex patterns. This conceptual approach may lead to placing an emphasis on direct physical intervention to try to alter these characteristics. Alternatively, however, one might conceptualize the failure of the child to move at the disability level, as a complex interplay of physical parameters, motivational factors that manifest themselves in passivity, and environmental factors that include inadequate social support for the child's attempts to reach for desired goals (such as a toy) independently when these attempts are effortful and qualitatively awkward. Adopting the latter conceptualization potentially shifts the priority from altering the physical impairments to altering the social factors if it is determined that they are more crucial to improving the overall function of the child.

A second major purpose of a functional assessment is to discriminate between normal and delayed functional performance. A pediatric functional assessment designed for this purpose must be based on a normative model and include content that will maximize the difference between children with normal and abnormal functional profiles. For example, the PEDI has been standardized on a normative sample, and standard normative scores for the functional limitation and disability components can be obtained for each scale. Initial data suggest that the PEDI effectively discriminates between children with relatively minor motor dysfunction and age-matched comparison children.[26]

Finally, conceptual frameworks also guide the choice of outcome measures for evaluation and efficacy research. These concerns have increased with the demand for accountability by education and health care providers and reimbursement agencies. Ideally, the measurement of change in a clinical setting would also be guided by a conceptual system that organizes the information about a particular child or group of children and suggests the appropriate ways to measure the effectiveness of various intervention efforts. A number of investigators have argued, however, that there is considerable confusion about the appropriate level of behavior to be measured. As a result, efficacy studies have used measures that cannot adequately represent meaningful changes in performance.[1,2] For example, if an intervention has been designed to facilitate functional movement, then the outcome measure should examine changes in functional skills, not changes in the physical impairments such as muscle tone that may (or may not) change with increases in skilled performance. Similarly, an intervention may significantly decrease a child's social disadvantage if it permits mobility through more flexible equipment. However, the physical parameters of the child's performance may remain essentially unchanged. Unless the outcome measure used is sensitive to the social effects, it could easily be decided that the intervention had no effect on function. Some of the confusion in outcome research reflects the lack of a sufficiently broad framework for describing children's function. In particular, a framework for representing the conceptual links between the physical parameters of impairment and functional performance is lacking.

•   •   •

With the increasing emphasis on functionally focused interventions, there is a critical need for a conceptual model to guide the description of function and disablement in young children. A working model to address this need has been presented that draws on existing frameworks in the adult literature but incorporates important distinctions between adult and child functional performance. This model incorporates the four levels of impairment, functional limitations, disability, and social role performance as well as developmental and contextual influences. This model should serve as the foundation for future measurement innovations by clarifying the issues that need to be addressed in both conceptualizing and developing assessment strategies for the different aspects of functional performance in infants and young children.

REFERENCES

1. Bundy A. The challenge of functional outcomes: Framing the problem. *Neuro-developmental Treatment Association Newsl.* July 1990:1–22.

2. Fetters L. Measurement and treatment in cerebral palsy: An argument for a new approach. *Phys Ther.* 1991;71:244–247.

3. Haley SM, Hallenborg S, Gans BM. Functional assessment in young children with neurological impairments. *Top Early Child Spec Ed.* 1989;9:106–126.

4. Harris SR. Efficacy of pediatric physical therapy in promoting family functioning and functional independence for children with cerebral palsy. *Pediatr Phys Ther.* 1990;2:160–164.

5. World Health Organization. *International Classification of Impairments, Disabilities, and Handicaps.* Geneva: World Health Organization; 1980.

6. Bagnato SJ, Neisworth JT, Munson SM. *Linking Developmental Assessment and Early Intervention: Curriculum-Based Prescriptions* 2nd ed. Rockville, MD: Aspen; 1989.

7. Wood PHN. The language of disablement: A glossary relating to disease and its consequences. *Int Rehabil Med.* 1980;2:86–92.

8. Granger CV. A conceptual model for functional assessment. In: Granger CV, Gresham GE, eds. *Functional Assessment in Rehabilitation Medicine.* Baltimore: Williams & Wilkins; 1984.

9. Kirshner B, Guyatt, G. A methodological framework for assessing health indices. *J Chronic Dis.* 1985;38:27–36.

10. Pope AM, Tarlov AR. *Disability in America.* Washington, DC: National Academy Press; 1991.

11. Nagi SZ. Some conceptual issues in disability and rehabilitation. In: Susman MB, ed. *Sociology and Rehabilitation.* Washington, DC: American Sociological Association; 1965.

12. Nagi SZ. Disability concepts revisited: Implications for prevention. In: Pope AM, Tarlov AR, eds. *Disability in America.* Washington, DC: National Academy Press; 1991.

13. Guccione AA. Physical therapy diagnosis and the relationship between impairments and function. *Phys Ther.* 1991;71:499–504.

14. Haley SM, Coster WJ, Ludlow LH. Pediatric functional outcome measures. *Phys Med Rehabil Clin North Am.* 1991;2:689–724.

15. Campbell SK. Framework for the measurement of neurological impairment and disability. In: Lister M, ed. *Contemporary Management of Motor Control Problems* (Proceedings of the IISTEP Conference). Alexandria, VA: Foundation for Physical Therapy; 1991.

16. Rogoff B. *Apprenticeship in Thinking.* New York: Oxford University Press; 1990.

17. Gallimore R, Weisner TS, Kaufman SZ, Bernheimer LP. The social construction of ecocultural niches: Family accommodation of developmentally disabled children. *Am J Ment Retard.* 1989;94:216–230.

18. Tharp R, Gallimore R. *Rousing Minds to Life: Teaching, Learning and Schooling in Social Context.* Cambridge: Cambridge University Press; 1989.

19. Haley SM, Coster WJ, Ludlow LH, et al. *Pediatric Evaluation of Disability Inventory (PEDI).* Boston: New England Medical Center. 1992. In press.

20. Uniform Data System for Medical Rehabilitation. *Functional Independence Measure.* Buffalo: State University of New York; 1987.

21. Haley SM, Ludlow LH, Gans BM, Faas RM, Inacio CI. Tufts Assessment of Motor Performance: An empirical approach to identifying motor performance categories. *Arch Phys Med Rehabil.* 1991;72:359–366.

22. Silverstein B, Kilgore KM, Fisher WP, Harley P, Harvey RF. Applying psychometric criteria to functional assessment in medical rehabilitation: I. Exploring unidimensionality. *Arch Phys Med Rehabil.* 1991;72:631–637.

23. Wright BD, Masters GN. *Rating Scale Analysis.* Chicago: Mesa; 1982.

24. Diderichsen J, Ferngren H, Hansen FJ, et al. The handicap code of the ICIDH, adapted for children aged 6–7 years. *Int Disabil Stud.* 1990;12:54–60.

25. Ferngren H, Lagergren J. Usefulness and interobserver agreement of a child adapted handicap code of WHO's ICIDH. *Int Disabil Stud.* 1988;10:155–158.

26. Feldman A, Haley SM, Coryell J. Concurrent and construct validity of the Pediatric Evaluation of Disability Inventory. *Phys Ther.* 1990;70:602–610.

Difficult and challenging behaviors in young children: A neurodevelopmental perspective for assessment and intervention

Brad D. Berman, MD
Assistant Director
Child Development Center
Children's Hospital Oakland
Oakland, California

CHILDREN WITH unique health needs and impaired or delayed developmental capabilities require understanding and support at multiple levels. In understanding these children, one needs not only to diagnose the illness or disability and to profile the child's strengths and weaknesses but also to address continuously the behavioral and developmental growth of the child. These children often display difficult behaviors such as aggression, tantrums, and testing of limits.[1] Interventions for these behaviors may be implemented at multiple sites, including the home, center-based programs, and schools. This article reviews a clinical approach to understanding these often challenging behaviors from a neurodevelopmental perspective, defined here as the influence of a child's biologic/neurologic functioning upon the growth and patterns of development within that child. This clinical approach also incorporates family and environmental factors that influence the expression of a child's behavior. Common behavioral interventions are then reviewed within the context of this neurodevelopmental approach.

MULTIFACTORIAL CLINICAL MODEL

The success of any one behavioral intervention will be dependent on an understanding of the health and neurodevelopment of the child, the environment in which he or she lives, and the capabilities of his or her caretakers to implement successfully the strategy. The evolution of a child's development as it influences behavior is best appreciated from a multifactorial perspective. The approach, then, is to formulate a profile of the child within the following areas: biology, development, and environment (Fig 1).

Biology

Biologic functioning and thus behavior may be influenced to a large degree by genetic factors. This may be seen, for example, in the oppositional and sometimes

Appreciation is extended to Shiva Berman, PhD, and Caroline Johnson, PhD, for their thoughtful review and suggestions.

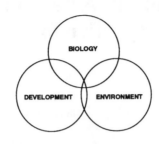

Fig 1. Multifactorial clinical model of child development.

aggressive behavior in children with Klinefelter's syndrome (XYY)[2] or with 18q syndrome.[3] The expression of temperamental traits may come in conflict with the child's environment, thus creating friction or real barriers for the child (ie, the goodness of fit model).[4] Neurologic function is primary in the expression of behavior and a child's response to intervention. This behavioral expression is seen most clearly in a child with an attention deficit-hyperactivity disorder, whose central neurologic difficulties with arousal, attention, impulsivity, and activity level may conflict with peer and adult expectations.[5]

It is also critical to evaluate the overall health of the child and any illnesses that may be ongoing. As a clinical example, a 16-month-old boy was admitted to Children's Hospital Oakland with failure to thrive, malnutrition with mild kwashiorkor, megaloblastic anemia, and profound apathy and generalized developmental delay at the 8-month level. The history for this child included treatment for congenital syphilis and disseminated tuberculosis. As his medical condition slowly stabilized and his nutritional status improved, he became more aware of and responsive to his surroundings, first with withdrawal and crying and later with gesturing to his nurses and physicians to hold him. Before discharge from the hospital, he was able, with only minimal intervention, to feed himself with a spoon, to drink from a cup, to play with a toy car, and to walk. There appeared to be linear progression in this child's development and behavior with clinical improvement and a stable environment.

Development

Various schematic models exist to describe a child's developmental unfolding that take into consideration the input of genetics and neurology as well as cognitive and emotional factors. Erikson's[6] stages of development blend psychoanalytic theory with neuromaturation and social experience. Cognitive development from infancy through childhood may best be understood through the work of Piaget, who described active change through a predictable progression of stages.[7] Gross motor, fine motor, and language development are intrinsic to this process as well,[8] influencing cognitive and emotional growth and thus behavior. How a child responds to his or her world is, to a large degree, a reflection of these developmental strengths and weaknesses. A discrepancy between chronologic and developmental capabilities in a child may lead to unexpected and challenging behaviors requiring an evaluative and therapeutic approach that accounts for these differences.

Environment

It is also critical to understand the family and environment within which the child lives and to identify sources of strength and resiliency as well as stressors that affect the child and family. Poverty, single parenthood, limited education, and lack of family or community resources may certainly influence family function and thus individual behavior.[9] Cultural perspectives and past experiences may influence a parent's response to common childhood behaviors in maladaptive ways, as seen with the vulnerable child syndrome.[10] For example, a parent's response to a common behavior such as breath-holding, often associated with pallor and cyanosis, can lead to difficult and dysfunctional behavior for child and parent. Had that parent experienced the death of another child or sibling due to respiratory complications? Is the parent's cultural belief that the child will lose his or her "wind" and thus become ill or die? Understanding the basis of parental worries or beliefs may shed light on the type and intensity of responses that parents have to their child's behaviors and may assist in creating workable suggestions to deal with such behaviors.

Because the focus of this article is on common behavioral interventions, a more thorough discussion of comprehensive assessment is not presented. The reader, however, is referred to Greenspan's[11] descriptions of assessing a child from a neurodevelopmental and contextual perspective, which encompass the major themes of infancy and childhood touched upon above.

BEHAVIORAL INTERVENTIONS

Behavioral interventions exist, both positive and negative, that have at their core the desire to discipline a child. Keeping in mind the definition of discipline, to teach, the goal is to help a child learn developmentally appropriate behaviors in a wide variety of situations. Brief descriptions of these common teaching, or disciplinary, interventions are now presented. It is also important to remember, when one is working with children and their families, to listen effectively to parental concerns and to acknowledge and validate parents' worries and frustrations. This is a vital step toward building a foundation of trust, cooperation, and alliance between parent and professional.[12,13]

Children are not born with a set of instructions regarding appropriate behavior in a wide variety of settings, including home, the neighbor's house, the center-based developmental program, or day care. Consequently, they must learn both what is expected of them and how they are actually to behave. Adult *modeling* of appropriate behaviors with *imitation* by a child and reinforcement through praise, affection, privileges, and even rewards is often effective for communicating expectations. Even gentle gestures such as patting a child on the back or momentarily stroking his or her hair after an appropriate action serve to communicate approval to that child.[14] Occasionally, the caregiver may need to practice paying attention to a child's good behavior and responding appropriately. A good method for practicing this is provided by Barkley[15] and is outlined in the box, "Paying Attention to Good Behavior."

Behavior therapy

As children advance developmentally, structured rewards contingent upon desired behaviors become more meaningful. *Behavior therapy* is based on the fol-

---

Paying Attention to Good Behavior

Select special time with child each day.
No other child should be involved with this special time.
Allow child to choose the play activity.
Relax and enjoy.
Ask no questions, and give no commands.
Offer positive statements, praise, and hugs about specific behavior immediately.
If misbehavior occurs, look away for a few moments.

Adapted from Barkley RA: *Defiant Children: A Clinician's Manual for Parent Training.* New York, NY: The Guilford Press; 1987.

lowing principles: All behavior is learned, behavior is shaped by consequences, behavior is more likely to be repeated if the consequence is positive, and behavior is less likely to be repeated if the consequence is negative.[16] (See the box, "Components of a Behavior Therapy System.") When used appropriately and in combination with other interventions, behavior therapy can be an effective approach for disruptive or aggressive behaviors in children with a spectrum of cognitive disabilities and developmental needs, including autism, communication impairment, and generalized developmental delay.[8] Biobehavioral disorders such as enuresis and encopresis are often amenable to this approach as well.[17] It is important to remember that, when one is designing a behavior therapy approach, the child must be able to understand what is wanted and be developmentally capable of performing the desired behavior. It is usually more effective to begin positively, with a series of guaranteed successes leading toward the goal of specific behaviors, than to overchallenge the child too early, with failures ensuing.

Extinction

A different version of behavior therapy for the suppression of unwanted behaviors is *extinction*. This is defined as the removal of reinforcement from a situation in which a response formerly occurred with the consequence that the probability of the previously reinforced response is eventually decreased. This *ignoring* of inappropriate behavior has two phases: a baseline phase and an extinction phase. In the baseline phase, the specific unwanted behavior is recorded with special note to the frequency of response and circumstances surrounding or leading up to the behavior. In the extinction phase, the frequency of behavioral occurrence is recorded as the adult selectively *ignores* or does not respond to the child when the undesired behavior occurs[18] (Fig 2). Although extinction is an effective and nonpunitive intervention, it requires a good deal of patience and concentration.

Components of a Behavior Therapy System

Rules: Adult statements regarding desired and undesired behaviors

Rewards/positive reinforcement: The presentation of a positive stimulus to reinforce or increase a wanted or desired behavior (eg, praise, attention, special activities with parent, star charts, treats, toys, money)

Negative reinforcement: The removal of a negative stimulus to reinforce or increase a wanted or desired behavior (eg, removal of an irritating noise or uncomfortable temperature)

Punishment: Ignoring the behavior, verbal disapproval, temporary isolation/time-out, temporary removal of a privilege

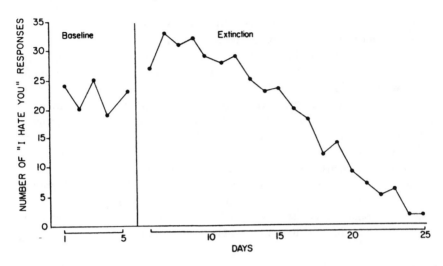

Fig 2. Recording of an undesired behavior in baseline and extinction phases. Reproduced with permission from Drabman RS, Jarvie G. Counseling parents of children with behavior problems: the use of extinction and time-out techniques. *Pediatrics.* 1977;59(1): 78–85.

Problems often arise that lead to premature abandonment of an effective and powerful intervention for the professional or caregiver. (See the box, "Extinction: Problem Areas.")

As a clinical example, RP was an 18-month-old boy seen for excessively clinging behavior and difficulty sleeping and eating. He was born at gestation week 37 with cyanotic congenital heart disease and pulmonary atresia. He had three surgical procedures to improve blood flow to the lungs with a particularly poor outcome after the second surgery. This was associated with developmental regression, especially in language and motor skills. He was irritable, inconsolable except when his mother held him, and dependent on her for most activities, including eating. A perception by hospital staff was that RP had become a vulnerable child given his parents' reluctance to challenge him. Underlying this reluctance was the parents' fear of harming their son physically, which might ultimately lead to his death.

In the initial phase of intervention, this family was validated and supported in their worries and frustrations. As RP began to improve clinically and developmentally, they too became open to more structured interventions, primary among which was extinction or selective ignoring, especially for disruptive eating behaviors such as throwing food. As they began to respond less to unwanted behaviors

---

Extinction: Problem Areas

Do *not* skip the initial baseline recording phase.
Adult perception of the behavior may be inaccurate.
Inconsistency in adult behavior may interfere with intervention.
The child may test the system (response burst).
Teach the child appropriate behavior.
Provide appropriate outlets for the child.
Ignore minor regressions to the old behavior.

---

in concert with rewarding for more appropriate actions, RP's eating and sleeping gradually became more functional and appropriate for age with an overall decrease in his irritability and his parents' frustration.

Time-out

Perhaps the most common behavioral intervention known to professionals and parents is *time-out*. It is a tried-and-true method of disciplining children of all ages and is effective in a variety of situations when used properly. Christophersen[19] suggests that the critical feature of time-out is first to ensure that the child understands *time-in*. He describes this as frequent, brief, nonverbal physical contact as a child is engaged in a desired activity or behavior. This may be a brief pat on the head while the child is playing, a gentle stroke on the back while the child is listening quietly in circle time, or a simple smile or a frequent touch on the hand or foot during an examination or therapy session. These frequent gestures communicate pleasantly acknowledgment and approval for desired behaviors and are useful with most children regardless of developmental or sensory abnormalities.

Once an infant or child is aware of time-in, the contrast to *time-out* in response to inappropriate behaviors becomes meaningful and easier to communicate. It is important to prepare in advance for the use of time-out, taking into account the child's age and neurodevelopment, and to be systematic and consistent when using it. General guidelines for this approach are presented in the box, "Time-Out: General Guidelines." Initially, a child may not be able to tolerate more than a 5- to 10-second time-out, which then can be gradually extended to longer times as suggested. Through selective use of this technique for specific behaviors, the child should be able to develop an appreciation of the contrast between normal activities with time-in responses and removal from these activities or adult interaction with time-out.[14]

There are, of course, pitfalls to the use of time-out that necessitate a closer look at how it is being used and in which circumstances (see the box, "Time-Out: Sug-

---

Time-Out: General Guidelines

Discuss with (teach) child appropriate and inappropriate behaviors.
Select time-out place: should be dull, away from distractors such as toys or television, and not frightening or dangerous.
Discuss in advance with child what time-out is for.
Length of time-out is generally 1 minute per year of age up to 5 minutes maximum.
Initiate time-out immediately when inappropriate behavior occurs.
After time-out is over, child begins with a clean slate.

---

gestions for Problem Areas"). For children with medical or developmental limitations, it is critical to ensure that the time-out techniques are appropriate and reasonable. A child with athetoid cerebral palsy might not be expected to sit in a time-out chair without body movements. The adult may be the individual who must break off contact and move away rather than the child who is confined to bed or technologically dependent. A young child with severe attentional difficulties may not be able to hold to time-out for longer than 30 seconds. In all cases, however, it is still possible to contrast the difference between time-in for appropriate behaviors and time-out when discipline is necessary.

Time-Out: Suggestions for Problem Areas

Explain time-out procedure to child initially. Rehearsal or practice run may be helpful.
Identify the behaviors you want to change; teach child alternative and acceptable ways to behave.
It may be fine to use one warning before time-out.
Decide on appropriate and realistic time limit in advance.
Time-out does not begin until child is in relative control.
Keep accurate track of time; a kitchen timer is helpful for this.
Do not scold or argue with child once time-out has begun.
Control teasing or interference from siblings or other children.
Should child leave time-out prematurely:
  • redirect child immediately to time-out area
  • provide one firm, clear warning about leaving time-out
  • possibly extend length of time in time-out or give additional punishment
  • resist child's desire to go to the bathroom or complaints of feeling hungry or tired
  • rarely, use physical restraint
  • avoid game of cat and mouse with child leaving time-out
It may help to redirect child to a different or more positive activity when time-out is completed.

Adapted in part from Barkley RA: *Defiant Children: A Clinician's Manual for Parent Training.* New York, NY: The Guilford Press; 1987.

As a clinical example, GB was a 36-month-old boy who presented to Children's Hospital Oakland with parental concerns of limited attention span, agitation and severe tantrums, difficulty sleeping, and overstimulation in the environment. He was a full-term infant adopted at birth. Within the first 2 months of life, GB developed group B streptococcal sepsis twice, the second time with meningitis. Problems consequent to the meningitis included mild right hemiparesis, which slowly resolved, and a seizure disorder treated successfully with carbamazepine. His developmental profile included generalized delay of 10 to 12 months with particular weaknesses in communication and fine motor skills. He had a low frustration level, was highly sensitive to environmental stimuli, and was both impulsive and active. Significant psychosocial stressors to this family included a parent on disability and a change in the family's medical insurance necessitating a corresponding change in their pediatrician and subspecialists.

Interventions included participation in a center-based program, speech/language therapy, and parental support. GB continued to act out at home and in the program, however, often interfering with the activities of other children and adults. An appreciation of FB's temperament and neurodevelopment was necessary before any consistent behavioral approach could be designed. The amount of stimulation he was provided in a group was decreased with a greater focus on individual therapy in a quieter atmosphere. Rules were simplified for expected behaviors at home and at the center, were clearly communicated to BG in a way he could understand, and often were repeated. Time-in, time-out, and selective extinction became the main interventions for setting limits and teaching him appropriate behaviors. Only a few specific behaviors were addressed at any time, and time-out initially consisted of 10- to 15-second breaks in engagement between GB and parent or professional. Continued support and communication between parents and staff were necessary to ensure consistency in approach toward GB and to help transitions flow more smoothly.

Tantrums and aggression

Two specific behaviors mentioned frequently as being particularly frustrating to parents and professionals are temper tantrums and aggression. An in-depth exploration of etiologic factors leading to these behaviors is not provided here. These behaviors, however, are often developmentally and contextually appropriate expressions of frustration and anger, requiring at some level both understanding and acceptance. Guidelines for tantrums are designed to allow this expression in ways that are acceptable yet neither harmful nor shameful to the child (see the box, "Temper Tantrums: General Guidelines"). Occasionally, children who are developmentally at risk may require direct adult intervention to help contain the expression and length of the tantrum. This might include holding or rocking them

---

Temper Tantrums: General Guidelines

Ensure child's physical/emotional safety.
Pay no attention, positive or negative, to child.
Do not reason with child during the tantrum.
Do not resort to restraining and spanking; they do not generally help.
Reunite after tantrum.
Do NOT give in.

---

and perhaps distracting or transitioning them to a new activity after the tantrum has gone on as long as deemed appropriate. Additionally, anticipating when a child will be at greatest risk for tantrums may help avoid them altogether. This is especially true during certain physical states, including hunger and fatigue, and during certain activities with which the child might become particularly frustrated.[20,21]

Aggressive behavior is defined as actions intended to cause injury or anxiety to others; these include hitting, kicking, destroying property, quarreling, attacking verbally, and resisting requests.[22] There are both individual and environmental risk factors that critically influence these behaviors, and the reader is referred to Campbell[23] for a further discussion of aggressive behavior problems. Some adult interventions may exacerbate the aggression rather than ameliorate it. These include further modeling of aggressive behavior (eg, biting a child back in response for biting another or overmatching a child verbally through excessive shouting).

Aggressive Behavior: General Guidelines

Assess and treat underlying causes of these behaviors.
Establish control when necessary.
Make allowances for behavior when child is under stress.
Acknowledge and validate child's feelings.
Emphasize that sometimes child must face and learn to cope with reality.
Reduce frustrating experiences when possible.
Keep rules simple, clear, and to a minimum.
Provide positive outlets for acceptable expressions of aggression.
Possibly give one-to-one attention to acting-out child.
Teach child acceptable behaviors, including alternatives to unacceptable behavior (with explanation of why behavior is unacceptable), coping skills, relaxation techniques, and obtaining help when needed.
Plan ahead, and *anticipate* at-risk situations.

Adapted from Hendrick J. *The Whole Child: Early Education for the Eighties.* St. Louis, Mo: Times Mirror/ Mosby; 1984.

Undesirable approaches to addressing these behaviors may include an *authoritarian* or narrowed stance, *overpermissiveness,* or *inconsistency.* Keeping in mind that working with children with a tendency toward aggression may be quite difficult, as seen for example in a subgroup of children with attention deficit-hyperactivity disorder with associated oppositional-defiant characteristics,[24] general guidelines do exist to help deflect, redirect, or teach a child more appropriate behavior (see the box, "Aggressive Behavior: General Guidelines").

•   •   •

The challenge in living and working with children is often in supporting their developmental drives and needs while coping with the frustrating and difficult behaviors that these engender. There is sometimes a fine line between acceptable and dysfunctional behavior, requiring flexibility, firmness when necessary, and understanding. Appropriate expectations for children, whether they have special needs or not, must stem from a neurodevelopmental perspective that takes into account the interplay of their unique biologic and developmental features with environmental influences. In doing so, one may find clues to understanding and responding to their behavior, and thus help foster and promote their growth and development.

REFERENCES

1. Dixon SD, Stein MT. *Encounters with Children.* Chicago, Ill: Year Book Medical; 1987.
2. Mandoki MW, Sumner GS. Klinefelter syndrome: the need for early identification and treatment. *Clin Pediatr.* 1991;30:161–163.
3. Wertelecki W, Gerald PS. Clinical and chromosomal studies of the 18q syndrome. *J Pediatr.* 1971;78:44.
4. Chess S, Thomas A. *Temperament in Clinical Practice.* New York, NY: Guilford; 1986.
5. Goldstein S, Goldstein M. *Managing Attention Disorders in Children.* New York, NY: Wiley; 1990.
6. Erikson EH. Eight ages of man. In: *Childhood and Society.* 2nd ed. New York, NY: Norton; 1985:44–52.
7. Crain W. Piaget's cognitive-developmental theory. In: *Theories of Development.* Englewood Cliffs, NJ: Prentice-Hall; 1980.
8. Capute AJ, Accardo PJ. *Developmental Disabilities in Infancy and Childhood.* Baltimore, Md: Brookes; 1991.
9. Shonkoff JP, Jarman FC, Kohlenberg TM. Family transitions, crises, and adaptations. *Curr Probl Pediatr.* 1987;17:508–533.
10. Green M. Vulnerable child syndrome and its variants. *Pediatr Rev.* 1986;8:75–80.
11. Greenspan S. *The Clinical Interview of the Child.* New York, NY: McGraw-Hill; 1981.
12. Glascoe FP, MacLean WE, Stone WL. The importance of parents' concerns about their child's behavior. *Clin Pediatr.* 1991;30:8–11.

13. Allmond BW, Buckman, W, Gofman HF. *The Family Is the Patient.* St. Louis, Mo: Mosby; 1979.
14. Christophersen ER. *Little People: Guidelines for Common Sense Child Rearing.* 3rd ed. Kansas City, Mo: Westport; 1988.
15. Barkley RA. *Defiant Children: A Clinician's Manual for Parent Training.* New York, NY: Guilford; 1987.
16. Block RW, Rash FC. *Handbook of Behavioral Pediatrics.* Chicago, Ill: Year Book Medical; 1981.
17. Howe AC, Walker CE. Behavioral management of toilet training, enuresis, and encopresis. *Pediatr Clin North Am.* 1992;39:413–432.
18. Drabman RS, Jarvie G. Counseling parents of children with behavior problems: the use of extinction and time-out techniques. *Pediatrics.* 1977;59:78–85.
19. Christophersen ER. Discipline. *Pediatr Clin North Am.* 1992;39:395–411.
20. Needlman R, Howard B, Zuckerman B. Temper tantrums: when to worry. *Contemp Pediatr.* 1989;6:12–34.
21. Schmitt BD. *Your Child's Health.* New York, NY: Bantam; 1987.
22. Hendrick J. *The Whole Child: Early Education for the Eighties.* 3rd ed. St. Louis, Mo: Times Mirror/Mosby; 1984.
23. Campbell SB. *Behavior Problems in Preschool Children.* New York, NY: Guilford; 1990.
24. Barkley RA. *Attention Deficit Hyperactivity Disorder.* New York, NY: Guilford; 1990.

Observing play: An appropriate process for learning and assessment

Rebecca R. Fewell, PhD
Professor of Pediatrics and
  Psychology
University of Miami
Coral Gables, Florida

Michelle P. Glick, BA
Graduate Student
Department of Psychology
University of Miami
Coral Gables, Florida

THE NEED FOR information about the abilities of infants and toddlers has challenged physicians, investigators, test designers, and program staff for many decades. Gesell and Cattell were among the first to formalize measures to determine how a given infant's performance compared to that of other infants.[1] Gesell[2] believed that physical and mental development could be seen through continuous stages. Through careful observations of a small sample of children during the 1920s, Gesell documented predictable growth trends at key ages and in several domains of development. Building on Gesell's work, Cattell[3] designed the Cattell Infant Intelligence Test to provide a standard measure of mental ability that could serve as a downward extension of the Stanford-Binet Test. The need for additional and more precise means of assessing the development of infants advanced rapidly in the 1980s as program specialists alerted funding agents to the importance, from the perspective of both child development and cost savings, of special education services from infancy. This resulted in the passage in 1986 of Public Law 99-457, which included a section specially designed for children birth through 2 years of age.

PL 99-457 includes specific requirements for the assessment of young children with special needs. The law requires that assessment be administered by qualified examiners and include testing in specific domains of development; use of multiple sources to gather information, including standardized testing, observation in naturalistic conditions, and determination of the perceptions of other significant persons; test procedures and materials that are free from cultural or racial bias; and procedures administered in the child's or parent's native language or preferred mode of communication. Results, when reported on a child's individualized family service plan, must include a statement of the child's present level of development in each of the domains.[4] Likewise, the results of these assessments are used to determine a child's eligibility for services and to develop an appropriate plan for intervention.

Among investigators and program specialists, the proliferation of services has heightened concerns over the efficacy of the assessment process, particularly as programs enroll children who are both younger and more severely disabled. Cicchetti and Wagner attribute this concern "to the paucity of assessment instruments that provide a rich enough picture of the developmental organization of children with atypical development."[5(p246)] Others provide a litany of reasons why traditional measures are inappropriate[6-9]; they call for alternative and more child-friendly procedures, measures that assess quality of performance as opposed to presence of behavior, and tools for assessing skills in young infants and toddlers with disabilities.

PLAY AS AN ASSESSMENT PARADIGM

In the last few years a number of investigators have advocated the use of play-based assessment as a promising procedure to address many of the problems with traditional, standardized assessment measures.[5,9-13] Wolery lists four reasons why play is being suggested for assessment and for the facilitation of learning: "(a) play is an enjoyable activity, (b) play may facilitate development of other behaviors, (c) play normalizes children's interactions with the environment, and (d) play has practical value."[13(pp428-429)] Fewell and Kaminski[10] indicate that play assessment is long overdue; they suggest that assessment during play may result in valid information about children's typical skills and may lead to more useful information than standardized testing. Linder[12] advocates the use of arena assessment and a transdisciplinary team approach so that all domains of development can be assessed in the context of play. Given that the play paradigm is not commonly used for assessment purposes, it is important to have a clear understanding of what play is and what one is examining in the context of play.

PLAY: A DEFINITIONAL ISSUE

Johnson et al[14] report that play is easy to recognize but hard to define. Researchers and program specialists have provided different perspectives on what constitutes play given differences in discipline and purposes for using play. At one end of a possible continuum of play behavior, Johnson et al[14] and Belsky and Most[15] distinguish between exploration and play, indicating that exploration involves unfamiliar objects rather than familiar ones and is done to gain information about an object rather than to use it for stimulation. At the other end of this continuum are distinctions between games involving compliance with externally imposed rules, which is a violation of the spontaneity normally associated with play. For the purposes of this article, the following definition of play is used: Play "is a spontaneous activity that involves interactions with objects in a pleasurable manner."[10(p147)]

ATTRIBUTES OF PLAY

Cognitive attributes

Cognitive development has been the focus of descriptions of play. Piaget[16] described three categories of play occurring in different stages of development.

Practice play occurs in the sensorimotor period and involves repetitive motor manipulations on objects. Symbolic play occurs in the preoperational period and involves the use of symbols to represent objects not present and the use of objects to substitute for other objects. Games with rules occur in the concrete operations period and involve adhering to rules. Smilansky[17] added three other types: functional play (repetitive movements made on objects), constructive play (objects used to make something), and dramatic play (engagement in pretend play). Researchers have found support for the ordering of Smilansky's categories.[18,19]

Self-awareness attributes

The content and context of symbolic play are of particular concern to investigators interested in the child's growing understanding of self and other. Fenson and Ramsey[20] described three stags: decentration, decontextualization, and integration. Decentration involves the child's extension of his or her play routine to include recipients of play actions other than his or her own body, as might be seen when a child gives a doll a bottle rather than pretending to drink from the bottle himself or herself. Benner[21] defines decontextualization as the child's engagement in play that transcends the immediate environment. For example, a child will pretend that a blue block is a bowl of ice cream. Integration is the successful engagement in multi-step enactments of routines such as setting the table, pouring a drink, and then giving the drink to a doll.[10]

Social attributes

The social attributes of play have been the focus of a number of investigators. Parten[22] identified different stages in a child's development of social participation skills during interactions with peers in play. These stages begin with unoccupied behavior, in which a child observes any interesting action and plays with his or her own body but does not engage in interactions with others. The stage of solitary play occurs next and is characterized by play alone with toys different from those of others in the vicinity. In the stage of parallel play, the child plays alongside others with the same or related toys or engages in a similar, albeit solitary, activity. Associative play occurs when children play in a group in a common activity but no roles are taken. Cooperative play is characterized by organized activities for achieving some goal. Barnes[23] found evidence supporting the original development of Parten's[22] levels of social play. Those interested in examining these characteristics of play will find useful a recording form developed by Johnson et al[14] that permits data collection for the combination of Smilansky's[17] cognitive play and Parten's[22] social play.

Mastery attributes

Child competence and mastery motivation are other behaviors readily observed in play. Jennings et al[24] found that continuity of play is related to indices of mastery motivation. It appears that the desire to complete a task that might be difficult (eg, unbuttoning a doll's dress, screwing a top on a bottle, or balancing blocks in building a structure) is evident in the play of infants and young children and is predictive of later competence.

Language attributes

Perhaps the behavior most often reported in the literature as observed through play is language. McCune-Nicolich[25] postulates parallel structural development between language and symbolic play with correspondences occurring across five levels of play (presymbolic games, autosymbolic games, single-scheme symbolic games, combinatorial symbolic games, and combinatorial symbolic play with planning). Ogura et al[26] examined the play and language of 18 children with Down syndrome and their mothers. They found the degree of symbolization in play to be related differently to expressive and receptive measures when controlling for chronological age. In the measures of sequential complexity, a strong association was found between the maximum number of symbols contained in sequential play and the longest utterance of content words. These researchers found support for only two of five levels of play and corresponding stages of language as proposed by McCune-Nicolich.[25]

Beeghly et al[27] reported four parallels between symbolic play and early language development. This finding is quite similar to that of Ogura,[28] who reported developmental correspondences between the onset of 6 language landmarks (the emergence of first words, naming words, vocabulary spurts, word chains, nonproductive two-word utterances, and productive two-word utterances) and the onset of 13 subcategories of play. In addition, she found that language and play both reflected the development of underlying symbolic ability and both developed in a parallel manner at the single-word stage.

Rogers states that "play is such an all-encompassing activity for young children that virtually all areas of development—cognitive, motor, social, emotional, language—can be observed in a child's play."[29(p11)] Judging from the studies that attest to the identification of domain-specific skill attributes referenced in this section, there is considerable evidence to support Rogers's statement.

THE ASSESSMENT OF PLAY SKILLS

Most of the instruments or observational coding systems for assessing play skills have been developed by investigators for use in particular studies of play and must be obtained directly from them.[30–35] Table 1 provides a brief description of some of the more commonly known scales and coding procedures developed specifically for examining play.

Upon examination of the various tests and procedures, one can see differences along three dimensions: structure in toy selection and presentation, specificity in coding and scoring, and procedure for eliciting behaviors form the child. Differences in these variables manifest in the amount and type of information one receives from the assessments. The technique best suited to the purpose of the assessment must be chosen by the examiner and may vary according to one's discipline.

Selection and presentation

Play scales and procedures vary widely along the structure and presentation dimension. Highly structured procedures can be traced to research origins and to work with normally developing children. Procedures with less structure were developed for use in the assessment of children with special needs.[10,13] Although much of the spontaneity of play and the information one can gain from observing play are compromised in the highly structured scales, the precision needed in research is ensured. The less structured scales are more useful in settings in which child preferences, learning styles, and functional information are needed in addition to scores on a developmental dimension.

In the area of toy selection and presentation, the Westby Symbolic Playscale[34] is the least structured of the instruments in Table 1. A large room is set up with toys arranged in the following five areas: infant stimulation, household, store, creative play, and gross motor. Children enter the room individually or in groups of up to four children. If adequate time is available, the examiner allows the child to explore freely; if, however, timely results are necessary, the examiner presents certain toys to the child. The toys are not placed in particular places or given to the child in a particular order. No specific toys are required, but the Westby Symbolic Playscale[34] describes a few examples of toys found in each area.

The Play Assessment Scale[33] (PAS) is also low in the structure dimension. The instructions include a list of suggested toys arranged in sets for use with children of various developmental ages. Sets are positioned singly and without time constrictions. Examiners are free to add other toys or to mix the toy sets. The toys are placed on the floor in a random arrangement, and the child is invited to play as he or she chooses.

The remaining procedures are more structured. All specify the toys to use and provide standard placements of the toys with regard to the child's position. Perhaps the most structured presentation is the Largo and Howard[30] procedure, in which 12 sets of specific toys are presented to the child while he or she is seated at a table.

Scoring or coding

All the procedures provide some definitions or criteria for scoring or coding behavior. The procedures differ in the degree of specificity. The McCune-Nicolich[31] and the Lowe and Costello[35] procedures list criteria scored for each

Table 1. Play scales and procedures

Instrument or source	Age (months)	Description
Developmental progression in play behavior of children between 9 and 30 months[30]	9–30	Specific toys are presented to the child in a specific order. The child plays spontaneously, is asked to perform specific behaviors, and is asked to imitate behaviors.
From exploration to play: A cross-sectional study of infant free play behavior[15]	7–20	A 12-step sequence of play development is used with a specific set of play toys. The child is observed with the mother, who responds to the child but does not direct play.
A Manual for Analyzing Free Play[31]	6–36	Observation of the child with specific toys. The mother responds but does not initiate. Scored according to detailed descriptions of the child's behavior with specific toys.
Play Assessment Checklist for Infants[32]	9–30	Observational checklist to measure aspects of play with specific toys. Form includes specific spaces for information such as mood, toy preferences, and motivation.
Play Assessment Scale[33]	2–36	Experimental measure of play development with 45 developmentally sequenced items. Opportunity to use verbal cues and modeling. Yields a play age.
Westby Symbolic Playscale[34]	9–60	Observation of one to four children interacting in a large room with five centers: infant stimulation, household, store, creative play, and motor. Developed to assess language acquisition but includes space for social play.
Symbolic Play Test[35]	12–36	Procedure that presents the child with four groups of toys and scores behaviors according to specific actions with specific toys. Yields an age-equivalent score.

action that a child might exhibit with an individual toy. A specific score is derived. Procedures by Belsky and Most,[15] Largo and Howard,[30] and Bromwich et al[32] are less specific. Definitions of categories are stated in general terms, and each category can be scored for any toy interactions. These procedures do not yield a quantitative score. The procedure of Bromwich et al[32] employs a range of specificity in coding. Some items refer to specific toys, and others are just behavioral observations of a child's temperament while playing. This assessment does not yield a particular score. The PAS[33] provides a description of the action criteria but does not require a specific toy. In addition, this scale includes examples of interactions with several toys that would yield a positive score and examples that are not to be scored positively. The PAS yields quantitative scores, including a total raw score that can be converted to a play age.

The advantage of the broader criteria is that they ensure that the child has ample opportunity to demonstrate a skill. The child has choices of toys, of space, and of time. Without time constraints, there are more opportunities for the child actually to demonstrate each of the interactions or to engage in interactions several times with different objects or circumstances. In addition, these less structured scoring systems permit the gathering of valuable information that is obtained from observations but is not reflected in a single score. Strengths of single standard scores are the ease of measuring child change over time and the validity of the findings when a standard exists for comparison.

Eliciting procedures

How children are instructed to interact with the toys within the context of play can have an effect on the response that the child makes in play. For most of the procedures, children are simply invited to play, and their interactions are recorded or coded. The PAS[33] and Largo and Howard[30] formats provide procedures for eliciting behaviors from the children after the children have had the opportunity to interact with the materials spontaneously. The PAS includes a procedure for eliciting and scoring responses by means of a series of gradual prompts. Fewell[33] reports that the information gathered and the scores obtained under these prompted conditions can be used to help teachers, parents, or others determine appropriate ways to facilitate play development in a child.

ASSESSMENT THROUGH PLAY

Up to this point, we have limited our review to the assessment of play as a developmental domain of behavior. We have cited studies that examined developmental domains of behavior (eg, language) while play is also observed, however. Virtually all domains of development can be observed easily while a child is engaged in play routines. This suggests that play is a promising model for assessment that is applicable to all aspects of a child's development. This idea has been proposed and presented by Linder[32] in her Transdisciplinary Play-Based Assessment Model (TPBA). The model involves using a team approach to assess the development of a child between 6 and 72 months of age while the child plays. Usually one member of the team serves as the play facilitator, interacting with the child. Assessments in the following domains are suggested: cognitive, social-emotional, communication and language, and sensorimotor. The model includes six phases: unstructured facilitation, structured facilitation, child-child interaction, parent-child interaction, motor play, and snack. Sessions are videotaped, and observations are recorded on observation worksheets developed for each domain of development. Useful information about developmental milestones are not directly linked to the observation system. There are no comparable developmental skills on play as a domain; play in this model is a means to an end, not an end in itself. All information obtained is qualitative but can be associated with developmental ages when noted for the various developmental skills listed.

PLAY AND DEVELOPMENTAL ASSESSMENT CASE STUDY

Given both the various scales and procedures listed in Table 1 and the TPBA's practical procedure for assessing behavior in traditional domains (ie, language, cognition, motor skills, and social behavior) while children are engaged in play routines, a logical combination of these two procedures might be useful. The combination of domain observations during the observations of play would not substitute for the precise assessment that is necessary to determine program eligibility. The proposed procedure is a format for using observational methods to gather information similar to that obtained through traditional, more structured testing. It is important to note that information gathered complements, but does not substitute for, other needed data.

We now provide a case study in which staff used the play setting to gather information about the development of play skills and to observe developmental skills from other domains while the child was playing. In addition, staff used traditional, more structured assessment measures to complete the evaluation of the child. We include both sets of scores for review.

John was born prematurely. He weighed 2130 g, had been exposed in utero to cocaine and alcohol, and had chronic lung disease, apneic episodes, and gastrointestinal reflux. After 15 months in a shelter for children under state care, he was released to his grandmother. He began intervention in a program in the shelter at 13 months and then continued in a center-based program 25 hours per week. At 28 months of age his skills had improved, and he was determined no longer to need services for children with known handicaps but to be eligible for services for children at high risk for developmental delay. John was mainstreamed full time into a class (25 hours a week) for normally developing toddlers. The battery of standard assessments traditionally administered to the high-risk children was administered to John in addition to the PAS.[33] John's play was videotaped for about a half hour in his toddler classroom with his peers both indoors and outdoors. From this videotape his mean length of utterance was calculated, and his skills were observed and charted with the age levels in the TPBA model. Results of these assessments and observations are listed in Table 2.

In the case study we included the PAS as a standard test because we did specifically administer that test. We scored the TPBA scores from the child's free play. One can see from Table 2 that the standard scores are similar but not exactly consistent with the scores obtained through play assessment and observations during play. It is interesting to note that John's scores ranged within domains from exactly the same to differences of 6 months. Higher performance scores were found on cognitive measures in the more structured, traditional testing procedures than during the free play procedures. His play domain score, as measured by the PAS, fell midway between the traditional, structured procedures and the free play procedures. In contrast, higher scores were found on the gross and fine motor observations during the free play procedures than on the structured procedures. The

Table 2. Results of assessments and observations

Domain/instrument	Score	Observations per TPBA
Cognition		
Developmental Activities Screening Inventory	25	19
Play		
Play Assessment Scale	22	
Language–Receptive		
Receptive Expressive Emergent Language Scale	24	23
Language–Expressive		
Receptive Expressive Emergent Language Scale	24	24
Mean Length of Utterance	28	24
Motor–Gross		
Peabody Developmental Motor Scales	20	25
Motor–Fine		
Peabody Developmental Motor Scales	26	29*
Social–Emotional		
Vineland	19	22

*Not from TPBA age ranges. Information provided was inconsistent with behavior observed. Scoring was based on the Hawaii Early Learning Profile and the Carolina Curriculum for Preschoolers with Special Needs.

higher scores were obtained when John was free to manipulate objects of his own choosing and to move about the environment in his preferred manner. These findings could be helpful to examiners who must select a test that is not likely to penalize John yet will still enable needed information to be gathered. From this initial assessment, the examiner will gain information about the conditions under which John is most likely to perform positively.

•   •   •

There is considerable evidence to support simultaneous use of play observations. Team members can observe a child playing and can assess the development of the child's play skills as well as an array of other developmental skills (eg, cognition, language, and motor skills) as they occur spontaneously. The results complement findings from traditional measures and provide information that is helpful for instruction and curriculum selection.

Play has always been the mainstay of curricula for normally developing children in child care and preschool programs. Recently, textbooks on the assessment and instruction of young children with special needs have begun to include chapters on play.[11,36–38] If play is to be used in the assessment and instruction of children with special needs, then it is important that persons in all disciplines begin to study how play can be used for assessment of domains skills and how their disciplines relate to play. Because play is not the unique study of any particular discipline, it is ideal for coalescing team members and giving them a body of information that is certainly of interest to family members.

Much research needs to be done to determine the validity of play assessment and of the information gathered through play. We need information about process, procedures, the ages of children when play assessment is most appropriate, and whether assessment should be done with individual children or small groups. We will need play scales and procedures that are standardized and readily available if this exciting activity is to become an accepted part of a child's experience in both assessment and early intervention.

REFERENCES

1. Fewell RR. Assessing handicapped infants. In: Garwood SG, Fewell RR, eds. *Educating Handicapped Infants.* Gaithersburg, Md: Aspen; 1983.

2. Gesell A. *The Mental Growth of the Preschool Child: A Psychological Outline of Normal Development from Birth to the Sixth Year, Including a System of Developmental Diagnosis.* New York, NY: Macmillan; 1925.

3. Cattell P. *Cattell Infant Intelligence Scale.* New York, NY: Psychological Corporation; 1960.

4. Early intervention programs for infants and toddlers with handicaps; final regulations (34 CFR Part 303). *Federal Register.* June 22, 1989;54:119.

5. Cicchetti D, Wagner S. Alternative assessment strategies for the evaluation of infants and toddlers: an organizational perspective. In: Meisels SJ, Shonkoff JP, eds. *Handbook of Early Childhood Intervention.* Cambridge, Mass: Cambridge University Press; 1990.

6. Bailey D. Assessment and its importance in early intervention. In: Bailey DB, Wolery M, eds. *Assessing Infants and Preschoolers with Handicaps.* Columbus, Ohio: Merrill; 1989.

7. Brooks-Gunn J, Lewis M. Assessing young handicapped children: issues and solutions. *J Dev Early Child.* 1981;2:84–95.

8. DuBose RF. Assessment of severely impaired young children: problems and recommendations. *Top Early Child Spec Educ.* 1981;1:9–22.

9. Fewell RR. Trends in the assessment of infants and toddlers with disabilities. *Except Child.* 1991;58:166–173.

10. Fewell RR, Kaminski R. Play skills development and instruction for young children with handicaps. In: Odom SL, Karnes MB, eds. *Early Intervention for Infants and Children with Handicaps.* Baltimore, Md: Brookes; 1988.

11. Fewell RR, Vadasy PR. *Learning through Play.* Allen, Tex: Developmental Learning Materials; 1983.

12. Linder TW. *Transdisciplinary Play-Based Assessment.* Baltimore, Md: Brookes, 1990.

13. Wolery M. Assessing play skills. In: Bailey DB, Wolery M, eds. *Assessing Infants and Preschoolers with Handicaps.* Columbus, Ohio: Merrill; 1989.

14. Johnson JE, Christie JF, Yawkey TD. *Play and Early Childhood Development.* Glenview, Ill: Scott, Foresman; 1987.

15. Belsky J, Most R. From exploration to play: a cross-sectional study of infant free play behavior. *Dev Psychol.* 1981;17:630–639.

16. Piaget J. *Play, Dreams, and Imitation in Childhood.* New York, NY: Norton; 1962.

17. Smilansky S. *The Effects of Sociodramatic Play on Disadvantaged Children: Preschool Children.* New York, NY: Wiley; 1968.

18. Rubin KH, Watson KS, Jambor TW. Free-play behaviors in preschool and kindergarten children. *Child Dev.* 1978;49:534–536.

19. Johnson JE, Ershler J. Developmental trends in preschool play as a function of classroom programs and child gender. *Child Dev.* 1981;51:995–1004.

20. Fenson L, Ramsey DS. Decentration and integration of the child's play in the second year. *Child Dev.* 1980;51:171–178.

21. Benner SM. *Assessing Young Children with Special Needs.* New York, NY: Longman; 1992.

22. Parten MB. Social participation among preschool children. *J Abnorm Soc Psychol.* 1932;27:243–269.

23. Barnes KE. Preschool play norms: a replication. *Dev Psychol.* 1971;5:99–103.

24. Jennings K, Harmon R, Morgan G, Gaiter, J, Yarrow L. Exploratory play as an index of mastery motivation: relationships to persistence, cognitive functioning and environmental measures. *Dev Psychol.* 1979;14:386–394.

25. McCune-Nicolich L. Toward symbolic functioning: structure of early pretend games and potential parallels with language. *Child Dev.* 1981;52:785–797.

26. Ogura T, Notari A, Fewell R. The relationship between language and play in Down syndrome children. *Jpn J Dev Psychol.* 1991;2:17–24.

27. Beeghly M, Hanrahan A, Weiss B, Cicchetti D. Development of communicative competence in children with Down's syndrome. Presented at the biennial meeting of the Society for Research in Child Development; April 1985; Toronto, Canada.

28. Ogura T. A longitudinal study of the relationship between early language development and play development. *J Child Lang.* 1991;18:273–294.

29. Rogers SJ. *Developmental and Clinical Aspects of Young Children's Play.* Monmouth, Ore: Western States Technical Assistance Resource; 1982.

30. Largo RH, Howard JA. Developmental progression in play behavior of children between nine and thirty months. I. Spontaneous play and imitation. *Dev Med Child Neurol.* 1979;21:229–310.

31. McCune-Nicolich L. *A Manual for Analyzing Free Play.* New Brunswick, NJ: Rutgers University; 1980.

32. Bromwich RM, Fust S, Khokha E, Walden MH. *Play Assessment Checklist for Infants.* Northridge, Calif: California State University; 1981.

33. Fewell RR. *Play Assessment Scale.* Miami, Fla: University of Miami; 1991.

34. Westby CE. A scale for assessing children's pretend play. In: Schaefer CE, Gitlin K, Sandgrund A, eds. *Play Assessment and Diagnosis.* New York, NY: Wiley; 1991.

35. Lowe M, Costello A. *The Symbolic Play Test.* Windsor, England: NFR-Nelson; 1976.

36. Bailey DB, Wolery M. *Assessing Infants and Preschoolers with Handicaps.* Columbus, Ohio: Merrill; 1989.

37. Gibbs ED, Teti DM. *Interdisciplinary Assessment of Infants.* Baltimore, Md: Brookes; 1990.

38. Odom SL, Karnes MB, eds. *Early Intervention for Infants and Young Children with Handicaps.* Baltimore, Md: Brookes; 1988.

Communication and language assessment for young children

Barry M. Prizant, PhD
Professor
Division of Communication Disorders
Emerson College
Boston, Massachusetts

Amy M. Wetherby, PhD
Associate Professor
Department of Communication
  Disorders
Florida State University
Tallahassee, Florida

A COMPREHENSIVE assessment is the first step in determining a young child's need for early intervention services that address communication enhancement. Early intervention for young children with communication difficulties is important because of the significant role that communication and language play in children's ability to develop relationships, to learn from others within the context of social engagement, and to function with greater independence with increasing age.[1] Early identification and intervention also serve a preventive function against a number of additional difficulties that may be closely related to, and may result from, early language and communication disorders.

First, families of children with communication problems may experience significant stress and confusion related to difficulties in identifying, acknowledging, and understanding their child's problem.[2] Problems in early identification of communication disorders may result from the inherent difficulty in establishing clearly defined criteria for determining the presence of communication problems in young children. This difficulty is due, in part, to great variability in the appearance of first words and in the rate of language acquisition even in normally developing children.[3] An absence of definitive criteria may result in delayed referral by primary care professionals, even when a problem is suspected by caregivers.[4] It is not uncommon for professionals to disagree as to whether there is any cause for concern when a child begins to demonstrate delays in development of communication skills. Caregivers of children with communication problems also may disagree over whether a problem exists and whether professional guidance should be sought.[5] Significantly delayed referral is more likely to occur when communication and language delays do not coexist with significant physical, sensory, or cognitive disabilities.

Second, the behavior of many young children with communication difficulties may pose significant challenges for parents. Paul[6] found that parents of 2-year-old children with slow expressive language development (SELD) perceived greater behavioral disturbances in areas of conduct, activity, and attention in their children compared to parents of matched controls even though the SELD children were cognitively within normal limits on nonverbal measures. On the basis of extensive family interviews, Bristol and Schopler[7] identified sources of stress re-

Inf Young Children 1993; 5(4): 20–34
© 1993 Aspen Publishers, Inc.

ported by parents of preschool children with significant social and communication disorders. Major sources of stress included the children's lack of effective communication, lack of response to family members, and behavior management problems.

Third, a significant relationship has been found among preschool language disorders, emotional and behavioral disorders, and late academic problems. Aram and Hall[8] found that 60% of children who displayed language disorders at a preschool level required special education placement during later childhood. Studies have documented co-occurrence rates of 50% to 60% for language and communication disorders and emotional/behavioral disorders in children and adolescents.[9] Specific to preschoolers, Stevenson and Richman[10] found that 59% of 3-year-olds with expressive language delays were reported by their parents to have significant behavioral disturbances. Although conclusive data are not available, it is likely that early identification and intervention would serve to alleviate stress for caregivers. Moreover, it has been suggested that communication intervention at an early age may prevent or mitigate later learning problems and emotional or behavioral disturbances.[11,12]

ASSESSMENT PRACTICES

Assessment and intervention should be viewed as interdependent processes. Ideally, parents should be integrally involved in assessment and intervention by participating in activities, by sharing their perceptions of their child's abilities, and by prioritizing intervention needs. It is beyond the scope of this article to include a comprehensive and detailed discussion of language and communication assessment. Recent resources provide additional information about language and communication assessment for infants, toddlers, and preschool children.[13-20]

Purposes and goals of assessment

The most obvious goal of a communication assessment for a young child is to determine whether a problem exists. Children who are suspected of having delays in communication development should be referred for a screening initially and, if deemed necessary, a comprehensive communication evaluation.[21] The box entitled "Checklist of Expected Communicative Behaviors" may be used as a guideline for early referral.[22]

Establishing a child's developmental level of communicative and language functioning helps determine whether a problem exists as well as the child's eligibility for services. This type of information in and of itself, however, provides minimal specific direction for intervention planning or for working with caregivers. In this discussion, we focus on goals and strategies of assessment that contribute most directly to intervention planning and the intervention process.

Checklist of Expected Communicative Behaviors*

EXPRESSIVE   RECEPTIVE

By 6 months

1. Vocalizes any sounds
2. Produces a range of vocalizations (eg, crying, cooing)
3. Produces various facial expressions

1. Turns toward voice
2. Startles at loud sounds
3. Can be comforted by caregiver's voice

By 12 months

1. Babbles with various consonantlike sounds (eg, ba-ba, ga-ga)
2. Takes turns vocalizing
3. Imitates vocalizations or gestures
4. Uses gestures and vocalizations purposefully to affect others' behavior

1. Ceases activity when told no
2. Can participate in familiar social games (eg, peek-a-boo)
3. Consistently locates source of sound in environment
4. Looks at or acts on objects mentioned by adult

By 18 months

1. Produces various sounds that may sound like words or short sentences
2. Uses various gestures and vocalizations to request objects and to direct attention
3. Produces a few meaningful words

1. Responds to his or her name
2. Responds to names of objects within sight
3. Responds to simple requests (eg, come here, sit down, stand up)

By 24 months

1. Uses at least 10 to 15 words meaningfully
2. Uses 2-word sentences meaningfully, including simple questions
3. Speech is present and at least 50% intelligible to caregivers

1. Responds consistently to many names of objects in immediate environment
2. Retrieves some objects out of sight upon request
3. Responds to two-step requests (eg, get the ball and bounce it)

By 36 months

1. Produces sentences of 3 to 5 words
2. Talks about past and future events
3. Asks questions with what, who, and where
4. Has vocabulary of 100 to 200 words
5. Speech is greater than 75% intelligible to caregivers

1. Responds to what, who, and where questions
2. Points to many different pictures in a book on request
3. Responds to questions or comments about objects/events outside immediate context
4. Shows interest in other persons' conversations

*Child should be referred for evaluation if most behaviors have not been observed by the specified age (based on direct observation or caregiver report).

Reprinted with permission from Prizant B, Wetherby A, Roberts J. Communication problems in infants and toddlers. In: Zeanah C. ed. *Handbook of Mental Health.* New York, NY: Guilford, in press. Copyright 1993, Guilford Publishers.

These goals include identifying the unique learning and communication style, strengths, and needs of the child; identifying functional intervention targets; and collaborating with caregivers on setting goals.

Principles of assessment

Communication and language assessment should be guided by a number of basic principles. These principles reflect the complexity and multidimensional nature of the process of communication. They also reflect the fact that communication is first and foremost a social activity that occurs in virtually all settings that a child encounters. Furthermore, communication and language development and the process of communication are highly transactional in nature, involving mutual influences between a child and persons and events in the child's life over time.[23,24] Finally, communication development is closely related to other aspects of development, including cognitive and socioemotional development. Thus, assessment should address these relationships. Principles of assessment are as follows.[25]

Principle 1: *Assessment involves gathering information about a child's communicative behavior across situational contexts over time; assessment is an ongoing process, not a one-time episodic event.* It has been well documented that a child's communicative abilities vary greatly as a function of many factors, including but not limited to the environment or setting in which a child is observed, the persons interacting with the child, and the familiarity of the situation to the child.[34] For example, a 10-month-old may use early communicative gestures at home with its mother to request continuation of a game of peek-a-boo but may not be observed to do so with strangers or in unfamiliar situations. A 14-month-old at emerging language levels may first use words during familiar routines in motivating and secure environments (eg, mealtime at home), but it may take a few months before those first words are used at mealtime in a day care setting. Thus, communication assessment should account for the normal variability observed in communicative functioning in young children across contexts. This is especially true for children with delays or identified disabilities because slower acquisition of communicative abilities as well as limited generalization may account for great variability across contexts.

Ideally, assessment involves gathering and coordinating information through questionnaires or interviews from persons who interact regularly with a child in different contexts. These may include direct care staff at a day care center, parents, educational staff in an integrated preschool setting, or speech-language pathologists. This requires that assessment be an ongoing process. A description of a child's communicative abilities and needs will not be completed until, and indeed may change significantly as, information from different sources is collected and integrated. Understanding a child's full range of communicative abilities across settings informs intervention efforts.

Principle 2: *A number of strategies should be used for collecting information.* To ascertain a child's communicative strengths and needs as well as to determine the learning opportunities available to the child, strategies such as direct assessment, naturalistic observation, and interviewing of significant others should be combined.[26] The use of various strategies reflects currently recognized best practices in early intervention for all assessment domains.[21,27]

Direct assessment involves professionals interacting directly with a child, typically with standardized instruments or checklists. It may also involve less structured play procedures to collect a language and communication sample for later analysis. When time for naturalistic observation is limited, specific sampling procedures or communicative temptations[28] may be used to entice child-initiated communication as a more efficient means of gathering information. Direct assessment may occur within a transdisciplinary practice model[29] or by means of interdisciplinary or multidisciplinary models. Naturalistic observation is characterized by nonintrusive data collection by observing or videotaping a child in relatively familiar life routines and activities while the child is interacting with familiar persons. Finally, information may be collected by interviewing significant others who have the opportunity to observe and interact with the child on a regular basis.[30]

It is important to recognize that each of these strategies has the potential to provide qualitatively different information about a child's communicative abilities that may ultimately be integrated to construct a more holistic picture of a child's communication system. Another positive feature of using different assessment strategies is that one may be more confident in assessment findings if similar communication patterns are observed across contexts.

Principle 3: *A number of tools or methods may be used in assessment and should be selected on the basis of a child's developmental level, the purpose of the assessment, and the assessment strategies used.* For example, a communication interview protocol or checklist focusing on developmental milestones may be used when one is interviewing caregivers or other familiar persons. Information provided may help determine developmental levels and provide direction for intervention. An observational checklist may be used during naturalistic observation or during direct assessment and also can provide information regarding communication status and intervention planning. Developmental checklists and standardized instruments focusing on communication milestones typically are used primarily for determining eligibility for services by delineating general developmental levels. Detailed listings and discussions of communication assessment instruments are available.[18,19]

Videotape analysis is a method that is being used increasingly for communication and language assessment. It is especially relevant for early communication assessment because subtle communicative behaviors including verbal, vocal, and nonverbal behaviors may need to be documented during a child's interactions with others. Other advantages of videotaping include the ability to observe a child's behavior in many contexts without actually being in those contexts, the ability to use videotapes with caregivers as an educational tool, and the ability to document progress over time. Clearly, the selection of assessment instruments and strategies will depend on time constraints, purposes of the assessment, and team philosophy and composition.

Principle 4: Communication assessment must account for conventional as well as unconventional communicative behavior. For some young children, the acquisition of conventional verbal or nonverbal means of communication is especially difficult or challenging. Because of the nature of their disability, some children may not follow expected developmental progressions and may acquire idiosyncratic and even socially unacceptable means to communicate their intentions. Idiosyncratic means may include subtle or difficult-to-read behaviors that can only be understood by those who know the child well. Such behavior has been documented in children with multiple disabilities[31] and in children with social-communicative disorders such as autism.[32] Socially unacceptable forms of communication including aggression and tantrums have been observed in children and adolescents with developmental disabilities.[33,34] Frameworks and instruments that document intentional but idiosyncratic or socially unacceptable forms of communication as well as conventional forms of communication are available and provide a more complete picture of a child's communication system.[28,35,36]

Principle 5: Parents or primary caregivers should be considered expert informants about their child's communicative competence. It is not uncommon for caregivers to report that they observe patterns or levels of communication in their young children that differ from those observed by professionals who conduct an assessment. Generally, this discrepancy is minimized when the assessment includes observations of the child during familiar routines in the home environment. As noted, communication abilities are naturally variable across contexts, and caregivers have opportunities to observe and interact with their child far more frequently in familiar and emotionally secure situations than professionals. Thus, caregivers are assumed to be most knowledgeable about their child's abilities, and professionals must refine their interviewing skills to elicit this vital information from caregivers.[30,37]

Principle 6: Developmental research on the sequence and processes of language and communication development should provide the framework for assessing a child's communicative abilities. Familiarity with sequences and processes of communication and language development is essential for a number of reasons. First, although individual differences exist in language acquisition, close to 30 years of research have documented relatively invariant sequences and stages of development[3] and thus can provide an organizational framework for documenting a child's abilities and progress in development.[13] Second, an intervention plan should be based on a child's current level of ability, with developmentally appropriate skills being targeted in setting short- and long-term goals. Of course, goal setting is greatly influenced by a child's functional needs and caregivers' priorities. Unless these factors are cast within a developmental framework, however, goals and expectations may be unrealistic and, in short term, would probably be unattainable. Third, knowledge of developmental sequences and processes enables professionals and caregivers to model language and communication in daily interactions to facilitate a child's communicative growth. Many caregiver-focused intervention programs provide information about processes and sequences in language and communication development as a first step in helping caregivers support their child's communicative growth.[38–40]

Principle 7: *Assessment should be linked directly to intervention.* Program planning should be based on ongoing assessment that documents changes in a child's communication and language behavior. Such documentation provides feedback in evaluating the effectiveness of approaches to enhance communicative competence. Alternative strategies and goals, when needed, can be developed in collaboration with caregivers to address a child's emerging communicative needs within the context of the child's developmental strengths and weaknesses. Additionally, caregivers' active involvement and participation in assessment activities may contribute significantly to their understanding of their child's communicative strengths and needs. Thus assessment may serve as a form of intervention. For example, caregivers may become more aware of their child's subtle or difficult-to-read communicative signals during the assessment process. As a result, they may implement interactive strategies that are conducive to sustaining social and communicative exchange, leading to more successful interactions that can enhance both the child's and the caregivers' sense of competence. Positive effects of caregiver observation and participation have been documented in early neurobehavioral assessment[41] and are now being advocated in early communication assessment.[42]

LIMITATIONS OF AVAILABLE INSTRUMENTS

Wetherby and Prizant[4] reviewed characteristics of instruments that address communicative and related abilities of young children that were reported to be used most frequently in graduate programs in speech-language pathology.[43] They noted that the instruments are characterized by a number of limitations. First, there tends to be a focus on communicative milestones and forms (eg, gestures and words) and limited attention to the functions or purposes of communication. Typically, minimal attention is given to the wide range of preverbal communicative strategies available to young children (eg, the range of conventional gestures). Second, some instruments rely solely on either caregiver report or direct assessment of a child. Caregiver report is invaluable, but a small minority of caregivers may have difficulty judging their children's competence (eg, adolescent or cognitively impaired caregivers). On the other hand, when direct assessment is used, a child is typically placed in a respondent role (eg, responding to commands or being required to name objects) with little opportunity to be observed in more natural reciprocal interactions. Third, a child's use of social-affective signals (eg, communicative gaze and expressions of positive and negative affect), which play an important role in regulating communicative interactions, are rarely considered an aspect of communicative competence. Finally, the instruments most typically provide developmental ages or quotients rather than a profile of a child's relative strengths and weaknesses.

An alternative to relying solely on formal instruments is to utilize various strategies (eg, caregiver interview, direct child-centered assessment, and ongoing naturalistic observation) that result in a profile of a child's developmental strengths and needs across a number of domains.[4,42]

DOMAINS OF ASSESSMENT

As noted, language and communication assessment traditionally has focused on a child's behavior with an emphasis on the sophistication of communicative means or forms (eg, gestures, sounds, words, and multiword utterances) and level of comprehension of speech.[43] With expanding views of communication development, child-focused assessment is now considered only one dimension of a comprehensive communication assessment. Current best practice recognizes that communication and communication development are transactional processes, demanding that a child's typical interactions with communicative partners and the quality of learning environments be addressed.[24,44] Thus a comprehensive communication assessment needs to address child abilities in communicative interactions and to identify aspects of communicative partner behavior that support or limit successful communicative exchange. Additionally, qualities of learning environments that support or restrict communicative growth need to be identified.

ASSESSMENT OF CHILD ABILITIES

An assessment framework delineates specific content areas or domains of a child's communicative behavior and related abilities that are to be assessed and that, when considered in total, provide a portrait of a child's communicative strengths and needs. Some information may be developmental in nature (eg, level of a child's linguistic comprehension or understanding); other information may be more qualitative (eg, use of nonverbal signals such as communicative gaze and affective expressions to regulate interactions). The Communication and Symbolic

Behavior Scales (CSBS)[28] represent one example of an instrument that measures both development and quality aspects of preverbal and early linguistic communication and related abilities of young children. The CSBS was standardized on a normative sample of 350 8- to 24-month-old children. On the basis of analyses of communication and play behavior in semistructured and relatively unstructured play contexts, a child's behavior is analyzed and rated on 22 scales. Analyses result in composite scores in the domains of communicative function, gestural and vocal communicative means, reciprocity, social-affective signaling, and verbal and nonverbal symbolic behavior. Information about the representatives of the assessment is obtained through a detailed caregiver interview and a caregiver perception rating, which are completed before and after the direct assessment, respectively. These results yield a profile of relative strengths and weaknesses for intervention planning (see the box, "Assessment Domains in the CSBS"). In its current form, the CSBS is most useful for intervention planning. A simplified scoring version is under development to accommodate clinicians with significant time constraints. Additionally, a future screening version will be designed primarily for early identification.

A more generic framework delineating specific content areas in assessment of communication and related abilities is presented in the box entitled "Framework for Early Communication and Language Assessment." The specific type of information provided in each area can be obtained through formal and/or informal procedures. Approaches will vary according to a child's developmental level of communicative functioning. The major domains include the following.

Expressive language and communication

The primary focus in this domain is documentation of communicative means, or the behaviors by which information is communicated; and communicative functions, or the purposes for which a child communicates.[43] For developmentally young, preintentional children, communicative means may include nonverbal and vocal behaviors such as body posture, facial expression, limb extension, hand gestures, directed gaze and gaze aversion, cry and cooing vocalizations, and intonated vowel and/or babbling vocalizations. These signals may function to inform a receiver of the child's physiologic and emotional state, level of alertness, focus of attention, interest in interacting with or receiving comfort from other persons, interest in obtaining objects, or desire to have events continue or cease. A framework for analyzing communicative functions expressed by young children,[28] based on the work of Bruner,[45] is presented in the box entitled "Early Communicative Functions."

Although a young child may not produce signals with the intention of affecting other persons' behavior in specific ways, it has been documented repeatedly that

Assessment Domains in the CSBS

COMMUNICATIVE FUNCTIONS

1. **Behavioral Regulation**—communicative acts used to regulate behavior of another person to obtain or restrict an environmental goal.
2. **Joint Attention**—communicative acts used to direct another's attention to an object, event, or a topic of a communicative act.
3. **Sociability of Functions**—proportion of communicative acts used for social interaction plus joint attention.

COMMUNICATIVE MEANS—
GESTURAL

4. **Conventional Gestures**—gestural communicative acts including giving, showing, pushing away, open-hand reaching, pointing, waving, nodding head, and shaking head.
5. **Distal Gestures**—gestural communicative acts in which the child's hand does not touch a person or object (eg, open-hand reaching, pointing at a distance, waving).
6. **Coordination of Gesture and Vocal Acts**—communicative acts that are composed of a gesture and a vocalization.

COMMUNICATIVE MEANS—
VOCAL

7. **Vocal Acts without Gestures**—vowels or vowel-plus-consonant combinations that are used as a communicative act and are not accompanied by a gesture.
8. **Inventory of Different Consonants**—the total number of different consonants produced as part of communicative acts.
9. **Syllables with Consonants**—vocal communicative acts that are transcribable vowel–plus–consonant combinations.
10. **Multisyllables**—vocal communicative acts that contain two or more syllables.

RECIPROCITY

11. **Respondent Acts**—communicative acts that are in response to adults' conventional gestures or speech.
12. **Rate**—the frequency of communicative acts displayed per minute.
13. **Repair Strategies**—repetitions or modifications of a previous communicative act produced when a goal is not achieved.

SOCIAL/AFFECTIVE SIGNALING

14. **Gaze Shifts**—alternating eye gaze between a person and an object and back (eg, person-object-person or object-person-object).
15. **Shared Positive Affect**—clear facial expressions of pleasure or excitement.
16. **Episodes of Negative Affect**—clear vocal expressions of distress or frustration.

VERBAL SYMBOLIC BEHAVIOR

17. **Inventory of Different Words**—the total number of different words used (ie, spoken or signed) in communicative acts.
18. **Inventory of Different Word Combinations**—the total number of different multiword combinations produced in communicative acts.
19. **Language Comprehension**—a measure of comprehension of contextual cues, single words, and multiword utterances.

NONVERBAL SYMBOLIC BEHAVIOR

20. **Inventory of Different Action Schemes**—the total number of different action schemes (eg, brushing and feeding) used with objects in symbolic play.
21. **Complexity of Action Schemes**—the child's use of action schemes with objects toward self or other agents and sequencing of different action schemes in pretend play.
22. **Constructive Play**—a measure of the child's ability to use objects in combination to construct a product (eg, a tower).

Reprinted with permission from Wetherby AM, Prizant BM. *Communication and Symbolic Behavior Scales.* Chicago, Ill: Riverside Publishers; 1993. Copyright 1993, Riverside Publishers.

Framework for Early Communication and Language Assessment

I. *Expressive language and communication*
   A. Communicative means (ie, gestural, vocal, verbal, other)
   B. Communicative functions
   C. Semantic complexity of language and range of vocabulary (if present)
   D. Morphologic and syntactic complexity of language (if present)
   E. Reciprocity in communication (ie, responsivity, rate of communicative acts, persistence, repair)

II. *Receptive language and communication*
   A. Orientation to sound and speech
   B. Nonlinguistic response strategies
   C. Linguistic comprehension

III. *Speech production*
   A. Quality of vocal production
   B. Quality of speech production
   C. Oral structure and oral-motor and speech function

IV. *Language-related cognitive abilities*
   A. Symbolic play and object exploration
   B. Constructive play
   C. Attentional capacities
   D. Imitation

V. *Social-affective behavior*
   A. Use of gaze for social referencing
   B. Expression of positive affect
   C. Expression of negative affect

---

caregivers respond to such signals as if they were intentional.[36,44] The process by which caregivers assign or impute intent to early communicative signals is considered important in fostering communicative development.[45]

For developmentally more advanced children who communicate through prelinguistic means, intentional use of idiosyncratic and conventional gestures as well as vocalizations and emerging word forms (if observed) should be documented. For children who are using language-based systems, including speech, sign language, or graphic systems (eg, communication boards), several parameters should be documented: range of vocabulary, semantic and syntactic complexity, and communicative functions. Range of vocabulary refers to the number of different words and word classes (eg, object words, action words, and modifiers or descriptors) that children use meaningfully. Semantic complexity refers to the types of semantic functions or meaning categories expressed in language-based systems. Syntactic complexity refers to the structural or grammatic complexity of multiword forms for children beyond early language stages. In all cases noted above, communicative functions should continue to be assessed. In addition, the

Early Communicative Functions

Behavioral Regulation
Request objects/actions
Protest

Social Interaction
Request social routine
Request comfort
Call
Greet
Show off
Request permission

Joint Attention
Comment
Request information
Provide information

Reprinted with permission from Wetherby AM, Prizant BM. *Communication and Symbolic Behavior Scales* (Standardized Edition). Chicago: Riverside Publishers; 1993. Copyright 1993, Riverside Publishers.

rate of communicative acts and a child's ability to persist in repairing communication breakdowns should also be documented.

Receptive language and communication

A child's ability to receive and respond to others' communicative signals is the second domain that should be addressed in assessment. Initially, an audiologic screening and, if deemed necessary, a full audiologic assessment relevant to the child's chronologic age and developmental level should be conducted by an audiologist to assess hearing status.[46] Informal behavioral observation of young children may also contribute information about a child's functional hearing. Relevant observations include whether a child shows any startle response to loud environmental sounds, localizes or orients to speech or environmental sounds, or can be soothed or comforted by a caregiver's voice. Preverbal children's ability to approximate sounds or intonation patterns in imitation also provides additional informal evidence of receptive status.

At higher levels of ability, children are able to respond to communicative gestures and vocalizations of others, and with the support of situational cues they demonstrate comprehension of words used in highly routinized and familiar activities. Chapman[47] has identified such nonlinguistic response strategies in young children, which can be observed from about 8 months of age. True linguistic comprehension is evidenced when children can comprehend words without situational or nonverbal cues, especially when words refer to persons, objects, and events outside the immediate environment. A child's ability to comprehend more complex utterances with a wider range of vocabulary referring to spatially and temporally distant events is assessed for developmentally more advanced children.

Speech production

Many young at-risk children or children with developmental disabilities may have difficulties in acquiring and using speech as a primary mode of communication. This may be due to severe cognitive impairment or severe to profound hearing loss. It may also be due to specific neuromotor speech disorders, including dysarthria, which is a paralysis or paresis (ie, weakness) in the oral musculature often observed in children with cerebral palsy or other identified neurologic disorders; and developmental dyspraxia, a dysfunction in the ability to plan the coordinated movements to produce intelligible sequences of speech sounds. Dysarthria and apraxia may co-occur in young children and may range from conditions mildly affecting speech intelligibility to severe conditions rendering speech unintelligible or precluding speech development. When there are concerns regarding the integrity of oral motor functioning, assessment should address the status of speech and vocal production to determine whether introduction of an augmentative nonspeech mode of communication may be beneficial.

Factors that should be considered when one is evaluating the potential for speech as a primary mode include (1) the child's ability to produce various sounds or to produce imitative approximations of words with various speech sounds, (2) the child's current level of intelligibility in spontaneous speech (if present), (3) past or recent history or problems in chewing or swallowing, (4) presence of abnormal reflexive patterns (eg, hyperactive gag reflex), (5) ability to produce controlled and differentiated oral-motor movements (eg, movements of the jaw, tongue, and lips), and (6) interest in speech and motivation to use speech. A complete oral function assessment should be conducted by a qualified speech-language pathologist and/or occupational therapist, but informal observations about vocal control for speech, patterns of chewing and swallowing, and other indicators of oral motor function are useful in making decisions about the need for nonspeech systems.

Language-related cognitive abilities

For a number of reasons, communication and language abilities should always be considered in the context of a child's cognitive abilities. First, communication and language development correlate strongly with aspects of cognitive development, including symbolic play development and understanding of cause-effect relations.[3] By profiling a young child's communicative abilities relative to nonverbal cognitive abilities and capacities, information is obtained about the nature of a communication or language delay. For example, a child with age-appropriate symbolic play and limited expressive language development may be showing evidence of a more specific expressive language delay not due primarily to a cognitive impairment. Such information has great implications for intervention planning. When one is interpreting more general measures of cognitive functioning for young children with language impairments, it is always important to consider the extent to which the assessment relies on the child's following verbal directions or responding verbally so that potential confounding effects of the language disability can be ruled out.

Second, communication is the means by which children express their knowledge and understanding of other persons and events in their world. Thus, language use reflects and is dependent upon a child's world knowledge.

Finally, as noted above, the choice of augmentative communication systems, which may be influenced by levels of cognitive/representational ability, requires some estimation of cognitive abilities. Guidelines for assessing language-related cognitive abilities in young children are available.[29,48,49]

Social-affective behavior

Communicative interactions are regulated, to a great extent, by social-affective signals. These signals include facial expression, vocalizations, and other observable behaviors reflecting attentional, emotional, and physiologic states. Young children also use gaze socially to reference or monitor the attention of others and to signal attention to others. Some children with social and communicative impairments may demonstrate limited use of gaze shifts to regulate interactions, and their emotional states may be difficult to read because of limited range of affective expression.[42] Because these signals influence communicative interactions, communication assessment should incorporate social-affective signals. The domain of assessment is especially crucial for infants and developmentally young children who may demonstrate limited intentionality or conventionality in their communicative signaling.

ASSESSING THE BEHAVIOR AND ABILITIES OF COMMUNICATIVE PARTNERS

Communicative partners include parents, other caregivers, educators, therapists, and others who interact with a child on a regular basis. Partners demonstrate a wide range of strategies and behaviors that may serve to support and facilitate a child's communicative growth or, in some cases, may hinder communicative transactions and possibly constrain growth. In extreme cases, some partners may develop maladaptive interactive styles that are thought to be detrimental to a child's communicative and socioemotional development.[50] For young children, primary caregivers' style and the degree of match or mismatch with the child's abilities are of primary importance.

The strengths and weaknesses of various communicative partners in supporting communicative interactions may be observed and documented during observations of familiar daily living and play activities. Dimensions of partner style that are relevant include degree of acceptance or rejection of a child's communicative attempts,[51] use of directive or facilitative styles of interaction,[51,52] and use of specific interactive strategies such as responding contingently to the child's behavior, providing developmentally appropriate communicative models, maintaining the topic of the child's initiations, and expanding or elaborating on communicative attempts.[51,53] The primary purposes of assessing partner style are to help partners develop an awareness of strategies that they are using that appear to facilitate successful and positive interactions and to help them recognize and modify interactive styles that may limit successful communicative exchange. There is no optimal or correct communicative style for all children. Factors such as the child's developmental level, extent of disability, attentional capacities, and social motivation must be taken into account. A partner's level of comfort in using a particular style and cultural influences on interactions with young children must also be considered.

The match between a partner's style and a child's ability to participate actively and successfully is of overriding concern.[38] A successful match is predicated on a partner's sensitivity to a child's communicative signals and the child's ability to respond to the partner's interactive and communicative overtures. Use of a more directive style may help keep some children focused and participating actively, whereas this same style may hinder successful communication for other children. When interactive matches are successful, the result is a sense of efficacy for both the child and the partner.[4] This mutual sense of efficacy has great implications for the emotional well being of the child, the caregivers, and their relationship. Literature on approaches and strategies for assessing different dimensions of the partner–child interaction is available.[38,51,53–55]

ASSESSMENT OF LEARNING CONTEXTS

In addition to the interactive factors noted above, other situational or contextual factors play an important role in communication development and therefore should be considered in any assessment.[53] These include the degree to which the following characteristics are present: joint activity routines (JARs), needs to communicate for assistance, and opportunities for choice making and protesting.

JARs[56] or social routines[57] are predictable and repetitive activities requiring active involvement, reciprocal and exchangeable roles, a mutual focus of attention, turn taking, and communicative exchange focused on a common theme or end goal. JARs may be as simple in structure as early mother–child social games such as peek-a-boo or songs or as complex as the social games that may be observed in preschool settings. JARs allow young children to participate and communicate actively, with the necessary contextual and interactive support allowing for the greatest degree of participation. Thus, the identification of JARs in children's daily experiences is indicative of opportunities for communicative growth.

Children also must have needs to communicate to obtain assistance or desired objects as well as opportunities to reject or protest in socially acceptable ways.[43,53] It is from these experiences that children learn to communicate for a wide range of communicative functions or purposes.[58] Finally, opportunities for decision making and choice making have been associated with higher degrees of communicative initiation and spontaneity in older children with disabilities.[59,60] Such opportunities for social control are now considered important characteristics of environments that support communicative growth for young children.[61] Thus, opportunities for successful communicative interactions and communicative and language growth, as indicated by the specific characteristics noted above, should be documented in assessment to help determine whether any environmental adaptations or modifications should be made as part of an intervention plan.

PRIORITIZING COMMUNICATIVE NEEDS

A child's communicative needs can be prioritized by interviewing caregivers and by observing the child in everyday situations. Caregivers can be asked to identify the communicative skills that they feel would be most helpful to their child and to the family. Specific information to help prioritize needs may include situations in which a child is most frustrated by limitations in communication and situations in which a child cannot participate fully because of communicative problems. Caregivers may also be asked to identify their own concerns or needs relative to supporting their child's communicative development. Goals for helping caregivers feel more competent as communicative partners may be incorporated into broader intervention efforts.

FROM ASSESSMENT TO INTERVENTION

Once a child's profile of communicative strengths and needs has been documented and caregiver priorities and needs have been determined, an intervention plan and specific goals and strategies for communication enhancement may be derived with caregivers. Goals should address the specific communicative means and functions to be targeted and modifications in partner behavior and social-communicative contexts that would be most facilitative of communication development. As with assessment, caregivers ideally play an active and significant role in communication enhancement efforts. Such efforts may take place within regularly occurring caregiving and play routines within the family context in addition to services provided by professionals.

•   •   •

In summary, communication and language assessment for young children involves a team effort among caregivers, family members, and various professionals. The ultimate goals of assessment are to provide a profile of a child's strengths and needs and to determine any modifications in interactive styles and in learning environments that may be necessary for optimal communicative growth. A comprehensive assessment is essential in helping caregivers and professionals develop a better understanding of a child's strengths and needs and in providing specific direction for communication enhancement efforts. To these ends, it is important that early childhood professionals view communication in the broad sense of nonverbal and socioemotional communication, not merely verbal abilities, and refer early when there are concerns about development. When assessment reveals problems in language and/or communication development, communication enhancement efforts should receive high priority because of the developmental interdependence between communication and language development and social, emotional, and cognitive aspects of a young child's development.

REFERENCES

1. Prizant B, Wetherby A. Toward an integrated view of early language and communication development and socioemotional development. *Top Lang Disord.* 1990;10:1–16.

2. Prizant BM, Meyer EC. Socioemotional aspects of communication disorders in young children. *Am J Speech Lang Pathol.* In press.

3. Bates E, O'Connell B, Shore C. Language and communication in infancy. In: Osofsky J, ed. *Handbook of Infant Development* (2nd ed). New York, NY: Wiley; 1987.

4. Wetherby A, Prizant B. Profiling young children's communicative competence. In: Warren S, Reichle J, eds. *Causes and Effects in Communication Disorders.* Baltimore, Md: Brookes; 1992.

5. Gottlieb M. The response of families to language disorders in the young child. *Semin Speech Lang.* 1988;9:47–53.

6. Paul R. Language delay and parental perceptions. *J Am Acad Child Adolesc Psychiatr.* 1991;29:669–690.

7. Bristol M, Schopler E. A developmental perspective on stress and coping in families of autistic children. In: Blacher J, ed. *Families of Severely Handicapped Children.* New York, NY: Academic Press; 1984.

8. Aram D, Hall N. Longitudinal follow-up of preschool communication disorders: Treatment implications. *School Psychol Rev.* 1989;18:487–501.

9. Prizant B, Audet L, Burke G, Hummel I, Maher S, Theadore G. Communication disorders and emotional/behavioral disorders in children. *J Speech Hear Disord.* 1990;55:179–192.

10. Stevenson J, Richman N. The prevalence of language delay in a population of three-year-old children and its association with general retardation. *Dev Med Child Neurol.* 1976;18:431–441.

11. Baker L, Cantwell D. A prospective psychiatric follow-up of children with speech/language disorders. *J Am Acad Child Aolesc Psychiatr.* 1987;26:546–553.

12. Guralnick M, Bennett F. *The Effectiveness of Early Intervention for at-risk and Handicapped Children.* New York, NY: Academic Press; 1987.

13. Lahey M. *Language Disorders and Language Development.* New York, NY: Macmillan; 1988.

14. Lund N, Duchan J. *Assessing Children's Language in Naturalistic Contexts* (3rd ed). Englewood Cliffs, NJ: Prentice-Hall; 1993.

15. Olswang, L, Coggins T, Carpenter R, Stoel-Gammon C. *Assessing Linguistic Behaviors in Young Children.* Seattle, WA: University of Washington Press; 1987.

16. Paul R. Assessing communication skills in toddlers. *Clin Commun Disord.* In press.

17. Richard N, Schiefelbusch R. Assessment. In: McCormick L, Schiefelbusch R, eds. *Early Language Intervention.* Columbus, Ohio: Merrill; 1990.

18. Roberts J, Crais E. Assessing communication skills. In: Bailey D, Wolery M, eds. *Assessing Infants and Children with Handicaps.* Columbus, Ohio: Merrill; 1989.

19. Rossetti L. *Infant-toddler Assessment: An Integrative Approach.* Boston, Mass: College-Hill; 1990.

20. Schuler A. *Assessing Communicative Competence.* New York, NY: Thieme-Stratton; 1989.

21. Meisels S, Provence S. *Screening and Assessment: Guidelines for Identifying Young Disabled and Developmentally Vulnerable Children and Their Families.* Washington, DC: National Center for Clinical Infant Programs; 1989.

22. Prizant B, Wetherby A, Roberts J. Communication disorders in infants and toddlers. In: Zeanah C, ed. *Handbook of Infant Mental Health.* New York, NY: Guilford. In press.

23. Sameroff A. The social context of development. In: Eisenburg N, ed. *Contemporary Topics in Development.* New York, NY: Wiley; 1987.

24. Sameroff A, Fiese B. Transactional regulation and early intervention. In: Meisels S, Shonkoff J, eds. *Handbook of Early Childhood Intervention.* Cambridge, Mass: Cambridge University Press; 1990.

25. Prizant B, Bailey D. Facilitating the development of communication skills. In: Bailey D, Wolery M, eds. *Teaching Infants and Preschoolers with Handicaps.* Columbus, Ohio: Merrill; 1992.

26. Prizant B, Wetherby A. International communicative behavior of children with autism: theoretical and practical issues. *Aust J Hum Commun Disord.* 1985;13:21–59.

27. Neisworth J, Bagnato S. Assessment in early childhood special education: a typology of dependent measures. In: Odom S, Karnes M, eds. *Early Intervention for Infants and Children with Handicaps: An Empirical Base.* Baltimore, Md: Brookes; 1988.

28. Wetherby A, Prizant B. *Communication and Symbolic Behavior Scales.* Chicago, Ill: Riverside; 1993.

29. Linder T. *Transdisciplinary Play-Based Assessment.* Baltimore, Md: Brookes; 1990.

30. Schuler A, Peck C, Willard C, Theimer K. Assessment of communicative means and functions through interview: assessing the communicative capabilities of individuals with limited language. *Semin Speech Lang.* 1989;10:51–61.

31. Yoder P. Relationship between degree of infant handicap and clarity of infant cues. *Am J Ment Defic.* 1987;91;639–641.

32. Prizant B, Wetherby A. Communicative intent: a framework for understanding social-communicative behavior in autism. *J Am Acad Child Adolesc Psychiatr.* 1987;26:472–479.

33. Carr E, Durand V. The social communicative basis of severe behavior problems in children. In: Reiss S, Bootzin R, eds. *Theoretical Issues in Behavior Therapy.* New York, NY: Academic Press; 1985.

34. Wetherby A, Prutting C. Profiles of communicative and cognitive-social abilities in autistic children. *J Speech Hear Disord.* 1984;27:364–377.

35. Donnellan A, Mirenda P, Mesaros R, Fassbender L. Analyzing the communicative functions of aberrant behavior. *J Assoc Persons Severe Handicaps.* 1984;9:201–212.

36. Wetherby A, Prizant B. The expression of communicative intent: assessment guidelines. *Semin Speech Lang.* 1989;10:77–91.

37. Winton P. Effective communication between parents and professionals. In: Bailey D, Simeonsson R, eds. *Family Assessment in Early Intervention.* Columbus, Ohio: Merrill; 1988.

38. MacDonald J. *Becoming Partners with Children.* San Antonio, Tex: Special Press; 1989.

39. Mahoney G. Enhancing the developmental competence of handicapped infants. In: Marfo K, ed. *Parent–Child Interaction and Developmental Disabilities.* New York, NY: Praeger; 1988.

40. Manolson A. *It Takes Two To Talk* (2nd ed). Toronto, Ontario: Hanen Early Language Resource Center; 1992.

41. Brazelton B, Cramer B. *The Earliest Relationship.* New York, NY: Addison-Wesley; 1990.

42. Prizant B, Wetherby A. Assessing the communication of infants and toddlers: integrating a socioemotional perspective. *Zero Three.* 1990;11:1–12.

43. Prizant B, Schuler A. Facilitating communication: theoretical foundations. In: Cohen D, Donnellan A, eds. *Handbook of Autism and Pervasive Developmental Disorders.* New York, NY: Wiley; 1987.

44. McLean LS. Communication development in the first two years of life: a transactional process. *Zero Three.* 1990;11:13–19.

45. Bruner J. The social context of language acquisition. *Lang Commun.* 1981;1:155–178.

46. Roush J. Early intervention: expanding the audiologist's role. *ASHA.* 1991;33:47–49.

47. Chapman R. Comprehension strategies in children. In: Kavanagh J, Strange W, eds. *Speech and Language in the Laboratory, School and Clinic.* Cambridge, Mass: MIT Press; 1979.

48. Casby M. Symbolic play: development and assessment considerations. *Infants Young Child.* 1992;4:43–48.

49. Westby C. Children's play: reflections of social competence. *Semin Speech Lang.* 1988;9:1–13.

50. Field T. Affective and interactive disturbances in infants. In: Osofsky J, ed. *Handbook of Infant Development* (2nd ed). New York, NY: Wiley; 1987.

51. Duchan J. Evaluating adults' talk to children: assessing adult attunement. *Semin Speech Lang.* 1989:10:17–27.

52. Marfo K. Maternal directiveness in interactions with mentally handicapped children: an analytical commentary. *J Child Psychol Psychiatr.* 1990;31:531–549.

53. Peck C. Assessment of social communicative competence: evaluating environments. *Semin Speech Lang.* 1989;10:1–15.

54. Comfort M. Assessing parent–child interaction. In: Bailey D, Simeonsson R, eds. *Family Assessment in Early Intervention.* Columbus, Ohio: Merrill; 1988.

55. Clark G, Seifer R. Assessment of parents' interactions with their developmentally delayed infants. *Infant Ment Health J.* 1985;6:214–225.

56. Snyder-McLean L, Solomonson B, McLean J, Sack S. Structuring joint action routines: a strategy for facilitating communication and language development in the classroom. *Semin Speech Lang.* 1984;5:213–228.

57. McCormick L. Sequence of language and communication development.. In: McCormick L, Schiefelbusch R, eds. *Early Language Intervention.* Columbus, Ohio: Merrill; 1990.

58. Prizant B, Wetherby A. Providing services to children with autism (0–2 years) and their families. *Top Lang Disord.* 1988;9:1–13.

59. Peck C. Increasing opportunities for social control by children with autism and severe handicaps. *J Assoc Persons Severe Handicaps.* 1985;10:1–15.

60. Houghton J, Bronicki G, Guess D. Opportunities to express preferences and make choices among students with severe disabilities in classroom settings. *J Assoc Persons Severe Handicaps.* 1987;12:18–27.

61. Theadore G, Maher S, Prizant, B. Early assessment and intervention with emotional and behavioral disorders and communication disorders. *Top Lang Disord.* 1990;10:42–56.

Assessing infant interaction skills in interaction-focused intervention

Lydia A. Aydlett, PhD
Research Fellow
Frank Porter Graham Child
    Development Center
University of North Carolina at
    Chapel Hill
Chapel Hill, North Carolina

THE FIELD OF early intervention is in a state of flux. Considerable controversy surrounds a growing movement away from the traditional structured, clinician-controlled, lessonlike processes to a more naturalistic, interaction-focused intervention.[1] Two lines of reasoning propel this transition. First, at a theoretical level, the highest quality of life for children of any level of functioning and their caregivers is obtained when children are able to interact adaptively. The more children are able to accommodate the social customs and conventions of family and community life, the more gratifying their presence to those around them. Furthermore, for children to obtain satisfying relationships with others, they must be able to communicate their needs, satisfactions, and dissatisfactions effectively. These abilities originate in the give and take of early reciprocal interactions and depend upon the appropriateness of those interactions for their optimal expression.

Second, at a practical level, the current movement toward a full inclusion of children with disabilities into regular early childhood settings requires the reconciliation of two educational traditions. Many early childhood special education and early intervention programs have emphasized didactic and behavioral techniques and the creation of programs with discrete goals and activities.[2] In contrast, contemporary models of infant and early child development emphasize children's active engagement in their environment. The key to optimal development is the quality and quantity of interactions that children experience while actively engaged.[3] Considerable empiric support is accumulating for the effectiveness of child-oriented, interactively responsive methods with infants and young children who have developmental disabilities.[3]

As in all intervention efforts, assessment is the starting point in providing interaction-focused intervention to handicapped or at-risk infants and toddlers.[4] This article addresses measures currently used to assess mother–infant dyadic interaction and measures that assess infant skills in this interaction context. Problems with using the mother–infant interaction context as the sole means of assessing infant interaction skills are outlined, and multimethod assessment, including observations of infant social behavior during clinician–infant interaction, is proposed. Finally, currently available techniques for assessing infant interactive be-

The author would like to thank Kris Huntington, Robin McWilliam, and Barbara Goldman for their assistance with this manuscript.

Inf Young Children 1993; 5(4): 1–7
© 1993 Aspen Publishers, Inc.

havior are discussed, and conclusions are drawn about the most appropriate skills to assess during infancy and their utility in the intervention context.

ASSESSING MOTHER–INFANT INTERACTION

Historically, observations of mother–infant interaction have been used to infer interaction skills in infants. Many mother–infant interaction scales have been developed, the majority being created to answer specific research questions. Recent reviews of these scales[5,6] indicate that most focus on the mother's contribution to the dyadic interaction, especially the degree to which she is sensitive and responsive. For example, the Parent/Caregiver Involvement Scale[7] is useful for assessing caregiver behavior, particularly in families with young, high-risk, or disabled children. The scale has been used with both biologically impaired and environmentally at-risk children (training materials are available from the authors). Although the scale measures the appropriateness of the mother's behavior to the child's development and interest, it does not directly assess the child's contribution to the interaction. Yet, parental behavior changes as a result of stimulation and reinforcement from the child.[8]

Several scales have included the assessment of infants' abilities to interact and communicate with their mothers. These scales vary in the setting for interaction, the degree to which the mother's behavior is evaluated, and the child behaviors deemed significant. Some of the infant behaviors assessed in this context are also assessed in clinician–infant interaction. As a rule, however, the assessment of infant skills during mother–infant interaction is limited. For example, the NCAST Teaching and Feeding Scales measure the contingent, reciprocal nature of caregiver–child interactions by observations during unstructured feeding or semistructured play.[9] The infant behaviors coded by this instrument fall into two categories: the clarity of infant cues (eg, the modulation of emotional states, the coordination of infant gaze with other behaviors, and the appearance of infant engagement and disengagement), and the infant's responsiveness to the parent (eg, positive and negative responses to the parent's actions).

A scale initially developed for use with infants who have Down syndrome has been used with other populations of handicapped infants.[10] This scale measures infant play maturity, social and object initiative, interest, affect, and social responsivity. Crawley and Spiker[10] have demonstrated relationships between infant development and social behavior and between infant social behavior and maternal behavior.

Dunst and Lowe[11] and Holdgrafer and Dunst[12] have focused on the manner in which children's early social interactions lead to the acquisition of formal language production. Their model of infant expressive communication development is derived from 20-minute observations of low-structured mother–infant interactions. This scale focuses on identifying the level of the child's expressive communication. At each of the identified seven communication levels, behavior state, recognitory, contingency, instrumental, triadic, verbal-contextual, and verbal-decontextual, the infant's ability to engage and terminate social interactions with his or her caregiver is observed and classified. For these investigators, engagement and termination behaviors are fundamental to interaction, and the methods that children use change in form with age and ability. The authors consider information from this scale appropriate for determining a child's needs and goals for intervention.[12]

Is the mother–infant context enough?

Typically, mother–infant exchanges are the most familiar interactive contexts available to the infant. Customary practice emphasizes observing mother–infant interaction to provide an accurate picture of infant interactive skills. If assessment is ultimately to provide information about the infant's status and his or her needs for intervention, however, the infant's interactive abilities must be determined. Even when observations are made of infant reciprocity, the skills of the infant cannot be determined wholly on the basis of the effectiveness of the mother–infant interchange. This is true in part because mothers support and structure infants' interactive behaviors[13] and in part because mothers' behaviors are dependent upon infants' behaviors both for timing and for content.[14] Adept mothers have been observed to keep their low-functioning infants engaged and responsive by carefully working within the infants' capacities. Depressed mothers give their infants few responses and little support for their social behaviors. Consequently, their infants function routinely at a lower level than their peers.[15] The support that mothers provide for infants' interactions, and the mothers' dependence upon infant cues for their own responses, complicate efforts to obtain a clearer, less confounded picture of infants' interactive capacities. By assessing the infant in varied contexts, for example with both a caregiver and with the clinician, we can clarify the contribution of the infant to interchanges.

An alternative approach

If infant behavior during mother–infant interaction is viewed as one set of social and communicative behaviors, and if infant behaviors during clinician–infant interaction are viewed as a complementary set, these two forms of assessment each provide information to the clinician that is necessary for a more comprehensive understanding of the infant's ability to engage in social interactions. The set of infant social behaviors observed when the infant interacts with a familiar caretaker may vary in the degree to which it overlaps with the set of infant social behaviors observed when the infant is interacting with a clinician. The extent of overlap in the two behavioral sets is dependent upon the infant's developmental status, the similarity of the two interactive contexts, the degree of infant disability, the measures used, and the extent to which the infant's partners are similar in obtaining and maintaining the infant's engagement and reciprocity. The degree of dissimilarity between the two sets of infant behaviors indicates a potential range of social behaviors and the infant's response to the interactive challenge of a new partner.

ASSESSING CLINICIAN–INFANT INTERACTION

Procedures for assessing the child's social and communicative competence outside the mother–infant interaction context are in the formative stage of development. There is no single instrument that can be recommended as a comprehensive assessment of interactive skills in infants and young children at this time. The few techniques that are available vary as to the age for which they are appropriate, the formality or informality of the assessment process, and the methods used to obtain a sample of the child's behavior. Therefore, it behooves the practitioner to review the methods available and glean procedures from them that yield *functional* information. Such information should not be used to classify children or to assume an underlying dimension of social competence. The psychometric soundness of these instruments has not been thoroughly tested, in part because traditional methods may not be appropriate. The instruments discussed here do not result in an overall score representing an underlying concept. Instead, they offer samples of behavior in various dimensions of interaction. Each assessment must be evaluated on the basis of its utility in an intervention setting. Does it tell you what you want to know? Is an assessment functional in providing information for enhancing children's social interactions?

To assist the practitioner in exploring infant social skills, a review of noteworthy infant behaviors found on various instruments is now presented. Although the exact level of a child's social and communicative development cannot be determined in this way, the purpose of such an assessment is to develop sufficient understanding to enhance the infant's interactive skills, relationships, and overall development.

The following instruments address infant interaction, communication, and/or social skills and offer guides to meaningful behavior. Two instruments that rate characteristic infant behavior patterns are the Infant Behavior Record[16] and the Carolina Record of Individual Behavior.[17] These are most often used in observing the infant during developmental assessments or other adult–infant interactions, including clinician–infant interactions. Infant social behaviors that are rated include responsiveness to persons (mother and examiner), expressive and receptive communication, cooperativeness, fearfulness, consolability, reactivity, and endurance.

The Neonatal Behavioral Assessment Scale (NBAS),[19] first published almost 20 years ago, was intended as a global assessment of the newborn's autonomic, motor, state, and social attention systems. It is an interactive assessment with the adult/clinician facilitating the infant's performance. The information gained ideally reflects the infant's capacities and limits in contributing to the caregiving environment.[19] Brazelton[18] believes that the infant's state of arousal is a tool for signaling a state of engagement or disengagement. The infant signals engagement by maintaining quiet alertness when receiving appropriate social stimulation and signals disengagement by habituating to noxious light and sound when sleeping. The infant's effectiveness in and manner of signaling responsiveness to the environment are evaluated during recovery from birth and the delivery process. Brazelton et al[19] believe that the best use of the NBAS might be to identify each infant's capacity for receiving and utilizing environmental, especially social, stimuli. How the infant demonstrates this capacity is reflected in scores on 28 behavioral items, each of which is scored on a 9-point scale. Serial NBAS examinations are recommended because Brazelton[18] believes that the recovery curve, rather than a single examination, best reflects the infant's current and predicted capacities. Indeed, predictive validity is poor without multiple assessments. This scale is extremely important as a conceptual guidepost, but its use is constricted by applicability only in the first month of life.

In the new Communication and Symbolic Behavior Scales,[20] clinician–infant interaction procedures are developed for analyzing interactive behaviors and related communicative, cognitive, and social-affective abilities in children from 8 to 24 months. Standard procedures are used to elicit various infant behaviors. The procedures include communicative temptations, sharing books, and probes of symbolic play, language comprehension, and combinatorial play. This scale records verbal and preverbal communicative acts and analyzes their functions along a continuum of sociability. Three categories of functions are delineated: behavioral regulation (eg, protests and requests), acts used for social interaction (eg, requesting comfort and social routines), and acts used for joint attention (eg, commenting and requesting information). In addition, children's social-affective signaling, reciprocity, language comprehension, and nonverbal symbolic behavior are profiled. How clearly a child can signal his or her emotional state to a partner is considered from the standpoint of both the clarity of the signal and whether the signal is shared with others by the infant's coordination of it with gaze at his or her partner. This assessment has been published in a research form and is currently being field tested for publication (additional information is available from the publisher).

To document age-related levels of interactive functioning in young infants, Aydlett[21] assessed 30 infants at 6, 8, and 10 months with a semistructured protocol. The intent was to develop a method of using a programmed clinician to document changes in social behavior at these ages and to make tentative comparisons to data gathered from mother–infant observations. Methods and analyses were drawn from a number of clinical and research sources.

At each session, each mother was videotaped interacting with her infant; this was followed by the examiner interacting with the infant. In the clinician–infant play, the clinician imitated the infant's actions, creating a gamelike interaction with a sequence of turns. A 10-second disengagement probe assessed infants' reactions to the suspension of their partner's engagement.

This simple interactive process distinguished infants by age on three important dimensions. As the infants aged, they increased in their ability to engage in intentional social interaction; they took more turns in bouts of play while coordinating their actions or vocalizations with gaze at their partner. Second, they became more sophisticated in their ability to respond to their partner's disengagement; they were increasingly able to follow their partner's gaze, and they made more overtures to reinstate play as they got older.

Furthermore, because of the structured nature of the protocol, this tool provided alternative information from that acquired with a more traditional mother–infant interaction measure.

WHEN, WHAT, HOW, AND WHY: QUESTIONS ABOUT THE PROCESS

An emphasis on child factors raises several specific questions. When should child interactive skills be assessed, what behaviors should be included, and how might the information gained be evaluated and used?

When?

Assessment of interactive skills should begin as soon as possible. For children who are referred as neonates because of biologic or environmental risk factors, assessment can begin at birth. For those who are referred for developmental problems, assessment of interactive skills should be included in any developmental assessment package. Knowledge about the infant's ability to interact with others is essential in planning interventions geared to the child's level of understanding and ability to respond.

A second issue in the timing of interactive assessment is that assessment should be serial; that is, it should occur repeatedly over time in infancy. This is true for two reasons. First, assessment in infancy should result in inference making rather than diagnoses.[4] Basing such inferences on repeated measures of infant behavior guards against making inferences that are inaccurate. Infant behavior is easily disrupted by physical and environmental factors; multiple samples of a single infant's abilities increase the likelihood that an inference about the infant's pattern of development is accurate. Second, in the development of social and communicative domains, human behavior is more malleable than that in development of motor and cognitive domains. It is sensitive to the quantity and quality of stimulation available and to progress in other developmental domains. As intervention proceeds, working with an accurate image of the child's skills increases the chance that his or her capacities are challenged and provides the interventionist with necessary information for programming.

What and how?

What do we need to know about infants to enhance their interactions and development, and how do we get the information we need? As described above, it is important to gather information from multiple sources to increase the effectiveness of intervention efforts. Some important infant behaviors can be observed in both mother–infant and clinician–infant interaction contexts, and some are more easily observed in one or the other setting.

The infant's emotional and affective responsiveness is an important target for observation. In this domain, the overall level and quality of affect are noted. Is this customarily a sober or a happy infant? How does the infant signal his or her emotional state? Does the infant respond differently to social and nonsocial stimulation? Is the response different for familiar and unfamiliar people? How and how well does the infant modulate affect (ie, does the infant go quickly from laughing to crying, or does the infant give gradual cues about increasing distress and pleasure)? Does the infant indicate pleasure when others' interactions are contingent on his or hers?

A second area to observe is infant attention and engagement. How long does the infant attend to social interactions? Can he or she maintain attention through several bouts of turn-taking? How subtle or exaggerated do the partner's responses need to be for the infant to respond? Children's interactive behaviors serve two functions: to engage others in social interaction, and to terminate interactions with them.[10] Engagement behaviors are infant behaviors that elicit and maintain the responsiveness of others and therefore sustain the infant's interaction with another person. Termination behaviors interrupt the other's responsiveness and provide the infant with control over the amount of social stimulation he or she receives and the opportunity for reengagement.[11] How the infant signals engagement and how difficult the infant is to engage are instructive to the interventionist in planning strategies.

Other infant abilities identified as crucial to the development of children's social and communicative competence include the ability to express understandable signals to others that become more conventional and specific with maturity. The mode of signaling, the intensity of signals, and the clarity of the infant's cues are critical observations to be made. The tempo of successful interaction is also noteworthy; attention should be paid to the lag between the clinician's action and the infant's response and to the pause necessary for the infant to notice the partner's next action.

Overall, social-interactive assessment must evaluate the infant's ability to participate actively in reciprocal interactions, to repair communicative breakdowns, and to signal emotional states.[22] Many of the behaviors described above can be observed during other traditional infant assessments (eg, cognitive, speech, and motor). if the clinician's attention is focused on other skills, videotaping or observer scoring should be utilized. It may be necessary to include specific age-appropriate probes to evaluate the full range of social/communicative functioning. For example, intentionally interrupting an interactive episode with a 12-month-old infant gives the clinician an opportunity to see the infant's affect when expectations are violated and to observe his or her ability to reengage the clinician.

Why?

Of what use is social-interactive assessment for families and interventionists? For the interventionist, knowing the infant's interactive capacities is essential to planning developmental interventions that engage the infant's attention and are therefore effective in increasing skills. Furthermore, interventionists can assess the match between an infant's capacity and the caregiver's response. Many caregivers adapt easily and precisely to their infants, and some have difficulty reading their infants' cues, timing their responses, and keeping their infants' attention. Being able to assess progress and improvement in this domain reinforces both parents and clinicians in their efforts to assist infants in developing interactive skills.

Communicating with others is always easier when we know, in the vernacular, where they are at or where they are coming from. This is especially true in families with infants at risk for developmental disorders. By knowing infants' social/communicative and interactive abilities, families can learn to pay attention to their infants' idiosyncratic signals of engagement and disengagement, can assist the infant in regulating emotional states, and can understand what is of interest to the infant and how to optimize the quality and duration of interactive episodes. This knowledge enhances the "goodness of fit" between infants and their caregivers. Ultimately, knowing and responding appropriately to infants' interactive capacities help families and their children achieve satisfying relationships. Satisfying relationships grow when families have suitable expectations for their children's abilities to adapt to family life and when they understand more clearly their children's needs and joys.

REFERENCES

1. Bromwich R. *Working with Parents and Infants: An Interactional Approach.* Baltimore, Md: University Park Press; 1981.

2. Odom S, McEvoy MA. Mainstream at the preschool level: potential barriers and tasks for the field. *Top Early Child Educ.* 1990;10:48–61.

3. Mahoney G, Robinson C, Powell A. Focusing on parent–child interaction: the bridge to developmentally appropriate practices. *Top Early Child Educ.* 1992;12:105–120.

4. Rossetti LM. Infant-toddler assessment: a clinical perspective. *Infant-Toddler Intervent.* 1991;1:11–25.

5. Barnard KE, Kelly JF. Assessment of parent-child interaction. In: Meisels SJ, Shonkoff JP, eds. *Handbook of Early Intervention.* Cambridge, Mass: Cambridge University Press; 1991:278–302.

6. Towle PO, Farran DC, Comfort M. Parent-handicapped child interaction observational coding systems: a review. In: Marfo K, ed. *Parent-Child Interaction and Developmental Disabilities.* New York, NY: Praeger; 1988.

7. Farran D, Kasari C, Comfort FM, Jay S. *Parent/Caregiver Involvement Scale.* Greensboro, NC: University of North Carolina; 1986.

8. Bell RQ. A reinterpretation of the direction of effects in studies of socialization. *Psychol Rev.* 1968;75:81–95.

9. Barnard KE. *Instructor's Learning Resource Manual.* Seattle, Wash: NCAST Publications, University of Washington; 1979.

10. Crawley SB, Spiker D. Mother-child interactions involving two-year-olds with Down Syndrome: a look at individual differences. *Child Dev.* 1983;54:1312–1323.

11. Dunst C, Lowe L. From reflex to symbol: describing explaining, and fostering communicative competence. *Augment Altern Commun.* 1986;21:11–18.

12. Holdgrafer GE, Dunst CJ. Developmental changes in early communicative competence. *Infant-Toddler Intervent.* 1991;1:255–273.

13. Bruner J. *Child's Talk: Learning To Use Language.* New York, NY: Norton; 1983.

14. Stern D. *The First Relationship: Mother and Infant.* Cambridge, Mass: Harvard University Press; 1977.

15. Field T, Healy B, Goldstein S, et al. Infants of depressed mothers show depressed behavior even with nondepressed adults. *Child Dev.* 1988;59:1569–1579.

16. Bayley N. *The Bayley Scales of Infant Development.* New York, NY: Psychological Corporation; 1969.

17. Simeonsson RJ, Huntington GS, Short RJ, Ware W. The Carolina Record of Individual Behavior: characteristics of handicapped children. *Top Early Child Spec Educ.* 1982;2:43–55.

18. Brazelton TB. Neonatal behavioral assessment scale. *Clinics in Developmental Medicine.* Philadelphia, Pa: Lippincott; 1984.

19. Brazelton TB, Nugent JK, Lester BM. Neonatal Behavior Assessment Scale. In: Osofsky JD, ed. *Handbook of Infant Development.* New York, NY: Wiley; 1987:780–817.

20. Wetherby A, Prizant B. *Communication and Symbolic Behavior Scales* (research edition). San Antonio, Tex: Special Press; 1990.

21. Aydlett LA. *A Method for Exploring the Interactive Capacities of Infants.* Chapel Hill, NC: University of North Carolina; 1989. Thesis.

22. Theadore G, Maher SR, Prizant BM. Early assessment and intervention with emotional and behavioral disorders and communication disorders. *Top Lang Disord.* 1990;10:42–56.

Assessment and treatment of sensory- versus motor-based feeding problems in very young children

Marjorie Meyer Palmer, MA
Speech Pathologist
Clinical Instructor
Department of Pediatrics
University of California, San Francisco
San Francisco, California

Melvin B. Heyman, MD, MPH
Chief
Pediatric Gastroenterology and Nutrition
Associate Professor
Department of Pediatrics
University of California, San Francisco
San Francisco, California

THE IDENTIFICATION and treatment of abnormal oral-motor patterns have been well documented in children with cerebral palsy.[1,2] Isolated movements of the lips, tongue, and jaw have been carefully described in a developmental sequence so as to enable easy categorization of normal and abnormal oral-motor patterns.[3] Neurodevelopmental and other motor-oriented therapies have been useful in the treatment of motor-based feeding disorders. A variety of handling and positioning techniques has provided a more normal base for the development of appropriate oral feeding patterns.[4]

With advances in medical technology infants of younger gestational ages and with more medical complications are surviving. Many preterm infants require long-term intensive care and multiple medical procedures during their hospital stay. Placement of an endotracheal or tracheostomy tube may be necessary for infants to survive and, in some cases, long-term ventilation may be required. Other infants have congenital anomalies or disease (eg, necrotizing entercolitis) requiring gastro-intestinal surgery. Commonly these infants are not able to be fed by mouth due to the severity or chronic nature of their illness. They may require intravenous, nasogastric, or gastrostomy tube feedings.

For those infants whose primary medical conditions resolve, clinical signs of cerebral palsy and related oral-motor dysfunction may not be present. Deviant feeding patterns, however, do not arise just from physical disability and are not solely the outcome of clinical syndromes such as failure to thrive.[5] Neurodevelopmental treatment or the use of more traditional facilitation techniques is, therefore, not usually successful for the remediation of feeding disorders in these infants and children. Behavioral management programs have been used with some success for children who have food refusal.[6-8]

Oral feeding problems in infants and young children without neuromuscular dysfunction may occur at any stage of feeding development. On discharge from prolonged hospitalization, some are non-oral feeders, some are able to accept only liquid from the bottle, and others can tolerate strained food from the spoon but are

Inf Young Children 1993; 6(2): 67–73
© 1993 Aspen Publishers, Inc.

unable to manage textured foods. Oral intake may be poor and weight gain may be slow. Many infants seem disinterested in food or just not hungry. Feeding transitions are difficult for them, and they are not able to adapt to changes in food texture, utensil, or placement of food in the mouth. On examination, oral-motor patterns are usually normal, which further confuses the issue of why these children will not eat or transition to a more developmentally appropriate feeding level. Medical diagnostic work-ups often fail to determine the etiology of the oral feeding aversion.

Long-term use of nasogastric tube feedings interferes with the development of successful oral feeding.[9–12] Reluctance to swallow has been reported in patients who have had trauma to the mucosa of the mouth or pharynx.[13] The effect of early oral trauma on swallowing has been termed "conditioned dysphagia."[14] Any aversive stimulation to the nasal and pharyngeal region may be considered traumatic and may result in avoidance behaviors such as gagging, vomiting, or physically expelling the food.[14] Brushing the teeth may also be a problem.

The authors hypothesize that such trauma to the oral and pharyngeal regions alters sensory perception and that sensory awareness in the pharyngeal area is depressed in order to withstand the initial trauma.

MOTOR VERSUS SENSORY-BASED FEEDING DISORDERS

In order to properly treat an oral feeding aversion it first must be determined whether the aversion has a motor or a sensory base. Sensory functions of the oral cavity are more difficult to evaluate than motor functions. There are limited means to test oral sensory abilities and no well-defined norms.[15] Clinical examination using such tools as the Neonatal Oral-Motor Assessment Scale[16,17] and the Pre-Speech Assessment Scale[3] may serve to rule out oral-motor dysfunction.

When neurologic findings are negative and no oral-motor dysfunction is detected, the oral feeding disorder can be assumed to have a primary sensory base. A sensory-based oral feeding disorder may be the residual of the treatments required for underlying conditions such as cardiac defects, diaphragmatic hernia, chronic lung disease, tracheoesophageal fistula, esophageal atresia, and necrotizing enterocolitis.

Adults are often able to describe the sensory aspects of their disorder in a way that children cannot. It would be useful, therefore, to have a clinical rating scale for the diagnosis of oral-sensory feeding disorders in infants and young children.

ASSESSMENT

A diagnostic checklist has been developed that offers some suggestions to help differentiate between oral feeding disorders with a motor versus a sensory base (see the boxes entitled "Oral-Sensory Feeding Disorders" and "Oral Feeding Dis-

---

Oral-Sensory Feeding Disorders

Birth to 3 months
    Unable to sustain a suckle pattern; habituates to the nipple
    Feeds better in a less than alert state with eyes closed, usually at night
    Demonstrates "nipple confusion" if offered bottle and breast
    Although suck is intact, unable to differentiate changing tastes offered through the nipple
    Poor oral intake; infant falls off the growth curve
Over 3 months
    Normal oral-motor patterns
    Able to swallow liquids, particularly water, but demonstrates difficulty with textures
    Tolerates own fingers in the mouth but no one else's
    Tongue retracts in response to touch
    Gag is hypersensitive
    Volitional open mouth posture occurs when food is placed in the mouth
    Holds food under tongue or in buccal cavity to avoid swallowing
    Able to sort out small pieces of solids from sauces and gravies; expels solid food pieces
       while swallowing liquids
    Able to bite and chew solids in mouth but unable to do so in the oropharyngeal area

---

orders Assessment"). Once a basis for the feeding disorder has been determined, an appropriate treatment program can be initiated.

The Neonatal Oral-Motor Assessment Scale (NOMAS) may be used to assess infants in intensive care and special care nurseries who are poor oral feeders. It is useful up to 3 months of age, when oral reflexes begin to diminish.[16–18] This scale differentiates disorganized from dysfunctional sucking patterns. By definition, oral-motor "dysfunction" is represented by abnormal movements of the tongue and jaw that interrupt the normal feeding process.[19] "Disorganization" is indicated by an incoordination of the total sucking activity.[20] Although sensory problems do occur in infants who demonstrate oral-motor dysfunction, this article focuses on

---

Oral Feeding Disorders Assessment

	Sensory	Motor
1. Normal oral-motor patterns	Yes	No
2. Liquids are easier to manage than textures or strained food	Yes	No
3. Mixed consistencies are difficult	No	Yes
4. Able to chew solids well	Yes	No
5. Gags when food approaches or contacts lip	Yes	No
6. Holds food to avoid swallowing	Yes	No
7. Hypersensitive gag for solids with normal liquid swallow	Yes	No

those infants without evidence of oral-motor dysfunction who may or may not be categorized as disorganized feeders early on.

Infants with oral-sensory perception differences may exhibit one or more of several characteristics during nippling. It is important to note that at some time, however briefly, these infants are able to produce a normal nutritive suck pattern. Infants who are unable to sustain a suck because of habituation to the stimulus of the nipple have been described as having a congenitally decreased intra-oral sensory awareness.[21] Their suck pattern, when present, consists of normal oral-motor components.

Often an infant may reportedly nipple more consistently and demonstrate increased oral intake when in a less than alert state with eyes closed. Such an infant nipples better late at night, possibly due to the decreased environmental stimulation at night compared to the bright lights and activity of daytime feedings.

Normal infants are usually adaptable, and their instinct for survival is strong. They are able to transfer from breast to bottle without difficulty. Infants with alterations in their sensory perception are unable to make the transfer and present with "nipple confusion."[22]

Another indication of an oral-sensory alteration in infants is the ability to detect changing sensory cues introduced through the nipple (eg, 5% glucose water versus 15% glucose water). A strong adverse reaction to the change may also indicate oral-sensory alternation. Normal-term infants are able to detect and respond to subtle changes in nutrient delivered the same nipple.[23]

Infants over the age of 3 months whose oral-motor movements are no longer reflexive demonstrate a wider variety of characteristics indicative of a sensory-based oral feeding disorder. A nonoral feeder may frequently choose to swallow water but is uncomfortable swallowing other liquid that has sensory cues and, most likely, will not even drink juice. Water is most like saliva and therefore is most easily tolerated by the mouth and pharynx. Such children may tolerate their own fingers inside the mouth, but demonstrate severe adverse reactions to anyone else's fingers. This aversion may be a defensive response secondary to early negative oral experiences.

Another manifestation of the defensive nature of these children is the retraction of the tongue in response to touch. Sensory receptors on the dorsum of the tongue may be intact; thus, the tongue remains the most sensitive area inside the mouth. A hypersensitive gag may be present and very often, if the child has had a history of gastroesophageal reflux without surgical correction, the gag will easily trigger vomiting.

Once food is presented to the inside of the oral cavity, another typical defensive reaction of the child with sensory problems is to hold the mouth open so as to diffuse the stimulus and to prolong necessary manipulation of the food. Food may be allowed to collect under the tongue or in the lateral sulcus, where it is purposefully maintained in order to prevent or delay swallowing.

These infants and children present with normal oral-motor patterns and have the mechanical ability to sort out small pieces of solid food from any gravy or sauce in which the solid might be contained. They often will swallow only the liquid consistency while expelling the solid piece of food from the mouth. In addition, although they are capable of biting and chewing solid food, the food is usually expelled from the mouth rather than swallowed in order to protect the pharynx from stimulation.

TREATMENT

Due to the sensory nature of this type of oral feeding disorder, a sensory-base treatment protocol for the management of oral feeding disorders is recommended (see Table 1).

A feeding baseline should initially be established (ie, what the child is able to tolerate without discomfort or distress). Establishing a baseline includes choosing an appropriate food texture and amount, utensil, and placement of food. Some children will be able to tolerate only one drop of water delivered by sterile clinic dropper to the lip, while others will tolerate 6 oz of strained food on a spoon. Each child begins the program at an individualized level of tolerance and success. Such a baseline is useful at any stage in the developmental continuum where an oral-sensory disorder exists, whether the child is a non-oral feeder or is able to eat strained food but will not yet bite or chew solids.

Transitions should occur slowly and in a subtle manner. To wean a child from water to juice, ½ tsp of juice may be added to 4 oz of water and gradually increased. To wean a child from strained food to solids, ½ tsp of wheat germ may be added to 4 oz of strained food. This action will gradually thicken the food and increase the consistency over time. When the change in taste or consistency is subtle and not overwhelming, the transition is more likely to be tolerated. The new liquid or consistency may be increased each week or as the child is able to tolerate the change. Gagging, choking, or vomiting is an indication that the stimulus is too strong and is not being tolerated well. It is important to maintain a forward direction working only in small increments; the new taste or texture should be increased and not decreased over time. When gagging occurs no further increases in the new food or liquid should be initiated until the child is able to manage the current level of input successfully.

For many children placement of food or liquid is best tolerated in the buccal cheek cavity, just outside the molar surfaces. Avoidance of the dorsum of the tongue appears to elicit fewer defensive reactions. The child is then able to move the bolus into the lingual cavity, which serves to increase the child's control and comfort over the oral feeding situation.

This approach has been successful in weaning children from tube to oral feedings as well as in helping them to progress through the stages of feeding transition (ie, liquid to strained food and strained food to semi-solids and solids).

Table 1. Palmer/University of California, San Francisco Oral-Sensory Protocol Daily Feeding Summary

Name _____ Date _____

BASELINE ASSESSMENT: FIRST DATE OF STUDY

Time	Texture	Amount offered	Amount swallowed	Utensil	Placement	Amount fed by tube	Feeder
	___ Liquid ___ Thick liquid ___ Strained ___ Semi-solid ___ Soft solid ___ Hard solid	___ Swipes (<30) ___ ounces	___ mL (<30) ___ ounces	___ Finger ___ Dropper ___ Syringe ___ Tongue depressor ___ Bottle ___ Spoon ___ Cup	___ Lower lip ___ Cheek ___ Gums ___ Tongue	___ mL (<30) ___ ounces	
	___ Liquid ___ Thick liquid ___ Strained ___ Semi-solid ___ Soft solid ___ Hard solid	___ Swipes (<30) ___ ounces	___ mL (<30) ___ ounces	___ Finger ___ Dropper ___ Syringe ___ Tongue depressor ___ Bottle ___ Spoon ___ Cup	___ Lower lip ___ Cheek ___ Gums ___ Tongue	___ mL (<30) ___ ounces	
	___ Liquid ___ Thick liquid ___ Strained ___ Semi-solid ___ Soft solid ___ Hard solid	___ Swipes (<30) ___ ounces	___ mL (<30) ___ ounces	___ Finger ___ Dropper ___ Syringe ___ Tongue depressor ___ Bottle ___ Spoon ___ Cup	___ Lower lip ___ Cheek ___ Gums ___ Tongue	___ mL (<30) ___ ounces	

(continued)

Table 1. Continued

Time	Texture	Amount offered	Amount swallowed	Utensil	Placement	Amount fed by tube	Feeder
	____ Liquid	____ Swipes (<30)	____ mL (<30)	____ Finger	____ Lower lip	____ mL (<30)	
	____ Thick liquid	____ ounces	____ ounces	____ Dropper	____ Cheek	____ ounces	
	____ Strained			____ Syringe	____ Gums		
	____ Semi-solid			____ Tongue depressor	____ Tongue		
	____ Soft solid			____ Bottle			
	____ Hard solid			____ Spoon			
				____ Cup			

During the course of the treatment it may be necessary to increase the oral transit speed. Because children with oral-sensory problems would prefer to hold or pocket the food somewhere in the mouth rather than to swallow, it may be helpful to offer some liquid or strained food or to introduce several spoonfuls in rapid succession in order to speed oral transit. In contrast, this technique is contraindicated for children with neuromuscular involvement or oral-motor dysfunction.

Distraction and the use of a "mealtime toy bag" are often successful in diminishing the gag reflex, vomiting, and defensive behavior. A child who is stimulated by auditory, visual, or tactile input may swallow more easily at mealtimes because focus has been removed from the discomfort that occurs when a liquid or solid bolus contacts the pharynx.

Children with sensory-based feeding disorders should be given a variety of foods for self-feeding; they should also be offered liquid to drink from a cup, strained food on a spoon, and solid finger foods. As the program progresses, so too will the child's desire and willingness to explore a variety of tastes and textures.

• • •

A thorough evaluation of both oral-motor and oral-sensory function should serve as the basis for all clinical diagnoses and decisions regarding oral function during drinking, chewing, and swallowing.[15] Following the differential diagnosis of a motor-versus sensory-based oral feeding disorder, an appropriate treatment plan should be formulated and therapeutic intervention begun.

Because infants and children with sensory-based feeding disorders demonstrate normal oral-motor patterns, they do not require the "hands-on" facilitation techniques generally used for children with oral-motor dysfunction (see the box entitled "Oral Feeding Disorders Treatment"). In fact, such an approach may serve only to heighten their already existing sensory defensiveness. Instead, infants and

---

Oral Feeding Disorders Treatment

	Sensory	Motor
1. If oral transit time is slow, introduce liquid or strained food to speed up	Yes	No
2. Stuffing the mouth is recommended	Yes*	No
3. Introduce a variety of tastes and textures for self-feeding at times other than mealtimes	Yes	No
4. Use a tongue facilitator to aid chewing	No	Yes
5. Use auditory, visual, and tactile input to decrease food sensitivity	Yes	No
6. Use "hands-on" facilitation techniques	No	Yes

*Use with caution and only when the patient is adequately prepared. Careful candidate selection is required.

children with sensory-based problems should be treated with an approach based on their level of sensory tolerance. Starting with a liquid or food texture that is acceptable to the child and carefully choosing the placement, amount, and utensil to be used help to decrease the defensive reactions and normalize the oropharyngeal sensation. Much of the reluctance to become an oral feeder or to move through the feeding transitions may be due to the decreased sensory perception in the pharynx. Thus, the pharynx is often the area most in need of remediation in infants and children with oral-sensory feeding disorders.

REFERENCES

1. Morris SE. Interacting frameworks in the assessment process. In: Palmer MM, ed. *The Normal Acquisition of Oral Feeding Skills: Implications for Assessment and Treatment.* New York, NY: Therapeutic Media; 1981.

2. Salek B, Braun MA, Palmer MM. *Early Detection and Treatment of the Infant and Young Child with Neuromuscular Disorders.* New York, NY: Therapeutic Media; 1982.

3. Morris SE. *The Pre-Speech Assessment Scale.* Wauwatosa, Wis: C.P. Project, Curative Rehabilitation Center; 1980.

4. Mueller HA. Feeding. In: Finnie NR, ed. *Handling the Young Cerebral Palsied Child at Home.* New York, NY: E.P. Dutton; 1975.

5. Iwata BA, Riordan MM, Wohl MK, Finney JW. Pediatric feeding disorders: behavioral analysis and treatment. In: Accardo PJ, ed. *Failure to Thrive in Infancy and Early Childhood: A Multidisciplinary Approach.* Baltimore, Md: University Park Press; 1983.

6. Greer RD, Dorow L, Williams G, McCorkle N. Peer-mediated procedures to induce swallowing and food acceptance in young children. *J Appl Behav Anal.* 1991;24:783–790.

7. Lamm N, Greer RD. Induction and maintenance of swallowing responses in infants with dysphagia. *J Appl Behav Anal.* 1988;21:143–156.

8. Riordan MM, Iwata BA, Finney JW, et al. Behavioral assessment and treatment of chronic food refusal in handicapped children. *J Appl Behav Anal.* 1984;17:327–341.

9. Cataldi-Betcher EL, Seltzer MH, Slocum BA, Jones KW. Complications occurring during enteral nutritional support: a prospective study. *J Parenter Enteral Nutr.* 1983;7:546–552.

10. Benda G. Modes of feeding low-birth weight infants. *Semin Perinatol.* 1979;3:407–415.

11. Bazyk S. Factors associated with the transition to oral feeding in infants fed by nasogastric tubes. *Am J Occup Ther.* 1990;44:1070–1078.

12. Reeves-Garcia J, Heyman MB. A survey of complications of pediatric home enteral tube feedings and discussion of developmental and psychosocial issues. *Nutrition.* 1988;4:375–378.

13. Griffin KM. Swallowing training for dysphagic patients. *Arch Phys Med Rehabil.* 1974;55:467–470.

14. Discipio WJ, Kaslon K, Ruben RJ. Traumatically acquired conditioned dysphagia in children. *Ann Otol Rhinol Laryngol.* 1978;87:509–514.

15. Sonies BC, Weiffenbach J, Atkinson JC. Clinical examination of motor and sensory functions of the adult oral cavity. *Dysphagia.* 1987;1:178–186.

16. Braun MA, Palmer MM. A pilot study of oral-motor dysfunction in "at-risk" infants. *Phys Occup Ther Pediatr.* 1985/86;5:13–25.

17. Palmer MM, Crawley K, Blanco I. The Neonatal Oral-Motor Assessment Scale: a reliability study. *J Perinatol.* 1993;13:28–35.

18. Bosma J. Human infant oral function. In: *Symposium on Oral Sensation and Perception.* Springfield, Ill: Charles C Thomas; 1967.

19. Morris SE, Oral-motor development: normal and abnormal. In: Wilson JM, ed. *Oral-Motor Function and Dysfunction in Children.* Chapel Hill, NC: University of North Carolina at Chapel Hill; 1977.

20. Crook CK. The organization and control of infant sucking. *Adv Child Dev Behav.* 1979;14:209–252.

21. Dubignon J, Cooper D. Good and poor feeding behavior in the neonatal period. *Inf Behav Dev.* 1980;3:395–408.

22. Lawrence RA. Breastfeeding the infant with a problem. In: *Breastfeeding: A Guide for the Medical Profession.* 2nd ed. St. Louis, Mo: Mosby; 1985.

23. Lipsitt LP. The study of sensory and learning processes of the newborn. *Clin Perinatol.* 1977;4:163–186.

Recognizing and coping with tactile defensiveness in young children

Carol J. Sears, PhD, OTR/L
Associate Professor
Special Education Program
Graduate School of Education
George Mason University
Fairfax, Virginia

THE IMPORTANCE of touch cannot be overly emphasized. "Every human being comes into this world needing to be touched, and the need for skin contact persists until death. . . ."[1(p24)] Touch is recognized as the first and most important sensory stimulus received by the newborn and an essential ingredient in his or her normal development.[2-4] Furthermore, Montagu[5] maintains that a child's mental and physical health depend on the child being handled, caressed, carried, and coddled, activities in which tactile stimulation plays a major role. When functioning normally, the tactile system provides a child with an avenue for rich interaction with and exploration of the surrounding environment. However, an abnormally functioning tactile system may result in a child demonstrating aversive responses or overreactions to touch sensations,[6] responses that register pain, fear, and discomfort rather than the pleasure, anticipation, or joy associated with most tactile experiences. "When one sees a newborn baby being soothed by loving touch, . . . the sensory experience can be described as poetry beyond analysis. Yet for some children, this communication through touch and movement can go unnoticed, bring terror, feel like a threat demanding 'fight or flight' defense."[7(p7)]

Ayres defined these feelings of discomfort and attempts at withdrawal from certain types of tactile experiences as tactile defensiveness.[8] She hypothesized that tactile defensiveness was "a sensory integrative dysfunction in which tactile sensations cause excessive emotional reactions, hyperactivity, or other behavior problems."[2(p181)] Normally, when sensory integration occurs, the brain automatically organizes and interprets sensory information received from the body and the environment, and as a result of this process, appropriate responses are demonstrated.[2,9] However, when a sensory integrative dysfunction occurs, there is a breakdown in the ability of the central nervous system to integrate input from sensory modalities, such as touch, owing to an irregularity in brain function.[2] As a result of this abnormal processing, unusual movements and behaviors may be observed. Unfortunately, "many of these behaviors are often attributed to personality, emotional make-up, or behavioral tendencies"[6(p10)] resulting in the possible misclassification and inappropriate treatment of a child.

Unless tactile defensiveness is recognized and treated as early as possible, these children will be at high risk for social, learning, and emotional problems that can and often do impact on their adult lives. Subjects in Kinnealy and Oliver's study of adults with tactile defensiveness reported early as well as continuing aversive ex-

Inf Young Children 1994; 6(4): 46–53
© 1994 Aspen Publishers, Inc.

periences with tactile stimuli, which suggests that their tactile defensiveness was an unidentified, long-standing problem.[10] The purpose of this article is to heighten the awareness of parents, caregivers, and professionals to the presence of tactile defensiveness in infants and toddlers and to suggest ways to help them cope with this condition if it is present.

CAUSES OF TACTILE DEFENSIVENESS

Ayres hypothesized that tactile defensiveness is caused by an imbalance of two afferent tactile pathways: a protective system and a discriminative system; the former predominates over the latter.[8,11] She proposed that the protective system responds to tactile stimuli with movements, alertness, and a high degree of affect, while the discriminative system interprets the tactile stimuli for cognitive purposes. When the protective system predominates, it overwhelms the discriminative system's cognitive-oriented activities, and its resulting overt behaviors are considered to be characteristics of tactile defensiveness. More recent investigation has led to the conceptualization of tactile defensiveness as part of a larger puzzle called *sensory defensiveness*. Wilbarger and Wilbarger described this puzzle as " a constellation of symptoms concerning aversive or defensive reactions to non-noxious stimuli across one [eg, tactile] or more [eg, tactile, visual and auditory] sensory modalities."[12(p4)] The hypothetical cause of sensory defensiveness, the more inclusive puzzle, is attributed to the overreaction of normal protective senses to harmless sensory experiences, overreactions that sometimes appear as irrational behaviors.[13] The causes of sensory defensiveness are still under investigation.

According to Mastrangelo,[13] sensory defensiveness may be acquired through trauma such as physical or sexual abuse, result from sensory deprivation, or be present at birth. Teratogenic drugs, used by substance-abusing mothers, can also affect the unborn infant's central nervous system. The resulting observable behaviors in these at-risk infants are very similar in nature to behaviors identifying infants with sensory integrative dysfunction such as tactile defensiveness.[14] Further investigations may indicate that these infants are also demonstrating sensory integrative dysfunctions. Whatever the cause, "enough cases of tactile defensiveness have been documented for us to be confident that this is truly a neurologically-based condition. . . ."[6(p10)] A word of caution is in order at this point. Necessary medical procedures may also cause hypersensitivity to touch; for example, "hypersensitivity, resistance to touch, may be caused by overstimulation to the oral area due to long-term tube feedings, or intubation."[15(p58)] Therefore, it is necessary to acknowledge any possible medical complications or procedures that could affect the processing of tactile sensations before an infant or child's aversive reactions to tactile stimuli are attributed to this neurologically based condition.

CHARACTERISTICS OF TACTILE DEFENSIVENESS

One of the most important steps in treating tactile defensiveness is to develop an awareness of its unique symptoms and behaviors. Behavioral reactions characteristic of tactually defensive individuals were compiled from numerous sources and listed in the accompanying boxes to provide parents, caregivers, and other professionals with observable examples of behaviors indicative of this condition.[2,7–12,16–22] These observable behaviors have bene arbitrarily divided into the categories of activities of daily living (ADL) and social/emotional reactions for purposes of discussion. The behaviors may range from quiet withdrawal to outright hostility, while the response itself may be due to something as subtle as an unexpected draft or a soft breeze against the skin. Surprisingly, these children often seem unaware of cuts and bruises until they are brought to their attention. Paradoxically, these children need to be touched as much as other children.[16]

Reactions to activities of daily living

Examples of observable behaviors characteristic of defensive reactions to activities such as self-care, dressing, and eating are given in the box, "Examples of Reactions to Activities of Daily Living." While defensive reactions are not limited to the

---

Examples of Reactions to Activities of Daily Living

1. Has difficulty suckling or eating solid foods
2. Dislikes having ears cleaned, brushing teeth, using toothpaste
3. Experiences great discomfort when nose/ears are cleaned with swabs
4. Responds with alarm, withdrawal, or scratching when face is wiped with a napkin or cloth
5. Dislikes dental work
6. Dislikes skin creams and powders
7. Has an aversion to face washing or baths
8. Demonstrates hypersensitivity to water temperature
9. Has an aversion to haircuts and having hair washed and combed
10. Avoid walking barefoot in sand, grass, and water
11. Avoids crawling on a carpet
12. Prefers wearing shoes to being barefoot
13. Has an aversion to nail cutting
14. Avoids using the palms of hands by manipulating objects with fingertips only
15. Avoids using hands for prolonged periods of time
16. Prefers to be covered, regardless of temperature
17. Dislikes the feel of new clothing
18. Dislikes the feel of certain textures such as wool and synthetics
19. Reacts defensively to rough bed sheets, blankets, or nightclothes
20. Reacts defensively to high-frequency sounds, specific odors, or bright lights

mouth, hands, and feet, these are the most tactually sensitive parts of the body, as sensory receptors for tactile stimuli are more abundant in these areas.[23,24] These children may be extremely defensive around the head and face, especially within and around the mouth, although they may "mouth" objects and clothing excessively.

Because the degree of tactile defensiveness affecting feeding and eating activities may be severe enough to threaten survival, it will be discussed in greater depth than the other aspects of ADL. Wilbarger described an infant who became so agitated when touched that "even the nipple given to him during feeding seemed irritating."[7(p8)] As a result of this oral sensitivity, some infants consume a minimal amount of breast milk, pulling on the nipple only long enough to raise their blood sugar before spitting the nipple out.[21] Oral sensitivity may also be responsible for a hyperactive gag reflux that complicates the intake of liquids and solid foods well beyond infancy.[17] Proper nutrition is not the only concern. Montagu[5] stressed the importance of breast-feeding in the consolidation of the symbiotic bond between mother and child as the foundation for the development of all social relationships. "The communication the infant receives through the warmth of the mother's skin constitutes the first of the socializing experiences of his life."[5(p73)] When early and relatively consistent patterns of abnormal feeding behaviors such as those just described are observed, it is imperative that a professional trained in the assessment and treatment of sensory integrative dysfunctions treat the child and design a team treatment plan to be implemented as soon as possible. Training of parents, caregivers, and professionals who are in close contact with the infant will ensure appropriate and consistent treatment of the feeding problem and its cause.

Intake of solid foods may also present a problem, as various textures, such as that of tapioca, can be aversive to some children.[18] Young children may reject pieces of meat, textured or hard vegetables and fruit, or hot and cold food and liquids and accept only relatively smooth, soft foods such as gelatin that do not cause discomfort to their hypersensitive oral areas. However, foods such as oatmeal and yogurt may be avoided because of their soft, slimy textures.[13] Continued behaviors such as spitting food out, withdrawal, anger, crying, or arching of the body may signal the child's aversion to a food. Recognition of these negative behaviors as possible defensive reactions to that specific food or type of food should alert the caretaker, and that food should be removed from the child's present diet. Food should not be forced on these children, as their reluctance to accept it may be due to oral defensiveness.[21] Removal of the foods causing the child's aversive reaction should make mealtime a much more pleasant experience for both parent or caregiver and the child. That specific food may be tried again when oral tolerance has been developed for it. Oral hypersensitivity within the mouth can be minimized or normalized through the use of various therapeutic approaches such as rubbing the inside of the mouth, using firm pressure, and an acceptable "tool" such as a finger to do so. Speech pathologists and occupational therapists usually have a repertoire of techniques for desensitizing such areas and can train parents and others in using them effectively.

Oral hypersensitivity to tactile stimulation in an around the mouth may also cause difficulty with the use of eating utensils because of their various textures, sizes, and shapes. Selection of appropriate utensils should take into consideration the types of textures already accepted by the young child and the least intrusive size and shape that can be used. The utensil is a foreign object that must become familiar and tolerable to the child; therefore, developing tolerance to the utensil before using it to carry food to the child's mouth is essential. Therapists can demonstrate appropriate methods to develop tolerance to both foods and utensils. However, building tolerance for new foods and utensils should be accomplished separately before the two are combined. A food already tolerated by the child should be combined with the use of a newly tolerated utensil, or vice versa. In other words, simultaneous introduction of new foods and unfamiliar utensils should not be attempted because of the possibility of the child's aversive reaction to this combination. The child's reactions will quickly indicate whether the selected combination is successful. The child's avoidance of anticipated touch by other people or objects (eg, withdrawal from the oncoming spoon and from the caregiver holding it) may further complicate feeding. The adult feeding the child should be positioned in front of or at an angle within the child's visual field so that the young child can anticipate and prepare for the oncoming utensil and food.

Tactile defensiveness involving the hands and fingers may also directly affect the child's ability to finger-feed. Finger-feeding may be unsuccessful because of the child's reluctance to touch or handle foods with his or her fingers and may be complicated by oral hypersensitivity. If the goal is development of the ability to finger-feed, it is important to observe which foods the child can tolerate handling and eating, and those foods should be used to begin finger-feeding. It is not uncommon for the child to demonstrate aversive behaviors if he or she is forced to engage in finger-feeding intolerable foods. Again, these aversive reactions may result in disastrous mealtimes at home or in nursery or preschool situations. A program planned to build tolerance and to desensitize hands and fingers to tactile experiences should be initiated prior to attempting finger-feeding if problems are noted in this area.

There are a number of variables to consider before making final decisions as to the possible causes of feeding problems and to select the best remedial or compensatory techniques to be used. "Successful intervention must consider the unique characteristics of the child . . . the environment . . . the caregiver . . . and the feeding equipment. . . ."[15(p59)] If not treated appropriately, defensive reactions to tactile stimulation of the mouth and facial areas and to food handling can extend well beyond early childhood. For example, adults in Kinnealy and Oliver's study reported problems with lipbalms, lipstick, greasy makeup, and dental care, as well as difficulty in touching foods and preparing dinner.[10] Recognition and treatment of early behaviors will assist in normalizing the child's developmental progress in eating and independence, as well as minimizing or eliminating consequent problems in his or her adult life.

While it is beyond the scope of this article to provide such an in-depth discussion about other activities of daily living, several examples are provided to demonstrate methods of addressing defensiveness in these activities. For example, before cutting or combing a child's hair, Hamill[16] suggests a firm, slow scalp massage, which should decrease the hypersensitive reaction of the scalp. Do not lightly tousle the child's hair, at any time, as this activates the defensive response of the child. When bathing the child, firmly rub his or her body with a towel or washcloth, as the tactually defensive child is able to tolerate and often seeks firm pressure. Follow the young child's lead in selection of types and textures of clothing. This child may prefer clothes that cover most of his or her body, thereby ensuring protection from direct tactile contact. Embroidered sunsuits are cute, but overalls and a long-sleeved shirt may provide comfort and security for the child and result in more pleasant behavior, which could encourage better mother–child bonding and development of early socialization skills. Unfortunately, these children often demonstrate poor sleep patterns that affect the entire family. Infant snugglers, backpacks, sleeping bags, and tucked-in heavy blankets usually prove helpful in providing comfortable, and comforting, sleeping environments, which often contribute to the development of better sleep patterns.[7,16]

Social/emotional reactions

Some of the atypical social and emotional responses that often accompany tactile defensiveness are given in the box, "Examples of Social/Emotional Reactions." However, the box does not show the impact of tactile defensiveness on activities that contribute to the normal development of the social and affective domains. For example, play is the most important occupation of the young child. "In almost every occupation we engage in and in every role we assume we give and receive messages about the ways we should behave toward one another. We first learn to give and receive those cues in play."[25(pp1,2)] However, tactually defensive young children are unable to participate in play and play activities in a normal way. Their play and exploratory activities are limited because of their fear and anticipation of being touched by others, as well as their possible intolerance of some play materials, such as plastic or fuzzy toys, water, and sand. For example, an infant or toddler may withdraw from or reject new toys presented by loving parents and relatives, and efforts to play with the child may fail because of the infant's fear of being touched or because of the great discomfort caused by the "feel" of the toys. Unfortunately, unless diagnosed, these symptoms can precipi-

---

Examples of Social/Emotional Reactions

1. Dislikes hugging, kissing, holding, or cuddling
2. Dislikes being picked up and often struggles when this occurs
3. Becomes distressed and uncomfortable when physically close to people
4. Dislikes being tickled
5. May initiate touch but objects to being touched by others
6. May have very poor peer and adult relationships
7. Reacts negatively to friendly pats, rumpling of hair, soft stroking of back
8. May rub or scratch the spot that someone has touched
9. Is involved in or appears to pick frequent fights
10. Has trouble making friends
11. Becomes verbally or physically hostile or aggressive
12. May become withdrawn
13. Demonstrates excessive weeping
14. Demonstrates emotional lability or anger
15. May react negatively to and avoid normal child's play
16. Is easily irritated or enraged when touched by siblings or playmates
17. Pinches, kicks, or otherwise hurts self or others
18. Frequently bumps or pushes others
19. Bangs head on purpose
20. Prefers solitary play
21. Avoids water or sandbox play
22. Dislikes crowded areas such as playgrounds or shopping malls
23. Avoids crawling or walking barefoot in sand, grass, or on carpet

---

tate poor parent and family relations with the child and among adults. The infant or toddler may be described as "finicky," "irritable," or "peevish" and may be less than welcome at family gatherings or seldom visited by close family members.

When questions arise as to the appropriateness of a toy, observe the child's preferred toys, manipulatives, blankets, and clothes and analyze their attributes. The child may repeatedly select specific textures such as smooth, soft, spongy, or hand. A teddy bear may be the favorite toy for more reasons than we know! Clues such as these can dictate further toy selections and eliminate the introduction of unfamiliar or disagreeable materials from the play environment. By combining careful toy selection with appropriate, nonthreatening touch and movement by adults, play between parent or relative and a young child can be cultivated.

A young child's interaction with his or her peers is often limited because of this condition. Solitary play and maintenance of distance from others are often protective techniques resulting from the constant anticipation of being touched. This apprehension may contribute to later age-inappropriate social interactions with peers and adults.[20] Accidental brushes or bumps from other children or adults may be interpreted by the tactually defensive child as aggressive or hostile acts, resulting in anger, weeping, or retreating even further from others. When a young tactually defensive child is participating in a group activity or is playing near other young children, it is important to be aware of his or her location in relation to the others. Placing the young child so that he or she is to the side of or behind others and can visually anticipate any touching will provide more security for the child by minimizing the fear of unexpected touch. This need for distance does not disappear in adulthood. Many tactually defensive adults report a continuing need to maintain their own space owing to a feeling of discomfort when interacting with people who stand too close or who touch when they talk. This need for space is also reflected in existing problems with crowded places such as malls, busses, and elevators.[10] If tactually defensive adults verbalize their difficulties with these crowded situations, then we should not be surprised if young tactually defensive children indicate the unacceptability of these same environments through the only language available to them—aversive behaviors.

Tactile defensive reactions can greatly affect healthy parent–child relationships. The infant or toddler may push away from the mother's gentle "butterfly" kiss or soft, light smoothing of hair. Thus the child appears to reject the mother's affection when, in reality, he or she is rejecting the way the mother's affection is being expressed. A firm kiss would be more readily accepted and shared by both parent and child. A parent's or relative's light embrace, meant to be a sign of love and approval, may be met with hostility or physical rejection, while a spanking may appear to be reinforcing to that child.[9] This contradictory behavior is due to the nature of the light embrace, which arouses the child's defensive reaction. On the other hand, the deep pressure of the spanking tends to inhibit the arousal, thereby appearing to calm the child.[11] Instead of a light embrace, a slow, firm "bear hug" would be a much more comfortable way to express affection, as the firm touch/pressure appears to lessen the defensive behavior of the child. The infant or toddler may also prefer a firm touch moving slowly down his or her body and in the direction of hair growth on arms and legs, which appears to have a calming effect, rather than a touch moving up against the direction of hair growth, which would activate the defensive response.[16]

•   •   •

Unless tactile defensiveness is recognized, diagnosed, and treated appropriately in the early formative years, Wilbarger and Wilbarger[22] may well have summarized the present and future world of the tactually defensive infant and toddler—and a frightening world it is! They claim that "defensiveness results in varying degrees of stress and anxiety. The child may perceive the world as dangerous, alarming or at the very least irritating. Memories can be stored as traumatic experiences. Relationships can be exaggerated."[22(p3)] In four all-encompassing sentences these authors have clearly described outcomes that will complicate these children's lives and the lives of their families and friends and affect their interaction with their environment. However, awareness of the presence of tactile defensiveness, use of techniques to cope with this condition, and application of early intervention programs on the part of parents, caregivers, and professionals can ensure that these youngsters have the opportunity to participate in normal experiences throughout their lives.

REFERENCES

1. Simon S. *Caring, Feeling, Touching.* Allen, Tex: Argus Communications; 1976.

2. Ayres AJ. *Sensory Integration and Your Child.* Los Angeles, Calif: Western Psychological Services; 1979.

3. Colton H. *The Gift of Touch—How Physical Contact Improves Communication, Pleasure and Health.* New York: Seaview/Putnam; 1983.

4. Springer I. "Akin to magic" volunteers help fragile babies to thrive. *AARP Bull.* 1991;32(1):9.

5. Montagu A. *Touching: The Human Significance of the Skin.* 2nd ed. New York, NY: Harper & Row; 1978.

6. Mailloux Z. Tactile defensiveness: some people are more sensitive. *Sensory Integration Q.* 1992;20(3):10.

7. Wilbarger P. Planning an adequate "sensory diet" application of sensory processing theory during the first year of life. *Zero to Three.* 1984;5(1):7–12.

8. Ayres AJ. Tactile functions: their relation to hyperactivity and perceptual-motor behavior. *Am J Occup Ther.* 1964;18(1):6–11.

9. Lerner J, Mardell-Czudnowski C, Goldberg D. *Special Education for the Early Childhood Years.* Englewood Cliffs, NJ: Prentice-Hall; 1982.

10. Oliver BF. The social and emotional issues of adults with sensory defensiveness. *Sensory Integration Special Interest Section Newsletter.* 1990;13(3):1.

11. Ayres AJ. *Sensory Integration and Learning Disorders.* Los Angeles, Calif: Western Psychological Services; 1972.

12. Frick S. Sensory defensiveness: a case study. *Sensory Integration Special Interest Section Newsletter.* 1986;12(2):4–6.

13. Mastrangelo R. Sensory defensiveness: roadblock to function. *Adv Occup Therapists.* 1991;(29):16.

14. Hyde AS, Trautman SE. Drug-exposed infants and sensory integration: is there a connection? *Sensory Integration Special Interest Section Newsletter.* 1989;12(4):1–2, 6.

15. Raver SA: *Strategies for Teaching At-Risk and Handicapped Infants and Toddlers: A Transdisciplinary Approach.* New York, NY: Merrill; 1991.

16. Hamill JS. Tactile defensiveness: a type of sensory integrative dysfunction. *J Rehabil.* 1984;50:95–96.

17. King-Thomas L. Evaluation of oral-motor functioning. *Developmental Disabilities Special Interest Section Newsletter.* 1980;3:31–32.

18. Larson KA. The sensory history of developmentally delayed children with and without tactile defensiveness. *Am J Occup Ther.* 1982;36(9):590–596.

19. Royeen CB. Domain specifications of the construct tactile defensiveness. *Am J Occup Ther.* 1985;39(9):596–599.

20. Sears CJ. The tactiley defensive child. *Acad Ther.* 1981;16(5):563–569.

21. Wilbarger P, Royeen CB. Tactile defensiveness. Symposium presented in November 1987; Washington, DC.

22. Wilbarger P, Wilbarger JL. *Sensory Defensiveness in Children Aged 2–12.* Santa Barbara, Calif: Avanti Educational Programs; 1991.

23. Kinnealy M. Aversive and nonaversive response to sensory stimulation in mentally retarded children. *Am J Occup Ther.* 1973;27:6–11.

24. Mailloux Z. Explore the sense of touch. *Sensory Integration Q.* 1992;20(2):10.

25. Bundy A. Play: the most important occupation of children. *Sensory Integration Special Interest Section Newsletter.* 1992;15(2):1–2.

Nutritional assessment of the young child with cerebral palsy

Maureen A. Fee, MD
Developmental Pediatrician
Division of Developmental and
  Behavioral Pediatrics
St. Christopher's Hospital for Children
Assistant Professor of Pediatrics
Temple University School of Medicine
Philadelphia, Pennsylvania

Edward B. Charney, MD
Developmental Pediatrician
Division of Child Development and
  Rehabilitation
Children's Hospital of Philadelphia
Children's Seashore House
Associate Professor of Pediatrics
University of Pennsylvania School of
  Medicine
Philadelphia, Pennsylvania

William W. Robertson, MD
Orthopedic Surgeon
Division of Orthopedic Surgery
Children's Hospital of Philadelphia
Children's Seashore House
Associate Professor of Orthopedics
University of Pennsylvania School of
  Medicine
Philadelphia, Pennsylvania

CHILDREN RESPOND better to educational and therapeutic interventions if they are well nourished. The child with cerebral palsy is no exception to this rule. Cerebral palsy is a disorder of posture and movement secondary to a static lesion of the developing brain. There are many nonmotor disabilities associated with cerebral palsy, including cognitive deficits, seizure disorders, sensory impairment, and poor nutritional status.

Various methods can be used to assess a child's nutritional status, such as standardized growth charts, laboratory values, and documentation of the intake of calories and nutrients. Studies have shown that children with cerebral palsy have decreased growth, abnormal laboratory values, and decreased caloric and nutrient intake.

In 1951, inadequate caloric intake was described as contributing to the poor nutritional status of children with cerebral palsy.[1] In that same year, the "reversed swallowing wave," prolonged feeding time, and intolerance for solids were outlined.[2] In 1960, Sterling reviewed the height and weight of 100 children with cerebral palsy and found that they were less than the 10th percentile in 69% and 62% of the children, respectively.[3] Hemoglobin and serum iron levels were also found to be below the norm.[4]

A poor nutritional status can result in apathy, which in turn can decrease a child's interest in social and educational activities. Malnutrition is also associated with an increased rate of infections. The malnourished child with cerebral palsy who requires orthopedic surgery presents additional concerns: Protein depletion is associated with impaired wound healing,[5] sepsis, pneumonia, prolonged weakness, and delayed physical rehabilitation.

Inf Young Children 1988; 1(1): 33–40

There has been an ongoing question about whether the poor growth in children with cerebral palsy is related to inadequate caloric intake or rather to a disturbed growth center in the brain. If poor growth is due to inadequate caloric intake, the provision of adequate calories should improve the child's growth. Shapiro et al demonstrated that by ensuring adequate calories via a gastrostomy, they could significantly increase the number of children who achieved adequate growth and a better nutritional status.[6] Another group showed that nasogastric feedings of malnourished children with cerebral palsy increased not only their weight but also their skinfold thickness and midarm circumference, indicating an increase in lean and fat tissue.[7]

EVALUATION OF NUTRITIONAL STATUS

Clinical evidence of malnutrition (Table 1) occurs relatively late and is usually preceded by anthropometric measurements and laboratory values.

Anthropometric measurements

Growth

During the first two years of life, growth is rapid. The healthy, full-term newborn will double his or her weight in five months and triple it by the end of the first year. During this time, there is a rapid increase in subcutaneous tissue as well. Although growth in the second year of life is still rapid, there is a relative deceleration such that the child gains an average of 2.5 kg in weight and 12 cm in length.[8] The growth of an individual child is best monitored using standardized growth charts adapted from the reference standards for normal children prepared by the National Center for Health Statistics.

These reference standards do not apply to children with chronic disabilities, and there are no specific norms or growth charts for children with cerebral palsy. Length measurements can be difficult to obtain because of contractures. Caloric requirements can vary with the degree of disability; it has been suggested that since severe motor dysfunction is often associated with short stature, the caloric requirements of children with cerebral palsy should be expressed in calories per centimeter of body height rather than per kilogram of body weight.[9] An extensive variation in energy expenditure has also been noted, with less energy expended in children with spasticity and more in those with athetosis.[10] At times, incremental growth charts that assess linear growth per unit time can be helpful in following deviations from the average for a given age.[11]

Body composition

Estimates of total body fat can be made by measuring skinfold thickness with calipers.[12] The estimate will vary depending on the site measured and the age and

Table 1. Clinical evidence of malnutrition

Area	Finding	Possible nutritional inadequacy
Overall body	Low body weight, short stature	Calories
	Edema	Protein
Hair	Looseness, sparseness, dullness	Protein
Skin	Xerosis, follicular keratosis	Vitamin A
	Solar dermatitis	Niacin
	Petechiae, purpura	Ascorbic acid
Subcutaneous tissue	Decreased subcutaneous tissue mass	Calories
Nails	Spoon-shaped appearance	Iron
Eyes	Dry conjunctiva, keratomalacia	Vitamin A
Lips	Angular stomatitis	Riboflavin, iron
	Cheilosis	B-complex vitamins
Gums	Swelling, bleeding	Vitamin C
Tongue	Glossitis	Niacin, folate, riboflavin, vitamin B_{12}
Skeletal system	Costochondrial beading	Vitamins C and D
	Bone tenderness	Vitamin C
Muscles	Decreased muscle mass	Protein, calories

sex of the person. Skinfold thickness should be followed as a trend rather than as a single recording and in general is more useful for monitoring obesity than for monitoring malnutrition. The limb circumference (ie, midarm circumference) in children 1 to 4 years old reflects their current protein (muscle) and caloric (fat) nutritional status, whereas in older children it also reflects "use hypertrophy" and obesity. Since muscle mass is an indirect measure of protein reserves (during malnutrition, a reduction in muscle size occurs as a compensatory mechanism to provide amino acids for gluconeogenesis and synthesis of hepatic proteins), estimates of limb muscle size have been used to assess nutritional status in children.

Laboratory values

Normal hemoglobin values vary from 11 to 14 gm/dL depending on the person's age and sex. A mean corpuscular volume less than 90 µL is associated with iron deficiency, whereas a value greater than 96 µL is associated with folate and or vitamin B_{12} deficiency. Total serum protein (normal range, 5.5 to 6.5 g/dL) is not a sensitive index because elevated values can occur secondary to dehydration or increased immunoglobulin levels with infection. However, serum albumin (normal range, 3.3 to 3.5 g/dL) is a fairly sensitive index of visceral protein status. A magnesium level below 1.3 mEq/L is indicative of malnutrition, as are a lymphocyte count less than 2,000/μL and a delayed cutaneous hypersensitivity reaction, both of which are characteristic of an altered immune status.

CAUSES OF NUTRITIONAL INADEQUACY

Documentation of caloric intake

Most often, the consumption of adequate calories results in growth. Thus the initial phase of the assessment is an attempt to obtain a comprehensive dietary history using the previous 24 hours as a sample of usual daily intake. In this way, the frequency, timing, and content of meals and snacks can be recorded as well as any circumstances surrounding the feeding time (eg, location and position when fed). Additional questions are required regarding the concentration of formula, episodes of choking or vomiting, the length of feeding time, and the amount of food lost from the mouth. A calorie count can then indicate whether adequate calories are being consumed. If adequate calories are being offered and retained, a further medical evaluation is needed to determine possible endocrine, pulmonary, or cardiac causes. In the young child with cerebral palsy, however, the poor weight gain is more likely to be secondary to inadequate caloric intake.

Once the calorie count is completed, it is possible to determine whether adequate calories were offered to the child.

Inadequate calories

The most easily remedied situation may involve inadequate calories being offered by the caregiver. This may be due to a variety of factors including limited financial resources resulting in the inappropriate dilution of the formula or a very early introduction of whole milk, a poor understanding of nutritional issues such as substituting water for formula or a too early introduction of solids, or the limited emotional capacity of the caregiver resulting in a disturbance of the child–adult dyad at feeding times.

Adequate calories offered but not consumed

A more difficult situation to identify and correct is that of adequate calories being offered but not consumed. In the child with cerebral palsy this may be due to a variety of factors such as dental problems, refusal of food, or oral motor dysfunction.

Dental problems

Dental problems are both an etiology and an outcome of poor nutrition. Inadequate matrix formulation results from inadequate intake of protein, vitamins A, D, and C, calcium, phosphorus, or fluoride. This can lead to caries that can cause pain and infection, resulting in a further decrease in oral intake.

Refusal of food

Refusal of food may be a behavioral problem. Lack of prior experience with oral feeding (eg, if the patient was fed exclusively with a tube in the early months) will interfere with the association of eating with pleasure. Some have suggested a "critical" or "sensitive" period of infancy, during which solids or liquids must be introduced or else behavioral feeding difficulties will arise in the future. Prior experience with forced feeding or tube placement may set up an aversive feeding situation. In some children, the resistance to oral feeding may be an issue of control.

The best treatment of refusal of food is prevention of the situations leading to such behavior, for example, providing nonnutritive sucking experiences temporarily paired with tube feedings. Once the behavioral disorder is established, behavioral modification techniques can help by breaking feeding into small, learnable steps, decreasing the child's anxiety, and modifying the parent–child interaction.[13]

Oral motor dysfunction

Because of the oral motor dysfunction seen so often in young children with cerebral palsy, spillage of food can prevent calories from being consumed. Those children who are at risk for significant oral motor dysfunction display primitive or abnormal reflexes such as the jaw thrust, lip retraction, tongue retraction, tongue thrust, and tonic bite. In addition, they also display an abnormal oral-facial tone. The developmental feeding sequence is delayed. Aspiration can occur secondary to swallowing dysfunction. Clinical evidence of aspiration includes a wet, gurgling vocal quality with feedings; coughing and sputtering; frequent respiratory illness; and weak, breathy vocalizations and cries.

Documentation of oral motor function is accomplished with videofluoroscopy of the three phases of swallowing: oral, pharyngeal, and esophageal. Proper positioning is essential during the study; the young child should be placed upright with the head and trunk in a good position in a radiolucent seating arrangement. Also, the feeding therapist (speech–language clinician or occupational or physical therapist) should provide food with a variety of textures during the study. Some children can safely swallow appropriately thickened food in an upright position, yet these same children may aspirate liquids or not tolerate oral feedings in a semireclining position.

Inadequate caloric retention

Vomiting

Another reason for inadequate intake of calories in a child with cerebral palsy is vomiting. In some children there is a hyperactive gag reflex that can be elicited even at the anterior third or half of the tongue. If this is activated, the result may be vomiting of the food just consumed.

Rumination

Rumination may also play a part in the inadequate intake of calories in the child with cerebral palsy. In the child whose neurologic function is intact, the onset is usually seen at 3 to 12 months of age, but in the child whose neurologic function is impaired, the onset may not be seen for several months or even years. Rumination is often associated with gastroesophageal reflux (GER) and hiatal hernia, in which cases the underlying disorders also need to be addressed. Other theories include a problem with attachment and self-stimulation with the resulting release of endorphins.[14] Behavioral modification can be applied here as well.

Gastroesophageal reflux (GER)

GER is commonly seen in the young child with cerebral palsy. This population is at high risk for all of the complications of GER such as poor weight gain, esophagitis (and resulting iron deficiency anemia), and aspiration pneumonia. Once GER is suspected from the clinical history and examination, it should be evaluated with barium sulfate radiography of the swallow and the upper gastrointestinal tract, a radionucleotide scan using labeled formula, pH probe studies, and manometry. If GER is documented, it can be treated with proper positioning and thickened feedings, with medications such as metoclopramide hydrochloride or bethanechol chloride, or with surgical procedures such as Nissen's operation (fundoplication). Since an underlying anatomic obstruction such as malrotation may be causing the vomiting, GER should be documented radiographically rather than just clinically.

REFEEDING AS AN INTERVENTION EFFORT

In the malnourished child with cerebral palsy who has been receiving inadequate calories, the cause of the inadequate intake must be considered in order to determine the route and content of refeeding.

Oral versus tubal route

For oral refeeding to be considered, the risk of aspiration must be minimal as determined clinically and videofluoroscopically with various textures of foods. Also, the evaluation must indicate that an adequate intake of calories is possible with the proper choice of high-calorie, correctly textured foods, feeding therapy, and special techniques learned by the caregivers. In addition, it is necessary that the feedings be accomplished in a reasonable period of time so that they will not fatigue the child or stress the caregiver.

If the above requirements are not met, then it will be necessary to accomplish the goal of refeeding through tube feeding. The choice of nasogastric (NG tube) versus gastrostomy should be based on the reason for tube placement, the expected duration of tube feeding, and the family's preferences. An NG tube can be considered when caloric intake has been poor because of prematurity, when tube feeding is expected to be of short duration, when continuous nocturnal feedings are used, or when parents are more comfortable with it than with a gastrostomy. An NG tube is contraindicated in cases of intractable vomiting, delayed gastric emptying, or significant GER. In small infants, an NG tube can occlude the nasal passages. Additional complications include nasopharyngeal trauma, aspiration, and an increase in GER. For some families, it is also cosmetically unacceptable.

A gastrostomy can be considered if the patient is unable to suck or swallow, has congenital anomalies of the esophagus, or will require long-term tube feeding, or if the parents are better able to deal with a gastrostomy than an NG tube. It is contraindicated in cases of severe GER without an accompanying surgical procedure, intractable vomiting, or inadequate gastric emptying. Complications of gastrostomy tube placement include obstruction of the pyloric outlet, bleeding, wound dehiscence, postoperative ileus, intestinal adhesions, and peritonitis. The incisionless, or percutaneous, gastrostomy has decreased the morbidity considerably and has enabled some children to undergo a gastrostomy who would not otherwise have been candidates.[15]

Dietary recommendations

Once it has been determined that the route of refeeding should be oral, the clinician should attempt to increase both the volume and caloric concentration of food consumed by the child. The volume can be increased by giving more frequent feedings, as well as by enhancing the child's oral motor skills through a structured feeding program by a speech pathologist or occupational or physical therapist. The caloric concentration can be increased by concentrating infant formulas to 24 to 30 kcal/oz. Various supplements such as Polycose (2 kcal/mL) can be added to standard formulas to increase their caloric concentration. A nutrition consultation may be beneficial for the child who is eating primarily solid foods to advise the caregiver in the selection of higher-calorie foods.

If the gastrostomy or NG route is chosen, the child can be given puréed foods or a proprietary formula once he or she is old enough to stop taking infant formulas (> 1 year or > 20 lbs).

A puréed diet can be a complete diet and has the advantage of being low in cost. However, it is time-consuming to prepare, is more viscous, and requires a large-bore feeding tube. Solids can settle out and the nutritional composition can be inconsistent.

The commercially available preparations (Table 2) are complete and convenient but expensive. The complete polymeric formulas of standard density require

Table 2. Some commercial nutritional preparations

Polymeric (standard density)	Polymeric (high density)	Monomeric
Citrotein	Ensure Plus	Criticare HN
Compleat-B	Isocal HCN	Vital HN
Compleat-Modified	Magnacal	Vivonex HN
Ensure	Sustacal Liquid	Vivonex Standard
Instant Breakfast	Travasorb MCT	
Isocal Standard		
Isotein HN		
Osmolite		
Precision LR		
Sustacal Liquid		

normal gastrointestinal function. Additional water may be needed because of the solute load. They may not meet the vitamin or mineral requirements of very small children; therefore, vitamins and minerals must be added or an infant formula continue to be used. The polymeric formulas can be administered through a gastrostomy or NG tube, or across the jejunum via continuous infusion. Those of high density cannot be used transpylorically because of their high osmolality. As with the standard density formulas, additional water may be needed because of the high renal solute load. Again, they may not meet the high vitamin and mineral requirements of very small children so that supplements are needed. Monomeric or elemental diets have a high osmolality (and so cannot be used transpylorically) and are especially helpful if the child's gastrointestinal function is impaired.

Discontinuation of tubal feedings

Even before tube feedings are instituted, parents ask when they can be discontinued. Before this mode of alimentation can be discontinued in favor of total oral feeding, the problem necessitating it (eg, absent sucking or swallowing reflex) must be resolved. Also, the child must be able to maintain his or her weight with oral feeding alone—especially during an intercurrent illness—and must be given ample time (six months) to demonstrate this.

Complications of refeeding

Certain complications can arise from rapidly refeeding a malnourished child. If the volume is expanded too rapidly, the child can experience fluid overload. Vomiting can occur if the rate of infusion is too fast, the volume too great, the osmolality too high, the tube improperly placed, or the gastric emptying delayed. In addition, diarrhea can occur from lack of bulk in the diet, an excessive infusion rate, or high osmolality, though some children become constipated. Temporary carbohydrate intolerance, which can result in glucosuria, needs to be monitored in order to avoid nonketotic, hyperosmolar dehydration.

The most serious potential complication is congestive heart failure. Atrophy of the cardiac muscle occurs during inanition. Thus the heart volume is decreased on chest radiography because of the decreased muscle mass as well as the decreased cardiac volume secondary to decreased blood volume, decreased cardiac output, and hypometabolic state. With repletion, cardiac output is increased secondary to increased fluid volume and increased extracellular volume, a hypermetabolic rate. This can result in congestive heart failure. In addition, there may be an "early repletion syndrome" seen in the first three weeks of repletion since the increase in cardiac mass lags behind the generalized increase in body mass, thus leaving a heart with an increased workload but without the concomitant increased muscle mass needed.[16] The recommendations to minimize the risk of congestive heart failure include a low sodium regimen, a slower infusion rate, and close monitoring of cardiac function.

•   •   •

Some children with cerebral palsy display poor weight gain. Providing adequate calories improves their nutritional balance. Various causes for their inadequate caloric intake have been identified, such as vomiting, refusal of food, and spillage. Refeeding a malnourished child is often successful using a combination of dietary manipulation, feeding therapy, and tube feeding, but it must be monitored closely. Further investigation is still needed regarding growth parameters and the criteria for optimal nutrition in children with cerebral palsy since all growth charts and reference standards currently available are for the normal population.

REFERENCES

1. Peeks S, Lamb MW: Comments on the dietary practices of cerebral palsied children. *J Am Diet Assoc* 1951;27:870–876.

2. Phelps WM: Dietary requirements in cerebral palsy. *J Am Diet Assoc.* 1951;27:869–870.

3. Sterling HM: Height and weight of children with cerebral palsy and acquired brain damage. *Arch Phys Med Rehabil* 1960;41:131–135.

4. Berg K, Isaksson B: Body composition and nutrition of school children with cerebral palsy. *Acta Paediatr Scan [Suppl]* 1970;205:41–52.

5. Haydock DA, Hill GL: Impaired wound healing in surgical patients with varying degrees of malnutrition. *J Parenter Enter Nutr* 1986;10:550–554.

6. Shapiro BK, Green P, Krick J, et al: Growth of severely impaired children: Neurological versus nutritional factors. *Dev Med Child Neurol* 1986;28:729–733.

7. Patrick J, Boland M, Stoski D, et al: Rapid correction of wasting in children with cerebral palsy. *Dev Med Child Neurol* 1986;28:734–739.

8. Nelson WE, Behrman RE, Vaughan VC (eds): *Nelson Textbook of Pediatrics*. Philadelphia, W.B. Saunders, 1987.

9. Culley WJ, Middleton TO: Caloric requirements of mentally retarded children with and without motor dysfunction. *J Pediatr* 1969;75:380–384.

10. Eddy TP, Nicholson AL, Wheeler EF: Energy intakes and dietary intakes in cerebral palsy. *Dev Med Child Neurol* 1985;7:377–385.

11. Roche AF, Himes JH: Incremental growth charts. *Am J Clin Nutr* 1980;33:2041–2052.

12. Walker EW, Watkins JB: *Nutrition in Pediatrics*. Boston, Little, Brown, 1985.

13. Blackman JA, Nelson CL: Reinstituting oral feedings in children fed by gastrostomy tube. *Clin Pediatr* 1985;24:434–438.

14. Chatoor I, Dickson, L, Einhorn A: Rumination: Etiology and treatment. *Pediatr Ann* 1984;13:924–929.

15. Mazo H, Chen CL, Wessen DE, et al: Incisionless gastrostomy for nutrititional support. *J Pediatr Gastroenterol Nutr* 1986;5:66–69.

16. Heymsfield SB, Bethel RA, Ansley JD, et al: Cardiac abnormalities in cachectic patients before and during nutritional repletion. *Am Heart J* 1987;95:584–593.

The syndrome of autism: Update and guidelines for diagnosis

B.J. Freeman, PhD
Professor of Medical Psychology
Department of Psychiatry and
  Biobehavioral Sciences
University of California, Los Angeles
Los Angeles, California

IN 1943 DR LEO KANNER, Professor of Child Psychiatry at Johns Hopkins School of Medicine, published a description of a unique group of children. These children had failed to develop normal relationships, were upset by changes in their environments, and showed abnormalities in speech and language.[1] The "autism" or self-centeredness in these children was recognized as a pathognomonic feature of their illness, and the terms autistic and autism came to denote their illness. Similar patterns were soon identified in children throughout the world.

In the subsequent five decades, much progress has been made in validating Kanner's concept of autism. It is now well recognized that the syndrome differs from other severe disorders of childhood in both its clinical features and course. When specific etiologic mechanisms have not yet been identified, it is now clear that autism is a heterogeneous syndrome with multiple biologic etiologies. Current consensus is that any agent or event that can produce damage to the central nervous system (CNS) can produce the syndrome of autism.

As when diagnosing any severe condition, it is necessary to be skillful and to go slowly. If not absolutely sure (for instance, when children are less than 2 years old or because symptoms and history are not clear on first review), it is best to tell the parents the three hardest words to say in any language, "I don't know." Then, arrange to see the child again in a few weeks or a month. Several such clinical snapshots may be necessary before you can obtain a mental movie of the child's development—a movie of sufficient detail to reveal the developmental disturbances and symptoms indicative of autism. It is preferable to go slowly and be certain, than either to miss another diagnosis or needlessly alarm a family by saying autism is present. Autism is a "hard" diagnosis to make, just as leukemia is "hard" to diagnose, because historically it has been associated with such a bleak prognosis. Its presence must not be denied when it is there, however. The diagnosis must always be made judiciously and with all due humility and sensitivity for the feelings of autistic persons, their parents, and their siblings. The purpose of this article is to provide an overview of how to make this hard diagnosis in the preschool child.

DEFINITION OF THE SYNDROME

Only a few short years ago children with the syndrome of autism were labeled as having childhood psychosis, severe emotional disability, atypical ego development, childhood schizophrenia, symbiotic psychosis, early (primary) or late (secondary) onset autism, or mental retardation with autistic features. Therapy was

Inf Young Children 1993; 6(2): 1–11
© 1993 Aspen Publishers, Inc.

just as idiosyncratic, ranging from parentectomy and psychoanalysis to electro-convulsive therapy (ECT) and lobotomy (stun and lacerate physical toxins). Most pathetically, the same children were often prescribed alternating courses of these widely differing "therapies" as their families floundered from clinic to clinic vainly seeking help for their children.[2]

Fortunately, as we enter the 1990s the situation has improved dramatically. In 1978, the Autism Society of America formulated a definition of the syndrome of autism.[3] It represented a consensus among professionals from different countries and disciplines and formed the basis for a similar and overlapping definition published in the American Psychiatric Association's *Diagnostic and Statistical Manual (DSM-III* and *DSM-III-R).*[4,5] Currently, these definitions are being refined even further and a new edition of the manual will be available next year.[6] These definitions are based on assumptions and facts that contradict some cherished mis-beliefs about autism and may require revision and updating of current thinking. For example, it is now agreed that

- *Autism is a clinical (behaviorally defined) syndrome.* It is considered a clinical syndrome because objective pathognomonic biomedical markers common to all cases have not been identified yet. Like all syndromes (eg, pneumonia, epilepsy, hypertension, diabetes), autism is assumed to be composed of many subtypes, each with different etiologies and possible treatments.

- *Autism is a spectrum disorder.* The concept of a spectrum or continuum of symptoms is enormously complex. While the expression of symptoms ranges from severe to mild, the concept of a continuum of symptoms is not simple. The manifestation of social and other impairments varies widely in all combinations of subtype and severity. Although most subtypes have not been named as separate syndromes, some (eg, Rett's syndrome[7]) have. The mistake most often made in diagnosis is the failure to recognize all the possible combinations of symptoms that can occur.

- *Autism is a developmental diagnosis.* As with all diagnoses made in childhood, expression of symptoms varies with both the age and developmental level of the person affected. Thus, autism is lifelong. While symptoms fluctuate, abate, change, and some may even disappear, once autistic, always autistic. Autistic persons have a normal life expectancy, and the majority require lifelong social support systems due to their developmental handicaps and continuing symptomatology.

- *Autism is a retrospective diagnosis.* While symptoms can appear as early as the first months of life, some children will display normal development until 12 to 24 months of age. Because most children are not seen until later and some persons are not seen until they are adults, it is not possible to make a differential diagnosis until a careful developmental history is obtained. This history should cover all aspects of development and a person's life course.

- *Autism is ubiquitous.* Autism occurs in all parts of the world, in all races and colors, and in all types of families. No social or psychologic characteristics of parents or families have proven to be associated with autism. Boys are affected more often than girls by a ratio of four or five to one, and some families have more than one autistic child.
- *Autism frequently occurs in association with other syndromes, specific diseases, and developmental disabilities.* The most common co-occurring condition is mental retardation. For example, approximately 70% of all autistic patients also have the syndrome of mental retardation (ie, score below 70 on intelligence quotient [IQ] testing). This finding occurs because the brain pathology that produces the symptoms of autism also affects cognitive development and symbol processing.[8] Epilepsy, motor incoordination, fragile X, and severe allergies are other frequent concurrent syndromes.[9] As persons with autism develop into adolescence, many will become anxious or depressed as a result of social pressures. There is no reason to believe that having autism precludes other forms of psychopathology.

It is critical to apply these principles when interpreting current criteria for diagnosing autism. Failure to do so can lead to a lack of recognition of the syndrome or misdiagnosis. In turn, parents may receive misinformation and patients may receive improper treatment.

The *DSM-IV*[6] criteria for autism state that in order to make the diagnosis of autism a child must show abnormal development prior to the age of 3 years as manifested by delays or abnormal functioning in social development (ie, gross and sustained impairment in social interaction), language or its use in social communication or play (ie, gross and sustained impairment in communication), and restricted patterns of behaviors, interests, and activities. Subtypes of autistic disorder, listed as other pervasive developmental disorders, include Rett's syndrome, Heller's syndrome, Asperger's syndrome, atypical autism, and atypical pervasive developmental disorder.[6]

These diagnostic criteria often result in confusion when applied to preschool-age children. Terms such as childhood onset pervasive developmental disorder and atypical pervasive developmental disorder often cloud the diagnostic picture of autism. Dahl and associates[10] have suggested that the main differences among these groups are degrees of impairment. Thus, it is more useful clinically to consider these different groups along a continuum of autistic disorder rather than as suffering from different conditions requiring different treatments.

DEVELOPMENT OF THE SYNDROME

Pregnancy and delivery factors

Several studies of pregnancy and delivery factors have been published and point to an increase in perinatal hazards in autism. For example, Gillberg and

Gillberg[11] compared 25 autistic and 25 controls on an "optimality" scale comprised of 30 pre-, peri-, and neonatal factors. They found that the mothers of autistic children showed reduced optimality, especially regarding prenatal factors. Maternal age, generalized maternal edema, pre- or post-maturity, mediation, and uterine bleeding during pregnancy were the adverse factors most often recorded. Furthermore, autistic patients with high IQs had the same reduced optimality scores as did those patients with very low IQs.

More recently, Mason-Brothers and coworkers[12] examined pre-, peri-, and neonatal factors in 287 pregnancies. They concurred with the findings of Gillberg and Gillberg[11] that no single factor was correlated with autism. In fact many of the adverse pregnancy factors occurred at the same rates in both autistic and normal populations. It is now well recognized that no single pre-, peri-, or neonatal factor can account for all cases of autism, and that any event that causes damage to the CNS may also produce autism.[13]

Developmental appearance of symptoms

It is now clear that just as autism must be viewed as a continuum, it must also be viewed developmentally. The development of autistic children is characterized by various peculiarities including lags and spurts,[14] regressions,[15,16] and unevenness across domains of functioning.[3,17] As a result of these peculiarities, researchers have not utilized traditional developmental models to study autism. Recent research[18-22] on developmental issues in atypical populations, however, has indicated that even autistic children can be studied within traditional models. For example, because the majority of persons with autism are also mentally retarded,[3] it becomes important to separate behaviors that may be due to mental retardation from those that are unique and thus diagnostic of autism.[21,22] In addition, it is also important to study basic issues regarding developmental processes such as sequences and profiles in autism.

In a recent study, Burack and Volkmar[23] assessed aspects of developmental sequences and structures in low- and high-functioning autistic and nonautistic developmentally delayed children. Specifically, they examined sequences, regressions, and profiles of development. Results indicated few differences among the groups in sequences of development. As previously reported,[3] however, the autistic children were more likely than nonautistic children to display developmental regressions and unevenness across developmental domains. These authors hypothesize that autistic children may show greater variation in transitions from one stage of development to the next or the extent to which an individual autistic child has mastered the developmental skills or milestones. Much more research is needed, however, to delineate the development of the various domains of functioning and how they relate to each other. Thus, when taking a history it is necessary to ask questions regarding irregularities of development in the motor, speech and language/cognitive, and social domain. Table 1 contains a partial listing of symptoms that may emerge at various developmental stages in these three areas.

As mentioned previously, extensive clinical experience reveals that characteristic symptoms and developmental delays are usually present during the first year of life.[3] In some carefully documented cases, however, apparently normal development for 12 to 24 months precedes the onset of symptoms. In these later cases, parents may associate the onset of symptoms with a specific medical illness (eg, infection, unexplained high fever, or seizure onset). Such illnesses may be relevant etiologically to the autism, but attempts to establish the validity of these relationships have not been successful.[9]

Motor development may be precocious, retarded, or characterized by spurts followed by plateaus. Previously acquired skills may be lost. Generalized hyperactivity is often seen, as are sleep-pattern disturbances (eg, the child will only sleep for 3 or 4 hours at a time).[3]

Disturbances in the responses to sensory stimuli include generalized hyper- and hyporeactivity and an alternation of these two states over periods ranging from hours to months. Thus, unusual sensitivity to auditory, visual, tactile, proprioceptive, and vestibular stimulation, paradoxically, is accompanied often by pursuit of these sensations. This inability of autistic persons to modulate sensory input appropriately results in the development of various repetitive habits, mannerisms, and gestures, referred to as motility disturbances, which are included as symptoms under a restricted repertoire of activities in the *DSM-IV*.[6]

Disturbances of speech and language include both verbal and nonverbal communication. Speech may be absent, delayed in onset, or peculiar. If present, speech may be characterized by echolalia or parroting. In early infancy, the child may fail to cry or stop babbling. Autistic children will often use a word once and then not use it again. Parents often report that the child can talk but refuses to do so. In addition, autistic children fail to develop a normal system of gesturing. They will often direct an adult's hand to make their needs known. As the children get older, they may develop speech but have absent or limited symbolic capacities.

Specific cognitive capacities, such as rote memory or visual-spatial skills, may be intact, but there is a failure to develop abstract reasoning and concepts. This situation is often confusing for parents and persons unfamiliar with autism. For example, a 2-year-old child may be able to do complex jigsaw puzzles but not be able to speak.

Disturbances in social skills are characterized by a failure to develop appropriate responsivity to people and to assign symbolic meaning to objects. These symptoms include emotional remoteness, nonuse of eye contact, and indifference to being held. It is important to remember that it is not that autistic persons "do not relate" as is commonly said, but rather than they often relate to people and objects in very peculiar ways. Furthermore, an autistic child may alternate between relat-

Table 1. Areas of disturbances

Age (months)	Sensory-motor (restricted repertoire of activities)	Speech-language cognitive development	Social (relating to people and objects)
Birth 0–6	Persistent rocking Inconsistent response to stimuli	No vocalizing Crying not related to needs Does not react differentially to adult voices	No anticipatory social responses (when sees or hears mother) Does not quiet when held Poor or absent eye-to-eye contact Fails to respond to mother's attention and crib toys
6–12	Uneven motor development Difficulty with response to textures (eg, problems transitioning to table foods) Failure to hold objects or attachments to unusual objects (or both) Appears to be deaf Preoccupation with fingers Over- or under-reaction to sensory stimuli (or both)	Babbling may stop Does not imitate sounds, gestures, or expressions Does not relate needs Does not give objects when requested to do so	Unaffectionate, difficult to engage in baby games Does not initiate baby games Does not wave "bye-bye" No interest in toys Flicks toys away Does not show distress when mother leaves room Absent or delayed social smile Does not repeat activities that he or she enjoys Does not extend toys to other people Does not differentiate strangers from family
12–24	Loss of previously acquired skills Hyper- or hyposensitivity to stimuli Seeks repetitive stimulation Repetitive motor mannerisms appear (eg, hand flapping, whirling)	No speech or occasional words Stops talking Gestures do not develop Repeats sounds noncommunicatively Words used inconsistently and may not be related to needs	Withdrawn Does not seek comfort when distressed May be overdistressed by separation No pretend play or unusual use of toys (eg, spins, flicks, lines up objects) Imitation does not develop No interest in peers

(continues)

Table 1. Continued

Age (months)	Sensory-motor (restricted repertoire of activities)	Speech-language cognitive development	Social (relating to people and objects)
24–36	Unusual sensitivity to stimuli and repetitive motor mannerisms continue Hyperactivity or hypoactivity (or both)	Mute or intermittent talking Echolalia (eg, repeats television commercials) Specific cognitive abilities (eg, good rote memory, superior puzzle skills) Appears to be able to do things but refuses Leads adults by hand to communicate needs Does not use speech communication	Does not play with others Prefers to be alone Does not imitate Does not show desire to please parents
36–60	Repetitive behaviors may decrease or occur only intermittently	No speech Echolalia Pronoun reversal Abnormal tone and rhythm in speech Does not volunteer information or initiate conversation May ask repetitive questions	Above continue but may become more interested in social activities Does not know how to initiate with peers Upset by changes in environment Delay or absence in thematic play

ing and responding appropriately and "totally tuning out." Mood swings also occur for no apparent reason. The child may start to laugh or cry in the absence of obvious external causes.

In summary, the development of autistic children is primarily characterized by two traits. First is inconsistency, the hallmark of the syndrome, in both development and response to the environment. Inconsistency should alert the diagnostician that further evaluation may be indicated. Second, autistic children, like normal and retarded children, follow laws of child development. Specific behavioral features such as the ability to initiate language and social skills, engage in symbolic play, and successfully complete tasks are related directly to the overall mental age of the child. Evidence does indicate that, in contrast to nonautistic mentally retarded children, autistic children may have more serious problems in the development of symbolic play, abstract reasoning, and nonverbal communication skills.

DIAGNOSTIC PROCEDURE

Differential and early diagnosis of autism are critical because the prognosis for autistic children has changed markedly since Kanner's[1] initial work. Identifying and diagnosing autism early can provide access to appropriate services [24] that results in a better prognosis.[8] In addition, parents benefit from having a label to put on their child's problem. It helps them understand why the child is having difficulties and helps to focus treatment efforts.[25] In spite of the recognized advantage of differential diagnosis, there is still a reluctance among professionals to "label" a child.

Konstantareas[26] recently identified several problems relative to the diagnostic process and reluctance to label a child. These problems include failure to recognize the full range of the symptoms, attempt to minimize severity of the disorder, inadequate feedback counseling, and failure to make appropriate recommendations. To avoid these problems the diagnostic process should include a flexible, tolerant, and empathetic attitude toward the child and family. Once the differential diagnosis includes autism, the special evaluations outlined in the box, "Components of an Evaluation in the Diagnosis of Autism," must be undertaken to assess organic, cognitive, intellectual, psychologic, and family factors. The diagnosis of autism should be based on direct observation of the child in both structured and unstructured situations as well as a careful developmental history.

Components of an Evaluation in the Diagnosis of Autism

Medical factors
- Developmental history
- Maternal medical records
- Child's medical records
- Medical and neurologic evaluations as indicated
- Audiometric and visual screening

Cognitive-intellectual assessment
- Nonverbal skills
- Verbal skills
- Educational assessment

Psychologic and social-adaptive skills

Family and social factors

ASSESSING MEDICAL FACTORS

A variety of biologic conditions, including congenital rubella, tuberous sclerosis, Down syndrome, viral infections, fragile X, and Rett's syndrome, has been shown to occur in association with autism.[9] While the majority of these conditions do not respond to specific interventions, they may have important implications, especially genetic, for families. Thus, it is important to rule out these conditions or diagnose them if they coexist with autism. In order to accomplish this, the first strategy is to obtain developmental and medical data. Tactics include interviewing all relatives, teachers, and other significant adults in the child's life, reviewing home movies and photograph albums, making home visits, and obtaining all permanent records. Flexibility and imagination are necessary ingredients in gathering a historical picture, and the importance of piecing together as complete a picture as possible cannot be overemphasized. Other tests may include medical and neurologic evaluations (eg, computed axial tomography, magnetic resonance imaging, and electroencephalograms). Special studies for metabolic and congenital syndromes may be necessary if indicated. Comprehensive visual and auditory examination should always be performed.

ASSESSING COGNITIVE AND INTELLECTUAL FACTORS

The use of standardized tests to assess cognitive development in autistic children has been very controversial. Initially, Kanner assumed that autistic persons had normal intelligence, although they were unassessable on standardized tests. Autistic persons could not be tested due to particular problems associated with their intellectual capabilities and their unique behavior problems. These arguments were buttressed by observations that some severely regressed autistic persons occasionally said or did something that indicated to the tester that they were "bright" or had "cognitive skills" hidden behind their "autistic wall." A notion that autistics were like "idiot savants" and had "islands of intelligence" or "splinter skills" gained much popularity during the 1940s and 1950s.

There is now ample evidence that most autistic persons indeed can be assessed accurately on standardized tests and can benefit from structured special education programs. Today most investigators agree that cognitive and intellectual capacities can be assessed on standardized tests and that the large majority of autistics function in the retarded range.[2,7]

Standardized IQ tests for autistic persons remain useful prognostic indicators. This finding is only true, however, when special tactics for assessments are tailored to each person. In particular, tests should assess verbal and nonverbal skills separately and should be appropriate to the developmental level of functioning rather than the age of the patient. Tests must be administered individually by experienced examiners. Maximum performance must be elicited by use of ancillary techniques such as those derived from behavior therapy.

ASSESSING PSYCHOLOGIC FACTORS

Psychodiagnostic interviews may be useful to determine an autistic person's general level of personality development as well as specific strengths and weaknesses. This assessment may help to determine overall management strategies and long-term planning. Psychodynamic understanding of key family members also is often necessary to aid in these undertakings.

The level of a child's social-adaptive behavior also must be assessed. As with cognitive tests, one must be careful to use only tests that are appropriate to developmental levels of functioning and to assess social-adaptive behaviors independently of cognitive functioning. In normal persons, there is a strong correlation between cognitive abilities and social functioning. However, this correlation does not usually exist with autistic persons who may show age-appropriate cognitive capacities on a highly structured test, but be unable to utilize these skills in day-to-day living situations.[27] Thus, systemic and structural behavioral observations may be a preferable strategy to assessing socio-adaptive behavior on tests.

ASSESSING FAMILY FACTORS

Careful clinical assessment of parents and siblings is a necessary ingredient of the diagnostic evaluation. Parents of autistic children have been shown in many studies to react to the diagnosis in a similar fashion as the parents of other developmentally delayed children. Their difficulties are often compounded by the fact that their autistic children look normal and at times can conduct themselves in socially appropriate ways. A child in a wheelchair evokes sympathy in a supermarket, whereas an inconsolable screaming autistic child may evoke hostility. Social strains can precipitate mental disruption and psychopathology in brothers and sisters. Referral for psychiatric evaluation and supportive treatment may be necessary in extreme cases.[28]

Finally, one must always keep in mind the sequence that all families go through when advised they have a developmentally delayed child:
1. denial (No, it cannot be true, the child will grow out of it.),
2. distortion (The child's just a little slow, but Einstein did not talk until he was 5 years old.),
3. projection (It is the obstetrician's fault; help us sue this physician.),
4. search for magical cure (Mega-vitamins, auditory training, and chiropractic manipulations will cure my child.),
5. exclusion (The child needs to be sent away to an institution never to be seen again.) or denial (buttressed by completely tailoring the family's life to the child's handicap), and
6. adjustment and acceptance.[2]

In the face of these reactions, appropriate supportive counseling may be necessary. It is important to remember, however, that everyone adjusts to having a handicapped child at a different rate. If a clinician is to help parents, then the clinician must be careful not to project personal values onto families.[29]

PRINCIPLES OF MANAGEMENT

Who can make the diagnosis of autism? The optimal situation is, of course, a multidisciplinary setting with specially trained persons in the areas listed in the Box. The reality is that this setting may not always be available to autistic persons and their families. It is important to remember that diagnosis at this point is a "clinical art" not a science. There is no checklist for diagnosis. Thus, the most important criteria for a diagnostician are knowledge of the syndrome, recognition of the implications for a family, and a willingness to work with a family.

The fact that autism is a lifelong disorder with a highly variable course necessitates a long-term clinician–family relationship punctuated by periodic reevaluations. The stage should be set for this during initial feedback sessions with parents. Explain that a long voyage lies ahead and tacks in several directions will be required. Consultations with medical, behavioral, educational, and other specialists will be required along the way, and different routes and harbors must be found. For example, autistic children may develop seizures and for a while require anticonvulsant medication. Periods of severe behavior problems may require intervals of strict behavioral control or psychotropic medications. Living at home during early adolescence may prove impractical. A solid, mutually respectful, and cooperative professional–family relationship is the fulcrum on which such changes can be weighed and implemented over time. One final recommendation for proper management is that professionals must become advocates for the children, join local chapters of the Autism Society of America, join professional advisory boards of parents and school organizations, testify before and lobby government agencies for appropriate services, and speak before parent groups. Most important, professionals must continue their education by attending seminars on autism, subscribing to journals devoted to autism, and joining the Autism Society of America.

THE PROGNOSIS OF THE SYNDROME

Several investigators have traced the natural course of the syndrome. Between 7% and 28% of autistic children who showed no clinical evidence of neurologic disease in early childhood, developed seizures by age 18 years.[30] Approximately 50% of all autistic children function in the retarded range throughout life, and initial cognitive test scores are highly predictive of later outcome.[31] Children with seizures and other indicators of specific organic brain dysfunction tend to be the most retarded, undeveloped, and ultimately impaired. The second prognostic group, approximately 25%, contains children whose motor development is relatively normal and who develop communicative language before the age of 5 years. Children in this group usually become extremely shy, introverted, and passive when adolescents. They will need continued supervision in living situations, but can often function in supported employment. The third prognostic group (approximately 25%) have normal intelligence, are able to live and work independently, and, in rare cases, may marry and have children.[32] These persons will continue to show significant personality, social, and specific cognitive impairment, however. More recent studies[8,33] are more optimistic. With increased expansion of social, vocational, and residential support services in the community, persons challenged with autism increasingly will be able to maximize their potential.

•   •   •

This article highlights some of the issues faced by professionals in the diagnosis of autism. These issues are extremely complex and require equally complex solutions. The future of autistic persons largely depends on early identification and continuing proper management. This responsibility belongs to both parents and professionals. With love, understanding, early intervention, and education, people with autism can and do lead happy and productive lives and can be integrated into society. The problem is that society is not always tolerant of persons who are different. It is up to us as parents and professionals to educate society and increase the understanding and appreciation of these very special people.

REFERENCES

1. Kanner L. Autistic disturbances of affective contact. *Nerv Child.* 1943;2:217–250.

2. Freeman BJ, Ritvo ER. The syndrome of autism: establishing diagnoses and principles of management. *Pediatr Ann.* 1984;13:284–296.

3. Ritvo ER, Freeman BJ. National Society for Autistic Children definition of the syndrome autism. *J Pediatr Psychol.* 1977;4:146–148.

4. American Psychiatric Association. *Diagnostic and Statistical Manual of Mental Disorders.* 3rd ed. Washington, DC: American Psychiatric Association; 1980.

5. American Psychiatric Association. *Diagnostic and Statistical Manual of Mental Disorders.* 3rd ed, rev. Washington, DC: American Psychiatric Association; 1984.

6. American Psychiatric Association. *Diagnostic and Statistical Manual of Mental Disorders.* 4th ed. Washington, DC: American Psychiatric Association. In press.

7. Philippart M. Clinical recognition of Rett syndrome. *Am J Med Genet.* 1986;24:111–118.

8. Freeman BJ, Rahbar B, Ritvo ER, Bice TL, Yokota A, Ritvo R. The stability of cognitive and behavioral parameters in autism: a twelve year prospective study. *J Am Acad Child Adolesc Psychiatry.* 1991;30:479–482.

9. Ritvo ER, Mason-Brothers A, Freeman BJ, et al. The UCLA–University of Utah epidemiologic survey of autism: the etiologic role of rare diseases. *Am J Psychiatry.* 1990;147:1614–1621.

10. Dahl EK, Cohen DJ, Provence S. Clinical and multivariate approaches to the nosology of pervasive developmental disorder. *J Am Acad Child Adolesc Psychiatry.* 1986;25:170–180.

11. Gillberg C, Gillberg IC. Infantile autism. A total population study of reduced optimality in the pre-, peri- and neo-natal period. *J Autism Dev Disord* 1983;13:153–166.

12. Mason-Brothers A, Ritvo ER, Pingree C, et al. The UCLA–University of Utah epidemiologic survey of autism: pre-, peri-, and post-natal factors. *Pediatrics.* 1990;86:514–519.

13. Schopler E, Mesibov G, eds. *Neurobiological Issues in Autism. Current issues in autism.* New York, NY: Plenum; 1987.

14. Fish B, Shapiro T, Halpern F, Wile R. Prediction of schizophrenia in infancy. *Am J Psychiatry.* 1965;121:768–775.

15. Harper J, Williams S. Age and type of onset as critical variables in early infantile autism. *J Aut Child Schizophr.* 1975;5:25–35.

16. Hoshino Y, Kaneko M. Yashima Y, Kumashiro H, Volkmar F, Cohen D. Clinical features of autistic children with setback course in their infancy. *Jpn. J Psychiatr Neurol.* 1987;41:237–246.

17. Volkmar F, Sparrow S, Goudreau D, Cicchetti D, Paul R, Cohen D. Social deficits in autism: an operational approach using the Vineland Adaptive Behavior Scales. *J Am Acad Child Adolesc Psychiatry.* 1987;26:156–161.

18. Hodapp R, Burack J, Zigler E. *Issues in Developmental Approaches to Mental Retardation.* New York, NY: Cambridge University Press; 1990.

19. Cicchetti D, Beeghly M. *Down Syndrome: The Developmental Perspective.* New York, NY: Cambridge University Press; 1990.

20. Sigman M, Mundy P. Symbolic processes in young autistic children. In: Cicchetti D, Beeghly M, eds. *Symbolic Development in Atypical Children: New Directions for Child Development.* San Francisco, Calif: Jossey-Bass; 1987.

21. Volkmar F. Burack J. Sequences and structures of development in autistic children (poster). Presented at meeting of American Academy of Child and Adolescent Psychiatry; October 1989: New York, NY.

22. Freeman BJ, Ritvo E, Schroth P. Behavior assessment of the syndrome of autism: behavior observation system. *J Am Acad Child Psychiatry.* 1984;23:588–594.

23. Burack JA, Volkmar FR. Development of low- and high-functioning autistic children. *J Child Psychol Psychiatry.* 1992;33:607–616.

24. Gallagher J. Public policy and its impact on autism. In: Schopler E, Mesibov G, eds. *Diagnosis and Assessment in Autism.* New York, NY: Plenum; 1988.

25. Akerley M. What's in a name? In: Schopler E, Mesibov G, eds. *Diagnosis and Assessment in Autism.* New York, NY: Plenum; 1988.

26. Konstantareas MM. After diagnosis, what? Some possible problems and diagnostic assessments. *Can J Psychiatry.* 1989;34:549–553.

27. Freeman BJ, Ritvo ER, Yokota A, Childs J. WISC-R and Vineland Adaptive Behavior Scale scores in autistic children. *J Am Child Adolesc Psychiatry.* 1988;27:428–429.

28. Marcus L, Schopler E. Working with families from a developmental perspective. In: Cohen D, Donnellan A, Paul R, eds. *Handbook of Autism and Pervasive Developmental Disorders.* New York, NY: Wiley; 1987.

29. Cutler B, Kozloff M. Living with autism: effects on families and family needs. In: Cohen D, Donnellan A, Paul R, eds. *Handbook of Autism and Pervasive Developmental Disorders.* New York, NY: Wiley; 1987.

30. Rutter M. Autistic children—infancy to adulthood. *Semin Psychiatry.* 1970;2:435–450.

31. Freeman BJ, Ritvo ER, Needleman R, Yakota A. Stability of cognitive and linguistic parameters autism: a five-year prospective study of autism. *J Am Acad Child Psychiatry.* 1985;24:459–464.

32. Ritvo ER, Freeman BJ, Mason-Brothers A, Ritvo A. Clinical characteristics of mild autism in adults. *Compr Psychiatry.* 1993; in press.

33. Venter A, Lord C, Schopler E. A follow-up study of high-functioning autistic children. *J Child Psychol Psychiatry.* 1992;33:489–507.

Communication-based assessment and intervention for prelinguistic infants and toddlers: Strategies and issues

Billy T. Ogletree, PhD
Assistant Professor
Department of Human Services
Western Carolina University
Cullowhee, North Carolina

Debora Burns Daniels, MA
Coordinator for Speech and Language
　Services
Children's Rehabilitation Unit
The University of Kansas Medical
　Center
Kansas City, Kansas

SINCE THE PASSAGE of Public Law 99-457 (Education of the Handicapped Act Amendments of 1986), the early identification and treatment of at-risk children have become national priorities. In response, individual states have initiated the development and implementation of comprehensive interagency programs to address the needs of infants, toddlers, and their families.[1] When in place, these programs are intended to assist with the evaluation and facilitation of cognitive, motor, and communicative and social development in children at risk for disabilities.

The successful implementation of Public Law 99-457 will require well-prepared, collaborative professionals. Unfortunately, many existing service providers have limited educational or practical experiences with children under the age of 3 years. Others are unfamiliar with "cutting edge" service delivery approaches or models and principles. If left unaddressed, this lack of preparedness could jeopardize early identification and intervention efforts.

Professional preparedness and collaboration are largely dependent on early interventionists' knowledge across disciplines with respect to the abilities and needs of young children. The purpose of this article is to provide early intervention team members with an overview of issues related to prelinguistic communicative development and the assessment and treatment of communicative impairments in infants and toddlers. This information is vital in light of the fact that communication impairments are often the initial indicator of primary handicapping conditions such as mental retardation or hearing impairment and are frequently associated with other areas of developmental delay.[2]

What follows is a review of social communication development during the prelanguage period (ie, birth to approximately 18 months of age). While the emergence of social communication is probably necessary for the development of language, it is not sufficient. Specifically, it does not account for the early development of language form (ie, phonology, morphology, and syntax). Language form, though not the focus of this article, should be a critical component of communication-based assessment and intervention with infants and toddlers. For more infor-

Inf Young Children 1993; 5(3): 22–30
© 1993 Aspen Publishers, Inc.

mation in this area, the reader is referred to the work of Stoel-Gammon,[3] Vihman,[4] and Bates et al.[5]

PRELINGUISTIC COMMUNICATION

Bates and coworkers[6] provided a framework for describing prelinguistic communication. Borrowing terminology from speech act theory,[7] they defined three states of early communicative growth. Infants function in the "perlocutionary stage" from birth to approximately 8 months of age. During this period, children's actions are preintentional (ie, nonpurposeful), yet may have systematic effects on their listeners. For example, an infant's cry may be interpreted as a request for feeding or a desire to be changed, depending on the context in which the cry occurs. Near 9 months of age, children enter the "illocutionary stage" as they gesture and vocalize to express needs and desires intentionally (ie, purposefully). The illocutionary child may request a desired object by reaching, vocalizing, and alternating his or her eye gaze between an adult and the object. Finally, at approximately 13 months of age, the communicative behaviors of children reflect movement into the "locutionary stage" of development. This period is characterized by intentional symbol use, typically referential words.

From this framework, it is apparent that an important accomplishment of the child during the prelinguistic period is the development of intentional communication. It has been suggested that prior to first words, children communicate intentionally for a variety of reasons.[7,8] These reasons, or communicative intentions, have been grouped by Bruner[9] into three categories:

1. behavioral regulation, including efforts to obtain the assistance of others in the pursuit or restriction of a goal,
2. social interaction, including efforts to direct the attention of others to oneself, and
3. joint attention, including efforts to establish shared attention with others.

Research examining prelinguistic intentional communication has helped to describe the emergence of intentions within each of the categories described by Bruner.[9] Efforts have demonstrated that prior to the emergence of words, children express a full range of intentions through gestures and vocalizations.[7,8,10–13] Furthermore, there is strong evidence suggesting that prelinguistic intentional communication is a necessary precursor to the development of language.[8,9]

Three theories have been postulated explaining the origins of intentional communication. One views communicative intent as an innate human capacity present from early infancy.[14,15] Another suggests that intentional communication is an acquired social skill where the infant, through a process of discovery with the communicative partner, learns rules and procedures for successful interactions.[8,16–18] A third position proposes that intentional communication results from the primary caregiver's interpretation of infant behavior from birth.[19-23] According to this perspective, the caregiver encourages the emergence of intentionality by first providing meaning for infant actions and later referencing that meaning with the infant.

Each of these positions seems necessary to explain the origin of communicative intent. For example, the presence of consistent sound patterns in infant cries,[24] infant preferences for human faces and voices,[25] and the ability of infants to follow a caregiver's line of regard[26] are critical innate aspects of emerging intentionality. Innate infant preparedness alone, however, cannot account for intentional communication. These abilities must be fostered through the infant's development of social rules and action formats within the communicative dyad (ie, the caregiver–child relationship). Furthermore intentionality is largely dependent on the presence of the primary caregiver, who creates opportunities for communication and interprets infant behavior.

In summary, the prelinguistic period is a time of considerable communicative growth. Prior to first words, children communicate intentionally for a variety of reasons with increasingly complex signals. In turn, this early signaling appears to establish the groundwork for the development of language. Given the suggested relationship between prelinguistic communication and later language development, the assessment and treatment of communication impairments during the prelinguistic period should be a priority for persons serving infants and toddlers.

ASSESSMENT ISSUES

Rossetti defines assessment as "any activity, either formal or informal, that is designed to elicit accurate and reliable samples of infant–toddler behavior from which inferences relative to developmental skill status may be made."[27(p45)] Given normal developmental variance and problems with eliciting representative communication behaviors from young children, the assessment of prelinguistic communication can pose a particular challenge for early interventionists. Central to this challenge are the following three issues: (1) the communicative abilities to be evaluated, (2) the means for evaluating these abilities, and (3) the use of the evaluation findings in determining treatment appropriateness.

Assessment targets

Assessment objectives should be selected with reference to a child's chronologic age and developmental functioning level. The box entitled "Assessment Targets for Prelinguistic Children" lists possible assessment targets for children functioning at each of the stages of prelinguistic communicative development postulated by Bates and associates.[6]

Assessment Targets for Prelinguistic Children

Perlocutionary functioning
　Physical competence
　　Hearing
　　Vision
　　Vocal development
　　Gestural development (upper extremity movement)
　Behaviors
　　Affective displays (positive and negative)
　　Gaze shifts
　　Attempts to gain and share attention
　　Turn taking within social exchanges
　Caregiver variables
　　Sensitivity to child behaviors
　　Consistency of responses to child behaviors
　　Provision of communicative opportunities
Illocutionary and Locutionary functioning
　Expression of communicative intent
　　Communicative intentions
　　Communicative means (gestures, vocalizations)
　Symbolic abilities
　　Comprehension of words and simple word combinations
　　Use of words and simple word combinations
　　Number of words
　　Types of words and word combinations
　　Phonetic composition of words
　　Single and multiple action play schemes

For the perlocutionary child (birth to 8 months of age), appropriate targets are those aspects of early development thought to contribute to the emergence of communicative intent. These targets include the child's physical competence (hearing and vision status and vocal and gestural development), socioemotional communicative behaviors[28,29] (emotional displays and efforts to gain attention and share affective states), and the caregiver's sensitivity and responsiveness within the caregiver–child dyad.[19]

Assessment objectives for children functioning at the illocutionary and locutionary stages of development (9 months of age and above) should include both the expression of communicative intent and verbal and nonverbal symbolic abilities. Wetherby and Prizant[30] stress the importance of evaluating communicative intent along vertical and horizontal dimensions. While a vertical analysis evaluates the sophistication of communicative signaling from the use of gestures and vocalizations through the emergence of language, a horizontal analysis considers the range of communicative intentions expressed by children. As mentioned earlier, normally developing children regulate behavior, reference joint attention, and engage in social interaction prior to the emergence of first words.[10,13]

Symbolic abilities emerging in locutionary children include the comprehension and use of words and word combinations and the development of nonverbal symbolic behavior (eg, play). Benedict's[31] evaluation of early lexical (ie, word) abilities suggests that during the first 18 months, reasonable targets for comprehension assessment are common action words and labels. Assessment targets related to verbal symbol use should include the number, phonetic composition, and types of words or word combinations used. Nonverbal symbolic assessment targets should include those play behaviors known to parallel specific achievements in communication development such as the use of single and multiple action play schemes. These behaviors typically occur as children begin to use words and word combinations.[32,33]

Evaluation methods

A variety of methods is available for the assessment of prelinguistic communication including formal test administration, observation of communicative competency, and parental or other report (eg, medical records, anecdotal reports of teachers or family members).[27] Unfortunately, these methods are not without limitations.

Wetherby and Prizant[34] identified the following problems with most formal assessment instruments for infants and toddlers:

- they target the forms of communication (ie, the use of gestures, signs, words, and multiword phrases) rather than the functions these forms express (eg, requesting, protesting, commenting, and so forth),
- they fail to analyze preverbal gestures and vocalizations,
- they may not assess social-affective signaling,
- they do not allow for the profiling of strengths and weaknesses across the domains of speech, language, and communicative functioning,
- they may rely solely on parent report,
- they are primarily clinician directed, limiting opportunities for the observation of initiated communication, and
- they may not use parents as active participants in the assessment process.

The more informal assessment methods such as child observation and informant report can also be problematic. For example, observations can reflect atypical child behavior, while the reports of parents and others may be affected by a lack of informant subjectivity.

To minimize problems associated with assessment, methods should be combined to form an evaluation battery or protocol. An effective protocol reliably identifies the typical communicative behaviors used by infants and toddlers and provides information to assist with decisions regarding the need for and potential direction of intervention. The protocol not only focuses on the child, but also evaluates the ecology of the communicative environment. Assessment protocols for children functioning within each of the stages of prelinguistic communicative development postulated by Bates et al[6] are provided in the box entitled "Assessment Protocols for Prelinguistic Children."

An assessment protocol for the perlocutionary child should include direct caregiver–child observation, the administration of a formal assessment measure, and a caregiver interview. Observation of the child should allow for the evaluation of vocal and gestural development and caregiver–child interactions (eg, turn taking, caregiver response sensitivity and consistency). Optimally, observations should occur within a context familiar to the child and consist of nondirective and directive segments (ie, segments where the caregiver follows the child's lead and introduces objects or action formats into interaction).

Formal test administration should include one or more of several informant- or observation-based assessment measures (eg, the Communication and Symbolic Behavior Scales,[35] The Receptive-Expressive Emergent Language Scale-Revised,[36] the Infant-Toddler Language Scale,[37] the Sequenced Inventory of Communication Development,[38] and the Birth to Three Checklist of Learning and Language Behavior[39]). Selection of assessment measures should be made on the basis of the measure's completeness with respect to the evaluation of the assessment targets mentioned earlier. Although a discussion of specific measures is beyond the scope of this article, the reader is encouraged to refer to the work of Wetherby and Prizant[34] for a brief overview of the characteristics of commonly used assessment measures.

Assessment Protocols for Prelinguistic Children

Perlocutionary functioning
   Caregiver–child observation
   Formal assessment measure
   Caregiver interview
Illocutionary and locutionary functioning
   Caregiver–child observation
   Child behavior sampling
      Expression of communicative intent
      Communication and language comprehension
      Play
      Emerging expressive language (locutionary)
   Formal assessment measure
   Caregiver interview

The caregiver interview should address the typical communicative behaviors and abilities of the child, the communicative needs posed by the child's environment, and the representativeness of caregiver or child behaviors observed earlier in the protocol. Examples of interview formats are provided by Bates[8] and Wetherby and Prizant.[35]

An assessment protocol for the illocutionary or locutionary child should not differ significantly from that for the perlocutionary child. One major difference should be the inclusion of procedures to sample child behaviors. Sampling should target the child's expression of communicative intent (ie, the communicative intentions conveyed by the use of gestures, vocalizations, words, or word combinations) in addition to his or her emerging communication and language comprehension and play behaviors. One formal assessment measure providing comprehensive sampling procedures is the Communication and Symbolic Behavior Scales.[35] The locutionary child's assessment protocol should also include analyses of emerging expressive language abilities including utterance length and vocabulary diversity.

Treatment appropriateness

Given that the predictive interpretation of early communication-language assessment results is, at best, tenuous,[27] decisions regarding treatment appropriateness for infants and toddlers can be difficult. Such decisions are often made according to a discrepancy model. That is, treatment is recommended if a child's communicative functioning is discrepant with his or her developmental level. Of course, communication-based treatment is also frequently recommended for children where discrepancies do not exist.[40]

Data are being reported that provide insight into possible early indicators of communication or speech and language impairment and should be useful in treatment decisions. The box entitled "Indicators of Possible Communication Impairment" lists these indicators for each of the stages of prelinguistic communicative development identified by Bates and coworkers.[6]

Indicators of communication and speech and language impairment for the perlocutionary child include demographic factors, perinatal history, and interactional variables. Tomblin and associates[41] reported numerous demographic factors associated with communication impairments. In their study, children with poor communication abilities were typically male, occupied later birth order positions, had fathers with limited educational attainments, and were from families with histories of speech and language deficits. Aram and colleagues[42] reported that very low birth weight (<1.5 kg) was a common finding in the histories of children with impaired speech and language. Furthermore, numerous aspects of child and caregiver–child behavior have been identified as early indicators of communica-

---

Indicators of Possible Communication Impairment in Prelinguistic Children

Perlocutionary functioning
   Demographic factors
      Sex (typically males)
      Later birth order
      Family history
   Perinatal history
      Very low birth weight (<1.5 kg)
   Interactional variables
      Poor visual discrimination
      Limited turn taking
Illocutionary and locutionary functioning
   Communicative behaviors
      Low or high rates of communication
      Predominant uses of regulatory communicative intentions
      Predominant use of gestures
      Limited use of isolated vocalizations
      Limited use of vocalizations with consonants
      Limited use of respondent communicative acts
      Few comments
      Increased maladaptive behaviors
      Reduced phonologic maturity

---

tion impairment, including poor visual discrimination by the infant and limited turn taking within the caregiver–child dyad.[43]

Wetherby and coworkers[44] provided several indicators of communication impairment for children functioning at the illocutionary and early locutionary stages of communication development. Their preschool subjects with handicaps often displayed unusually low or high rates of communication when compared to typical peers. These authors suggested that low rates of communication may indicate a delay in the acquisition of intentional communication, while high communicative rates may signal language that is impaired relative to overall communication development (ie, impaired language in comparison to robust nonsymbolic communicative abilities). Other possible indicators of communicative impairment evidenced by these handicapped subjects included predominant use of regulatory communicative intentions (ie, communicative acts to request and protest) and gestures and limited use of isolated vocalizations, vocalizations with consonants, and respondent communicative acts (ie, communicative behaviors that respond to a previous topic, answer a question, or imitate a previous communicative behavior).

Paul[45] suggested additional indicators of speech and language impairment in her study of normally developing and language delayed children at the age of 2 years. Her findings revealed fewer comments, more maladaptive behaviors, and less phonologic maturity in children with slow expressive language development.

Carefully planned assessment protocols should provide data that can be interpreted according to the findings discussed above. In turn, the presence or absence of possible indicators of communication and speech and language impairment should assist with treatment decisions.

TREATMENT APPROACHES AND MODELS

Once intervention is recommended for an infant or toddler, a treatment approach and model must be selected and implemented. The child's needs and the needs and priorities of his or her family should be two critical factors contributing to these decisions.

Treatment approaches

Wilcox[46] suggests that intervention approaches with infants and toddlers and their families can be classified according to three orientations: remediation, prevention, and compensation. According to Wilcox, most early interventionists, including those providing communication-based services, use a remedial approach to intervention. In doing so, they identify areas of deficit and intervene with the overall objective of eliminating problems or mitigating their long-term effects. In contrast, prevention, as a service delivery approach, is designed to prevent developmental problems in children who are identified as "at risk" due to biologic or environmental factors (or both). Wilcox states that preventive approaches are "focused on facilitating or ensuring acquisition of functional skills in suspect areas, with particular consideration given to the fact that one skill deficit is likely to affect other skill areas."[46(p73)] A compensatory approach to intervention is used when a child presents with developmental deficits that are not likely to change. The goal is to compensate for disability through the provision of devices or strategies designed to improve functional skills. Examples of compensatory strategies include augmentative communication devices, wheelchairs, walkers, and so forth.

According to Wilcox, approaches to intervention are most often used in combination. Typically, prevention is the first approach used. Once a clear deficit is identified, however, remedial or compensatory approaches are initiated depending on the nature and expected long-term outcome of the child's disability. Wilcox suggests that three factors impact decisions regarding treatment approaches: (1) the point at which a child enters a program, (2) the degree of his or her disability, and (3) the child's intervention goals.[46]

With the selection of an intervention approach, service providers must determine their role within treatment. While some children might benefit from direct services, others may be better served through indirect methods (eg, consultation). It appears reasonable to suggest that the speech pathologist's role should be more direct within approaches emphasizing remediation and more consultative within preventive or compensatory approaches.

There are clear benefits to consultative communication-based treatment. For example, consultations designed to develop center-based and home-based intervention programs can result in increased services for children, the provision of services from familiar persons within natural contexts, and increased time for the speech pathologist to participate in collaboration and training opportunities with parents and professional peers. Of course, consultative treatment can only be effective if all those involved are committed to the treatment process.

Treatment models

The service delivery model is the structure governing intervention practices.[46] Typically, one of four models of intervention (ie, unidisciplinary, multidisciplinary, interdisciplinary, and transdisciplinary) is used in the provision of communication-based services to infants and toddlers. The unidisciplinary model is best characterized by independent service provision. Although popular, unidisciplinary services are limited by a lack of interprofessional collaboration (ie, interaction). As a result, treatments may not be "cutting edge" and are often poorly coordinated.

Unlike unidisciplinary services, the remaining models allow for some degree of collaboration. In a multidisciplinary model, professionals provide services independently, yet have a formal means of collaboration (eg, staffings). An interdisciplinary model, while allowing independent functioning, emphasizes a greater degree of interaction between professionals, typically resulting in joint decision making regarding treatment goals and strategies. Finally, a transdisciplinary model incorporates the concept of professional role release where disciplines share roles and responsibilities.[47]

Decisions regarding appropriate treatment models are impacted by a variety of factors including family needs and the availability and attitudes of professionals. Although collaborative models appear more compatible with Public Law 99-457, they may not be preferred by families or be possible given the lack of service providers in some regions and the unwillingness of some professionals to adapt service delivery styles.

●   ●   ●

The implementation of Public Law 99-457 requires that early interventionists become knowledgeable regarding the provision of "best practice" services to infants and toddlers. This article has provided an overview of prelanguage communicative development and issues critical to the assessment and treatment of communicative abilities in prelinguistic children. It is hoped that this information will assist professionals as they attempt to provide better services for young children and their families.

REFERENCES

1. Houle GR, Hamilton J. Public Law 99-457: a challenge to speech-language pathologists and audiologists. *ASHA.* 1991;33:51–54.

2. Miller J. Identifying children with language disorders and describing their language performance. *Contemp Issues Lang Intervention. ASHA Reports.* 1983;12:61–74.

3. Stoel-Gammon C. Normal and disordered phonology in two-year-olds. In: Paul R, ed. Late bloomers: Language development and delay in toddlers. *Top Lang Disord.* 1991;11:21–32.

4. Vihman M. Early phonological development. In: Bernthal J, Bankson N, eds. *Articulation and Phonological Disorders.* Englewood Cliffs, NJ: Prentice Hall; 1988.

5. Bates E, Bretherton I, Snyder L. *From First Words to Grammar.* Cambridge, Mass: Cambridge University Press; 1988.

6. Bates E, Camaioni L, Volterra V. The acquisition of performatives prior to speech. *Merrill-Palmer Q.* 1975;21:205–226.

7. Austin J. *How To Do Things with Words.* Cambridge, Mass: Harvard University Press; 1962.

8. Bates E. *The Emergence of Symbols: Cognition and Communication in Infancy.* New York, NY: Academic Press; 1979.

9. Bruner J. The social context of language acquisition. *Lang Communication.* 1981;1:155–178.

10. Carpenter R, Mastergeorge A, Coggins T. The acquisition of communicative intentions in infants eight to fifteen months of age. *Lang Speech.* 1983;26:101–116.

11. Dore J. A pragmatic description of early language development. *J Psycholinguist Res.* 1974;4:343–351.

12. Halliday MAK. *Learning How to Mean.* London, England: Edward Arnold; 1975.

13. Wetherby A, Cain D, Yonclas D, Walker V. Analysis of intentional communication of normal children from the prelinguistic to the multi-word stages. *J Speech Hear Res.* 1988;31:240–252.

14. Trevarthan C. Psychobiology of speech development. *Neurobiol Sci Res Bull.* 1974;12:570–585.

15. Trevarthan C. Communication and cooperation in early infancy: a description of primary intersubjectivity. In: Bullowa MM, ed. *Before Speech: The Beginning of Interpersonal Communication.* New York, NY: Cambridge University Press; 1979.

16. Bates E. *Language and Context: The Acquisition of Pragmatics.* New York, NY: Academic Press; 1976.

17. Bruner J. The ontogenesis of speech acts. *J Child Lang.* 1975;2:1–19.

18. Bruner J. Early social interaction and language acquisition. In: Schaffer HR, ed. *Studies in Mother–Infant Interaction.* New York, NY: Academic Press; 1977.

19. Dore J. The development of conversational competence. In: Schiefelbusch R, ed. *Language Competence Assessment and Intervention.* San Diego, Calif: College-Hill Press; 1986.

20. Newsome J. An intersubjective approach to the systematic description of mother–infant interaction. In: Schaffer HR, ed, *Studies in Mother–Infant Interaction.* New York, NY: Academic Press; 1977.

21. Shields MM. The child as a psychologist: contriving the social world. In: Locke A, ed. *Action, Gesture, and Symbol.* New York, NY: Academic Press; 1978.

22. Stern D. *The First Relationship: Infant and Mother.* Cambridge, Mass: Harvard University Press; 1977.

23. Vygotsky LS. *Thought and Language.* Cambridge, Mass: MIT Press; 1962.

24. Stark R. Features of infant sounds: the emergence of cooing. *J Child Lang.* 1978;5:1–12.

25. Wolf P. Observation on the early development of smiling. In: Foss B, ed. *Determinants on Infant Behaviors II.* New York, NY: Wiley; 1963.

26. Bruner J. On prelinguistic prerequisites of speech. Presented at the Stirling Conference on Psychology of Language; 1977.

27. Rossetti L. Communication assessment: birth to 36 months. *ASHA.* 1991;33:45–46.

28. Tronick E. Emotions and emotional communication in infants. *Am Psychol.* 1989;44:112–119.

29. Stern D. *The Interpersonal World of the Infant.* New York, NY: Basic Books; 1985.

30. Wetherby A, Prizant B. The expression of communicative intent: assessment guidelines. *Semin Speech Lang.* 1989;10:77–91.

31. Benedict H. Early lexical development: comprehension and production. *J Child Lang.* 1979;6:183–200.

32. McCune-Nicolich L. The cognitive bases of relational words in the single word period. *J Child Lang.* 1981;8:15–34.

33. Shore C, O'Connell B, Bates E. First sentences in language and symbolic play. *Dev Psychol.* 1984;20:872–880.

34. Wetherby A, Prizant B. Profiling young children's communicative competence. In: Warren S, Reichle J, eds. *Causes and Effects in Communication and Language Intervention.* Baltimore, Md: Paul H. Brookes; 1992.

35. Wetherby A, Prizant B. *Communication and Symbolic Behavior Scales-Research Edition.* Chicago, Ill: Riverside Publishing; 1990.

36. Bzoch K, League R. *Receptive-Expressive Emergent Language Scale-Revised.* Austin, Tex: Pro-Ed; 1990.

37. Rossetti L. *Infant-Toddler Language Scale.* East Moline, Ill: LinguiSystems; 1990.

38. Hedrick D, Prather E, Tobin R. *Sequenced Inventory of Communication Development.* Seattle, Wash: University of Washington Press; 1975.

39. Bangs T. *Birth to Three Checklist of Learning and Language Behavior.* Allen, Tex: DLM Teaching Resources; 1986.

40. Cole K, Dale PS, Mills PE. Defining language delay in young children by cognitive referencing: are we saying more than we know? *Appl Psycholing.* 1990;11:291–302.

41. Tomblin JB, Hardy JC, Hein HA. Predicting poor communication status in preschool children using risk factors present at birth. *J Speech Hear Res.* 1991;34:1096–1105.

42. Aram D, Hack M, Hawkins S, Weissman BM, Borawski-Clark E. Very-low-birth weight children and speech and language development. *J Speech Hear Res.* 1991;34:1169–1179.

43. Colombo J, Mitchell W, Horowitz FD. Infant visual attention in the paired-comparison paradigm: test-retest and attention-performance relations. *Child Dev.* 1988;59:1198–1210.

44. Wetherby A, Yonclas D, Bryan A. Communicative profiles of handicapped preschool children: implications for early intervention. *J Speech Hear Disord.* 1989;54:148–158.

45. Paul R. Profiles of toddlers with slow expressive language development. *Top Lang Disord.* 1991;11:1–13.

46. Wilcox J. Delivering communication-based services to infants, toddlers, and their families: approaches and models. *Top Lang Disord.* 1989;10:68–79.

47. Lyon S, Lyon G. Team functioning and staff development: a role release approach to providing integrated educational services for severely handicapped students. *J Assoc Persons Severe Handicaps.* 1980;11:250–263.

Infants exposed to cocaine in utero: Implications for developmental assessment and intervention

Jane W. Schneider, MS, PT
Assistant Professor
Programs in Physical Therapy
Northwestern University Medical
  School
Senior Physical Therapist
Children's Memorial Hospital
Chicago, Illinois

Dan R. Griffith, PhD
Developmental Psychologist
Perinatal Center for Chemical
  Dependence
Clinical Associate
Department of Psychiatry and
  Behavioral Sciences
Northwestern University Medical
  School
Chicago, Illinois

Ira J. Chasnoff, MD
Associate Professor of Pediatrics and
  Psychiatry and Behavioral Sciences
Northwestern University Medical
  School
Director
Perinatal Center for Chemical
  Dependence
Chicago, Illinois

DRUG ABUSE in the United States is beginning to be recognized and acknowledged as a significant societal problem. The use of cocaine and its derivatives occurs in all segments of US society regardless of race, ethnicity, or socioeconomic status. Furthermore, cocaine use during pregnancy is no longer an unusual phenomenon. In fact, it appears to be increasing.[1-3] A recent study by the National Association for Perinatal Addiction Research and Education[4] surveyed 36 hospitals around the country and found that at least 11% of women in the hospitals studied had used illegal drugs during pregnancy. Based on those figures, an estimated 375,000 newborns per year face health hazards from their mothers' prenatal drug abuse.

Specific hazards of prenatal cocaine use include increased rates of spontaneous abortion, abruptio placentae, intrauterine growth retardation, and in-utero cerebrovascular accidents. Attempting to determine the impact of prenatal cocaine exposure on development, however, is a complex issue. Many women whose drug of choice is cocaine are abusers of other drugs as well. It is often difficult to ascertain the frequency and amount of drug use. It is also acknowledged that the infant's environment as well as prenatal exposure to drugs will have a profound effect on subsequent development. Currently, data from both a research and an empirical perspective are being gathered to help clarify the effects of prenatal cocaine exposure.

The research on which this article is based was supported by a grant from the National Institute on Drug Abuse, National Institutes of Health (DA04-103-01).

American society has begun to more readily acknowledge drug abuse. Health care professionals can now begin to gather information concerning development following prenatal drug exposure, and at the same time begin appropriate intervention on behalf of exposed infants. This article describes motor development of cocaine-exposed infants, the impact on other areas of development during the newborn and early infancy stages, and intervention strategies appropriate for cocaine-exposed infants and their caregivers.

COCAINE: PROPOSED MECHANISMS OF ACTION IN UTERO

The placenta does not protect the fetus from cocaine exposure. Cocaine readily crosses from maternal to fetal circulation and may remain in the infant's system long after it has been excreted by the mother because immature liver and kidneys metabolize the cocaine more slowly. As cocaine is metabolized, it is broken down into norcocaine, a highly active metabolite with a high level of penetration into the central nervous system (CNS). Because norcocaine is water soluble, it does not readily pass back into the mother's system for excretion. It is theorized that an infant may continue to be exposed to cocaine and its active metabolites by reingestion of norcocaine through the amniotic fluid.[5]

Cocaine acts centrally on the CNS as a stimulant while peripherally causing vasoconstriction, tachycardia, and a rapid rise in blood pressure.[6-8] These physiologic effects are thought to occur in both mother and fetus, and therefore may explain increased rates of spontaneous abortion, abruptio placentae, and in-utero cerebrovascular accidents associated with cocaine use during pregnancy.[1,2,9,10] Documentation of specific CNS damage has been reported by Dixon and Bejar[11] on a sample of 28 cocaine-exposed infants. They found that 39% of that sample showed hemorrhagic cerebral infarcts documented by cranial ultrasound at birth. While the physiologic effects of cocaine on the adult have been well documented,[12] research is only now showing that the same and perhaps more severe effects may be experienced by infants exposed to cocaine in utero.

DESCRIPTION OF THE COCAINE-EXPOSED INFANT

As health care professionals encounter more newborn infants exposed to drugs prenatally, the initial task is to identify drug-exposed infants. Withdrawal syndromes are well-documented in infants born to heroin-addicted mothers; however, some controversy exists concerning the presence of a cocaine withdrawal syndrome.[13] Whenever prenatal exposure to drugs is suspected, urine toxicology screens of both mother and infant should be performed. Common clinical sings of prenatal cocaine exposure include hyperirritability, poor feeding patterns, high respiratory and heart rates, increased tremulousness and startles, and irregular sleeping patterns.[13] Relating these signs to a withdrawal syndrome may be a misnomer, since the infant may in fact still be experiencing the direct effects of cocaine exposure. Also, because some of these effects persist beyond the first few weeks of life, they may be indications of a more lasting CNS change rather than a withdrawal pattern.

Full-term cocaine-exposed infants have been tested as newborns and at one month of age using the Brazelton Neonatal Behavioral Assessment Scale.[14] Infants at both ages show depressed interactive abilities and poor state control when compared to drug-free infants of the same ages.[2,15,16] While these behavioral characteristics are not unique to cocaine-exposed infants, they have been noted as part of the cluster of characteristics that describe a large percentage of these infants.

Beyond the newborn period, the Movement Assessment of Infants (MAI)[17] has been used to assess motor development of full-term cocaine-exposed infants at four months of age. This test was chosen since it provides both a quantitative and qualitative assessment of motor development in the first year of life. Ongoing results of research suggest that many symptoms noted on the Brazelton examination in the newborn cocaine-exposed infant remain at four months of age on the MAI.[18,19] For example, frequent tremors, especially in the upper extremities, are still noted at four months of age. These infants display increased extensor muscle tone, especially in the lower extremities. Primitive reflexes normally integrated by four months are often still present. Using previously established risk categories, approximately 40% of the cocaine-exposed infants studied were designated "high risk" for motor developmental dysfunction as opposed to 2% of a control group (JW Schneider and IJ Chasnoff, unpublished data, 1989). This means that cocaine-exposed infants were approximately 40 times more likely to be designated "high risk" for motor developmental dysfunction than nonexposed infants.[18,19]

Preliminary results of eight-month-old cocaine-exposed *v* nonexposed infants suggest that while motor abnormalities have lessened by this age, they have not totally disappeared. Some of the cocaine-exposed eight-month-old infants, while able to crawl, were slow in moving, and stood bearing weight on their toes with stiff extension of their lower extremities. Future studies are needed to document motor development of cocaine-exposed infants in the first year of life and beyond.

DEVELOPMENTAL IMPLICATIONS OF COCAINE EXPOSURE

State control

The physiologic effects of cocaine on the newborn nervous system make state control difficult. Newborns have a variety of behavior states available to them and cycle through periods of sleeping (deep or light sleep), wakefulness (drowsy, quiet alert, active alert), and crying.[14] It is expected that newborns will spend some time in each of these behavioral states, that they will move smoothly from state to state, and that as they grow they will spend more time in quiet alert states and less time sleeping or crying. Many cocaine-exposed infants, however, do not show organized behavior states or smooth state changes, but rather tend to change rapidly from one extreme state (eg, deep sleep) to another (eg, frantic crying).

Four common behavioral patterns have been observed clinically in newborn cocaine-exposed infants.[15,16] Some infants, in response to any sort of stimulation, will pull themselves down into a deep sleep. These infants will not awaken in response to handling of any sort. While this is a protective mechanism for their fragile nervous system, it precludes any caregiver–infant interaction.

A second pattern presents as an agitated sleep state. These infants seem stressed by external stimulation (as evidenced by startling, color changes, whimpering) but do not wake up to attend to the stimulation.

Newborn cocaine-exposed infants demonstrate a third behavioral pattern by vacillating between extremes of state (sleeping or crying) during handling.[15,16] For example, when unwrapped from a blanket they immediately cry and show agitation, but when wrapped up again, they quickly fall asleep.

The fourth common behavioral pattern resembles a panicked awake state.[15,16] This is seen in an infant who can achieve an alert state for short periods but appears quite stressed while doing so and requires a lot of help from the caregiver to stay calm.

The descriptions of these four behavioral states make it clear that many newborn cocaine-exposed infants may be initially incapable of responding appropriately to their caregivers. Because they have such difficulty reaching and maintaining an alert state, their abilities to attend to either auditory or visual stimuli may be quite limited. Those cocaine-exposed infants who do reach alert states usually need outside assistance to stay calm, and then only attend to a stimulus briefly before showing signs of distress such as gaze aversion, increased respirations, or disorganized motor activity.[15,16]

The reciprocity normally present in the process of bonding may be very difficult for these infants.[20,21] Thus if inadequate behavioral interaction between infant and mother results, it places their relationship at risk, since studies have shown that the behavior of the newborn affects the caregiving he or she receives.[22,23] In effect, a negative cycle may be set up in which the behavior of the poorly organized, high-risk infant may suppress the optimal caregiving pattern necessary to facilitate his or her recovery.[24,25] The feelings of frustration and inadequacy that parents may experience in dealing with their fragile yet unresponsive infants may predispose them later to physical child abuse, as has been seen in other high-risk infant groups.[26]

Motor behavior

Looking beyond the newborn period to the age of four months, it is important to remember some of the key characteristics of normal four-month-old motor behavior. When supine, four-month-olds are very active. They can reach out easily to midline and finger one hand with the other. The infants' lower extremities are also very active. They can flex and extend their legs and kick reciprocally. The infants flex their legs in order to begin playing with and exploring their knees and feet. This is an important part of learning and contributes to the proper development of body image. Flexibility is a key descriptor of four-month-old motor development. They are developing control of both the flexor and extensor muscle groups without being dominated by either one. Even though a four-month-old cannot stand independently, when held in supported standing this flexibility is seen by a relaxed standing posture that incorporates both flexor and extensor muscle control.

The flexibility so evident in normal four-month-old motor behavior is often less apparent in some cocaine-exposed infants. When supine, these infants often lie in excessively extended postures, and movements of their extremities may be jerky and stiff.[18,19] While they do reach out for objects, the presence of tremors in the upper extremities may have an impact on their development of good eye-hand coordination. Many cocaine-exposed infants are less able to round their buttocks off the supporting surface or kick reciprocally.[18,19] This stiffness in their lower extremities prevents them from exploring their lower body either visually or with their hands. Visual and tactile exploration of body parts are important in the development of body image and contribute to the ability to move well in the environment (ie, motor planning).

The increased extensor muscle tone noted in the supine position is noted in other positions as well. Many cocaine-exposed infants display an exaggerated positive support reaction when held in an upright position.[18,19] This reaction is characterized by stiff extension of hips, knees, and ankles and weight bearing on the toes. This type of standing posture encourages abnormal alignment of the body parts and would impede development of appropriate balance control.

The above descriptions of the motor abilities of some cocaine-exposed infants suggest that they are mildly hypertonic infants with dystonic movement patterns. It is important that health care professionals be able to identify these characteristics in the cocaine-exposed infant and understand the effect of any detected behavioral or motor abnormalities on later development. Health care professionals can also provide appropriate intervention to mother and infant both before and after birth.

INTERVENTION

Intervention will be addressed by considering the infant's developmental phases from before birth through infancy. Within each phase, the focus is on enhancing infant development, and intervention with parents will be addressed from this viewpoint.

Prenatal program

Drug abuse programs now exist in most major cities across the country. Programs for the pregnant addict, however, are less prevalent. As awareness of the problem increases, programs such as the Perinatal Center for Chemical Dependence (PCCD) at Northwestern University Medical School in Chicago, Illinois, should become more available in drug-abusing pregnant women.

The PCCD is a comprehensive program staffed by a number of medical personnel, including physicians, nurses, a developmental psychologist, a physical therapist, a social worker, and drug dependency counselors. The PCCD provides prenatal and postnatal addictive care, obstetric care, and psychological care, as well as pediatric care for the infant. There is a heavy emphasis on education throughout the program, including topics such as Lamaze training, family planning, nutrition, having a healthy baby, parenting, infant–toddler series, a woman's issues and the law. It is hoped that programs such as this will provide more information about the effects of drug exposure on infant development while providing comprehensive care for those who seek it.

Newborn phase

The therapeutic techniques described below were chosen to address the specific needs of the cocaine-exposed infant.[27] These same techniques would be equally appropriate for any infant who displays similar clinical manifestations. The overall intervention goals of this period are to increase periods of alertness so that appropriate infant–caregiver interactions can occur. This broad goal can be accomplished by meeting each of the subgoals listed in Table 1.

Positioning

Even in the newborn nursery, cocaine-exposed infants can be positioned to improve their posture and movement patterns. The infant can be positioned on his or her side to overcome both increased extensor tone and the effects of gravity. The spine, including the head, should be flexed, bringing the infant away from the hyperextended position (Fig 1).[28] Upper extremities should be protracted at the shoulder girdle to encourage midline orientation. Lower extremities should be flexed somewhat to break up pelvic and lower extremity extensor tone. Rolled-up cloth diapers can be placed between the legs and along the spine to support and maintain the posture while allowing the infant freedom to move within the posture. Covering the infant with a blanket tucked in on each side of the mattress will help maintain this relaxed posture and thus encourage a more relaxed behavioral state.

Table 1. Summary of intervention goals and management related to period of development

Period of development	Intervention goals	Management
Newborn	Increase periods of alertness and interaction	
	Prevent hyperextended posture	Positioning in sidelying
	Decrease irritability, tremors, and overshooting	Swaddling and rocking
		Hydrotherapy graded auditory and visual stimuli
	Improve feeding patterns	Positioning and handling
	Improve feeding posture	
	Decrease facial and oral hypersensitivity	Tactile stimulation to facial and oral areas
	Improve parent handling	Observe Brazelton Model for appropriate behavior
		Demonstration and return demonstration of appropriate handling
Infancy	Improve movement patterns to enhance interaction and exploration	
	Decrease extensor tone	Supine flexion with lower extremity rotation
		Prevent extensor thrusting in sitting and standing
		Discourage supported standing
		Discourage use of jumpers and walkers
		Carry inflexed position
		Slow, gentle movement through space
	Increase antigravity strength	Prone positioning
		Pivoting in prone position
		Sitting with support for short periods
	Improve parent handling	Demonstrations and return demonstrations of appropriate play and carrying positions and handling techniques

Handling

A caregiver's first impulse might be not to handle the cocaine-exposed infant for fear of setting off an irritable response from the hypersensitive infant. However, proper handling is essential to help the infant improve state control and appropriate motor patterns. Initially an infant may need to be swaddled in a blanket in a semiflexed position. The warmth from the blanket appears to cause inhibition

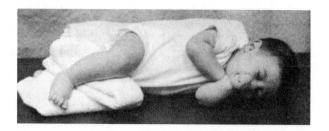

Fig 1. Infant in flexed sidelying position used to decrease extensor tone. Reprinted from Schneider JW, Chasnoff IJ: Cocaine abuse during pregnancy: Its effect on infant motor development—A clinical perspective. *Top Acute Care Trauma Rehabil* 1987;2(1):63.

---

of motor behavior.[29] In addition, the flexed position breaks up the extensor tone, decreases tremors and overshooting, and facilitates normal hand-to-mouth activity. In conjunction with swaddling, slow rocking may be necessary to calm the infant. Studies have shown that such vestibular proprioceptive stimulation frequently has the immediate effect of arresting crying, reducing irritability, and bringing the infant to a visually alert state.[30] This produces a sense of effectiveness in the caregiver that encourages social interaction.

While vestibular-proprioceptive input appears to have a strong effect on the infant's motor control, other forms of slow rhythmical input (eg, visual, auditory, tactile) could be used to "pacify" the infant.[31] Once the infant has become calm, he or she can be held in the en face (face-to-face) position to encourage visual tracking, vocalization, and playful interaction with the caregiver (Fig 2). Initially, this face-to-face interaction may be brief, since cocaine-exposed infants often have difficulty processing complex combinations of stimuli such as looking at the mother's face and listening to her voice at the same time. The infant may signal this sensory overload by crying or averting his or her gaze.

Another unique form of handling the cocaine-exposed infant to reduce irritability and improve motor control is the use of neonatal hydrotherapy. This consists of placing the infant in a small tub or bassinette filled with water 99°F to 101°F. Hydrotherapy techniques include handling to facilitate head in midline, hand-to-mouth activity, and flexion and rotation of the trunk. An overhead radiant heater should be used to decrease temperature loss during hydrotherapy. Vital signs should be carefully monitored for any signs of physiologic instability. Sweeney[28,32] has used hydrotherapy in an intensive care nursery setting and has found it to be effective in improving posture, muscle tone, behavioral state, and feeding behavior in premature infants. These outcomes are also appropriate for cocaine-exposed infants. If the infant responds well to this form of state control, it could easily be taught to the parents and adapted for home use.

Fig 2. Swaddled infant in en face position with mother. Reprinted from Schneider JW, Chasnoff IJ: Cocaine abuse during pregnancy: Its effect on infant motor development—A clinical perspective. *Top Acute Care Trauma Rehabil* 1987;2(1):64.

While swaddling, rocking, and other methods of calming may initially be necessary, it is important to use these methods only as needed and to begin to withdraw these additional techniques as soon as possible so that the infant learns to gain control over his or her state. For example, swaddling may initially be necessary every time the infant is handled. As the infant responds more to calming measures and begins to show self-calming abilities, swaddling should only be done when the infant seems unable to respond without this intervention.

Feeding

Poor feeding has been mentioned as a symptom in cocaine-exposed newborns.[13] Problems in oral motor control are again most probably related to abnormal extensor tone, disorganized movement patterns, and poor state control. Proper positioning and handling techniques described above should prepare the infant motorically and behaviorally to assume and maintain a more relaxed, flexed posture during feeding. Cocaine-exposed infants may also display oral hypersensitivity. Gentle but firm tactile stimulation around the face as well as within the mouth should help to decrease sensitivity and increase appropriate sucking behavior.

Parent education

This component of the intervention program is of paramount importance in enhancing normal infant development as well as ensuring a strong parent–infant bond. Parent education should begin early enough so that parents can learn appropriate and effective caregiving and avoid compounding the problems of the already at-risk infant. Having the parents observe the Brazelton Neonatal Behavioral Assessment appears to have a positive effect on later interaction with their infants.[33] This is probably because parents are able to see the positive characteristics and the strengths their infant possesses rather than focusing only on the weaknesses. While it appears that some drug-abusing mothers continue to deny their infant's problems, pointing out positive attributes as well as ameliorating problem behaviors will serve to strengthen the mother's bond with her infant.

Many cocaine-abusing mothers may not be physically or psychologically ready to observe the initial assessment done on their infants a few days after birth.[16] Information gained during this assessment, however, can be used to educate the mother about the competencies and needs of her infant. Most important to understand is how easily the cocaine-exposed infant can become overstimulated. Parents are taught to recognize common distress signs from overstimulation such as yawning, sneezing, hiccuping, gaze aversion, spitting up, color changes, and crying.[15]

When the infant is alert, they are instructed to try to engage the infant en face without speaking or moving too quickly. If the infant is fixing on them comfortably, they may try either speaking to the infant in a soft rhythmic voice or moving slowly in front of the infant without speaking. For some infants, any direct visual input may prove too stressful initially. In this case, parents are instructed to hold the infant in a vertical position against their chest with the infant facing away from the parent (Fig 3).[15] In this position, the infant may be held securely to prevent uncontrolled movements and can hear the parent's voice without needing to interact visually.

Whenever an infant does become distressed, parents are encouraged to see this as an attempt of the infant to ask for help and are taught the calming techniques (swaddling, pacifier, vertical rocking) discussed earlier. Repeated demonstrations of positioning and handling techniques to relax and being interacting with the infant, as well as return demonstration by the parents, are all part of the educational process.

More than teaching dos and don'ts, parents are taught to pay attention to their infant's cues during interactions and to respond as quickly as possible. Modeling of appropriate handling and feedback to parents on their handling and interactions help the parents to expand the infant's range of appropriate behaviors. Regardless of how competent a parent may seem, a follow-up session after the infant has been in the home setting for at least one week is recommended. Follow-up visits at one

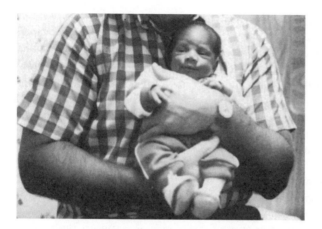

Fig 3. Infant held securely facing away from parent.

week and one month of age allow the infant's improvements in state control to be highlighted for the parents. Suggestions for appropriate progression of interactions with the infant to increase his or her responsiveness to more complex stimuli for long time periods are also given. These sequential intervention sessions help determine how appropriate the parent–infant interactions appear and how well the infant has fit into the family unit.

Infancy

The goal of intervention during this period is to have the infant move appropriately throughout his or her environment. By moving well, he or she will be able to interact well and explore his or her environment appropriately. Thus, infant motor abilities can have an impact on psychosocial and cognitive development. Since cocaine-exposed infants beyond the newborn period demonstrate increased muscle tone and retention of primitive reflexes, they may require intervention to move normally. This intervention can be in the form of practical suggestions for appropriate play and carrying positions or ways to handle infants to decrease muscle tone while encouraging normal movement.[30]

Play positions

When supine, cocaine-exposed infants show increased extensor tone. This tone causes decreased pelvic mobility and limits the infant's ability to lift the legs up to play with his or her knees or to kick reciprocally. Parents can be taught to lift the infant's pelvis up and flex the legs toward the chest, enabling the infant to overcome the extensor tone and to begin increased kicking movements with the lower extremities (see Table 1). From this position of supine flexion, the lower extremities can be rotated from side to side to further decrease extensor tone (Fig 4). The upper extremities may need to be brought down and forward (depressed and protracted) at the shoulder girdle to allow the arms to reach out to grasp objects. Parents should be warned against leaving their infants supine for long periods, since increased extensor tone and the effects of gravity make movement difficult in this position.

Prone is a good position for infants to develop antigravity extensor strength. Because cocaine-exposed infants have a preponderance of extensor tone, they usually enjoy this position and perform well in it. The infants should be encouraged to move in prone by placing colorful stimulating toys beside them, which prompts pivoting in the trunk to reach the toys.

Sitting is an appropriate developmental activity from approximately five months of age, and, in addition, infants may sit with the support of their parents from birth onward. One caution to parents is not to place infants in the sitting position for long periods of time, since newly developing trunk extensor muscles will not be capable of sustaining the erect position. In addition, cocaine-exposed infants often push backward into extension when sitting (or standing). This extensor thrusting should be prevented by bending the infant forward at the hips when-

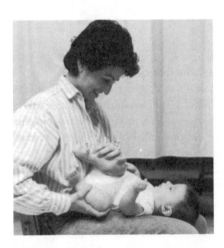

Fig 4. Lower extremity rotation in supine flexion position. Reprinted from Schneider JW, Chasnoff IJ: Cocaine abuse during pregnancy: Its effect on infant motor development—A clinical perspective. *Top Acute Care Trauma Rehabil* 1987;2(1):66.

ever thrusting occurs or is anticipated. If thrusting is allowed to continue, extensor tone (already abnormally high) will be further facilitated.

Supported standing allow infants to experience upright weight bearing throughout the lower extremities. Cocaine-exposed infants characteristically enjoy standing because it allows them to use their abundance of extensor tone. They can frequently be observed in rigid stand positions, including going up on their toes or thrusting head and trunk backward into extension. Despite their obvious enjoyment of standing, this position should not be encouraged since it reinforces their abnormal tone and movement patterns.

Use of infant assistive devices such as jumpers and walkers should be discouraged. Parents should be informed that thousands of injuries each year are related to the use of these devices.[34] As importantly, infants placed in these devices are not exercising their muscles appropriately, since they do not yet have the ability to hold themselves in proper postural alignment when placed in the upright position.[35] The leg actions of an infant in a walker have little relationship to walking skills. Rather than training an infant to walk, the walker may actually impede progress by inhibiting the infant from crawling around.[35] Walkers encourage hypertonic infants (like the cocaine-exposed infants) to further increase their extensor tone by pushing their feet against the floor and arching their trunks backward.[35,36]

Carrying

Since cocaine-exposed infants display primarily extensor tone, they should be carried in a more flexed position to counteract this. Fig 5 illustrates how the infant sits on the parent's hip while being supported by the parent's arm under the infant's thighs. The infant's arms are kept forward, which facilitates the hands coming to midline. This position controls the infant's tone while facilitating head and trunk control and the ability to reach and grasp objects.

Handling

Parents who have been taught to handle their infant so as to optimize interaction in the newborn period can now expand on those abilities as their infant grows and changes. The cocaine-exposed infant should no longer require swaddling to stay calm; he or she may, however, require more sensitive handling than normally required of a growing infant. For example, while rough-house play is enjoyed by most infants, cocaine-exposed infants may be more sensitive to quick rough movements and may respond by stiffening their bodies or crying. Slow, gentle swinging through the air should replace rapid movements in space during roughhouse play. In all cases, the infant's reactions (physically and behaviorally) should guide parents in assessing the appropriateness of their handling.

Parent education, which includes appropriate play, carrying, and handling techniques, changes according to the infant's needs. While many cocaine-exposed in-

Fig 5. Infant in flexed carrying position. Reprinted from Schneider JW, Chasnoff IJ: Cocaine abuse during pregnancy: Its effect on infant motor development—A clinical perspective. *Top Acute Care Trauma Rehabil* 1987;2(1):67.

fants may not require intensive physical therapy, monthly sessions may be necessary to demonstrate developmentally appropriate activities and to teach parents new handling skills. As always, return demonstrations from parents are important to confirm their level of skill and understanding.

•   •   •

It is clear from present research findings that cocaine exposure in utero is not an innocuous phenomenon. Physical and behavioral findings exist that are worrisome to the pediatric health care professional. Clinical experience has shown that some of these findings can be ameliorated with appropriate intervention.

Because of the tremendous potential for plasticity that exists within the human nervous system, it may be expected that hard neurological signs and gross motor dysfunction may not be apparent after 12 months of age. However, the early effects of cocaine on the developing nervous system may place the drug-exposed infant at high risk for minimal brain dysfunction, which involves an abnormal nervous system reorganization that may result in behavior and learning difficulties.[37-40]

Studies are needed to document motor development of cocaine-exposed infants later in the first year of life. Follow-up of these infants through preschool and early school years will help to identify any behavior or learning disorders that may be associated with intrauterine cocaine exposure.

REFERENCES

1. Bingol N, Fuchs M, Diaz V, et al: Teratogenicity of cocaine in humans. *J Pediatr* 1987;110(1):93–96.

2. Chasnoff IJ, Burns WJ, Schnoll SH, et al: Cocaine use in pregnancy. *N Engl J Med* 1985;313(11):666–669.

3. Madden JD, Payne TF, Miller S: Maternal cocaine abuse and effect on the newborn. *Pediatrics* 1986;77:209–211.

4. Chasnoff IJ: Drugs and women: Establishing a standard of care. *Ann NY Acad Med,* to be published.

5. Chasnoff IJ, Lewis DE: Cocaine metabolism during pregnancy (abstract). *Pediatr Res* 1988;23:257A.

6. Beuchimol A, Bartall H, Desser KB: Accelerated ventricular rhythm and cocaine abuse. *Ann Intern Med* 1978;88:519–520.

7. Resnick RB, Kestenbaum RS, Schwartz LK: Acute systemic effects of cocaine in man: A controlled study of intranasal and intravenous routes. *Science* 1977;195:696–697.

8. Richie JM, Greene NM: Local anesthesia, in Goodman LS, Gilman A (eds): *The Pharmacological Basis of Therapeutics.* New York, Macmillan, 1980.

9. Acker D, Sachs BP, Tracey KJ, et al: Abruptio placentae associated with cocaine use. *Am J Obstet Gynecol* 1983;146:220–221.

10. Chasnoff IJ, Bussey ME, Savich R, et al: Perinatal cerebral infarction and maternal cocaine use. *J Pediatr* 1986;108:456–459.

11. Dixon SD, Bejar R: Brain lesions in cocaine and methamphetamine exposed neonates (abstract). *Pediatr Res* 1988;23:405A.

12. Cregler L, Mark H: Medical complications of cocaine abuse. *N Engl J Med* 1986;315:1495–1500.

13. Newald J: Cocaine infants: A new arrival at hospital's step? *Hospitals* 1986;60(7):96.

14. Brazelton TB: *Neonatal Behavioral Assessment Scale: Clinics in Developmental Medicine No. 50,* Philadelphia, Lippincott, 1973.

15. Griffith DR: The effects of perinatal cocaine exposure on infant neurobehaviour and early maternal–infant interactions, in Chasnoff IJ (ed): *Drugs, Alcohol, Pregnancy and Parenting.* Lancaster, UK, Kluwer, 1988.

16. Griffith DR: *Neurobehavioral Assessment of the Neonate.* Read before the National Training Forum on Drugs, Alcohol, Pregnancy and Parenting. New York, August 1988.

17. Chandler LS, Andrews MS, Swanson MW: *Movement Assessment of Infants: A Manual.* Rolling Bay, Wash, Movement Assessment of Infants, 1980.

18. Schneider JW: Motor assessment and parent education beyond the newborn period, in Chasnoff IJ (ed): *Drugs, Alcohol, Pregnancy and Parenting.* Lancaster, UK, Kluwer, 1988.

19. Schneider JW: Motor assessment of cocaine-exposed infants at four months of age. Unpublished data, 1988.

20. Stern D: Mother and infant at play: The dyadic interaction, in Lewis M, Rosenblum L (eds): *The Effects of the Infant on Its Caregiver.* New York, Wiley, 1974.

21. Brazelton TB, Koslowski B, Main M: The origins of reciprocity: The early mother infant interaction, in Lewis M, Rosenblum L (eds): *The Effects of the Infant on Its Caregiver.* New York, Wiley, 1974.

22. Osofsky J, Danzger B: Relationships between neonatal characteristics and mother–infant interaction. *Dev Psychol* 1974;10:124–130.

23. Osofsky J: Neonatal characteristics and mother–infant interaction in two observational situations. *Child Dev* 1976;47:1138–1147.

24. Lester B: Behavioral assessment of the neonate, in Sell EJ (ed): *Follow-up of the High Risk Newborn—A Practical Approach.* Springfield, Ill, Charles C Thomas, 1979.

25. Mintzer D, Als H, Tronick EZ, et al: Parenting an infant with a birth defect: The regulation of self-esteem, in Powl J (ed): *Zero to Three.* Washington, DC, Bulletin of the Neonatal Center for Clinical Infant Programs, 1985.

26. Garborino J, Brookhouser PE, Authier KJ, et al: *Special Children Special Risks: The Maltreatment of Children with Disabilities.* New York, Aldine De Gruyter, 1987.

27. Schneider JW, Chasnoff IJ: Cocaine abuse during pregnancy: Its effect on infant motor development—a clinical perspective. *Top Acute Care Trauma Rehabil* 1987;2(1):59–69.

28. Sweeney JK: Neonates at developmental risk, in Umphred DA (ed): *Neurological Rehabilitation.* St Louis, Mosby, 1985.

29. Umphred DA, McCormack GL: Classification of common facilitory and inhibitory treatment techniques, in Umphred DA (ed): *Neurological Rehabilitation.* St. Louis, Mosby, 1985.

30. Korner A: Interconnections between sensory and affective development in early infancy, in Powl J (ed): *Zero to Three.* Washington, DC, Bulletin of the National Center for Clinical Infant Programs, 1985.

31. Wilhelm IJ: The neurologically suspect neonate, in Campbell SK (ed): *Pediatric Neurologic Physical Therapy.* New York, Churchill Livingstone, 1984.

32. Sweeney JK: Neonatal hydrotherapy: an adjunct to developmental intervention in an intensive care nursery setting. *Phys Occup Ther Pediatr* 1983;3:39–52.

33. Widmayer SM, Field TM: Effects of Brazelton demonstrations for mothers on the development of preterm infants. *Pediatrics* 1981;67:711–714.

34. Newsbriefs: Ban sale of baby walkers, CMA urges. *Can Med Assoc J* 1987; 136(1):57.

35. Various notes from readers: More on infant walkers. *Pediatr Notes* 1987;26:46.

36. Simpkiss MJ, Raikes AS: Problems resulting from the excessive use of baby-walkers and baby bouncers. *Lancet* 1972;1:747.

37. Touwen BC: Examination of the child with minor neurological dysfunction, ed 2, in *Clinics in Developmental Medicine,* no. 71. Spastics International Medical Publications, Lavenham Press Ltd, Lavenham-Suffolk England, 1979.

38. MacGregor SN, Keith LG, Chasnoff IJ, et al: Cocaine use during pregnancy: Adverse perinatal outcome. *Am J Obstet Gynecol* 1987;157:686–690.

39. Oro AS, Dixon SD: Perinatal cocaine and methamphetamine exposure: Maternal and neonatal correlates. *J Pediatr* 1987;111:571–578.

40. Drillen CM, Thomason AJ, Burgoyne K: Low birth-weight children at an early school age: A longitudinal study. *Dev Med Child Neurol* 1980;22:26–47.

The hearing-impaired infant and toddler: Identification, assessment, and intervention

Steven J. Kramer, PhD
Professor
Department of Communicative
 Disorders
San Diego State University
San Diego, California

Diane R. Williams, MA
Assistant Professor
Department of Communicative
 Disorders
San Diego State University
San Diego, California

ADVANCES IN audiologic evaluation techniques have markedly improved the ability to identify infants and toddlers with hearing impairments. Today, there is widespread use of noninvasive physiologic methods, specifically the auditory brain stem response (ABR) which has had extensive clinical application during the past 15 years. In addition, a much newer physiologic technique called otoacoustic emissions (OAE) is just beginning to establish its role in auditory clinical applications. These objective measures of auditory function can be used to identify auditory impairments at any age, even in neonates before hospital discharge. Behavioral testing of an infant's hearing ability using visual reinforcement audiometry (VRA) has also become clinically established for normally developing infants 6 months of age and older. The Joint Committee on Infant Hearing[1] (JCIH) and the American Speech-Language-Hearing Association (ASHA)[2] have endorsed early identification programs involving high-risk registers and ABR evaluations in the newborn period to confirm hearing loss and to initiate intervention at the earliest possible age, generally 3 to 6 months (see appendix for JCIH high-risk criteria for neonates and infants).

A newborn who fails an auditory evaluation in the hospital generally has a retest within 1 to 3 months to confirm an auditory impairment with sufficient validity to satisfy criteria for initiating early intervention services in accordance with PL 99-457.[3] Early identification of hearing impairment is beneficial in reducing the adverse impact of the hearing loss, especially on development of speech and language. Despite the availability of techniques for early identification, however, the average age at which intervention begins for hearing-impaired children has been found to be 18 to 30 months. Between 25% and 50% of children who were later found to have hearing impairments that were assumed to be related to congenital factors would not have been identified using earlier versions of the high-risk register and strategies for early identification.[4–6] In response to this problem, the most current recommendations by JCIH have added the recommendation to evaluate infants with high-risk factors specific to the 1- to 24-month age period, including parent concern regarding hearing, speech, or language delay, and to evaluate for neonatal risk factors associated with progressive or late-onset sensorineural hear-

Inf Young Children 1993; 6(1): 35–49

251

ing loss, trauma, neurodegenerative diseases, and infectious diseases related to hearing loss. For an excellent review and perspective on the most recent position statement of JCIH, see Diefendorf et al.[7]

Considerable attention by hearing health care professionals is being directed toward improving early identification programs so that more children with hearing impairment, including those with mild losses and unilateral losses, can receive appropriate intervention at the earliest possible age. Because the majority of the hearing-impaired infants are not deaf, it is important to be able to identify different degrees and types of hearing loss. Many children seen by early intervention professionals for other types of disorders may have mild or moderate hearing impairments that are undocumented but can have adverse effects on communication, psychosocial development, and academic performance. Early intervention professionals are in a position to make referrals for hearing evaluations if they have any concern about an infant's hearing ability. In addition, the multidisciplinary team needs to be aware of the consequences of hearing loss, even a mild loss, to develop appropriate intervention strategies. This article provides an overview of some of the current techniques for hearing evaluations and the strategies for early identification. In addition, information is provided regarding the relationship of different degrees of hearing loss to the resulting behaviors and to the specific needs the child might have relative to the early education environment.

AUDIOLOGIC EVALUATION TECHNIQUES

ABR

ABR is the most reliable objective evaluation method for use with infants younger than 6 months of age as well as for other children who are uncooperative or have developmental, cognitive, or physical involvements. Over the past 15 years, ABR has established itself as a routine clinical procedure for neonatal hearing evaluations, including those for premature infants.[5,8–10] Currently, ABR is the procedure recommended by JCIH and ASHA for use with high-risk infants. In recording an ABR, a series of abrupt-onset sounds (clicks) is delivered to the ear to produce synchronous neural responses from the auditory pathways, which are recorded from three electrodes, one taped on the forehead and one behind each ear. The infant's stimulus-related neural responses are extracted with an averaging computer from the ongoing random electrical brain activity. Generally, each averaged waveform takes about 1 minutes to collect, and a series of averaged waveforms is collected for different stimulus intensity levels until threshold is estimated for each ear. Including electrode attachment and quieting of the infant, the diagnostic ABR takes about 30 to 45 minutes. Because patient movement and other physiologic noise can contaminate ABR, testing of infants needs to be conducted while they are asleep, either naturally or by being sedated.

ABR occurs within a latency period of 10 msec relative to the stimulus delivered to the ear and at high stimulus levels is characterized by three prominent wave peaks labeled waves I, III, and V (Fig 1). ABR reflects synchronous neural responses of cranial nerve VIII from the inner ear (wave I) and subsequently portions of the lower brain stem pathways (waves III and V). Wave V is the largest ABR peak and the only peak measurable in normal ears for intensity levels as low as 20 to 30 dB normal hearing level (relative to adult behavioral thresholds for the clicks and designated nHL to distinguish from the audiometric pure-tone designation of HL). For assessment of peripheral auditory sensitivity in the absence of brain stem pathology, the lowest stimulus level that produces a wave V response peak is taken as an estimate of the infant's hearing threshold in the midfrequency range (1000 to 4000 Hz). If an ABR is obtained as low as 30 to 40 dB nHL, then the infant is considered to have normal peripheral auditory function. At high stimulus levels, the latency differences between the various wave peaks are used to provide information relative to neural function within the lower brain stem. ABR does not provide any information about midbrain or cortical auditory disorders and can be absent in cases of peripheral or low brain stem neuropathy, which affects the synchrony of neural discharges. ABR is a diagnostic test that can be used reliably to estimate hearing thresholds for each ear in the 2000- to 4000-Hz frequency range when broad spectrum click stimuli are used,[11] or it can provide more detailed frequency information from 500 to 8000 Hz when short-duration tones are used.[12] Inner ear disorders can be differentiated from middle ear disorders through characteristic latency changes in the waveform as a function of intensity or by comparing air-conducted ABR with bone-conducted ABR, as in audiometric behavioral evaluations.

OAE

In 1978, Kemp[13] first demonstrated that the inner ear emits a subaudible echolike sound in response to externally presented brief stimuli (transients). These inner ear echoes, generally referred to as evoked OAEs, travel back out of the ear and can be recorded with sensitive microphones placed at the entrance of the ear canal. The ability to measure OAE has been instrumental to a newly accepted theory of cochlear (inner ear) function in which the normal cochlea acts as an active mechanical amplifier, probably through motile activity of the outer hair cells.[14] In other words, during normal vibration of the cochlea's basilar membrane, the outer hair cells elongate and contract through some normal physiologic process in resonance with mechanical motion of the basilar membrane, thereby producing additional movement of the cochlear structures necessary for the good sensitivity and frequency selectivity of the normal ear. Damage to outer hair cells, as occurs in many sensory hearing losses, will eliminate the cochlear mechanical amplifier and thus eliminate the OAE. OAEs appear to be a byproduct of the non-

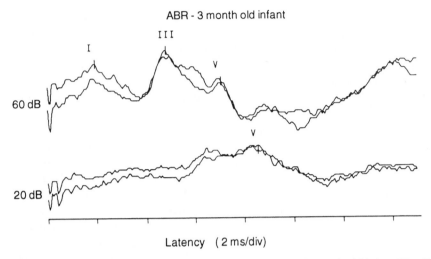

Fig 1. Click-evoked ABR waveforms from a normal-hearing 3-month-old infant. The 60 dB nHL waveform shows the typical wave peaks I, III, and V. At lower intensities, wave V is usually the only peak present and is the peak used for evaluation of auditory sensitivity. For this infant, wave V is present at 20 dB nHL, indicating normal auditory sensitivity at least for the middle to high frequencies. Calculations of interwave latency intervals (eg, I–V) are used to provide information about neural integrity of cranial nerve VIII and lower brain stem pathways.

linear preneural cochlear amplifier occurring as a part of the normal hearing process and are measurable in 98% to 100% of normal hearing ears, including those of newborn infants.[15,16]

OAEs are the newest objective measurement technique for evaluation of auditory function and, like ABR, are ideal for infants and other patients who are unable to be tested with more traditional behavioral hearing tests. The clinical applicability of OAE, especially in infants, has been well documented during the past 5 years,[17] and commercial OAE instruments recently have become available. The equipment and recording procedures for OAE are similar to those for ABR; the primary advantage of OAE is that electrode attachment is not required, so that a sleeping infant can generally be tested in about 5 minutes. Fig 2 shows an example of an OAE recorded in a neonate. The analysis for OAE converts the OAE waveform into its frequency components (spectrum) using a fast fourier transform (see upper right panel of Fig 2). In general, one looks for the presence of spectral components of OAE across the frequency range of 500 to 5000 Hz, which then can be related to normal peripheral auditory function in those frequencies. Numerous studies have demonstrated that OAEs are absent at frequencies where the hearing

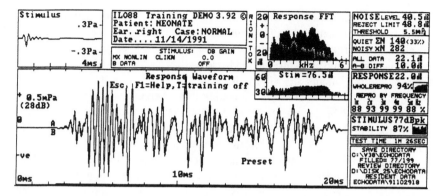

Fig 2. Click-evoked OAE waveform and analyses from a neonate. The larger panel shows the OAE waveform. In the upper right panel (response FFT), the data are presented as frequencies obtained by a fast fourier transform of the emission waveform. The black region in the response FFT represents the emission frequencies that are above the gray-shaded region, representing the noise. Recordings were made with an Otodynamics ILO88. Figure was provided courtesy of Otodynamics, LTD, United Kingdom.

---

impairment is greater than 30 dB HL. If OAE is absent, however, the actual thresholds for those frequencies cannot be determined (ie, the results would be the same for mild, moderate, or severe impairments). Another type of evoked OAE being investigated, called distortion-product OAE, uses two simultaneously presented primary pure tones (f1 and f2) that generate an inner ear distortion tone (2f1–f2), which can be extracted from the ear canal recording. By sweeping the primary pairs of tones through the frequency range, the distortion product OAE is recorded as a function of frequency, thereby providing more discrete frequency information.[18] An important factor that must be considered for OAE testing is that the outer and middle ears need to be functioning normally to allow the low-level emissions generated in the cochlea to be conducted outward and recorded in the ear canal.[19] Common middle ear problems in infants, such as otitis media, can result in a slight conductive hearing loss that would result in absent OAE.

Behavioral audiometry

Hearing screening of neonates through observation of behavioral responses to sound has not been successful and is not recommended by JCIH. Once the infant reaches a developmental age of 5 to 6 months, however, VRA techniques are relatively easy to apply and provide reliable audiometric information. The VRA technique uses an operant conditioning procedure that rewards infants with a visual stimulus (eg, an animated lighted toy animal) for performing a head turn (to look for the visual reinforcer) whenever they hear a tonal or speech stimulus. The sounds can be presented through earphones, bone conduction transducers, loudspeakers, or hearing aids. For infants 6 to 36 months of age, VRA is effective in getting accurate threshold information for low-level speech and tones, which even for 6-month-old infants are within 10 to 20 dB HL of adult thresholds.[20] With VRA, different degrees and types of hearing loss, even mild losses due to middle ear problems, can be documented and used for intervention decisions. If testing is done only with loudspeakers, however, ear-specific information is not possible, and the technique only provides information about the best-hearing ear; therefore, VRA with earphones at a later age would be necessary, or a physiologic test (ABR or OAE) would be required to provide more complete information. JCIH recommends VRA for assessment of infants 6 months of age or older. Because VRA requires processing through the entire auditory system, it can be used to complement the more limited ABR. For infants who do not or cannot cooperate for VRA, however, ABR is recommended to document auditory function appropriate for intervention decisions.

STRATEGIES FOR EARLY IDENTIFICATION

For more than 20 years it has been assumed that mass hearing screening of all newborn infants was not feasible, primarily because quick, simple behavioral testing is not valid in neonates and because ABR is too time consuming and expensive. The most popular early identification strategy that has evolved is one in which a subpopulation of high-risk infants is referred for ABR neonatal testing. For screening purposes, an infant passes the conventional ABR if a response is present at a 30- or 40-dB nHL screening level. Often an intensity series is conducted to characterize better the responses and to document thresholds for those who do not respond at 30 to 40 db nHL; the series only takes a few extra minutes. For infants who fail the ABR screening, a more complete diagnostic ABR should be done in 1 to 3 months. Many investigations have consistently demonstrated that about 10% to 20% of high-risk infants initially fail the neonatal ABR but that the majority are found to be normal at the ABR retest 1 to 3 months later. Those infants who have a bilateral sensorineural hearing loss requiring hearing aids represent about 2% to 4% of the high-risk population.[5,21] Even with the above strategy, however, many newborns may not be identified through the neonatal screening programs because they did not have an identifiable risk factor, because they had neonatal conditions associated with progressive or late-onset hearing loss, because they acquired their hearing loss, or because they were not tested as neonates. The new JCIH high-risk register for infants (1 to 24 months) may help in earlier identification of infants with hearing impairments.[7]

Another strategy under consideration for earlier identification of more infants is to improve and expand the use of neonatal objective screening tests. Most recently, given the speed of testing, OAE has tremendous potential as a screening method that could separate those with normal peripheral hearing (thresholds less than 30 dB HL) from those who would be referred for further diagnostic testing by ABR. Another available screening method is the use of an automated ABR (eg, ALGO-1, Natus Medical, Inc, Foster City, Calif) instrument that uses a preset screening intensity level and an internal computer template to which responses are automatically compared and registered as a pass or refer (Fig 3). Both OAE and

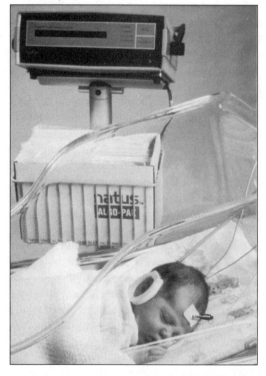

Fig 3. Automated ABR testing with an ALGO-1 neonatal screening instrument. The ALGO-1 is a battery-operated instrument that screens at a single intensity level (35 dB nHL) and automatically indicates pass or refer depending on the match between the recorded ABR and a stored template. Photo provided courtesy of Natus Medical, Inc., Foster City, California.

the automated ABR can be faster and more readily used by trained paraprofessionals or volunteers than conventional ABR.

A few published reports, primarily from European countries, have demonstrated that OAE is comparable to ABR screening results and recommend OAE as a more practical screening method because of its shorter test time. Kennedy et al[22] evaluated 370 high- and low-risk infants with OAE, ALGO-1, and conventional ABR. The follow-up confirmation test was a behavioral distraction test at 8 months of age ($n = 354$) and a questionnaire at 18 months of age ($n = 210$). Results showed that OAE was the quickest procedure (mean, 12.5 minutes) and that, although all three tests had similar neonatal failure rates, OAE had the highest sensitivity for those who were later confirmed to have a severe hearing impairment. Stevens et al[23] found a sensitivity and specificity of OAE of 93% and 86%, respectively, as validated by diagnostic ABR at age 3 months. Specific issues to be resolved are the effects of probe placement in the ear canal and the high incidence of middle ear problems on the OAE false-positive rate and whether OAE is cost effective in screening large populations of infants. Using the ALGO-1 automated ABR instrument, Jacobson et al[24] reported that this method would be acceptable for infants; the sensitivity and specificity were 100% and 96%, respectively, for a population of 224 intensive care newborns. With either OAE or automated ABR neonatal screening tests, those who fail must be followed by a diagnostic ABR to document the degree of auditory impairment. Although enough information can be obtained with the objective measures of hearing to initiate early intervention services, including the fitting of hearing aids, within the first 6 months of life, continued assessment is required and must include behavioral assessment with VRA beginning at 6 months of age. Assessment should continue until documentation of hearing status is completed across the frequency range for each ear, a process that may take several visits.

In view of the relatively late ages at which children in the United States are being identified and enrolled in intervention programs, and with the recent advances in objective screening methods, the issue of mass screening of all newborns has resurfaced. Last year, a Congressional committee was reviewing a bill known as the Newborn Hearing Screening Act introduced by Congressman James Walsh (D–New York) to mandate screening of all infants for hearing loss. The Walsh bill had several implementation problems that have kept it in committee, but ASHA and the American Academy of Otolaryngology–Head and Neck Surgery have met with Congressional staff regarding other versions of a federal bill for infant hearing screening.[25]

THE EFFECT OF HEARING LOSS ON COMMUNICATION

JCIH recommends, and PL 99-457 requires, that infants and toddlers diagnosed as having a hearing loss be evaluated by a multidisciplinary team.[7] Subsequently, an individualized family service plan (IFSP) should be prepared that is developed jointly by the family and the personnel involved in the provision of early intervention services, is based on a multidisciplinary evaluation to determine the child's initial eligibility, and includes a comprehensive description of the services needed to enhance the development of the child and the capacity of the family to meet the child's special needs. The five areas that must be evaluated by the multidisciplinary team and, if appropriate, included in the intervention program are cognitive development, physical development (including vision and hearing), speech and language development, psychosocial development, and self-help skills. Because language and speech delays secondary to hearing impairment can significantly affect the results of the evaluation and intervention goals in these five developmental areas, it is critical that all members of the multidisciplinary team be aware of the effects of early hearing loss on verbal communication. The importance of this issue prompted ASHA and the Council on Education of the Deaf jointly to draft a proposal regarding the knowledge and skills necessary for professionals providing services under PL 99-457 to hearing-impaired children. The joint proposal stated that each member should have "knowledge of normal language acquisition and effects of hearing impairment on communication and its concomitant effects on all other aspects of a child's development."[26(p2)]

Degree of hearing loss: Relationship to speech perception

The effects of perlingually acquired hearing loss on the speech, language, and psychosocial development and academic status of children have been extensively documented,[27] and these effects are strongly related to the child's ability to hear and understand speech. The most obvious effect of hearing loss is to decrease the availability of acoustic cues. A low-frequency loss may primarily affect the discrimination of vowels or vowel-like consonants (eg, *m*, *l*, and *r*), and a high-frequency loss primarily affects consonant discrimination.

Even a mild hearing loss can have a significantly negative impact on the discrimination ability of infants. Nozza and Sabo[28] found that 6- to 8-month-old infants could discriminate */ba/* from */da/* with 82% accuracy when the phonemes were presented at 57 dB HL (which is 7 dB louder than the average level for conversational speech). At 37 dB HL, however, these infants could make this discrimination with only 60% accuracy. This demonstrates that even a mild shift in hearing level of 20 dB, which could result from fluctuating otitis media or a sensorineural hearing loss, could reduce an infant's speech perception ability to close to chance.

Because amplification can make the majority of speech cues available for even children with severe losses, it is often assumed that, once aided, children with various degrees of hearing loss will have similar speech perception abilities. This overlooks the fact that progressively greater degrees of hearing loss produce progressively greater internal distortion of speech.[29] The effect of different levels of hearing loss on the ability to identify amplified speech was investigated by Boothroyd[30] using school-age children with prelingually acquired sensorineural hearing loss ranging from 55 dB HL (moderate loss) to 123 dB HL (profound loss). Progressively poorer speech discrimination ability as a function of the severity of hearing loss was demonstrated on all speech tasks. For example, children with a 55- to 74-dB hearing loss were able to identify phonemes (consonants and vowels) in an open-set monosyllabic word test with 66% accuracy, whereas children with a 90- to 104-dB HL hearing loss demonstrated a score of only 18%. The performances of the children with the greatest hearing loss (115 to 124 dB HL) were only at chance level on all speech tasks. Because the majority of children with profound hearing loss (90 dB HL or higher) do not have perceptual abilities that will allow them to learn language and academic material through audition and/or speech reading, they are enrolled in programs that use both oral and manual communication (total communication).

Because speech perception in quiet decreases with the severity of hearing loss, it is not surprising that the ability to identify speech in the presence of background noise decreases accordingly. Thus a child with a moderate sensorineural loss who could identify 66% of monosyllabic words in quiet (even when aided) would be able to identify still fewer words in background noise. An aided child with a profound sensorineural loss who could identify 18% of the words in quiet probably would not be able to identify any words in background noise. Because adults also experience degradation of speech, an adult who can understand a speech message despite the presence of noise tends to assume that a child can also understand it. Background noise has significantly greater detrimental effects on children, however. For example, one study[31] demonstrated that, in the presence of noise, infants from 6 to 24 months of age need the speech signal to be 10 times more intense than the intensity required by adults just to detect the signal. Thus an environmental sound that is easily detected by an adult in the presence of background noise might be inaudible to an infant or toddler.

Speech production

The sounds made by infants seem unrelated to the speech they hear up to approximately 4 months of age. In fact, the vocalizations of congenitally deaf infants are indistinguishable from those of normal-hearing infants until 5 to 6 months of age. Hearing-impaired infants demonstrate a decrease in the size of their consonantal repertoires over time and demonstrate fewer multisyllabic utterances containing true consonants. Because the vocal responses of infants begin to be of a reciprocal nature at around 4 months of age, this decrease in the vocalizations of children who cannot hear their own voices or those of their parents would be expected.[32] To restore the auditory feedback loop and the parent–child interactions needed to develop intelligible speech, children with congenital or early-onset hearing impairment must be promptly identified and fitted with amplification. Children with mild to moderate losses can usually be fitted with hearing aids that make most speech cues accessible, at least in quiet listening environments. Providing nearly normal hearing sensitivity, especially for the high-frequency range that is critical to consonant discrimination, is more difficult for children with severe to profound hearing losses. Thus the greater the degree of hearing loss, the poorer the clarity of the speech signal (especially the consonants) even when amplified, and the poorer the child's speech intelligibility is likely to be.[30]

The speech errors made by hearing-impaired children range from omissions and/or distortions of consonants for those with mild to moderate hearing loss to omissions, distortions, and substitutions of both consonants and vowels, voice disorders (inappropriate nasality and poor breath support), and disruptions in the rate and rhythm patterns of speech for those with profound hearing loss. The extent to which speech is intelligible is affected by many factors, including the age of onset, the type and degree of hearing loss, the age at which the loss is identified, the delay between the onset of the loss and the fitting of amplification, the appropriateness and consistency of amplification, and the age at which speech therapy is initiated.

Language

In general, the greater the degree of hearing loss, the greater its impact on the acquisition, development, and use of language, both receptive and expressive, oral and written.[27] As with speech perception and production, however, a wide range of factors (such as age of onset), in addition to the degree of the loss, affects the level of language proficiency achieved by a hearing-impaired child. The fact that the degree of hearing loss cannot be used accurately to predict the degree of language delay is exemplified by the language problems associated with unilateral hearing loss and the milder degrees of bilateral hearing loss (whether conductive or sensorineural in nature); that is, their effects on language are often significantly greater than anticipated based on the degree of the hearing loss.[33]

The listening demands of infants and toddlers with unilateral hearing loss typically are not great enough to cause immediate communication problems; indeed, children with a unilateral loss typically exhibit no speech or language problems in early childhood. In spite of this, they have academic failure rates (23% to 35%) that are significantly greater than the failure rates for the other children in their school districts (2.0% to 3.5%), and those with right-ear hearing impairment have academic failure rates 5 times higher than those with left-ear hearing impairment.[34] The greater risk for academic failure of children with unilateral hearing loss appears to be linked to their need for a louder speech signal to process the message comfortably and to their difficulty understanding speech in the presence of background noise. In addition, their difficulty localizing the speaker in the room reduces their ability to use the visual aspects of speech to complement the weaker auditory message they receive. These classroom communication problems increase the difficulty of acquiring auditorily presented information, tend to result in vocabulary deficits, and make the child more fatigued by the end of the school day.

In a prospective study of the effects of otitis media with effusion (OME), Friel-Patti and Finitzo[35] demonstrated a direct causal connection between hearing and language and an indirect causal connection between OME and language based on the relationship between OME and hearing. The number of days effusion was presented correlated negatively with receptive language at 12 months of age and with expressive language at 18 months of age. The children's average hearing over time correlated negatively with receptive and expressive language at 12 and 18 months, and from 18 to 24 months of age both receptive and expressive language scores were significantly related to hearing. Although the language performance of these children was not delayed in relationship to the anticipated performance for their chronologic ages, better language was associated with better hearing even in these middle-class children who were not otherwise at risk for language delay.

Although many children with significant histories of fluctuating otitis media are seen in clinics because of phonologic delays and other language problems, many other children with similar histories demonstrate no communication problems until they enter school. The latter group of children, along with children with unilateral hearing loss, often do well in one-to-one and small-group communication settings but show problems in coping with the greater listening and language demands of the classroom. Teachers are often perplexed by children with histories of otitis media who have passed hearing screening tests but demonstrate reading difficulties (including sound–symbol association and sound blending) and problems in the areas of auditory attention, auditory figure ground, and auditory memory. Children with fluctuating otitis media as well as those with sensorineural hearing loss demonstrate developmental delays in the acquisition of grammar due to their difficulty perceiving short unstressed words (eg, articles, prepositions, and conjunctions) and word endings (eg, the -s that signals subject-verb agreement, plurals, and possessives).[27] Because this decreased availability of cues makes it difficult even for an adult to recognize familiar words and grammar patterns, the significant negative effects of hearing loss on a child learning to use acoustic cues to categorize and recognize speech sounds, to learn vocabulary, and to extract the grammar of the language are obvious. In addition, hearing-impaired children have difficulty learning abstract concepts and multiple meanings of words.[27] The greater the hearing loss, the more purposeful the organization of language input required by parents, educators, and speech-language pathologists to facilitate the sequential, integrated development of auditory, speech, and language skills.[33] As these children grow older, the gap between their language levels and those of their normal-hearing peers tends to grow larger.[27]

INTERVENTION PROGRAMS

According to PL 99-457, the IFSP must include a statement of the specific intervention services necessary to meet the unique needs of the handicapped child and his or her family. Each hearing-impaired child and his or her family will present unique needs, but because of the effects of hearing loss per se the multidisciplinary team must consider the following in planning the intervention program of each hearing-impaired infant and toddler:

- How will appropriate management of health problems be ensured with regard to
    1. audition: Who will provide medical clearance for hearing aid use, management of otitis media or progressive hearing loss, cerumen management, and periodic hearing evaluations?
    2. vision: Does the child have a vision problem that will reduce the ability to utilize manual communication and/or the visual components of oral communication? Can a vision problem be identified that would assist in determining the etiology of the hearing loss and thereby assist in planning the intervention program?
- Can the use of a sensory device assist the child in compensating for the hearing loss? If so, which device is most appropriate: (1) Amplification (hearing aids, personal FM auditory trainers, and/or sound-field FM amplification systems), (2) a vibrotactile device, or (3) a cochlear implant? Who will select and fit the device and train the parents in its use?
- Which mode of communication (oral, aural, total communication, or manual communication using American Sign Language with English viewed as a second language) is most appropriate? This decision is based on factors such as the child's degree of hearing loss, auditory perceptual abilities, current language skills, nonverbal intelligence, family support, and attitude toward oral communication.[36]
- What type of parent education program will be used to
    1. provide information regarding the effects of hearing loss, the benefits and limitations of their child's sensory device, the care and use of the sensory devices, educational options, and criteria to use in selecting health care professionals?
    2. help the family adjust to having a hearing-impaired member?
    3. train the parents to facilitate speech-language development and to maximize the home auditory environment?
    4. teach behavioral management techniques?
    5. provide information regarding the legal rights of both the child and the parents?
- Who will pay for the evaluations, sensory devices, and intervention services if the state in which the child lives does not participate in Part H of PL 99-457?

SUMMARY AND RECOMMENDATIONS

Successful early intervention with hearing-impaired children has been greatly facilitated by current technology and screening methods. Audiologic techniques are available to test reliably any newborn's or infant's hearing. Despite the use of high-risk register and ABR screening programs, the average age at which hearing-impaired children are enrolled in intervention is still too high. Improvements in the high-risk register and the potential for screening more neonates with OAE hold promise for the future as health care professionals put forth a concentrated effort directed at lowering the age of identification and intervention with hearing-impaired infants and toddlers. Any infant suspected of having any degree of hearing impairment, either by parents or by health care providers, or who has one of the JCIH high-risk factors should be referred for audiologic evaluation without delay. Any degree of hearing loss during the first 36 months of life, whether it is a permanent sensorineural loss or a fluctuating conductive loss and whether it is present at birth or acquired postnatally, has the potential to influence detrimentally a child's acquisition of speech and language, psychosocial development, and later educational performance. With early identification and timely intervention, the effects of the hearing loss can be minimized.

The effects of hearing loss on communication have several implications for members of the multidisciplinary team. First, to allow hearing-impaired infants and toddlers to make maximum use of their residual hearing, the listening environment should be optimized by having speakers face the children when speaking to them, by minimizing the distance between the children and speakers, and by reducing background noise.

Second, obtaining the most accurate clinical picture of a particular hearing-impaired child requires adequate knowledge of his or her communication skills. In view of the information given above, the care provider can anticipate the degree of speech-language delay from the results of the audiologic evaluation. In addition, having an evaluation of the child's communication skills by a speech-language pathologist before the child is evaluated by other health care providers can prove extremely useful. Because evaluation and intervention procedures with infants are not based on verbal ability, the choice of tests or procedures need not be modified to compensate for the differences in the speech and/or language skills between hearing-impaired and normal-hearing infants. Similarly, few modifications are needed for hard-of-hearing 12- to 15-month olds: The examiner's understanding of the one-word productions characteristic of these children in this age group is facilitated by the context of games or the use of toys. Even at this young age, however, a child with a severe to profound loss may already be delayed in the area of speech-language production or may rely on manual rather than oral communication. Moreover, because tests administered to normal-hearing 12- to 36-month-old children are designed to evaluate the rapid acceleration of vocabulary and grammar that occurs during this time frame,[37] prior knowledge of the child's communication skills provides invaluable information to assist the examiner in selecting tests and appropriately modifying his or her language level and/or communication style for the hearing-impaired child in this age range.

Third, knowledge of the child's current level of oral language functioning and attitude toward oral communication is critical in planning an intervention program. Therefore, although performance IQ scores are regarded as having more validity than verbal IQ scores for estimating the intellectual potential of the hearing impaired, their performance on the verbal portions is useful in choosing an appropriate academic setting[27] and later in predicting concurrent academic achievement.[38]

Fourth, early intervention specialists should be aware that the delayed language associated with hearing loss affects not only the development of vocabulary and grammar but the pragmatic aspects of language as well (eg, adult–child interactions and turn-taking). Consequently, reduced communication ability may interfere with the development of age-appropriate social skills. This may be the basis for parents describing their school-age hearing-impaired children as having more serious problems interacting with others and establishing friendships than normal-hearing children and as having behavior problems characterized by aggression, impulsivity, immaturity, and resistance to discipline and structure.[38] In any event, knowledge of the relationship between delayed language and social skills will allow the formation of a more appropriate clinical picture.

Finally, cultural differences may also influence the development of language skills and the performance of the hearing-impaired child during evaluations other than those related to speech and language. Maxon and Brackett[33] noted that the extended infantile behavior accepted by many cultures may result in parents not viewing their hearing-impaired child's delayed communication skills as being widely variant from the norm. Other cultural variations include children averting their eyes when interacting with adults, a behavior that not only appears deviant to those not familiar with the discourse rules of the culture but that also prevents the child from making full use of contextual and situational cues during communication. Sensitivity to such cultural differences is required if the examiner is to separate the effects of hearing loss from cultural influences.

REFERENCES

1. Joint Committee on Infant Hearing. 1990 position statement. *ASHA*. 1991;33:3–6.
2. American Speech-Language-Hearing Association. Guidelines for audiologic assessment of children from birth–36 months of age. *ASHA*. 1991;33(suppl 5):37–43.

3. Early intervention program for infants and toddlers with handicaps; final regulations. *Fed Reg.* 1989;54:26306–26348.

4. Elssmann S, Matkin N, Sabo M. Early identification of congenital sensorineural hearing impairment. *Hear J.* September 1987:13–17.

5. Kramer S, Vertes D, Condon M. Auditory brainstem responses and clinical follow-up of high-risk infants. *Pediatrics.* 1989;83:385–392.

6. Stein L, Jabaley T, Spitz R, Stoakley D, McGee T. The hearing-impaired infant: patterns of identification and habilitation revisited. *Ear Hear.* 1990;11:201–205.

7. Diefendorf A, Reitz P, Cox J. The Joint Committee on Infant Hearing 1990 position statement: a closer look. *Infants Young Child.* 1992;5:v–xi.

8. Galambos R, Hicks G, Wilson M. The auditory brain stem response reliably predicts hearing loss in graduates of a tertiary intensive care nursery. *Ear Hear.* 1984;5:254–260.

9. Schulman-Galambos C, Galambos R. Brain stem auditory evoked responses in premature infants. *J Speech Hear Res.* 1975;18:456–465.

10. Swigonski N, Shallop J, Bull M, Lemons J. Hearing screening of high risk newborns. *Ear Hear.* 1987;8:26–30.

11. Hyde M, Riko K, Malizia K. Audiometric accuracy of the click ABR in infants at risk for hearing loss. *J Am Acad Audiol.* 1990;1:59–66.

12. Stapells D, Picton T, Perez-Abalo M, Read D, Smith A. Frequency specificity in evoked potential audiometry. In: Jacobson J, ed. *The Auditory Brainstem Response.* San Diego, Calif: College Hill: 1985:147–177.

13. Kemp D. Stimulated acoustic emissions from within the auditory system. *J Acoust Soc Am.* 1978;64:1386–1391.

14. Brownell W. Outer hair cell electromotility and otoacoustic emissions. *Ear Hear.* 1990;11:82–92.

15. Probst R, Coats A, Martin G, Lonsbury-Martin B. Spontaneous, click- and toneburst-evoked otoacoustic emissions from normal ears. *Hear Res.* 1986;21:261–275.

16. Prieve B. Otoacoustic emissions in infants and children: basic characteristics and clinical application. *Semin Hear.* 1992;13:23–35.

17. Lonsbury-Martin B, Whitehead M, Martin G. Clinical applications of otoacoustic emissions. *J Speech Hear Res.* 1991;34:964–981.

18. Lonsbury-Martin B, Martin G. The clinical utility of distortion-product otoacoustic emissions. *Ear Hear.* 1990;11:144–154.

19. Owens J, McCoy M, Lonsbury-Martin B, Martin G. Influence of otitis media on evoked otoacoustic emissions in children. *Semin Hear.* 1992;13:53–66.

20. Wilson W, Thompson G. Behavioral audiometry. In: Jerger J, ed. *Pediatric Audiology.* San Diego, Calif: College Hill; 1984.

21. Fria T. Identification of congenital hearing loss with the auditory brainstem response. In: Jacobson J, ed. *The Auditory Brainstem Response.* San Diego, Calif: College Hill; 1985:317–334.

22. Kennedy C, Kim L, Dees D, et al. Otoacoustic emissions and auditory brain stem responses in the newborn. *Arch Dis Child.* 1991;66:1124–1129.

23. Stevens J, Webb H, Smith M, Buffin J, Ruddy H. A comparison of oto-acoustic emissions and brain stem electric response audiometry in the normal newborn and babies admitted to a special care baby unit. *Clin Phys Physiol Meas.* 1987;8:95–104.

24. Jacobson J, Jacobson C, Spahr R. Automated and conventional ABR screening techniques in high-risk infants. *J Am Acad Audiol.* 1990;1:187–195.

25. American Speech-Language-Hearing Association. Discussions of infant hearing legislation strategies underway. *Audiol Update.* 1992;11:9–10.

26. Cherow E, Davila R, Dickman D. Education of children with hearing impairment. Presented at the American Speech-Language-Hearing Association Convention; November 1992; San Antonio, Tex.

27. Ross M, Brackett D, Maxon A. *Assessment and Management of Mainstreamed Hearing-Impaired Children: Principles and Practice.* Austin, Tex: Pro-Ed; 1991.

28. Nozza J, Sabo D. Screening in audiology: principles and practice. Presented at the Annual Convention of the American Speech-Language-Hearing Association; November 1991; Nashville, Tenn.

29. Anderson K, Matkin N. Relationship of degree of longterm hearing loss to psychosocial impact and educational needs. *Educ Audiol Assoc Newsl.* 1991;8:11–12.

30. Boothroyd A. Auditory perception of speech contrasts by subjects with sensorineural hearing loss. *J Speech Hear Res.* 1984;27:134–144.

31. Trehub A, Bull D, Schneider B. Infants' detection of speech in noise. *J Speech Hear Res.* 1981;24:202–206.

32. Stoel-Gammon C, Otomo K. Babbling development of hearing impaired and normally developing hearing subjects. *J Speech Hear Dis.* 1986;51:33–41.

33. Maxon A, Brackett D. *The Hearing Impaired Child: Infancy Through High-School Years.* Boston, Mass: Andover; 1992.

34. Oyler R, Oyler A, Matkin N. Unilateral hearing loss: demographics and educational impact. *Lang Speech Hear Schools.* 1988;19:201–210.

35. Friel-Patti S, Finitzo T. Language learning on a prospective study of otitis media with effusion in the first two years of life. *J Speech Hear Res.* 1990;33:188–194.

36. Geer A, Moog J. Predicting spoken language acquisition of profoundly hearing-impaired children. *J Speech Hear Dis.* 1987;52:84–94.

37. Bates E, Thal D. Normal and abnormal development: the early stages. Presented at the American Speech-Language-Hearing Association Convention; November 1992; San Antonio, Tex.

38. Davis J, Schum R, Bentler R. Effects of mild and moderate language, educational and psychosocial behavior of children. *J Speech Hear Dis.* 1986;51:53–62.

Appendix

Summary of JCIH high-risk registers

RISK CRITERIA FOR HEARING LOSS

The following risk factors are listed by the *Joint Committee on Infant Hearing* to identify neonates and infants at risk for hearing loss.

Neonates (birth to 28 days)

- Family history of childhood hearing loss.
- Mother had rubella (German measles), cytomegalovirus (CMV), toxoplasmosis, herpes, or syphilis present at birth of infant and/or during pregnancy.
- Birthweight less than 3 lb, 5 oz (1500 grams).
- Unusual ear, eye, head, or neck development, including cleft lip or palate, absent philtrum, low hairline, ear tags or pits, etc.
- Severe jaundice (hyperbilirubinemia) that required an exchange blood transfusion.
- Presence of bacterial meningitis.
- APGAR score of 3 or less at 5 minutes after birth, failure to initiate spontaneous respiration by 10 minutes, or hypotonia persisting to 2 hours of age.
- Need for prolonged mechanical ventilation of 10 or more days duration (eg, persistent pulmonary hypertension).
- Presence of syndromal characteristics associated with hearing loss (eg, Waardenburg's or Usher's syndrome).
- Certain ototoxic drugs or medications including, but not limited to, aminoglycosides used for more than 5 days.

Infants (29 days to 2 years)

- Presence of any of the criteria listed above for neonates at risk.
- Parents/caregivers have concern regarding hearing, speech, language, and/or developmental delay.
- Presence of neonatal risk factors that are associated with progressive sensorineural hearing loss (eg, CMV, prolonged mechanical ventilation, and heredity).
- History of head trauma.
- Presence of neurodegenerative disorders such as neurofibromatosis, myoclonic epilepsy, Werdnig-Hoffmann disease, Tay-Sachs disease, infantile Gaucher's disease, Niemann-Pick disease, any metachromatic leukodystrophy, or any infantile demyelinating neuropathy.

- History of childhood infectious diseases associated with sensorineural hearing loss (eg, mumps, measles).

COMMUNICATION DEVELOPMENT

0–4 months

Startles (jumps or blinks) to loud sounds.
Can be soothed by a familiar voice.
Says "coo" or "aaah" sounds.
Stops playing and appears to listen to sounds or speech.
Watches a speaker's face.
Usually awakens when sleeping quietly and someone talks or makes a loud noise.

6–9 months

Notices and looks toward interesting sounds.
Responds to soft levels of speech and other sounds.
Responds to "no" and his/her name.
Begins to understand "bye-bye" or "up" when used with a hand gesture.
Enjoys rattles and other sound-making toys for their sound, not for visual appeal.

10–14 months

Uses voice to get attention.
Begins to use single words.
Turns head in any direction to find an interesting sound or the person speaking.
Responds to name even when spoken softly.

15–23 months

Identifies sounds coming from another room or outside.
Enjoys music and tries to dance or make sounds to music.
Begins to follow two-part requests (get your toy and put it in the box).
Can point to body parts.
Imitates words.

24 months

Vocabulary should consist of 50–250 words.

36 months

Vocabulary should be well over 1000 words.

REMEMBER: HEARING CAN BE TESTED AT ANY AGE.

Reprinted with permission from the American Academy of Audiology.

Health, developmental, and psychosocial aspects of Down syndrome

Michael E. Msall, MD
Department of Pediatrics
Children's Hospital
Division of Developmental Pediatrics
  and Rehabilitation
School of Medicine and Biomedical
  Sciences
State University of New York at
  Buffalo
Robert Warner Rehabilitation Center
Albany, New York

Kathleen M. DiGaudio, MS, PNP
Department of Pediatrics
Children's Hospital
Division of Developmental Pediatrics
  and Rehabilitation
School of Medicine and Biomedical
  Sciences
State University of New York at
  Buffalo
Robert Warner Rehabilitation Center
Albany, New York

Anthony F. Malone, MD
Division of Developmental Pediatrics
Albany Medical Center and Center
  School for the Disabled
Albany, New York

DOWN SYNDROME (DS) is the most commonly known cause of mental retardation and congenital malformation.[1] DS occurs with a frequency of 1:600 to 1:800 live births.[2] It is increasingly a prenatal cause of concern on the part of women in their 40s who have deferred their families and are concerned about risks and ethical dilemmas of amniocentesis. It is a cause of concern to health professionals who discover abnormal maternal serum alphafetoprotein (MSAFP) or abnormal ultrasound during prenatal surveillance for birth defects in early pregnancy.[3,4]

Two recent medical reviews[5,6] and several medical monographs have targeted the complexity of health impairments over the life span of individuals with Down syndrome. Several psychoeducational and habilitation reviews have examined past and current efforts in early childhood intervention.[7-9] In this paper, DS will be viewed as a model disorder that provides opportunities for integrating biomedical, developmental, and family supports in early childhood. Guidelines will be offered for dealing with medical concerns that most impact on development. Communication guidelines for health and developmental professionals will be described to facilitate optimal habilitation of the whole child and empowerment of parents. Our format will include illustrative cases from our clinical practices to demonstrate stress points that occur prenatally, perinatally, postnatally, and through the first 3 years of life.

Presented in part at the 44th Annual Meeting of the American Academy of Cerebral Palsy and Developmental Medicine, Orlando, Florida, October 6, 1990.
Partial support of this study was provided by the Office of Mental Retardation and Developmental Disabilities of the State of New York (RF 150-6619D)

Inf Young Children 1991; 4(1): 35–45
© 1991 Aspen Publishers, Inc.

PRENATAL AND GENETIC

Case 1: A prenatal crisis. Mrs. Smith, a 28-year-old accountant, is pregnant for the first time. Dr. Jones has obtained routine prenatal blood work, including MSAFP. The MSAFP is found to be significantly decreased at 16 weeks gestation. He explains that the MSAFP value may be a miscalculation of dates or a normal variant. However, preliminary research suggests that in some cases a low MSAFP value may suggest a chromosome disorder. Mrs. Smith asks if the test means that she may be carrying a deformed child. Mr. Smith feels that he needs to find out what is wrong and wants absolute certainty of test results. Dr. Jones, after an extended discussion, suggests that a level 3 sonogram be performed and that Mr. and Mrs. Smith meet with the University Prenatal Genetics team.

One week later, a combined level 3 ultrasonography and prenatal genetics visit takes place at the University Hospital. Ultrasound reveals a 16-week fetus with shortened femur, normal gastrointestinal and normal cardiovascular anatomy. Extensive time is spent with both Mr. and Mrs. Smith, explaining the statistical association between low MSAFP and chromosome disorders.[4] Mr. Smith still requests absolute certainty. He expresses anger that medical science cannot tell him exactly if this pregnancy is affected by Down syndrome from ultrasound information. Mrs. Smith wants to know what Down syndrome children are like, what their abilities and disabilities are, and what supports exist for families.

Dr. Lyons, the pediatric geneticist, arranges an extended session with the genetics counselor and simultaneously refers the family to the educational director of an infant and preschool program.

Some of the guidelines for counseling families about genetic issues are
- It is an educational process with a nondirective orientation.
- The first goal is for a family to understand the nature of the genetic disorder, its natural history, and its treatment.
- The second goal is for the family to understand applicable genetics, including recurrent risks and available reproductive options, and to facilitate options consistent with informed decisions.

These guidelines are often not known to either primary care health professionals or early childhood professionals. They emphasize genetics counseling as a process of understanding information, probability, and decision making. Specific stress points for families occur because of several genetic myths:
- DS babies are born only to older women.
- Maternal behavior in pregnancy causes DS.
- In subsequent pregnancies, the risk of DS is very high.
- Genetic counseling is a coercive process specifying the decisions parents should make.
- The prognosis for DS is severe retardation with inevitable institutionalization, impossibility of academic learning, and limited motor abilities.

Many health and development professionals do not know that the majority of children with DS are born to women in their 20s. Because of the statistical association of advanced maternal age and DS, there is a tendency for mothers to feel that they are the cause of having a child with DS. Even when a woman is 40 years old, one cannot determine why only 1/100 pregnancies for this age group result in DS and 99/100 do not. In addition, in 20% of cases, the extra chromosome is of paternal origin.[1]

In trisomy 21, which occurs in over 95% of children with DS, the recurrence risk in subsequent pregnancies does not exceed 1%, though clinicians and families imagine the risk to be several orders of magnitude higher. In translocation DS, one of the parents may be a balanced translocation carrier. If a parent is a translocation carrier, the recurrence risk of DS varies depending on what parent carriers the translocation and the chromosome involved.

Because genetic counseling is a nondirective process, it is important that all professionals understand that reproductive options are selected by families based on their personal, religious, ethical, and family values. No genetics counselor explicitly says to a family statements such as, "If I were in your shoes, abortion would be the only option." However, because of the high levels of stress associated with discussion of genetic issues, it is important for both health and developmental professionals to offer ongoing support while recognizing that there are no easy answers when facing uncertainty.

NEONATAL STRESSES

Case 2: The first day. Mrs. Langdon, a 28-year-old primigravida woman, has delivered a full term 7-pound female infant at 7 PM on a Saturday. There was an uncomplicated pregnancy, labor, and delivery. The nursery evening nurse calls the pediatrician at home to express concern that the child is floppy and looks "mongoloid." The obstetrician has told the parents that all is well.

The purpose of this case is to address simultaneously the clinical diagnosis of DS and those health issues that are neonatal emergencies. For both physicians and nurses, the key concept to clinically recognizing that a child may have DS is the clustering of the neurological impairment of central hypotonia along with craniofacial and extremity dysmorphisms.[10]

Though many professionals feel that the diagnosis of DS can be made at a glance, this is the exception, not the rule. It is most important to systematically examine the whole child and list major and minor malformations. Low tone without weakness, also known as central hypotonia, is a major neurological finding and is present in 90% of infants with DS. Not all health professionals feel comfortable performing newborn neurological exams, but Dubowitz check sheets are excellent teaching and recording devices.[11] The most common minor malformations include small ears with overlapping of the helix, midface hypoplasia and wide space between first and second toes. These occur in 90% or more of individuals with DS.[10] Even with systematic evaluation, the diagnosis of Down syndrome can be difficult.

Four key questions must initially be addressed by health professionals: First, is there a chromosomal abnormality? Second, are there any indications of gastrointestinal malformation? Third, are there any cardiac malformations? Fourth, how does the physician communicate concerns and support the family in crisis?

The health professionals must be aware that the initial communication session is critically important for both sharing medical diagnostic issues and supporting the family. A spectrum of emotions takes place in families during these initial informing sessions and includes disbelief, sorrow, helplessness, anger, bitterness, guilt, and confusion.[12] Many of these initial emotions are so overwhelming that the capacity for parents to hear detailed information is not possible. This is often reflected in statements to nurses and developmental professionals such as "No one ever told me anything." In many cases, these parental statements reflect disbelief and would be more accurately expressed as "I can't believe this is happening to me." Unless professionals recognize these emotions, they will not understand barriers to receiving initial information about children with DS. Communication sessions throughout early childhood are required in order to facilitate family understanding and address individualized concerns.

The health professional must emphasize that the child is a child first and has a genetic difference second. He or she must also encourage parents to be parents of a newborn first and give opportunities for acknowledging how feelings of developmental uncertainty make it very difficult to sort out the myriad changes and challenges that a new child brings to a family. Linkage with the DS parent group at this early stage may be very helpful in presenting a more complete perspective.

If a child has a congenital gastrointestinal malformation, the family's initial crisis will include dealing with the stresses of neonatal surgery and the neonatal intensive care unit. The role of the health professional is to explain in lay terms the environment of the neonatal intensive care unit, the fears surrounding the vulnerability of children in that unit, especially fear of death, and the need to understand information from nurses, surgeons, neonatologists, and pediatricians. Visiting, holding, touching, assisting in care, and feeding are all important interactive times.

It is most important for health professionals to realize that infants with DS are often difficult feeders, whether breast or bottle fed. Craniofacial differences, such as shortened palate and midface hypoplasia, coupled with oral hypotonia, tongue thrust and poor lip closure can lead to difficulties with coordinated, sustained suck-swallow. Other factors, such as postextubation stridor, lack of experience with non-nutritive sucking, fears of disconnecting intravenous or nasogastric tubes, and dislodging of apnea monitors all contribute as barriers to making initial breast or nipple feeding difficult. Failure to support mothers during these initial feeding difficulties will often lead to further feelings of helplessness and overwhelmedness. Health and education professionals must explicitly acknowledge that breast feeding is the preferred feeding method and requires extensive family and professional support. Supporting mothers in a nonjudgmental manner for this difficult task can do much for building maternal confidence and establishing feelings that the child is a baby first and has an extra chromosome second.

The second major group of malformations impacting on children with DS is congenital heart disease. This occurs in 40% to 60% of children.[13] Approximately one-third of these malformations have endocardial cushion defects (atrioventricular [AV] canal), one-third are ventricular septal defects and the remaining one-third include Tetrology of Fallot, atrial septal defects, and patent ductus arteriosus. Prior to 1975, correction of endocardial cushion defects was not technologically feasible as this malformation involves complex midline and valvular cardiac structures.[13] In addition, significant mortality was associated with this lesion because of pulmonary hypertension and difficulty with infant valvular heart repair. Currently, pediatric cardiovascular surgical techniques and supportive care have advanced so that definitive repair of this most complex heart lesion is available in the first year of life.

Unfortunately, not all health professionals are aware of these advances. For this reason, all DS infants require an initial pediatric cardiology consultation with a pediatric echocardiogram. The noninvasive technology of pediatric echocardiography clarifies the diagnosis of congenital heart disease in the newborn period so that planned cardiac intervention strategies can take place. If a child with DS has an endocardial cushion defect, then myriad additional family crises will take place in the first 2 years of life. These are illustrated in the next case.

INFANCY

Case 3: Cardiac delays. Amy is 6 months old. She has Down syndrome and a complete atrioventricular canal. She has difficulty feeding and gaining weight. At age 2 months, she was hospitalized for viral pneumonia with congestive heart failure. Digoxin was initiated, and nocturnal nasogastric feedings begun. At 6 months, she weighs 10 pounds. She has a continuous nasal discharge. It takes her 40 minutes to drink 4 ounces of a special low-salt formula. Significant head lag is noted. In prone, Amy does not roll. She likes to put two hands on her bottle during feeding. The parents were told that definitive cardiovascular repair was not possible until the child weighed 15 pounds.

In this case, health and developmental professionals must address three questions. First, what are the priority issues for Amy's health? Second, what direction should intervention efforts take for Amy? Third, what is the interplay between health and developmental concerns?

One of the more important issues is to acknowledge the balance between supporting Amy's family and addressing her complex health and developmental impairments. The reason Amy takes so long to feed is that taking one ounce requires the cardiopulmonary endurance equivalent of running one mile. Amy's case requires that developmental professionals individualize their interventions to Amy's condition. The therapy and developmental curriculum geared to the child with DS and no underlying heart disease is not appropriate for Amy. The oral motor interventions for children with cerebral palsy are also not appropriate for Amy. In addition, a respiratory infection for Amy acquired from infant day-care or preschool setting can lead to serious and critical illness.

The major goals for Amy are to lessen the cardiopulmonary stresses in her life while promoting visual, verbal, nonverbal and fine motor activities and family supports. Amy's needs include positioning to avoid aspiration, careful nutritional monitoring, enriching experiences that are not physically taxing, and supports for her family to deal with the uncertainty of outcome in open heart repair. Creative use of videocassette, teleconferences, lending libraries, parent guidebooks, and curricula such as Learningames[14] can lead to family support and developmental opportunities within the context of Amy's individual needs. Many of these might be undertaken during home visits by infant educators and nurse specialists and as part of an integrated child life program during hospitalizations. Families with infants with complex medical needs may choose to defer formal center-based programming until a later date. Teamwork and developmental activities across settings are most important and involve collaboration, not competition, between medical, nursing, and developmental professionals.

DEVELOPMENTAL PERSPECTIVES

Case 4: Developmental counseling. Adam is 12 months old. He has attended an early intervention infant program since 3 months of age. His parents have received support from the Down Syndrome Parent Group since his first week of life. Adam sits well, babbles, and attains medium size objects. The father wonders if the child will ever walk. The mother is concerned that her parents do not help with babysitting as often as they help with her sister's 2-year-old. She is also concerned about how well Adam will talk as she has heard that having a large tongue will make speech difficult. The grandparents want to known if he is really retarded.

The key issues facing health and developmental professionals are how to communicate ongoing developmental strengths and weaknesses of children with DS. One approach is to consider prognosis in three areas: motor, communicative, and cognitive.

Certain motor development is characteristic in DS:
- Central hypotonia may reflect cerebellar and genetic differences.
- The low tone is not accompanied by weakness.
- All DS individuals walk.
- Cervical spine differences of atlantoaxial instability are present in 10% to 20% of DS individuals.

- One percent of all DS individuals develop symptomatic atlantoaxial instability.

A key framework for understanding motor development in DS is to understand central hypotonia. Central hypotonia is best defined as low tone without weakness.[15]

Though many DS early childhood intervention efforts focus on neurodevelopmental therapy for low tone, recent recommendations are to incorporate motor development in a full spectrum of developmental services, including oral motor, fine motor, communicative, cognitive, and family supports.[16,17] An important point of view is for the therapist to facilitate the parents' learning of the child's strengths. In particular, functional self-mobility is a strength for children with DS. All DS children without additional neurologic complications learn to walk. Failure to emphasize an empowering and developmental consultative role can often lead to parents' medicalization of developmental issues. Specifically, parents can misperceive the role of therapists so that they always believe that intensive one-on-one rehabilitative services are the only way to promote development in children with DS. We have often heard parents express the fear that unless their 6-month-old receives individualized physical therapy five times per week, this child will not walk. Often these parents are fearful that unless the child receives ongoing physical therapy at age 3, he or she will stop walking.

The major goals of motor intervention for children with DS can follow an AIMS-oriented format developed by Scrutton.[18] This format encourages targeted functional goals across settings by understanding accurate prognosis. Motor activities, being interactive and pleasurable for child and caretakers, are seen as opportunities for exploring the environment and natural settings for social imitative learning. In addition, achievement of goals can give parents confidence in their abilities to provide an environment that facilitates the next stage of development. Thus, a parent–therapist–infant educator partnership is emphasized.

A second developmental area to monitor closely and facilitate is communication. Children with DS have some degree of language difficulty. Expressive, receptive, and mixed developmental dysphasia are common. Overall, this spectrum of communication disorders reflects degrees of mental retardation, hearing loss, and central language processing difficulties. Fluctuating, intermittent hearing impairment from otitis media with effusion is universal and, though not fully understood, has been attributed to small middle ear space, hypotonia of musculature of the eustachian tube, and immunological differences.[19] In addition, as many as 20% of children with DS may have a sensory-neural hearing loss or a mixed hearing loss. Thus, ongoing hearing monitoring is required even if otolaryngological surgeries have taken place. Language and audiologic issues in DS may be summarized as follows:

- Expressive, receptive, and mixed developmental dysphasia are universal.
- Developmental articulation and voice disorders are common. In pilot studies these problems were not decreased by reconstructive surgery on the tongue.
- Ways of enhancing language development include total communication strategies in early childhood, whole word reading, and computer written language programs in early elementary school years.
- Hearing loss interfering with language development is present in 80% of children with DS. Most of this hearing loss is conductive. However, as much as 20% is sensorineural or mixed. Close monitoring of all aspects of hearing is required.
- Sensorineural and significant mixed hearing loss may increase with age and require amplification.

The heterogeneity of hearing and language disorders in children with DS again emphasizes that there is no universal speech curriculum for all children with DS. However, a variety of programmatic options for enhancing communication have been summarized and include intensive developmental language activities, total communication, and augmentative communication.[20–22] A rich and directly interactive communication experience should be the broad fabric on which intervention is based. Audiological monitoring in conjunction with pediatric medical management and otolaryngological consultation is essential.

The third developmental area to examine is overall cognitive development. The most recent comprehensive longitudinal study was performed by Pueschel and colleagues in Boston between 1974 and 1977.[23] This prospective study of 89 noninstitutionalized children found the following mean scores at age 3: Bayley MDI 58, PDI 53, Vineland Social Quotient 64, Receptive Language Quotient 52, and Expressive Language Quotient 46. Overall, this study built on Share's Los Angeles experience in the early 1960s, which demonstrated that most 3- to 5-year-olds with DS have IQs of over 50.[24] Share also emphasized that learning continued throughout childhood in DS and that actual achievement and social capability were higher than a numerical IQ score. These data are used so that health and developmental professionals both maintain a longitudinal perspective and facilitate strategies for optimizing independence despite levels of motor, communicative, and cognitive impairment.

MEDICAL MONITORING

Three additional medical problems may impact on children with DS and lead to nonoptimal development. The first is thyroid disease. Neonates with DS have approximately a thirty-fold increase for congenital hypothyroidism.[25] Acquired thyroid disease including autoimmune thyroiditis occurs in 10% to 20% of children with Down syndrome and its prevalence may increase during adolescence and adulthood. Specialized growth charts facilitate the tracking of height and weight in children with DS.[26] By using these charts, following up on results of neonatal screening, and having a high index of suspicion for the early signs of thyroid deficiency, additional disability in children with DS can be detected. Developmental professionals need to be aware that early signs of acquired thyroid deficiency include growth failure with relative obesity, constipation, lethargy, and lack of developmental progress. Since these signs often overlap with clinical findings in children with DS, ongoing clinical evaluation, baseline laboratory studies, and follow-up laboratory studies are required.

The second medical problem impacting on development is vision. As many as 77% of children with DS have a refractive error (myopia, hyperopia) or an astigmatism.[27,28] Children with disproportionate fine motor or perceptual delays require formal ophthalmological evaluation so that these disorders may be promptly treated. Other visual disorders include congenital glaucoma in 1% to 5%, congenital dense cataracts in 2% to 3%, nystagmus in 33%, and strabismus in over 50%. Monitoring strategies include sequential cranial nerve, fundoscopy, and acuity assessment. We currently recommend formal evaluation by a pediatric ophthalmologist by age 2 or sooner if any clinical or perinatal concerns arise. Just as there is no limit to the earliest age for assessing hearing in infants, new noninvasive technologies, such as Teller Acuity Cards, make assessment of functional vision possible well before the first birthday.[29,30]

The third medical problem impacting on development is ligamentous laxity of the transverse ligament of the first (C1) and second (C2) cervical vertebrae. This

---

Guidelines for Atlantoaxial Instability Screening in Medical, Developmental, and Rehabilitational Settings

Down syndrome children younger than 6 years require both developmental neurologic and radiographic screenings for AAI.

Between 2 and 6 years of age, AAOD must be measured in flexion, neutral, and extension prior to medical and rehabilitational procedures, including developmental therapies.

Prior to elective surgery procedures (eg, strabismus, middle ear tubes), children with DS require documentation of their functional motor abilities, developmental neurologic examination, and C-spine films.

Children with AAOD >5 mm require neurosurgical consultation with neurophysiologic and specialized neuroimagery studies.

Developmental neurologic examination protocols that are part of routine health monitoring in DS need to include high index of suspicion for AAI.

AAI = Atlantoaxial instability.
AAOD = Anterior arch of C1-odontoid distance.

Table 1. Down syndrome developmental health monitoring protocol for 0–3 years*

	Age in months						
	1	6		12	18	24	36
Genetic issues							
Chromosome analysis	X						
Genetic counseling	X			X		X	
Developmental assessment							
Neurodevelopmental	X	X		X	X	X	
Gross motor		X		X	X	X	
Language				X	X	X	X
Problem solving/fine motor				X	X	X	X
Activities of daily living							X
Cardiac evaluation							
(including echocardiogram)	X						
Dental evaluation							X
Thyroid studies							
Review state screening	X						
T3, T4, TSH						X	
C-spine films†							
Neutral						X	
Extension						X	
Flexion						X	
Referral to Down syndrome							
parents group	X						
Referral to education program		X		X			
Audiometry							
ABR		X	or	X			
Tympanometry		X		X	X	X	X
Sound field					X	X	X
Ophthalmological screening	X	X		X	X	X	X
Teller screening				X	X		X
Pediatric ophthalmology							
evaluation						X	
Special growth charts	X	X		X	X	X	X
Option of yearly influenza vaccine							
for children with heart or							
lung disease							

*No tests are to be performed yearly as routine screening. Tests are to be performed periodically. Tests may need to be done more frequently or sooner as clinically indicated. For example, in some centers pediatric ophthalmologists may request an initial ophthalmological examination by the first birthday.
†May be done prior to elective surgery at 12 to 24 months. In community hospitals with limited experiences with younger children, initial screening may occur later.

occurs in 10% to 20% of individuals with DS.[31] This can be detected by radiographic screening of the neck in flexion, extension, and neutral beginning at the 2nd year birthday.

Guidelines for screening for cervical spine problems in the preschool period are summarized in the boxed material.[32] Screening strategies exist so that those with atlantoaxial (AAI) instability can avoid any stresses on the head and neck that could cause additional disability. Those without AAI instability can be reassured and participate in developmentally appropriate physical activities. Monitoring for AAI stability provides opportunities for a partnership between health professionals and developmental therapists. The role of therapists is to report any functional losses. For example, a 3-year-old who has a change of gait with increasing spasticity and incontinence requires medical evaluation. These sings of potential spinal cord impairment must not be attributed solely to behavioral and environmental causes.

FAMILY SUPPORTS

Case 5: Anticipatory guidance for toddlers. Suzy is 2 years old. She successfully underwent surgical repair of her atrioventricular canal at age 12 months. Since surgery, she has made rapid progress in motor skills with attainment of independent ambulation, increased fine motor manipulative play, and increased verbal production of single words and jargoning. She awakens at 1 AM and 3 AM nightly. She returns to sleep if given a bottle of milk or taken into her parents' bed. In the daytime, frequent temper tantrums occur during feeding time of her brother.

This case illustrates the importance of anticipatory guidance for night awakenings and arrival of a new sibling. Too often after dealing with major stresses such as genetic diagnosis, cardiac surgery, and arrival of a new family member, typical childhood behavior problems with individual temperament and parent behavioral management challenges are forgotten. In addition, involving other family members, especially fathers and other siblings, in becoming more knowledgeable about appropriate social expectations is very important. In this way, social independence can be enhanced across caretakers and settings. Too often, the burden of 24-hour coordinator, programmer, and manager is expected of mothers.

•   •   •

We view DS as a model developmental disorder for a partnership between medicine, education, and families. We emphasize that DS is best viewed as a dual developmental disorder of communicative and cognitive impairment. Our perspective is that families need up-to-date information that acknowledges genetic and developmental differences and enhances their ability to focus on the whole child and optimize both his or her health and development. Our overall health monitoring guidelines are in Table 1. We have chosen case vignettes to illustrate the complexities of genetic guilt, developmental guilt, and medical and family challenges. We emphasize a health-educational partnership, not medicine versus education, so as to counter common developmental myths for children with DS.

We encourage all professionals systematically to examine their attitudes toward mental retardation, what stresses they themselves might experience if one of their family members had a developmental disability, and to become aware of community resources beyond one's own discipline. In particular, we emphasize that chromosome number, genetic information, and early intervention are not the end but the starting point for appreciating the complexity of development. In this way, strategies to enhance cognitive function, movement, communication, socialization, and parent support can be developed so as to emphasize the independence of children with DS. As we face the challenges of the 1990s, we must facilitate this partnership between health and developmental professionals and families.

REFERENCES

1. Epstein CJ. Down syndrome (trisomy 21). In: Scrivner CR, Beaudet AL, Sly WS, Valle D. eds. *The Metabolic Basis of Inherited Disease.* 6th ed. New York, NY: McGraw-Hill; 1989.

2. Hook EB. Epidemiology of Down syndrome. In: Pueschel SM. *Down Syndrome: Advances in Biomedical and Behavioral Sciences.* Cambridge, Mass: Ware Press; 1982.

3. Benacerrof BR, Gelman R, Frigoletto FD. Sonographic identification of second trimester fetuses with Down's syndrome. *N Engl J Med.* 1987;317:1371–1375.

4. DiMaio MS, Baumgarte A, Greenstein RM, Saal HM, Mahoney MJ. Screening for fetal Down's syndrome in pregnancy by measuring maternal serum alphafetoprotein levels. *N Engl J Med.* 1987;317:342–346.

5. Van Dyke DC. Medical problems in infants and young children with Down syndrome: Implications for early services. *Inf Young Child.* 1989;1:39–50.

6. Magill CJ. Down syndrome: Update for the primary care practitioner. *J Am Acad Phys Assist.* 1989;2:5–13.

7. Gibson D, Fields DL. Early infant stimulation programs for children with Down syndrome: A review of effectiveness. *Adv Dev Behav Pediatr.* 1984;5:331–371.

8. Guralnick MJ, Bricker D. The effectiveness of early intervention for children with cognitive and general developmental delays. In: Guralnick MJ, Bennett FC. eds. *The Effectiveness of Early Intervention for At-Risk and Handicapped Children.* Orlando, Fla: Academic Press; 1987.

9. Rynders JE, Horabin JM. Always trainable? Never educable? Updating educational expectations concerning children with Down syndrome. *AJMR.* 1990;95:77–83.

10. Carey JC. Chromosomal disorders. In: Rudolph AM. ed. *Pediatrics.* 17th ed. Norwalk, Conn: Appleton-Century-Crofts; 1982.

11. Dubowitz LMS, Dubowitz V. The neurological assessment of the preterm and full term newborn infant. In: *Clinics in Developmental Medicine.* No. 79. Philadelphia, Pa: Lippincott-Spastics International; 1981.

12. Bocian ME, Kaback MM. Crisis counseling: The newborn infant with a chromosomal anomaly. *Pediatr Clin North Am.* 1978;25:643–650.

13. Noonan JA. Chromosomal abnormalities. In: Long WA. ed. *Fetal and Neonatal Cardiology.* Philadelphia, Pa: W.B. Saunders; 1990.

14. Sparling J, Lewis I. *Learningames For The First Three Years.* New York, NY: Walker; 1979.

15. Dubowitz V. The floppy infant. In: *Clinics in Developmental Medicine*. No. 76. Philadelphia, Pa: Lippincott-Spastics International; 1980.

16. Harris SR. Transdisciplinary therapy model for the infant with Down's syndrome. *Phys Ther.* 1980;60:420–423.

17. Rogers MJ. Functional management of gross motor development of children with Down syndrome. *Dev Med Child Neurol.* 1990;90:32(suppl 62):44–45.

18. Scrutton D. Aim-oriented management. In: Scrutton D. ed. *Management of the Motor Disorders of Children with Cerebral Palsy*. Philadelphia, Pa: Lippincott-Spastics International; 1984.

19. Balkany TJ, Downs MP, Jafex BW, Krajicek MJ. Hearing loss in Down syndrome. *Clin Pediatr.* 1979;18:116–118.

20. Swift E, Rosin P. A remediation sequence to improve speech intelligibility for students with Down syndrome. *Am Speech Lang Hear Assoc.* 1990;21:140–146.

21. Kumin L. A survey of speech and language pathology services for Down syndrome: State of the art. *Appl Res Ment Retard.* 1986;7:491–499.

22. Miller J. Language and communication characteristics of children with Down syndrome. In: Pueschel SM, Tingey C, Rynders JE, Crocker AC, Crulcher DM. eds. *New Perspectives on Down Syndrome*. Baltimore, Md: Brookes Publishing; 1987.

23. Pueschel SM, Schnell RR, Cronk CE. Interrelationships of biological environmental and competency variables in young children with Down syndrome. *Appl Res Ment Retard.* 1980;1:161–174.

24. Share J, Koch R, Webb A, Gruliker B. The longitudinal development of infants and young children with Down syndrome (mongolism). *Am J Ment Defic.* 1964;68:685–692.

25. Fort P, Lifschitz F, Bellisario R, et al. Abnormalities of thyroid function in infants with Down syndrome. *J Pediatr.* 1984;104:545–549.

26. Cronk C, Crocker AC, Pueschel SM, et al. Growth Charts for Children with Down Syndrome: One month to 18 years of age. *Pediatrics.* 1988;81:102–110.

27. Mumma P. Ophthalmological concerns in Down syndrome. Paper presented at National Down Syndrome Congress, San Antonio, Texas, 1984. Cited in: Pueschel SM, Tingey C, Rynders JE, Crocker AC, Crutcher DM. *New Perspectives on Down Syndrome*. Baltimore, Md: Brookes Publishing; 1987.

28. Caputo AR, Wagner RS, Reynolds DR, Guo S, Goel A. Down syndrome: Clinical review of ocular features. *Clin Pediatr.* 1989;28:355–358.

29. Teller DY, McDonald MA, Preston K, Sebris SL, Dobson V. Assessment of visual acuity in infants and children: the acuity card procedure. *Dev Med Child Neurol.* 1986;28:779–789.

30. Mohn G, vanHof-vanDuin J, Fetter WPF, deGroot L, Hage M. Acuity assessment of nonverbal infants and children: Clinical experience with the acuity card procedure. *Dev Med Child Neurol.* 1988;30:232–244.

31. Pueschel SM, Scola FH. Atlantoaxial instability in individuals with Down syndrome: Epidemiological, radiographic and clinical studies. *Pediatrics.* 1987;80:555–560.

32. Msall ME, Reese ME, DiGaudio K, Griswold K, Granger CV, Cooke RE. Symptomatic atlantoaxial instability associated with medical and rehabilitation procedures in children with Down's syndrome. *Pediatrics.* 1990;85:447–449.

Index

A

Aggressive behavior, 134–135
  definition of, 134
  guidelines for handling of, 134
Albert Einstein Scale of Sensorimotor
  Development, 14
Assessment of Preterm Infant's
  Behavior, 26
Assistive listening devices, 7
Auditory brainstem response testing,
  3, 251, 252–253, 256–258
Autism, 208–219
  appearance of symptoms, 211–212
  characteristics of, 208–210
  cognition, 212
  cognitive assessment, 216
  common traits of autistic, 214–215
  co-occurring conditions, 210
  definitions of, 208–209
  diagnosis of, 215–217
  diagnostic criteria, 210
  and earlier normal development, 209
  family assessment, 217
  language disorders, 212, 213–214
  and life span, 209
  management of, 218
  medical assessment, 216
  motor development, 212, 213–214
  prenatal factors in, 210–211
  prognosis for, 218–219
  psychological assessment, 217
  social development, 212, 213–214
  as spectrum disorder, 209

B

Battelle Developmental Inventory
  Screening Test, 82–83
Bayley Scales of Infant Development,
  14, 16, 19, 30, 58, 71

Behavioral disturbance, and language
  dysfunction, 149–150
Behavioral observation audiometry, 2,
  255–256
Behavior therapy, 128–133
  components of, 129
  extinction, 129–131
  time-out, 131–133
Behind the ear (BTE) hearing aid, 6
Birth to Three, 85–86, 227
Body composition, measurement of,
  199–200
Body-worn hearing aids, 7
Brain electrical activity mapping,
  nature of, 26
Brazelton Neonatal Behavioral
  Assessment Scale, 17, 173, 237
Bruininks-Oseretsky Test of Motor
  Proficiency, 40

C

California First Year Mental Scale, 14
Callier-Azusa Scale, 31
Cardiac vagal tone, in measurement of
  arousal, 58
Caregiver assistance, in assessment
  measure, 118–120
Carolina Record of Individual
  Behavior, 172
Casati-Lezine Scale, 14
Cattell Infant Intelligence Test, 137
Central nervous system, and cocaine,
  236
Cerebral palsy
  and dental problems, 201
  food refusal in, 202
  and gastroesophageal reflux, 203
  growth problems in, 199